THE
AWAKENING
OF THE WEST

Also by Stephen Batchelor:

Alone With Others: An Existential Approach to Buddhism
The Faith to Doubt: Glimpses of Buddhist Uncertainty
The Tibet Guide

Translator:

A Guide to the Bodhisattva's Way of Life (Shantideva)
Echoes of Voidness (Geshé Rabten)
Song of the Profound View (Geshé Rabten)
The Mind and its Functions (Geshé Rabten)

Editor:

The Way of Korean Zen (Kusan Sunim)
The Jewel in the Lotus: A Guide to the Buddhist Traditions of Tibet

THE
AWAKENING
OF THE WEST
The Encounter of Buddhism
and Western Culture

Stephen Batchelor

Parallax Press
Berkeley, California

Parallax Press
P.O. Box 7355
Berkeley, California 94707

Cover design by Ayelet Maida/L racy Media, Inc.
Cover image of Gandhara Buddha courtesy of San Francisco Zen Center.
Maps by Pelorus Maps
Text typeset by Harper Phototypesetters Limited, Northampton, England.

Library of Congress Cataloging-in-Publication Data

Batchelor, Stephen
    The awakening of the west: the encounter of Buddhism and Western
culture/Stephen Batchelor.
        p. cm.
    Includes bibliographical references and index.
    ISBN 0-938077-68-6 (cloth) : $30.00. -- ISBN 0-938077-69-4 (paper
    : $18.00
    1. Buddhism--Europe--History.   2. Buddhism--Study and teaching-
-Europe--History.
BQ704.B38 1994
294.3'09182'1--dc20   94-8016
                                                         CIP

For Geshé Ngawang Dhargyey

*Toutes les histoires anciennes, comme le disait un de nos beaux esprits,
ne sont que des fables convenues.*
(All ancient histories, as one of our fine spirits put it, are
nothing but convenient fictions.)

Voltaire

ACKNOWLEDGMENTS

I would like to thank the following people who have contributed to making this book possible.

Fred von Allmen, Ajahn Amaro, Anando, Alexander Andreyev, Sr. Annabel, Maurice Ash, Roger Ash-Wheeler, Sr. Astrid, Gert Bastian, David Batchelor, Martine Batchelor, Mauro Bergonzi, Martin Baumann, Pierre-François de Béthune, Bhikkhu Bodhi, Oleg and Svetlana Borisov, John Bramble, Alexander Breslavetz, Jacques Brosse, Reinette and Kirk Brown, Heather Campbell, Richard Causton, Guy Claxton, Alessandra Cornero, Phillipe Coupey, H. H. the Dalai Lama, Dilgo Khyentse Rinpoché, Mary Finnegan, Ven. Gérard Godet, Hans Gruber, Charles Hadfield, Charles Hastings, Roger Hill, Edie Irwin, Paul Jaffe, Lama Jigmé Tsewang, Petra Kelly, Ursula King, Kittisaro, Arnold Kotler, Dharmachari Kulananda, Karl Ludwig Leiter, Louis van Loon, Hans Ludin, Bob Mann, Mimi Maréchal, Daniel Milles, Lama Monlam, Rev. Daishin Morgan, Vladimir Montlevich, Thich Nhat Hanh, Elena Nikolaeva, Nyanaponika Thera, Ole Nydahl, Lama Osel, Andrei Paribok, Ven. Thubten Pende, Corrado Pensa, Luciano Petech, Elizabeth Puttick, Andrew Rawlinson, Roland Rech, Mathieu Riccard, Sam Richards, Donald Rothberg, Jeremy Russell, Ven. Tenzin Khetsun Samaev, Rev. A.M.A. Samy, Sangharakshita, Karl Schmidt, Chris Shaw, Jeff Shore, John Snelling, Christof Spitz, Rosemary Staheyeff, Suryadas, Karen Thomas, Tom Tillemans, Peter Timmerman, Christopher Titmuss, Helen Tworkov, Jaroslav Vasilikov, Vimalo, Maurice Walshe, Tulku Pema Wangyal, Gay Watson, Russell Webb, Sylvia Wetzel.

CONTENTS

FOREWORD

Buddhism is more than an Asian religion. As the teachings of the Buddha become better known and practised in Western countries, it is vital to understand their place in Western history and culture. Stephen Batchelor's illuminating and timely account of the transmission of Buddhism to the West is essential reading for all who are concerned with the significance of religious experience in the modern world.

The Dalai Lama
November 1993

INTRODUCTION

I am going to tell the story of an encounter between two cultures. It is a story that has never been fully told before. And it is a strange story; for its plot is still unfolding and its ending is impossible to guess.

This is not, however, a tale about two obscure traditions that a scholar's archival burrowing and ingenious imagination have tenuously connected. Together the cultures in question have had a greater influence on humanity than any others in the course of history. Yet for more than two thousand years they grew up largely unaware of one another. Today it is hard to grasp that Europeans and Americans had no coherent conception of Buddhism until 150 years ago.

It is nonetheless a long story. For it is a drama of indifference and blindness, missed opportunities, arrogance and tragedy, political ambition and unfulfilled dreams that goes back to the time of Gautama Buddha, who died 543 years before the birth of Jesus.

This long, uncertain relationship of the West with Buddhism has been marked by five attitudes:

- blind indifference
- self-righteous rejection
- rational knowledge
- romantic fantasy
- existential engagement.

With the exception of a few ancient Greeks, until the 13th century Europe had no knowledge of or interest in the cultures of Asia. From the 13th until the end of the 18th century its attitude was almost entirely one of self-righteous rejection, instances of Buddhism generally being condemned as heathen idolatry. From the beginning of the 19th century the Westernn attitude split into two: one half dealt with Buddhism as a field of rational scientific knowledge, while the other half turned it into an object of romantic fantasy. Not until the beginning of the 20th century did a handful of Europeans engage with Buddhist traditions as *forms of practice* that addressed the dilemma of their existence. And only since the 1960s has that practice established itself in the West in the form of *sangha* — intentional spiritual communities.

These attitudes reflect not only broad historical phases in Europe's perception of Buddhism, but also psychological strata within the Western mind. Even those who have existentially committed themselves to the Dharma (what Buddhists call Buddhism) may still entertain romantic notions about enlightenment; attend courses to study Buddhism with rational objectivity from non-Buddhist professors; reject particular ideas as alien features of Asian culture; and be indifferent to aspects of the teachings that, they believe, do not concern them.

This story is complex, because the development of both Buddhist and Western culture is complex. Just as Buddhism has evolved from its earlier to its later schools, so the Western mind has moved through its own well-documented stages. In their own ways, both traditions have shown themselves as fluid and adaptable to change. And in their present encounter they both face the challenge of further change if they are to accommodate each other's insights.

In the way I have chosen to tell the story, these historical phases, psychological strata and evolutionary changes thread their way amongst each other, weaving a fabric that reveals a pattern as coherent as the vagaries of history allow. So instead of a single linear thread, stretching year by year from 543 BCE to 1992, the story flashes ahead and darts back in time.

To understand, for example, why a group of French men and women are meditating together in Paris on a winter morning in 1991, one needs to know why a Japanese Zen monk made an arduous journey to southern China in 1151. The story illustrates the curious interconnectedness of things (a theme, by the way, as familiar to 8th-century Hua-yen Buddhist philosophers in China as to playful post-modern poets in Pennsylvania).

Furthermore, the story tells of what happened during the writing of the story (from October 1990 to December 1992). For in a story whose plot is still unfolding and whose ending cannot be guessed, reality slips about like mercury, upsetting the neat conclusions of a week or a year before.

In May 1991, for instance, I visited Leningrad to research the condition of Buddhism in Russia. A year later the Communist Party was banned, the Soviet Union no longer existed, and Leningrad became St Petersburg again. Several chapters had to be revised because of events that outdated them: Ajahn Chah and Dilgo Khyentsé Rinpoché, two leading figures in the spread of Buddhism to Europe, died; while another was discovered as an eight-year-old boy in Tibet and enthroned as the 17th Karmapa. In September 1991, I chanced upon the obituary in *Le Monde* of the only other person to have written this story (*La Rencontre du Bouddhisme et de l'Occident* in 1952): Cardinal Henri de Lubac.

I have chosen to limit the events recounted here to the geographical boundaries of Asia and Europe. For historically Buddhism's encounter with the West has essentially been an encounter with *European* culture. Even today the dominant cultures of America and Australasia remain primarily European in their origins and values. Moreover, for justice to be done to the spread of Buddhism over the past century into the New World would make the text unacceptably complex. This is also largely unnecessary since a thorough account of Buddhism in the United States can be found in Rick Fields' *How the Swans Came to the Lake: A Narrative History of Buddhism in America*, and a comprehensive overview of Buddhism in Australia is available in Paul Croucher's *Buddhism in Australia (1848–1988)*.

Even with these qualifications, this book is still far from a comprehensive account of everything that has ever occurred in the course of the encounter between Buddhism and European culture. By necessity I have been selective. Some schools, notably the Pure Land sects of Japan and the Sakya tradition of Tibet, because of their limited followings in Europe today, have been largely omitted. I have sought to be impartial, but recognize the inevitable exercise of authorial privilege in the selection of material. I apologize in advance to any Buddhist reader who feels short-changed.

PROLOGUE

In the final dramatic weeks of 1989, with the Soviet-backed regimes of Eastern Europe collapsing around him, the Buddhist monk Tenzin Gyatso, the 14th Dalai Lama of Tibet, wrapped in burgundy robes, his breath condensing in the winter air, stood beside the already crumbling Berlin Wall. Silently, an old woman stretched out her arm and gave him a red candle. 'With some emotion,' he recalled

> I lit it and held it up. For a moment the tiny dancing flame threatened to go out, but it held and, while a crowd pressed round me touching my hands, I prayed that the light of compassion and awareness would fill the world and dispel the darkness of fear and oppression.

For the Dalai Lama, then in the thirty-first year of exile from his own country, this moment revealed not the triumph of one political system over another but a reassuring truth: 'No matter what governments do, the human spirit will always prevail.'

This conviction was confirmed a few weeks later when he landed in Czechoslovakia as the guest of Vaclev Havel, dissident playwright abruptly turned President and the first head of any European state in history to receive a Dalai Lama. On arrival in Prague he was greeted by a waving throng of emotional men and women before being whisked off to the Presidential Palace where he instructed the president and his aides in meditation. The 'God-King' found the 'Philosopher-King' to embody classic Buddhist virtues. The president was 'gentle and full of honesty, humility — and humour. He seemed quite unaffected by his new position.' His only discernible un-Buddhist quality was a singular devotion to beer and cigarettes, which prompted the Dalai Lama to pray for a second revolution in Czechoslovakia: one of 'less smoking at mealtimes'.

This meeting between two dissidents served as a celebration of human freedom after the fall of a totalitarian regime. It also occasioned the first spiritual exchange between a Buddhist monk and a European ruler since the Venerable Nagasena answered the questions of King Menander in the foothills of the Himalayas about 150 years before the time of Jesus. For in spite of the Dalai Lama's insistence on the pre-eminence of the human spirit over the policies of governments, the fortunes of Buddhism throughout its history have been inexorably tied to the support of sympathetic kings and emperors. Menander was one such king, who although born in what today is Afghanistan and the ruler over large parts of north-west India, was ethnically and culturally a Greek.

ONE

ASHOKA, GREEKS AND GNOSTICS

1

MENANDER:
GREEKS IN INDIA

Greek colonies are known to have existed in India at least
since the time of the Buddha in the 6th century BCE.
In a discourse from the *Middle Length Sayings*, the
Buddha tries to convince the young *brahman* Assalayana that the
Indian social castes are not divinely ordained but variable, as with
the Greeks where permanent membership of one of two castes
— master or slave — is far from guaranteed. While this reference to
Greeks shows that they were sufficiently known at the time to serve
as an example in educated discussion, both their location in the north-
west, far from where the Buddha lived and taught, and this sole
mention in the early Buddhist canon make it unlikely that any contact
ever took place between the Buddha and these displaced Europeans.

Who were these early Greek settlers? The historian Arrian tells
of how Dionysos, the subversive god of frenzy, conquered India
and founded cities, created laws and introduced the Indians to the
delights of wine. Although Dionysos is mythical, the presence of
his Greek devotees in India is not. It was their descendants that
Alexander the Great encountered in the city of Nysa in the Hindu
Kush during his Indian campaign (326 BCE). That they were
Ionian Greeks from Asia Minor (today the Aegean coast of Turkey)
is suggested by the Pali word for them: *Yona*.

At the time of the Buddha the Ionian Greeks had reached a peak
of intellectual development, yet were politically weak, struggling
for survival against Persia. The Ionian Pythagoras was an exact

3

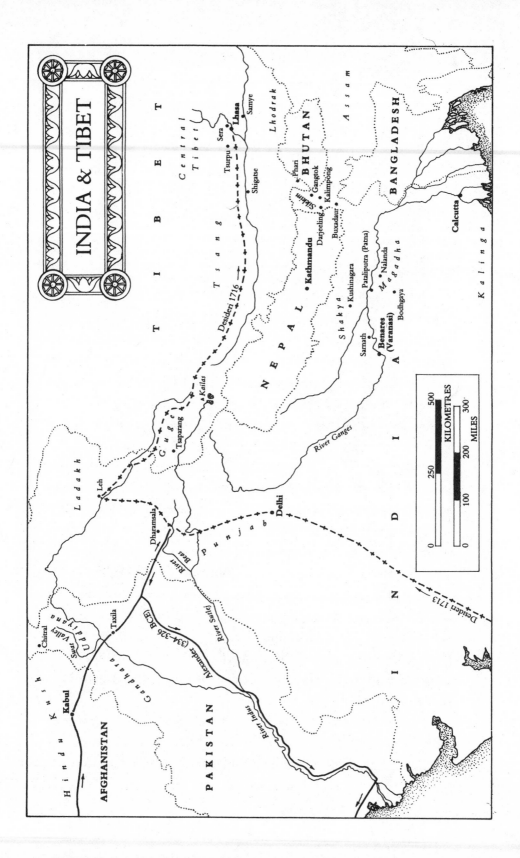

contemporary of the Buddha and professed a world-view with striking similarities to some of his Indian counterparts. Not only did he believe in rebirth and non-violence, he saw his teachings as implying a rigorous spiritual discipline based on renunciation, supported by a like-minded community and aimed at liberation from birth and death.

When Alexander embarked on his great expedition eastwards in the spring of 334 BCE, fired with his tutor Aristotle's inaccurate image of India as the end of the earth, he was setting out to conquer the world. His expedition included scientists and philosophers in addition to forty thousand soldiers. He saw himself not just as a military conqueror but as the conveyor of civilization. But progress was slow; it took him seven years to reach the Indus.

A few days' march after crossing the great river he came to Taxila, a ramshackle town renowned as a centre of trade and learning. Here he met 'gymnosophists', naked sages who lived austere and disciplined lives for the sake of spiritual insight. These were either Jain monks or *shramanas*, wandering ascetics of the kind the Buddha became on renouncing the world. Alexander was impressed by their feats of self-control and tried to recruit one of them, Dandamos, to join his company of philosophers. In response Dandamos remained silent, then asked Alexander: 'Why did you travel so far?' He continued:

> I have just as much of the earth as you and every other person; even if you gain all rivers, you cannot drink more than I. Therefore, I have no fears, acquire no wounds and destroy no cities. I have just as much earth and water as you; altogether I possess everything. Learn this wisdom from me: wish for nothing and everything is yours.

Pyrrho, Aristotle's nephew, who accompanied Alexander and returned to Greece to found the Sceptic school, may have been influenced by such Indian ideas. They did little to restrain Alexander.

Yet within a year the expedition ground to a halt at the Beas river (in the modern Punjab), defeated not by a native army but by a loss of morale among the troops. Alexander retreated. He died in Babylon eighteen months later at the age of thirty-two, leaving behind him an already disintegrating Indian empire.

For Alexander, 'India' meant not the Indian subcontinent, of which he had merely a hazy misconception, but the Indus valley alone. Had Alexander managed to cross the Beas (the penultimate eastern river of the Indus system), he would have been tantalizingly close to the western reaches of the Gangetic civilization, the homeland of Buddhism. By the time he arrived in Taxila, his knowledge of this region would certainly have improved, perhaps, as Plutarch says, from a young exile from the kingdom of Magadha called Chandragupta, who visited Alexander's camp and conferred with the Macedonian.

Chandragupta originated from the Mauryan clan, which at the time of the Buddha had ruled over the small republic of Maurya, just to the south of Shakya (in modern-day Nepal), where the Buddha was born. By the time of Alexander both these republics had been swallowed up by larger kingdoms and now formed part of Magadha, the dominant power in the region, with its capital of Pataliputra (modern Patna) strategically placed on a major confluence of the Ganges.

In 324 BCE Chandragupta deemed the time right for revolt against the corrupt rule of the prevailing monarchy. He wrenched the throne of Magadha from the king to found the Mauryan empire, which was to last for 137 years and for the first time unite the greater part of the Indian subcontinent. One of his first acts as king was to expel the disordered remnants of Alexander's forces and secure his western border at the Indus.

Chandragupta's India was a powerful, unified state, well equipped to withstand the Hellenic pressures from the west and to suppress any regional unrest from within. And it is through this empire that Europe had its first glimpse of a Gangetic civilization, conveyed by the *Indika* of Megasthenes, who served for more than ten years as an ambassador to the court of Chandragupta at Pataliputra, before returning to Greece to write his memoirs.

In addition to descriptions of the land and its customs, Megasthenes also talks of the philosophers he encountered in the Mauryan empire. He divides them into the *brachmanes* and the *sarmanes*, which correspond to the Sanskrit terms *brahman* and *shramana*. For Megasthenes the *brahman*s 'are best esteemed'

> for they are more consistent in their opinions. They live in simple style, and lie on beds of rushes or skins. They abstain from animal food and sexual pleasures, and spend their time in listening to serious discourse, and in imparting their knowledge.

The *shramana*s, however,

> live in the woods, where they subsist on leaves of trees and wild fruits, and wear garments made from the bark of trees. They abstain from sexual intercourse and wine. They communicate with the kings, who consult them by messengers regarding the causes of things, and who through them worship and supplicate the deity.

Megasthenes lived for an entire decade in the heartland of the Buddha's dispensation, less than two hundred years after the Buddha's death — but there is no mention in the *Indika* of Buddhist monks. At the time of Megasthenes, Buddhism was a small sect with no influential followers. Chandragupta, a staunch upholder of brahmanical values, was certainly no Buddhist. And Kautilya, Chandragupta's chief minister, fails even to mention Buddhism in his famous book on statecraft, the *Arthashastra*.

Yet within fifty years of Megasthenes' departure from India Buddhism had exploded across the subcontinent as the imperial philosophy of Chandragupta's grandson Ashoka. Europe, however, was to wait another fifteen hundred years (until 1255) before it received a first-hand report of Buddhism and its practices.

The empire that Ashoka controlled extended from the borders of Persia in the west to the Ganges delta in the east and as far south as present-day Goa. The only significant area of the subcontinent that remained out of his grasp was Kalinga to the south-east. During the first years of his rule he launched a brutal campaign to conquer this region.

Even as this campaign was being waged, other forces were at work in Ashoka's life, which were to result in his conversion to Buddhism. Although trained in the brahmanical philosophy of his grandfather, he had already been exposed to Buddhism. His first wife, Devi, was a Buddhist and already two years before the Kalingan victory Mahinda and Sanghamitta, his son and daughter by her, had entered the Buddhist order.

In the figure of Ashoka, Buddhism found the ideal catalyst to transform it from an obscure Middle-Indian sect into a budding world religion. That the Buddha himself saw his Dharma as having universal relevance is clear from the oft-repeated injunction to his monks:

Go forth, and walk for the welfare of many, for the happiness of many, out of compassion for the world, for the profit, for the welfare, for the happiness of gods and mankind. Let not two of you go by the same path. Expound the Dharma which is beneficent in the beginning, beneficent in the middle, beneficent in the end; teach it in its spirit and its letter.

8

However inwardly distressing the cost of Kalinga may have been to Ashoka, externally it fulfilled a key objective of the Mauryan dynasty: to establish an empire sufficiently unified, extensive and powerful to prevent any further Greek incursions from the west. Ashoka was now free to inaugurate a civilization based on the principles of the Buddha's Dharma of wisdom, tolerance and compassion.

While a Buddhist himself, Ashoka did not insist that his subjects convert to Buddhism. The edicts which he carved on rocks and pillars throughout the empire simply exhorted the people to practise the classic Indian ethical virtues. In this regard, Ashoka followed the Buddha's own attitude of tolerance:

> I do not call truth what the foolish confront each other with; they make their own view the truth; that is why they treat their opponents as fools.

Only in three edicts addressed to the Buddhist community does he employ Buddhist terminology and refer to Buddhist discourses.

Ashoka's personal endorsement of Buddhism nonetheless gave it an unprecedented authority in the empire and paved the way for its active dissemination throughout India and into Ceylon. Ashoka records having sent missions from India bearing his message of the victory of the Dharma to the Greek kings Antiochus II of Syria, Ptolemy II (Philadelphus) of Egypt, Antigonus Gonatas of Macedonia, Magas of Cyrene and Alexander of Epirus. There is no mention in Western sources, however, of the arrival of any such missions.

A strange symmetry of these times is that just as Alexander, the greatest Greek king, is overlooked in the Indian mytho-histories of the time, likewise Ashoka, the greatest Indian king, is ignored by the Greek historians. For the Indians, the forgetting of Alexander may indicate no more than the wish to expunge an embarrassing episode from their collective memory. With Ashoka it is more puzzling. For both his father and grandfather regularly received Greek envoys and appeared on the pages of Greek histories with Hellenized names. It is possible that Ashoka himself was a quarter Greek — he may have descended from a Greek princess given in marriage to Chandragupta. That Ashoka was close to the Greek communities in his empire is clear both on account of his having served as governor of the Greek centre of Taxila and, when he assumed power, having appointed a Greek prince to govern the district of Aparanta. He even sent a Greek monk called Dharmarakshita — certainly the first European known to have taken the robe — as a Buddhist envoy to the district.

Towards the end of his reign, Ashoka published an edict which addressed the community of monks and nuns, stressing the need for unity to prevail in the order. The picture this paints of Buddhism at the time is one where contending voices are struggling to be heard, where divisions are threatening to undermine whatever harmony the community may have enjoyed in the halcyon days before imperial favour descended upon it.

Ashoka's appeal was in vain. During the course of his rule the first major rupture occurred within the Buddhist community, dividing it into two principal streams: the 'Elders' (*Sthaviras*) and the 'Majority' (*Mahasamghikas*). Behind the doctrinal disputes lay a more fundamental divergence over the nature of authority and the ordering of spiritual priorities. The Majority demanded a greater say in the running of the community for the ordinary imperfect monks — even, it seems, for the laity. For the Elders such democratic tendencies were felt to threaten the very authority they believed to have been invested in them by the Buddha. This tension is at the root of the confusing division into the so-called 'Hinayana' and 'Mahayana' traditions of Buddhism that persists to this day.

To some extent the tension was already present at the time of the Buddha and only came to a head in Ashoka's reign. To resolve the dispute a council was called at Pataliputra — the third since the Buddha's passing. No agreement was reached and the split became official.

After a reign of thirty-six years, Ashoka succumbed to senility and died in 231 BCE. Once he had gone, the Mauryan empire started disintegrating and collapsed forty-two years later. The official encouragement of non-violence and Buddhism seems to have weakened the central military power needed to control such an empire. The final blow came when the last Mauryan king was assassinated by Pushyamitra, the commander-in-chief of his army.

Pushyamitra was a *brahman*, representing those still loyal to the memory of Chandragupta who felt disenfranchised and alienated during the Buddhist rule of Ashoka. As soon as he gained power, Pushyamitra found himself bogged down in combating internal rivalries and suppressing revolts. And it was in this confusion that Demetrius, the Greek king of Bactria (now Afghanistan), saw his chance to realize at long last the Greek dream of ruling India — with himself on the throne of Ashoka.

And, in the hazy memory of the West, as such was Demetrius remembered. The Latin historian Justin gave him the title *Rex Indorum* — King of India — a notion which echoed down the centuries to surface, via Boccaccio, in Chaucer's 'Knight's Tale' as 'grete Emetreus, the kyng of Inde'. What actually happened was both more complicated and tragic than the regal title suggests.

With apparently no danger threatening him from the west and the Mauryan empire at an end, Demetrius invaded India and by 182 BCE had occupied Taxila and secured Gandhara (in modern Pakistan). From here he launched an army eastwards headed by his general Menander.

Thus Menander became the first Greek conqueror to cross the Beas, the river at which Alexander turned back. He rapidly advanced into the heartland of the Gangetic civilization to besiege and occupy Patiliputra itself, the capital of Magadha where once Ashoka had ruled.

At this point fortune turned against the Greeks. Word reached them of an unexpected attack from the west on their poorly defended homeland of Bactria. They were forced to retreat. In the battles that ensued Demetrius was killed, leaving Menander to assume kingship of the portion of north-west India that remained in Greek control. Menander spent the rest of his days consolidating the realm and deepening his understanding of Buddhism.

Little is known of Menander's early life. He was born in a village in the Paropamisadae (Central Afghanistan) near the town of Alexandria-of-the-Caucasus. He proved to be the most successful of all Greek rulers in India, renowned as a brilliant general and administrator as well as a man of great intellectual sensitivity. He is the only Indo-Greek king to have survived as an identifiable personality in Indian literature as well as to have inspired legends recorded by a Western writer — Plutarch. In the figure of Menander we find a synthesis of Alexander and Ashoka, a person who was both a Greek hero and a Buddhist king.

Menander ruled from the city of Sagala, located somewhere in the Himalayan foothills between Uddiyana (the modern Swat valley in Pakistan) and Sialkot (in the Punjab). In Buddhist writings Sagala is depicted as a thriving and harmonious city serving as the centre of a society whose political and social structure was Greek but whose cultural and spiritual values were largely Buddhist.

Menander had never even been to Greece and had no formal relations with Athens. He was a Greek only in the sense that he embodied the administrative and cultural norms of Hellenic civilization. For many Greeks in his realm, Greece and all it stood for existed merely as part of their collective memory. Although they continued to build shrines to Greek gods, and amphitheatres in which to perform Greek plays, they did so out of attachment to their Hellenic identity rather than as a means of impressing a superior creed on a subservient race.

The reason why so few Greeks are recorded as having converted to Buddhism is due to the Greek mind's inability to comprehend the need for the kind of renunciation exhibited by Buddhist monks. In other respects, Buddhism suited the Greek settlers well. Its rejection of the caste system meant that Buddhists would be less prone to resurgences of Indian nationalism and more likely to support a tolerant, pluralistic and relatively decentralized Greek state.

For Indians the outstanding memory of Menander is that he alone among the Greek kings adopted Buddhism. One of the best-known texts in Pali (also preserved in Chinese) is the *Milindapanha – Menander's Questions –* the record of a dialogue between the king and a Buddhist monk called Nagasena.

The precise extent of Menander's commitment to Buddhism is open to question. Although the Pali text concludes in declaring how Menander renounced the world, became a monk and attained the state of an *arhat*, a more credible outcome is suggested by the king himself:

> As a lion captured in a golden cage stretches its neck outwards, even so do I, while remaining in the world, aspire for solitude. But if I left the world to take up the religious life, I would not live long, for I have many enemies.

That Menander did meet a violent end yet remained highly esteemed by his Buddhist subjects is confirmed by Plutarch:

> When Menander, who had ruled with moderation, met his death during an expedition, the villages celebrated his funeral

13

ceremony jointly; they put forth rival claims over his relics, and it was with difficulty that they came to the agreement that each city would receive an equal part of the ashes, and that each of them would have reliquaries of that king.

The learned Plutarch would have been unaware that such funerary honours were reserved by Buddhists for Buddhas and Universal Monarchs (*Chakravartin*) alone.

After Menander's death the stability he achieved was soon destroyed by external invasions and internal rivalries. Both the Greek and Indian records break off at this point, leaving just a mass of coins embossed with the names of otherwise unknown Greek kings. Several generations of Greeks continued to exert control over parts of Menander's fragmented kingdom, but were gradually sucked into the cultural and ethnic whirlpool of India. By the end of the 2nd century CE, 350 years after Menander's death, no distinctively Greek communities remained in north-west India.

As part of this process of assimilation, many Greeks became Buddhists. Due to them one lasting trace of Hellenism survived in India and throughout Asia: the depiction of the Buddha in human form.

For the first five hundred years after the enlightenment the Buddha was not represented as a human being. In the carved rock reliefs and sculptures that survive, he was suggested only through symbols — an eight-spoked wheel, an empty throne, a tree, a pair of footprints. This tradition emphasized the transcendence of the Buddha, his earthly human existence extinguished in Nirvana, about which nothing could be said in words or images. For the Greek Buddhists of Gandhara, in the process of transforming into

14

Indians, such a radical absence of the one who gave meaning to their lives must have been unsatisfactory. Thus the idea of depicting the Buddha in a form drawn from their collective Greek memory stirred in their minds. And it is not surprising that the form they selected was that of the god Apollo, who, as a youthful warrior, represents the ideal human form, while also standing for the virtues of healing, purity, moderation and self-knowledge.

Thus the Greeks, who cavorted into India with Dionysos, crossed the Indus under Alexander, stimulated the birth of the Mauryan dynasty of Chandragupta and Ashoka, penetrated the Gangetic civilization under Demetrius, and established a Graeco-Buddhist culture through Menander, evaporated after a thousand years having bequeathed the image of Apollo.

2

NAGASENA:
THE DHARMA

Will we ever know what words passed between the Dalai Lama and Vaclev Havel in the Prague winter of 1989? Possibly someone at the meeting took notes. Perhaps a tape-recorder gathered magnetic impressions in a corner of the room. One day something may appear in published form. But we do have a record — seven 'books' worth — of the discussions between King Menander and the Buddhist monk Nagasena.

We know a fair deal about Menander. But who was Nagasena? No one has a clue. The information given in *Menander's Questions* is largely hagiographic and comes from a part of the first book which is considered apocryphal. It serves to impress upon a devout reader the extraordinary sagacity and saintliness of Nagasena, but says little of the man. Given that Nagasena is so highly venerated by the narrator of *Menander's Questions*, one would expect at least a mention of him in other records. But there is none.

The question of Nagasena's identity is, however, explored by Menander at the opening of their dialogue.

'Who are you?' asks the king.

'I am Nagasena, sir', replies the monk. 'As such am I known to my fellow renunciates. But although my parents gave me this name, it is merely a denotation, a designation, an appellation, a conventional usage. Nagasena is only a name since there is no person to be found here.'

'But if no person can be found', retorted Menander, 'who gives

16

you robes and alms? Who is it that enjoys them? Who is it that keeps vows, practises meditation, and realises Nirvana? Let us take a closer look. Could it be that the hairs on your head are the Venerable Nagasena?'

'O no, sir.'

'Then what about the hairs on your body?'

'Impossible, sir.'

'How about your nails, teeth, skin, flesh, sinews, bones, marrow, kidneys, heart, liver, membranes, spleen, lungs, intestines, stomach, excrement, bile, phlegm, pus, blood, sweat, fat, tears, saliva, mucus or urine? Your brain perhaps?'

'None of them, sir.'

'So if you are not your body, might you then be a feeling of pleasure or pain, a perception, a mental impulse, or a state of consciousness?'

'No, sir.'

'If you are neither your body nor mind, do you somehow exist apart from your body and mind?'

'Not at all, sir.'

'In that case, Venerable One, you told me a lie when you said you were Nagasena. For I find no Nagasena. There is no Nagasena at all. Only a name.'

Then Nagasena asked: 'How did you get here, sir? By foot or in a vehicle?'

'In my chariot', said the king.

'If you came by chariot, sir, then show me this chariot. Is the axle the chariot?'

'Well, no.'

'Are the wheels the chariot?'

'No.'

'The body, the flag-staff, the yoke, the reins, the goad — are these the chariot?'

'No.'

17

'Then is there a chariot apart from these things?'

'No, Venerable Nagasena.'

'Then are not you, the king of India, also lying? For you said you came by chariot, but are unable to produce anything. So what is this chariot? It too is nothing but a name.'

Menander's entourage applauded Nagasena.

'No, Venerable Nagasena,' conceded the king, 'I am not telling a lie. For it is because of these parts that a chariot exists as a denotation, a conventional usage, a name.'

'Exactly', said Nagasena. 'And so it is for me, sir. Because of my body, feelings, perceptions, mental impulses and consciousness does Nagasena exist as a denotation, a conventional usage, a name. But ultimately there is no person at all to be found.'

Thus we are torn away from a linear progress of events and the identification of historical figures by their physical and mental traces in ancient records. Nagasena's dialectic plunges the Greek king into a view of the world that values deconstruction over construction, infinite transparent depth over finite opaque surfaces. The ground upon which history marches forward is snatched from beneath its feet, echoing the question of the naked sage Dandamos to Alexander: 'Why did you travel so far?'

The world Nagasena inhabited was dominated by a single all-important event: the awakening, four centuries previously, of a man called Gautama, the Buddha. During the vast cycles of time in which countless universes endlessly expand and contract, Buddhas periodically erupt onto the stage of human history to reveal the Dharma: the 'Law', the 'way things are'. Unlike divine interventions emanating from a source beyond history, such eruptions are the culmination of an individual's resolve to unlock the riddles of life, thereby gaining freedom from the bonds that lock them into the frustrating repetitions of anguish. On our own little speck of living matter called 'Earth', in this minute fraction of an aeon called 'history', Nagasena and his fellow monks believed Gautama to be such a person whose awakening had the power to reveal a way of life that would inspire generations for millennia to come. Exactly how long this dispensation would last was another matter. Some said five hundred, some two thousand, some five thousand years. For even the teachings of a Buddha were understood to be subject to the law of impermanence that governs all conditioned things.

That the awakening of Gautama coincided with the emergence of a stable and prosperous period within Gangetic civilization implies that Buddhas only appear in a world that has the psychological and spiritual maturity to understand what they have to say. The Dharma, like a sensitive plant, can only survive in an appropriate environment. Before such an environment has evolved and after it has degraded, the Dharma is absent. In global terms, this notion is mirrored by Karl Jasper's 'Axial Age': the period during which the Buddha, Confucius, Lao Tzu, Zoroaster and Socrates flourished more or less concurrently. From a Buddhist point of view, such concurrence could be seen as the simultaneous eruption of a trans-personal awakening, the epicentre of which was in Magadha, but whose reverberations extended throughout the civilized world.

For Nagasena, the Buddha was comparable to the vast ocean into which 'all rivers flow constantly and continually while it never increases or decreases in size'. The mind of the Buddha was 'all-knowing and all-seeing' and his body 'distinguished by thirty-two major and eighty minor marks of a Great Man, radiant with a golden-coloured skin and a halo spreading round him six feet in all directions'. This was how the community at Nagasena's time remembered the Buddha, a person whose impact on their world was of such enormity that he could only be represented allusively, in quasi-mythical form. For Nagasena the Buddha was not a brilliant philosopher, a yogic adept, or a divine incarnation, but one who had awoken to the very heart of what human life, individually and socially, was about.

For the Greeks, this Buddhist culture, which surrounded and intrigued them and into which they were being fatally drawn, was alien and perplexing.

'Nagasena,' asked Menander, 'what is the use of going forth into homelessness? What is the aim of the Buddhist life?'

'Why, sir, that suffering may cease and further suffering may not arise: that is why one becomes a monk. Utter Nirvana without any trace: that is the aim of this life.'

Such notions were as difficult for the ancient Greeks to comprehend as they are for contemporary Westerners today. A secular culture can grudgingly understand why people would devote themselves to improving their lot in a hypothetical future existence, but to consider Nirvana, the extinguishing of all trace of physical and mental existence as we know it, as the highest good, and to abandon the security and warmth of family life to achieve it: this is at best eccentric, at worst crazy. Indeed no Buddhist idea has proved as problematic for the European mind as that of Nirvana.

For Nagasena 'the world of men is dark', their lives 'a mass of anguish'. The Buddha was the first to reveal the extent of human suffering, to explain its origins, to realize its cessation and to describe the means whereby it could be brought to an end. This cessation, the end of suffering, is Nirvana. Far from being equated with death, it is deathlessness. No positive assertions about it can be made. Although it is said that the Buddha has entered Nirvana, one cannot say what has become of him. 'When the flame of a great burning mass of fire has gone out,' Nagasena rhetorically asks Menander, 'is it possible to point to that flame and say that it is either here or there?'

This does not mean that the Buddha is inaccessible. For although 'it is not possible to point to the Buddha who has gone home and say he is either here or there, it is possible to point to him by means of the Body of Dharma, for the Dharma was revealed by the Buddha'. And as Nagasena says elsewhere, quoting Gautama: 'he who sees the Dharma sees the Buddha'. Nirvana may be sheer transcendence from the standpoint of human suffering, but through the Dharma it is rendered immanent and immediate.

'Nagasena,' asked Menander matter-of-factly, 'have you seen the Dharma?'

But Nagasena refused to be drawn and replied obliquely: 'Disciples have to spend their entire lives with the Buddha as their guide, following the Buddha's discipline.' The only other comment he makes on the Dharma is that it is 'all-subtle'. In this sense 'Dharma' refers to the way things are, what is finally the case with life. Usually it means either what the Buddha taught or the way to practise what he taught. Much of *Menander's Questions* is taken up with Nagasena explaining to the king precisely what the practice of Dharma entails.

'Nagasena,' said Menander, 'how would you define faith?'

'Faith has two characteristics: clarifying and leaping. Imagine a mighty king who crosses a stream with an army of elephants, horses, chariots and infantry and then gives an order for his troops to pause for a drink. Since the water would be fouled and turbid from the crossing he would first have to clarify it with a special gem so that the mud subsides and the water becomes clear and settled. Faith is like such a gem: it clarifies the mind of defilements and renders it clear, pure and serene.

'As for leaping, imagine a crowd of people arriving on the bank of a river swollen by a violent storm, who, afraid of the width and depth of the torrent, hesitate to cross. But when a man appears who, knowing his own capacity and power, takes a great leap which safely brings him to the other bank, then the people too will leap. Likewise, when one recognises that the minds of others are freed, does one find the faith to leap towards such a state oneself.'

Faith, for Nagasena, is the lucid confidence in one's own capacity to discover the freedom of Nirvana. Although inspired by others, faith does not imply dependence on the salvific power of another person or god nor is it an uncritical assent to a set of beliefs. Far from being blind, it is characterized by an experience of clarity in which the confused turmoil of life is, at least momentarily, absent. Having taken this leap of faith, one embarks on a process of transforming one's life to optimize the possibility of realizing Nirvana. This begins with ethical integrity.

'Ethics', explains Nagasena, 'is the basis for all other skilful qualities. Just as vegetable and animal life grow and come to maturity in dependence upon the earth, so do faith, enthusiasm, mindfulness, concentration and wisdom grow and mature on the ground of ethics. Just as an architect first clears and levels the site on which he plans to build a town, then maps out the location of the streets, squares and buildings, so does he who intends to develop such qualities of mind prepare himself by establishing ethical integrity. And just as an acrobat makes sure the ground is smooth and level before a performance, so does an earnest practitioner refine his ethics before embarking on the path to Nirvana.'

Ethical integrity is the indispensable foundation upon which to nurture, construct and pliably display the qualities of mind needed to realize Nirvana. While the aim of ethics is inner freedom, the context is engagement with the world through one's deeds, speech and livelihood. Without having settled into a non-violent, responsible relationship with the world, spiritual development will flounder.

'Just as rafters in a roof', continues Nagasena, 'incline towards a ridge-pole, so do skilled mental states incline towards concentration.' An ethically stable mind naturally tends towards integration and focal unity. And when, through meditative discipline, such concentration becomes the prominent feature of

22

consciousness, statements such as: 'ultimately there is no person at all to be found' begin to make sense.

'How many factors of awakening are there?' asked Menander.

'There are seven factors of awakening, sir.'

'But how many of these factors actually awaken one, Nagasena?'

'Just one of them, sir: investigation into things.'

Which is what Nagasena demonstrated to the king in their dialogue about identity. Whether investigating the nature of a person called 'Nagasena', 'Menander', 'Ashoka' or 'Alexander', or simply the identity of a chariot, ultimately it is impossible to put one's finger on anything, physical or metaphysical, that tells you what a person or a chariot is. This inability to find any essence or substance drops one into a depth that continues infinitely into the heart of things, never halting at something but also never coming to a stop at nothing. Upon awakening to this middle way between the extreme of reification, on the one hand, and nihilism, on the other, one is finally freed from anguish. For Nagasena this open transparency of being is called 'selflessness', for others 'transparency'; for some it is equated with 'Nirvana', and for others the 'Body of Dharma' (*Dharmakaya*).

Intellectual comprehension of selflessness alone is insufficient to trigger the kind of awakening that liberates one from suffering. This requires wisdom based on concentration and ethical integrity.

'How would you define wisdom, Nagasena?' asked the king.

'Wisdom has two characteristics, sir: cutting off and illuminating. Just as someone harvesting barley takes hold of a handful of barley in the left hand and a sickle in the right, then cuts it off, so does one take hold of the mind with attention and cuts off distortion and disturbance with wisdom. And just as someone who brings a lamp into a dark house dispels the darkness with light, so when wisdom arises it dispels the darkness of ignorance and illuminates the noble truths, so that one sees clearly what is impermanent, what is unreliable and what is selfless.'

Such moments of wisdom sever erroneous perceptions of oneself and the world, undermine past habits and assumptions and break one free from the constrictive feelings associated with them. The experience is both cognitively *and* affectively liberating, symbolized by the radiance and warmth of light. And such awakening discloses not a divine 'other' but the truth of what is the case: impermanence, unreliability and selflessness.

'Venerable Nagasena,' said the king, 'where does wisdom dwell?'

'Nowhere, sir.'

'Then there is no wisdom?'

'Where does the wind dwell, sir?'

'Nowhere, Nagasena.'

'Then there is no wind?'

And so Menander, the Greek king of north-west India, sat at the feet of a Buddhist monk and grappled with a philosophy of life in some respects similar but in most ways dissimilar to his Hellenic view of the world. He who started his rule by storming Pataliputra and claiming Ashoka's throne, ended it by stamping out coins embossed with the eight-spoked Wheel of Dharma, and — if we literally translate 'Euthymedia', the Greek name for Sagala — by calling his capital 'Right Thought', the second limb of the Buddha's eightfold path. Menander, the invader and conqueror, is invaded and conquered from within by the philosophy of those he believed he controlled.

BASILIDES:
GNOSTIC CONNECTIONS

As its colonies were absorbed into India and the rest of its territories taken over by the Roman Empire, the disintegrating and anxious Greek world was confronted by the upsurge of a new religion from Palestine.

The time from the birth of Jesus until the establishment of Christianity as the official religion of the Roman Empire by Constantine in 330 was marked by a struggle for philosophical and religious dominance among three strands of thought: Greek, Christian and Gnostic. Rarely was one of them found in an unalloyed form. They came mixed with each other as well as with Judaic, Zoroastrian and even Indian elements.

During the same period, Buddhism was flourishing in India under the impact of such figures as Nagarjuna and Asanga and the Dharma was spreading eastwards through Central Asia to China as well as westwards into Persia. Commerce between Asia and the Roman Empire increased; luxury goods were imported from China; a community of Indian merchants was settled in Alexandria; an Indian holy man immolated himself in public in Athens; and a Ceylonese embassy reached the court of Claudius in Rome.

Cyprian, the 2nd-century Church Father and Bishop of Carthage, described these uncertain times with strikingly modern pessimism:

The world today speaks for itself: by the evidence of its decay it announces its dissolution. The farmers are vanishing from the countryside, commerce from the sea, soldiers from the camps; all honesty in business, all justice in the courts, all solidarity in friendship, all skill in the arts, all standards in morals — all are disappearing.

Although the Romans adopted many features of Greek civilization, a sense of degeneration and loss prevailed throughout the Hellenized world. The time was ripe for religious innovation and at least one prominent Greek thinker, Plotinus, looked to the East for inspiration.

Like many leading figures of the period, Plotinus lived in the cultural and commercial centre of Alexandria on the north African coast. He was the foremost proponent of Neo-Platonism, a combination of rationalism and mysticism that remained the principal way of interpreting Plato until after the Renaissance. At the age of thirty-nine Plotinus attached himself to the Roman army of Gordianus III, which planned to conquer Asia, in order to study at first hand the wisdom of India. The expedition failed, and he only reached Mesopotamia before being forced to return. However sympathetic Plotinus may have been to Indian ideas, there is no indication in his philosophy of any specifically Buddhist influence.

Out of reverence for the classics, Plotinus and his contemporaries still drew their knowledge of India from such works as the *Indika* of Megasthenes. In contrast to the proud classical period, when everything non-Greek was seen as 'barbarian', now it was believed that Greek civilization had its origins in the distant and barely known cultures of India and Egypt. The *brahman*s and the *shramana*s were held in high esteem and contemporary writers praised them endlessly.

One of the most fertile areas of cross-cultural exchange were the tales and legends conveyed orally by merchants, travellers and pilgrims who crossed each other's paths on the vast network of land and sea routes between India and Europe. There are many instances of the same story, dressed in different cultural garb, occurring as a Buddhist *Jataka* tale in India and as one of Aesop's fables in Greece. One tale which had wide currency in India in this period was that of the Buddha's life. It would have been told, in rough outline at least, by Indian merchants, perhaps even by a stray *bhikshu*, to Jews, Greeks and Romans they met on their travels. This, together with the high esteem granted to anything Indian, might account for the parallels between the story of Christ and that of the Buddha.

When Christian missionaries first noticed these similarities, they were disturbed by the possibility that the account of Jesus in the New Testament might not be the unique revelation they believed it to be. Both Gautama and Jesus had miraculous births, followed by the prophecy of a wise man about their future destiny (Asita for Gautama, Simeon for Jesus); both endured a severe fast and were tempted by demonic powers shortly before embarking on their mission (Mara for Gautama, Satan for Jesus); both fulfilled earlier expectations (Gautama as the successor of Buddha Dipamkara, Jesus as the Messiah); and both encouraged their followers to spread their message to the whole of humankind. The Apocryphal Gospels contain even more detailed parallels. In the telling of Jesus's life the early Christians may unwittingly have borrowed imagery from the story of Gautama.

It was from the Church Fathers that Europe heard the first mention of the Buddha. In his *Stromata*, Clement of Alexandria, one of the first to apply Greek ideas to interpret Christian doctrine, spoke of the origins of philosophy which 'flourished in antiquity among the barbarians, shedding its light over the nations. And afterwards it came to Greece'. After listing the prophets of Egypt, the Druids and the Magi, Clement continues:

27

The Indian gymnosophists are also in number. And of these there are two classes, some of them called Sarmanae and others Brahmans ... Some, too, of the Indians obey the precepts of Boutta; whom, on account of his extraordinary sanctity, they have raised to divine honours.

Apart from this passing reference, he says no more. His disciple Origen, however, makes one solitary and puzzling remark. He explains how Britain in the 3rd century was a favourable ground for Christianity because the island 'had long been disposed to it through the doctrines of the Druids and the Buddhists, who had already inculcated the unity of the Godhead'.

The third great religious movement of the time, which Plotinus, Clement and Origen alike were at pains to refute, was Gnosticism. Rather than a tradition or school, Gnosticism is more a tendency with certain common aspects, one of which is the emphasis on *gnosis*, i.e. direct spiritual understanding, accessible to an initiated élite, thereby allowing access to the inner meaning of a religious tradition. Another aspect is its dualistic view of the world, in which material existence is condemned as irredeemably dark and evil in contrast to a spiritual realm of purity, goodness and light. *Gnosis*, then, is the means to release oneself from the bondage of matter to a state of beatitude.

The Gnostic emphasis on transcendent liberation through one's own insight is indeed similar to the Indian idea of freedom (*moksha*) from the sorrowful round of birth and death (*samsara*) and the realization of Nirvana through knowledge (*vidya*). It is now widely accepted that the Gnostics incorporated ideas from oriental traditions.

The Gnostic system with the most likely mark of Buddhist influence is that of Basilides, who lived in Alexandria during the 2nd century and composed an *Exegetica* of twenty-four books, which is now lost. He was a Christian who sought to establish a Gnostic basis for his faith, only to be roundly condemned by

28

both Clement and Origen. In 1902 a theologian called J. Kennedy argued that Basilides' theory 'was Buddhist pure and simple — Buddhist in its governing ideas, its psychology, its metaphysics; and Christianity reduced to a semi-Buddhist ideal as a result'. Kennedy argues that Basilides learnt the principles of Buddhism from the Indian community in Alexandria and then built them into his own system of Gnostic-Christianity.

Some of the central notions in Basilides' system are strangely analogous to Buddhism. According to Clement, Basilides believed that 'pain and fear are as inherent in human affairs as rust in iron', and that 'the soul has previously sinned in another life, and endures its punishment here'. Yet the most distinctively Buddhist of his ideas are those regarding the nature of the self. For Basilides, 'the soul is not a single entity', an idea which led Clement to compare it to a Trojan horse full of warriors. Basilides believed that due to the admixture of *prosartemata* — parasitic emotions (similar to the *klesha* of Buddhism) — the rational psyche finds itself in a state of 'primitive turmoil and confusion', from which it must strive to free itself, a task which results in salvation for a minority of saints. Although Basilides' system was theistic, his definition of God approaches that of Nirvana: *ouk on theos* — 'non-being God', unknowable, unutterable and inconceivable.

In other respects, Basilides' thought is alien to Buddhism. He presents a typical Gnostic account of creation and sees the advent of Jesus as the unique, decisive event in that creation. His scriptural authorities are the gospels, the Pauline epistles and the Acts of the Apostles. If, either knowingly or unknowingly, he included Buddhist ideas, he did so as a committed Christian in search of a coherent philosophy of salvation, with which to argue for his faith in the uncertain climate of his age.

Further east in Babylonia, however, a form of Gnosticism arose which made explicit reference to the Buddha. This was the system of Mani, who declared:

Wisdom and deeds have always from time to time been brought to mankind by the messengers of God. So in one age they have been brought by the messenger called Buddha to India, in another by Zarathustra to Persia, in another by Jesus to the West. Thereupon this revelation has come down, this prophecy in this last age, through me, Mani, messenger of the God of truth to Babylonia.

Mani was convinced that he had been divinely ordained to initiate the one religion that would be able to heal the world's divisions and unite humankind.

According to Mani, all previous religions had become corrupted after the death of their founders, but Manichaeism (as it came to be known) would safeguard itself against such dangers. To this end Mani wrote seven books to record his doctrine with precision. He also saw the need for flexibility and allowed his teachings to adapt freely to the lands in which they spread, identifying the founders of the other faiths as precursors of himself.

Mani began his mission by travelling to north-west India, which at the time was a flourishing centre of Buddhism. It is possible that he modelled his order on the organization of the Buddhist communities he observed there. The relation between Mani's 'Elect' and 'Hearers', for example, is similar to that between monks and lay supporters in Buddhism. Mani spent the last thirty years of his life travelling through the Persian-dominated areas of the Middle East, spreading his teaching and establishing his order of Elect. Finally, hostility from the Zoroastrian priesthood at the Persian court caused him to be thrown into prison where he was duly martyred.

Manichaeism might be a dead religion today, but in the centuries after Mani's death it spread rapidly both westwards into north Africa and Europe and eastwards into Central Asia and China with such success that it seemed on the verge of becoming the world religion Mani had predicted. In the West Mani was presented as the final incarnation of Jesus, in the East as the Buddha of Light; his dualistic doctrine provided a convincing explanation for the apparent predominance of evil; his Elect impressed people with their renunciation and the enthusiasm of their mission. But its other-worldliness did not endear it to governments and it suffered persecution across the entire Euro-Asian landmass. It was condemned by Christians and Muslims alike and violently suppressed as late as the 13th century.

Manichaean views filtered into Christianity nonetheless through Augustine of Hippo, the most influential of the Church Fathers. Before being converted to the Christian faith by his mother, Augustine had for nine years been a Manichaean Hearer. That this doctrine would have held the attention of so commanding an intellect as Augustine's indicates the authority it held. Although Augustine came to detest Manichaeism and attack it in his writings, it is increasingly acknowledged that it provided the dualistic framework of his doctrines and informed his ideas about the sinfulness of sex and the depravity of humankind. These perceptions affected the entire moral climate of Christianity, from the early Roman church to the Puritanism of Calvin.

As Augustine lay dying in Hippo (modern Annaba, Algeria) in 430, the city was being sacked by the Vandals, a tribe from the north-east that had poured across the borders to plunder the enfeebled Roman Empire. The classical period of Hellenic civilization was over and Europe entered the 'Dark Ages', a thousand years of Christian dogmatism interrupted by flashes of mystical and scientific insight which would last until the Renaissance.

At the same time that Europe was becoming Christian, Asia was becoming Buddhist. In India the monastic universities of Nalanda and Vikramashila flourished, and by the 8th century Central Asia, China, Korea, Tibet and Japan were, in varying degrees, Buddhist. Yet this growth and consolidation of two of the world's major religions occurred in complete ignorance of each other. Absorption in their own doctrinal and institutional concerns, combined with the rise of Islam from the 7th century onwards, closed the possibility of communication between them — with one exception.

Sometime in the late 10th or early 11th centuries a monk called Euthymius from Mount Athos translated from his native Georgian into Greek the account of two Christian saints from India: Barlaam and Josaphat. The story tells of a powerful king called Abenes, who persecuted Christians, and had an only son called Josaphat. To the king's dismay the wisest astrologer of the land predicted that Josaphat would renounce the world and become a prophet of the Christian faith. So the king confined Josaphat to a palace and prevented him from seeing the true condition of humankind. The young man persuaded his father to let him out and as he toured the kingdom he saw a blind man, a cripple and an old man. Josaphat was shocked into a realization of the transient nature of life and lost interest in worldly pursuits.

At this point a Christian hermit called Barlaam appeared from Ceylon, disguised as a merchant. In the course of several discreet visits Barlaam converted Josaphat to Christianity. The king found out and forced Barlaam to flee. Alarmed by his son's conversion, the king tried to cure him of his world-renouncing ways by tempting him with beautiful women. Josaphat resisted the temptations. In despair the king decided to divide the realm between himself and his son. Although Josaphat's half prospered, the king's declined. At last the king was convinced of the truth of Christianity and, together with his court, was converted. After his father's death, Josaphat placed the kingdom in the hands of a retainer and departed to join Barlaam in Ceylon, where they lived out the rest of their days as saintly hermits.

This is, of course, the story of the Buddha's renunciation. The major difference is Josaphat's conversion by Barlaam, rather than 'working out his own salvation with diligence' as did the young Prince Siddhartha. Barlaam's teaching resembles Buddhist doctrine only in its broad theme of renunciation but rarely in its details. The Greek text of the story is further embellished with copious citations from the Bible and the Church Fathers.

It was widely believed in Europe that the story of Barlaam and Josaphat was an account of the second conversion of India to Christianity, the first having been achieved by the Apostle Thomas, who was credited with having founded the Church on the subcontinent shortly after the death of Jesus.

The version of Gautama's life upon which the Barlaam and Josaphat story is based came into being in the 2nd and 3rd centuries CE with works such as Ashvaghosa's *Buddhacarita*. This highly popular Sanskrit biography spread quickly through the Buddhist world and was translated into Chinese by 421. It most likely found its way westwards, not directly from India, but through the Manichaeans of Central Asia, who adapted the legend of the Buddha's renunciation to their own ends. An Arabic text of the story, translated from the Iranian Pehlevi dialect, appeared in the 8th century in Baghdad — home to a sizeable but secret Manichaean community. This was translated the following century into Georgian by Orthodox monks in Jerusalem, and given a Christian interpretation. Euthymius's Greek translation appeared about a hundred years later.

From the Greek it went into Latin and from the 11th century onwards found its way into French, German, Italian, Spanish, Provençal, Romaic, Dutch and the Scandinavian languages. As it spread through the Byzantine countries, Africa and beyond, an estimated eighty translations were made — including, ironically, a

Chinese translation from a Latin compendium of the lives of the saints brought to China by Jesuit missionaries in the 17th century.

Unbeknown to the devout admirers of this story, in worshipping Josaphat, they were paying homage to Buddha, the chief 'idol' of heathen Asia. Prior to his awakening the Buddha was known as the 'Bodhisattva' (Sanskrit), which became 'Budhasaf' (Arabic), then 'Iodasaph' (Georgian), 'Ioasaph' (Greek) and finally 'Josaphat' (Latin). Although never canonized, in the 16th century Barlaam and Josaphat were, by popular demand, assigned a place in the Roman Catholic roll of saints, their day being 27 November. A church was dedicated to Josaphat in Palermo, Sicily, while the church of Saint-André d'Anvers in France housed one of his relics. During the Reformation they were held up as justifications for monasticism. And Shakespeare drew on one of Barlaam's parables for his device of the 'Three Caskets', by which Portia chooses her suitor in *The Merchant of Venice*.

The first European to notice similarities between the story of Barlaam and Josaphat and its Indian original was a Portuguese historian, Diogo do Couto, in 1612. This insight did not cause him to doubt Josaphat's authenticity, but led him to conclude that Josaphat was the model on which the life of the Buddha was constructed. The whole story only came to light when the French scholar Laboulaye gave the first accurate account of its origins in 1859.

The legend or 'romance' of Barlaam and Josaphat unintentionally introduced into medieval Europe the rudiments of the Buddha's life. But since it was unrecognized as such and heavily overlaid with Christian dogma, it provided no information either about the Buddha or his teaching. It says more about European perceptions of Asia as a repository of holy men and wondrous events than anything else.

During the thousand-year period from the Buddha until Augustine the impact of Buddhist and Hellenic/Christian thought on each other was at best marginal. Their relationship was largely one of mutual ignorance and disinterest, tinged, in periods of self-confidence, with the assurance that all other peoples were barbarians, and, in periods of self-doubt, with the romantic notion that 'people of whom we know little or nothing have all the virtues we lack'.

Such is the veil which continued to obscure Buddhism from the West for nearly 2,500 years. Only during the 20th century has this veil been slowly lifted, allowing a more immediate encounter with the Dharma — in the very heartland of Europe.

4

BHIKKHU SANGHA:
THE ORDER OF MONKS

Dawn awakes with the faint cry of a rooster and, moments later, cobalt-blue light smouldering in the panes of the Victorian bay-window, sharpening the golden gleam of the Buddha's forehead. Floorboards creak, radiators strain and clunk, as nine shaven-headed monks sit immobile, cross-legged, wrapped in creased ochre robes. Lone birds stammer out their first notes. The light pales to grey and through the mist beyond the Buddha's head, unseen by the monks' downcast eyes, reach the gnarled fingers of an oak and the bluff summit of a cedar. The cooing of a wood-pigeon entreats them back to sleep. A cluster of leaves presses against a corner pane. The kitchen clatter of ill-fitting lids on aluminium pots signals the preparation of gruel.

So begins a spring day in Wat Pah Cittaviveka or Chithurst Forest Monastery, a converted 19th-century manor house situated amidst the pastoral affluence of West Sussex, England. These monks were born in America, Britain, Switzerland and Latvia but their spiritual roots go back to Magadha. Their presence in Europe can be traced, via a meandering two-thousand-year trail through Ceylon and Thailand, to the missions of Ashoka. The translated Pali texts in their library upstairs preserve the conversations between Menander and Nagasena.

The Arhat Mahinda, son of Ashoka, introduced Buddhism to Ceylon around 250 BCE. One of his first tasks was to construct a *sima* — the formal boundary for monastic ordination — with the king himself driving a plough along the lines drawn out by the monks. Then he ordained the first Ceylonese *bhikkhus* (monks), declaring that Buddhism could not be said to have taken root in the land until native Ceylonese had ordained and could recite the monastic rule (*vinaya*). Shortly afterwards, his sister Sanghamitta arrived in the island to institute the order of *bhikkhunis* (nuns).

Of the two strands into which Buddhism was dividing at the time of Ashoka, Mahinda and Sanghamitta represented the tradition of the Elders rather than that of the Majority. Over the ensuing centuries the Elders developed into numerous branches, the most resilient of which proved to be the Theravada. This school reached its most mature form in the 5th century CE in Ceylon with the commentarial syntheses of the Buddhist monk-scholar Buddhaghosa, who established Pali as the lingua franca of Theravada Buddhism.

It is less clear how Buddhism spread to South-East Asia. The indigenous Mon people of what is now Burma and Thailand had been introduced to diverse forms of the Dharma from India by the 4th or 5th centuries CE. In 832 the peninsula was invaded by Thai people from the region of Nan-chao in south-west China. The Thais spread through the area over the next four hundred years, eventually dominating the Mon and, following a massive exodus of Thais from China fleeing Kublai Khan's armies at the end of the 13th century, created independent kingdoms. They nonetheless assimilated Mon culture, including its forms of Buddhism.

The Thai kingdom of the central and southern part of the country was ruled from 1279—99 by Rama Khamhaeng, a righteous Buddhist monarch who followed the example of Ashoka in issuing edicts carved in rock to declare his enlightened policies to his subjects. Yet Rama Khamhaeng's son and successor Lö Tai felt that the Buddhism of his realm was still mixed with animism and superstition and looked to the Ceylonese forest tradition as the repository of the true Dharma. He dispatched a *bhikkhu* called Sumana there to receive ordination and training. When Sumana returned he spread the Ceylonese form of Theravada Buddhism throughout the kingdom of Sukhotai.

One of the first glimpses Europe received of such Theravada Buddhist monasticism was from Jean Marignolli, an envoy of Pope Benedict XII, who, having been dispatched to China in 1338, returned home via Ceylon and described the kind of life the *bhikkhus* led at the time of Sumana:

> These monks only eat once a day and never more and drink nothing but milk and water. They never keep food with them overnight. They sleep on the bare ground. They walk barefoot, with a stick, and are satisfied with a robe rather like that of our Friars Minor (Franciscans), but without a hood and with a cloak over their shoulder in the manner of the apostles. Every morning, they go in a procession to ask, with the greatest possible reverence, that rice be given them in an appropriate quantity for their number . . . . I speak of these things as a witness and, in truth, they welcomed me as if I had been one of them . . . . These people lead a very saintly life — albeit without Faith.

It was into such a Buddhist culture, little changed in the intervening seven hundred years, that Ajahn Chah was born on 17 June 1918, to a prosperous family in a village in the forested north-east of Thailand. After receiving monastic ordination at the age of twenty-one, he embarked on the usual course of studies in Buddhist doctrine and the Pali language. When his father died five years later, he realized that his learning had brought him no closer to the end of suffering. In 1946 he set off on foot with nothing but his robes, an almsbowl and the minimal requisites of a monk in search of a way of life more conducive to discovering the freedom of Nirvana. This quest led him to place greater emphasis on the monastic rule, which in the towns and cities was often lax, and to seek instruction in the *practice* of Buddhism, rather than contenting himself with knowledge of its doctrines.

His dilemma reflected a conflict that had beset the Theravada tradition throughout its history in Ceylon and Thailand. State support meant that the Buddhist order was guaranteed the material and social security needed to ensure the preservation of the Dharma. But in return the monks were to serve the interests of the State by establishing a moral and spiritual framework whereby the people would live in harmony and obedience. This caused the order to fracture into two parts: 'forest monks', who placed a premium on realizing Nirvana, and 'town monks', who chose to serve as village priests, administrators in city temples, or scholars and teachers. Once a *bhikkhu*'s role as a cleric superseded his religious aspirations, the very *raison-d'être* of being a monk — 'that suffering may cease and further suffering may not arise' — was undermined. Observation of the rule became largely a formality that went with the job and the practice of meditation a luxury for which there was little time and interest.

Such concerns led Ajahn Chah to the renowned meditation master Ajahn Mun. Although he spent very little time with this teacher, he learned something that transformed his understanding of Buddhism: *the true way of practice lies in mindfully seeing that everything arises in one's own heart.* This insight inspired him to spend the next seven years following the austere disciplines of the Forest Tradition, wandering through the countryside and meditating in jungles. In 1954 he returned to his home village and settled in the nearby woodland. His presence drew other monks to follow his example and they founded a monastery that came to be known as Wat Pah Bong.

It was to Wat Pah Bong that a newly ordained American monk, Ven. Sumedho, was taken to meet Ajahn Chah in 1967. In his former existence as Robert Jackman, Sumedho had served as a medical officer in the Korean war, completed a degree in South Asian Studies at Berkeley and taught English with the Peace Corps in Borneo. His first year as a novice in Thailand had been spent mainly in solitary retreat, where he had experienced an overwhelming sense of spiritual well-being but found himself incapable of coping with other people. As a foreigner he was used to being pampered by the Thais. When he arrived in Wat Pah Bong people said: 'He's American; he can't eat our kind of food!' Ajahn Chah responded with a mischievous grin: 'He'll have to learn.' Sumedho spent the next ten years under the guidance of his kind, humorous but uncompromising teacher, learning the principles that underlay Ajahn Chah's approach: living harmoniously in a community, practising mindfulness under all conditions, and ceaselessly letting go of clinging and conceit.

By 1974 the number of Westerners arriving to ordain and practise with Ajahn Chah led to the founding of Wat Pah Nanachat, a monastery dedicated to the training of Western monks. Sumedho was appointed abbot, the first Westerner to hold such a post in Thailand. But in 1977 this idyll in the Thai jungle was interrupted. Ajahn Chah received an invitation from the English Sangha Trust, a lay organization that since 1955 had been trying, as yet unsuccessfully, to establish an order of Western Buddhist monks in Britain.

Attempts to found a Theravada Buddhist monastic *sangha* (community) in England go as far back as 23 April 1908, when the first Buddhist Mission to Britain was welcomed at London Docks by members of the newly founded Buddhist Society of Great Britain and Ireland. This mission was headed by Allan Bennett, the second Briton to have ordained as a Theravada *bhikkhu*, and known since his ordination in Burma in December

1901 as Ananda Metteyya. (The first was Gordon Douglas, ordained by a Siamese monk as Bhikkhu Ashoka in 1899 or 1900. There are conflicting accounts of his fate: he either died of cholera six months after ordination, or founded a school and died in Burma in 1905.)

Prior to his departure for Asia in 1898, Bennett had been a close friend of the self-declared 'Wickedest Man in the World', Aleister Crowley, who described Bennett as 'the noblest and gentlest soul I have ever known'. Bennett became a prominent member of Crowley's Order of the Golden Dawn but his work as an aspiring magician was hampered by chronic asthma. He decided to travel to the warmer climes of Ceylon, the funds for which were solicited by Crowley from a colonel's wife with whom he was having an affair. Bennett, who arrived in Ceylon as a 'self-converted' Buddhist, soon decided to organize a mission to England to establish the Dharma in his homeland. To this end he travelled to Burma for ordination as a *bhikkhu*, at the conclusion of which he publicly announced his intention 'to carry to the lands of the West the Law of Love and Truth declared by our Master, to establish in those countries the Sangha of his Priests'. His return to England was heralded by the country's small cluster of Buddhists as an auspicious start to the spreading of the Dharma in Europe. Despite his noble bearing and erudition, Ananda Metteya was an uninspiring public speaker, and a mere six months later, his asthma worse than ever, he abandoned the Mission and returned to Burma. In 1914 ill-health forced him to disrobe and he came back to England, where he stayed until his death on 9 March 1923, promoting Buddhist ideas through his writings and occasional lectures.

Forty-seven years and two World Wars were to elapse before the next phase in implanting a Theravada monastic *sangha* in Europe began. On the Wesak (Buddha's enlightenment) day of 1954, an Englishman, William Purfurst, was ordained as Bhikkhu

Kapilavaddho in Thailand. The following year he returned to London and was instrumental in founding the English Sangha Trust. Within a few months four British *bhikkhus* were in residence at a *vihara* (monastery) in St John's Wood. But a year later Kapilavaddho succumbed to illness and was forced to disrobe. The small community struggled on, until only one *bhikkhu* (Pannavaddho) was left, who chose, in 1961, to settle in Thailand, where he has remained ever since under the Thai meditation master Ajahn Maha Boowa.

Three further attempts to create a Western monastic *sangha* followed. For two years the Hampstead Vihara (the location since 1962) in north London was under the direction of a Canadian monk Ananda Bodhi (formerly Leslie Dawson; latterly Namgyal Rinpoché), then for a further two years under the English monk Sangharakshita (Dennis Lingwood). Both these men, however, were not convinced of the value of a traditional Theravada-style monastic *sangha* in the West and left to pursue their own visions of how Buddhism should be taught and practised. In October 1967, Kapilavaddho, his health restored, took ordination once more and returned to the Vihara. After an energetic spell Kapilavaddho again fell ill and disrobed in 1970. He died on 19 December the following year at the age of sixty-five. The Vihara was soon empty of monks and, apart from periodic visits, was to remain so until Ajahn Chah's arrival in 1977.

With him Ajahn Chah brought Sumedho — now Ajahn Sumedho — and left his disciple in charge of three other Western *bhikkhus* in the Vihara, a cramped house at 131 Haverstock Hill, in the less salubrious end of Hampstead, that rattled with the groan of passing traffic. Unlike his predecessors Sumedho had two key factors in his favour: not only was he firmly committed to the need for a monastic *sangha*, he was vigorously healthy.

One morning the following spring, while out on the daily ritual with their begging bowls in search of non-existent alms, the *bhikkhus* attracted the attention of a jogger on Hampstead Heath who offered them a forest. This was Hammer Wood in West Sussex, that the jogger had bought with the intention to restore it to its original state. Recently he had realized that his plan was too ambitious to accomplish unassisted. Although not a Buddhist himself, he felt that these monks would be ideal wardens. By-laws, however, forbade any permanent structures to be built in the wood. The forest monks had a forest but nowhere to live. So the following year the English Sangha Trust sold the Hampstead property and purchased a dilapidated Victorian house about a mile from the woodland in the village of Chithurst. At this point Ajahn Chah returned from Thailand to see how his disciples were getting on.

Over the years the previous owners had let Chithurst House fall into ruin, retreating from the leaking roofs and decaying floors until only four of the twenty or so rooms were habitable. The electricity had long since failed, only one cold water tap worked, dry rot infested the woodwork, the cesspit had not been emptied for twenty-five years, more than thirty abandoned cars littered the gardens, and the house was packed with hoarded pre-war bric-à-brac. It took a week just to burn all the newspapers and magazines. Ajahn Chah gave his approval to the place and the monks and their lay supporters set to work on the task of restoring the building and the grounds.

For two years they put aside their monastic routines and turned into builders, carpenters, metal-workers and plumbers, pausing for contemplation only during the Rains Retreat or when funds ran out.

In 1981 three events signalled, if not completion of their task, at least that its end was in sight. In February the radiant half-ton golden Buddha arrived as a gift from a devout lay-supporter in Thailand and was manoeuvred into the newly prepared shrine room. On 3 June, Ven. Anandametteya, an elder from Sri Lanka, established a *sima* (monastic boundary) in the garden and conferred on Ajahn Sumedho the authority to perform ordinations. And on 16 July the first Theravada Buddhist ordination in Europe to be carried out by a Westerner took place as Ajahn Sumedho ordained three Western postulants as *bhikkhus*.

This flourishing of Buddhism in Sussex coincided with the collapse of Ajahn Chah's health in Thailand. Earlier that summer the diabetes which had affected him for years became suddenly worse and he was rushed to Bangkok for an operation. This was of little help. By the autumn he had lost his speech and shortly afterwards the use of his limbs. By the end of the year he was paralysed and bed-ridden.

By 1992, Chithurst House had been immaculately restored in every detail from the spiralling brick chimneys to the well-tended lawns, from the scrupulously polished floors, up the caringly recrafted banisters, to the sparkling bathrooms. In this sanctuary from the turmoil of modern life, where radio, television and newspapers are forgotten rather than banished, where the days are regulated by bells and lunar cycles instead of clocks and calendars, a vital stillness absorbs anxiety and precipitates 'wise reflection on the Dharma', silent meditation, bowing and chanting, in short: a life of awareness.

Chithurst is no longer an eccentric outpost of Thai Buddhism in a corner of England, but the nucleus of a growing monastic community throughout Europe. It has become a Buddhist 'seminary', where newly ordained monks are trained before being sent to serve in Amaravati, the main public centre north of London, or in the two smaller centres in Britain — in Harnham, Northumberland, and Honiton, Devon — or even to the newly opened *viharas* in Switzerland and Italy. At the time of writing, there are around fifty *bhikkhus*, nine ten-precept nuns and about thirty male and female postulants living in the different European centres.

The success of Chithurst has surprised not only sceptical outsiders, but even members of the English Sangha Trust. One of the stumbling blocks to Ananda Metteyya's mission in 1908 had been the sheer incongruity of the traditional lifestyle of a Buddhist monk in the context of British society. Perceptions had not changed greatly in the seventy years since. The very notion of shaven-headed *bhikkhus* in thin cotton robes and sandals going on a daily alms-round through English towns and villages, where not only Buddhism but monasticism and mendicancy in general are alien, seemed ludicrous. Surely the sensible thing to do would be to modify certain aspects of the monastic rule so that the contrast between the monks and the rest of society would be lessened. But Ajahn Chah and Ajahn Sumedho — as well as the ethnic Thai community in Britain — would hear nothing of it. If change comes, it will come in its own time, they said. Our sole task is to place unconditional trust in the rule and the Dharma. If the conditions are ripe in Europe, it will work; if not, then we'll go back to Thailand.

Throughout its history Buddhism has regarded the establishment of a monastic *sangha* — of at least five *bhikkhus* — as the indispensable condition for a country to qualify as a place where the Dharma has taken root. Symbolically, such a community represents the living presence of the Buddha's dispensation; in real terms, it shows a society sufficiently conscious of the value of the Dharma to support a community of men and women dedicated to its practice. Chithurst Forest Monastery may not be the first place in Europe to house a settled community of Buddhist monastics (ethnic Tibetan, Vietnamese, Sri Lankan and Thai monasteries have existed for some years), but it is the first such community to be run entirely by Western monks and nuns, with the wholehearted backing of an orthodox tradition.

How has Chithurst succeeded in establishing such a community in Europe? It was not a deliberately plotted campaign to implant Buddhism; the British supporters saw it as a gamble, the monks as merely a response to circumstances. The Thai community in Britain (as well as supporters in Thailand) may have seen it as a mission of sorts and were proud to witness an aspect of their culture received with enthusiasm in the West. But while they provided, and still provide, a great deal of funding, money alone cannot account for the coherence, vitality and growth of a religious community.

At the root of Chithurst Monastery lies the encounter between Ajahn Chah and the straggling procession of disaffected Westerners who drifted into Thailand during the 1960s and 70s. Ajahn Chah, himself a rebel against the lax clerical Buddhist establishment of the towns, appealed to these veterans of the hippy trail and the Vietnam War as someone who offered not only a radically simple and sane philosophy of life but an embodiment of it in his daily existence. The austere lifestyle he followed was infused not with the dour, world-denying outlook one might expect but with a sparkling, roguish and above all contented personality. Years of hedonistic excess, together with a loss of faith in Christianity, had led these young Europeans and Americans not to unfettered freedom but to spiritual despair. And this pot-bellied little monk, who looked more like a bullfrog than a saint, turned their world-view on its head.

The long hair and beards were shaved off, the embroidered Afghan shirts and baggy Indian trousers were exchanged for hand-dyed ochre robes, and total unrestraint was replaced by 227 rules of conduct. 'I know that you have had a background of material comfort and outward freedom', Ajahn Chah would tell them:

By comparison you now live an austere existence. Food and climate are different from your home .... This is the

46

suffering that leads to the end of suffering. This is how you learn . . . . I know some of you are well educated and very knowledgeable. People with little education and worldly knowledge can practise easily. But it is as if you Westerners have a very large house to clean. When you have cleaned the house, you will have a big living space. But you must be patient.

The explicit emphasis on a simple and harmonious community life and the implicit need to train with a teacher wiser than oneself are at the basis of Ajahn Chah's understanding. An inscription carved in a stone embedded in the lawn in front of the monastery's *sima* reads *Vinayo Sasanassa Ayu*: 'The rule is the life of the teaching.' No matter how uncomfortable or irrational the monastic rule may seem at times, unconditional confidence that it is vital to Buddhist practice is the act of faith upon which the community is founded. The danger of it becoming constricting and legalistic is avoided by emphasizing moment to moment examination of the mind and letting go of fixations. This combination of literal adherence to the rule with open-minded, warm-hearted awareness not only endeared Ajahn Chah to his Western disciples but also endears the monks and nuns at Chithurst to the lay community that supports them. Thus a relationship of mutual, freely offered provision is established: the community gives spiritual nourishment to the laity and the laity provide physical nourishment for the monks and nuns.

'If you want to really see for yourself what the Buddha was talking about,' Ajahn Chah would say, 'you don't need to bother with books. Watch your own mind.' This non-scholastic, experience-based approach to Buddhism is central to the community at Chithurst. It does not mean that books are forbidden — there is an extensive library of Buddhist scriptures in the monastery — but it teaches one to treat intellectual knowledge with caution. The absence of emphasis on Pali texts, especially the commentarial literature, has freed the Thai forest tradition to follow a strand of the Buddha's teaching which receives only scant attention in the recorded discourses: 'This mind, monks,' said the Buddha, 'is luminous, but it is defiled by taints that come from without.' In contrast to many Theravada Buddhist teachers, who tend to speak in terms of 'non-self' and 'Nirvana', Ajahn Chah, following his teacher Ajahn Mun, uses expressions like 'true mind' to designate a basic dimension of being that neither arises nor passes away; it just is:

> About this mind . . . in truth there is nothing really wrong with it. It is intrinsically pure. Within itself it is already peaceful. Our practice is simply to see the Original Mind. So we must train the mind to know the sense impressions, and not get lost in them. To make it peaceful. Just this is the aim of all this difficult practice we put ourselves through.

The Buddha is not a remote historical or metaphysical being but simply 'the One Who Knows, the one who has purity, radiance and peace in his heart'.

This positive approach, usually associated more with Zen or Tibetan Buddhism, may also account for the attraction of Ajahn Chah's teachings among Westerners. For a mind teetering on the edge of nihilism, traditional Buddhist doctrines of non-self and emptiness can seem threatening. To be told that fundamentally you are sane, radiant and at peace with yourself provides metaphors of reassurance with which to build a non-egoistic self-confidence as the basis for ethical and meditative practice.

Ajahn Chah is fully aware of the dangers of reification, of turning the 'Original Mind' into a subtle kind of self-centredness. When once asked whether something really did exist independently from the changing processes of body and mind, he replied:

There isn't anything and we don't call it anything — that's all there is to it! Be finished with all of it. Even the knowing doesn't belong to anybody, so be finished with that, too! Consciousness is not an individual, not a being, not a self, not an other, so finish with that — finish with everything! There is nothing worth wanting! It's all just a load of trouble .... You can call it 'Original Mind' if you insist. You can call it whatever you like ...

In 1991 Ajahn Chah entered the tenth year of his comatose existence, cared for by his disciples in a custom-built clinic in the forest at Wat Pah Bong. Paradoxically, during the period he had been silenced by disease the number of monasteries inspired by his example has grown to nearly a hundred world-wide. On 15 January 1992 Ajahn Chah died. His body, however, laid in state for a further year. Elsewhere in the monastery a perfect life-size wax replica of him sits on his favourite couch, frozen in time, teaching that all things are subject to change.

TWO

MONGOLS AND FRIARS, LAMAS AND ZEN

SHANTIDEVA:
THE BODHISATTVA

Eleven thousand years ago Cro-Magnon men and women crawled into the womb-like interiors of a cave near what is now the town of Rouffignac in the Dordogne region of south-west France. Lying on their backs they traced the outlines of animals — horses, bulls, rhinoceros, goats, mammoths — on the cave surface above them.

Not far from Rouffignac, on the banks of the Vézère, lies Le Moustier, a tiny village which, due to discoveries in a rock shelter behind the baker's shop in 1864, gave its name to the 'Mousterian' period of prehistory, which spanned more than a hundred thousand years. The baker's shop still stands at the point where a tiny road winds up the Côte de Jor, a forested ridge rising above the Vézère Valley. Tucked on a stone wall, invisible from the main road, is a small, cracked wooden board inscribed with the words 'Centre Bouddhique'.

If you had followed this road at the end of August 1991, having passed a number of Tibetan Buddhist centres and retreat facilities (the former visible, the latter invisible from the road), you would have reached a field containing a marquee capable of seating up to ten thousand people. Having checked your cameras and tape-recorders into the *consigne* and passed through the gate-like metal detectors, you would have been admitted inside where smiling hostesses would have shown you to a seat on a colour-coded floor. On the stage at the front amidst flowers, richly decorated hangings and Tibetan scroll paintings, seated on a brocaded throne would have been Tenzin Gyatso, the 14th Dalai Lama.

To the Dalai Lama's right hangs a large scroll painting of Avalokiteshvara, the Bodhisattva of Compassion, with one thousand arms radiating in a circle from his white eleven-headed body, and in the palm of each hand an eye; and to his left, beneath a tree that emerges through an opening in the stage floor, is a sand-mandala, an intricate symmetrical design composed by the Dalai Lama's monks of coloured grains of sand.

In his hand the Dalai Lama is holding a long page of Tibetan text which he has taken from a cloth-wrapped volume on a table at his side. He reads it rapidly in the refined inflections of the Lhasa dialect, pausing to comment on key passages. This is translated into French over the loud-speakers and in English, German and Spanish through remote-control headphone-sets, so that all of the four thousand people in the audience can follow the Dalai Lama's thoughts on the classic Buddhist text: *A Guide to the Bodhisattva's Way of Life (Bodhicaryavatara)*, composed in Sanskrit by the Indian poet Shantideva around the 8th century CE.

&c&

Of Shantideva himself little is known. By his time the Buddhism of Nagasena had expanded into several philosophical traditions and offered a diverse range of spiritual practices. While agreeing in principle with the earliest strata of Buddhist doctrine, the Buddhism of Shantideva had evolved over the centuries in the changing spiritual climates of India. From his writings we know that Shantideva was an exponent of the Madhyamaka philosophy of transparency (*sunyata*), formulated by Nagarjuna in the 2nd century CE and, in ethical attitude, a proponent of the ideal of the Bodhisattva — one who selflessly dedicates his or her life to Buddhahood for the welfare of all that lives.

54

In broad terms, this movement evolved from the views of the Majority at Ashoka's time. It now called itself the 'Great Vehicle' (*Mahayana*) — 'great' in that its concerns extended beyond personal salvation to include all beings. It contrasted itself to those Buddhist schools, who traced their origins back to the Elders of Ashokan times, whom it pejoratively labelled as 'Lesser Vehicles' (*Hinayana*). Although there are records of monks of both tendencies happily co-existing in monasteries in ancient India, the division between Mahayana and Hinayana hardened over time, the so-called 'Mahayanists' accusing the so-called 'Hinayanists' of selfish preoccupation, and the so-called 'Hinayanists' condemning their former confrères of degeneration and impurity. Even Mahayana texts, however, state that this division has nothing to do with one's allegiance to a particular school of Buddhism; but with the attitude of mind that motivates one's practice.

Shantideva lived at a time of internal political conflict and disarray in the Indian subcontinent after the break-up of the powerful Gupta dynasty, coupled with the external threat of Islam, the newly dominant religious culture that had rapidly expanded westwards as far as Morocco, eastwards as far as Sindh (in modern Pakistan), and northwards into Central Asia. There was no Chandragupta or Ashoka waiting in the wings to unify the subcontinent under a powerful new dynasty as when it was threatened by the Greeks. The freely wandering *bhikshus* of Nagasena's time had been replaced by vast monastic universities, most prestigious of which was Nalanda, in present-day Bihar, where 'five hundred' (which means 'a lot' in Indian literary convention) learned pandits taught and debated with several thousand monks from all over the subcontinent. The period is renowned for its advances in scholarship and philosophical analysis. It was also the time when Buddhism became top-heavy with institutions.

Shantideva's life is only recorded in outline — and more as

legend than biography. Like the Buddha, he is said to have been born into a royal family. Yet just before he was to be enthroned, he received a vision of Manjushri, the Bodhisattva of Wisdom, renounced his title and fled to Nalanda. Contrary to expectation for one with such auspicious beginnings, Shantideva failed to distinguish himself. In the eyes of his fellow monks he was a layabout proficient in only three things: eating, sleeping and defecating.

In order to rid the monastery of such parasites, a public examination was convened, where each monk would be invited to deliver a discourse to the community as a means of showing his degree of understanding. Those who fell below a certain level would be expelled. When Shantideva mounted the teaching throne, he started — to the amusement of the gathering — by asking whether he should present something that was already known or something original. The monks opted for the latter and, to their amazement, Shantideva proceeded to recite an eloquent thousand-verse poem, which he entitled *A Guide to the Bodhisattva's Way of Life*. And not only did this stream of inspired utterance pour forth from his mouth but when he recited the lines:

When neither something nor nothing remains in mind,
There are no other alternatives.
So without any object,
There is complete peace,

he ascended into the air until, his words becoming fainter and fainter, he vanished. The monks dispatched search-parties to recover this unrecognized prodigy. They found Shantideva in a remote corner of India, but, despite their entreaties, he refused to return to Nalanda. This was effectively his final contact with the Buddhist establishment.

Another tradition, that of the iconoclastic tantric *mahasiddhas*, goes on to tell how at this point Shantideva gave back his monastic vows and returned to the anonymity of laylife, taking employment for twelve years as a palace guard (armed with only a gold-painted wooden sword), until, having been 'discovered' again, he retreated to a remote mountain cave and lived out the rest of his years as a hermit. He also married a low-caste woman.

Whatever the historical legitimacy of these accounts, they confirm the underlying principles of Shantideva's legend. The example of Shantideva stands as a model Buddhist life of his times. He is a true individual, one who follows his own insights and intuitions (symbolized by his receiving 'visions' of Manjushri, the archetypal form of wisdom), first by rejecting the expectations of the world and then those of the monastic establishment. His life is a critique of the institutionalization of the Buddhist order, which he purifies, as it were, through his poem, by forcefully restating the principles of the Bodhisattva's way of life. While certain monks may have been capable of reforming themselves in the light of his understanding, the institutions were beyond salvation. The authentic Buddhist life was to be found outside the monastic walls, in a return to the world, to a practice based on personal insight and expressed through protean forms of life, some of which might outwardly appear shocking. At one point in his later life he is observed killing and eating deer. When challenged, he replies: 'I am no butcher; I am a healer.' To prove his point, he opens his cave door, out of which 'animals streamed into the sunshine, seeming to multiply as they ran, covering the hills and valleys, until finally they vanished into nothing' — a practical illustration of the insubstantiality of all things.

The leitmotif of Shantideva's life is his yearning for anonymity — as a prince, as a monk, as a tantric adept. His legends stress the need for the concealment of spiritual genius. He embodies the ideal of the Chinese Taoist sage, who realizes the paradoxical truth that to be most effective in the world means to disappear, unrecognized, into the world. Such a person, says Chuang Tzu, 'will not harm others, but he makes no show of benevolence or charity'.

> He will not wrangle for goods or wealth, but he makes no show of refusing or relinquishing them . . . . His actions differ from those of the mob, but he makes no show of uniqueness or eccentricity . . . . All the titles and stipends of the age are not enough to stir him to exertion; all its penalties and censures are not enough to make him feel shame.

A similar sentiment is found in one of the key passages of Shantideva's poem. Having recognized the essential identity of all forms of life, Shantideva remarks:

> Even when I have done things for the sake of others,
> No sense of amazement or conceit arises.
> It is just like having fed myself;
> I hope for nothing in return.

What is it about *A Guide to the Bodhisattva's Way of Life* that makes it so appealing even today? What has caused it within the last decade to have been translated or retranslated into English, French, German, Spanish and Estonian? It is the compelling humanism of the text, the author's intensely personal tone, that speaks across time and culture to the concerns and aspirations of our age. It is not an 'easy' text to read: many of its metaphors are alien, some of them extreme, much of its tone bespeaks a devotionalism apparently at odds with its psychological acuity, and many of its philosophical passages are, to say the least, obscure. Yet in contrast to so many Buddhist writings, whose lofty abstraction and repetition renders them remote and even cold, Shantideva's poem, even when one rebels against its imagery, overcomes such reservations with its passion.

The theme that animates the text throughout is that of *bodhicitta*, a Sanskrit term variously rendered as the 'thought (*citta*) of enlightenment (*bodhi*)', the 'spirit of enlightenment', the 'awakening mind' — all of which fail to capture the richness of the idea. It is defined, rather drily, as 'the selfless aspiration to attain enlightenment for the sake of all living beings'. *Bodhicitta* is what inspires someone to be a Bodhisattva, a person whose life is dedicated not merely to the ending of their own suffering, but to the uprooting of all suffering, irrespective of whether it is 'mine' or 'yours'. Since, in Buddhist terms, the optimal fulfilment of one's own and others' welfare is found in Buddhahood, a mode of being in which wisdom and compassion are both fully integrated and manifest, it is to the realization of Buddhahood that one dedicates one's life. *Bodhicitta* is not merely the initial motivating force, but also the selfless way of life thus motivated. 'There are two aspects to *bodhicitta*:' says Shantideva, 'the thought that aspires to awaken and the process of awakening itself.' The difference between the two is like the difference between 'wanting to go somewhere and actually going there' — and clearly the 'doing' of awakening is more valuable than merely aspiring to it.

Shantideva speaks of 'seizing' this *bodhicitta* by consciously committing one's life to such a goal, but he also recognizes that it has arisen in him miraculously. He compares himself to 'a blindman who has chanced upon a jewel in a heap of rubbish', and considers his promise to assume the burden of liberating all beings from pain as 'the words of a lunatic'. But the depth of his commitment is such that he must find a way of honouring it. This leads to a prolonged reflection on the nature of ethical responsibility.

For Shantideva the justification for an ethical life is to preserve and strengthen the *bodhicitta*. The key factors are constant mindfulness of one's resolve and awareness of the means to best focus that resolve in each situation. Mindfulness is compared to 'a watchman at the gateway of consciousness', constantly on guard against any impulse that threatens to override the vulnerable resolve of *bodhicitta*. Such impulses are like 'thieves in search of an opportunity to rob one of this virtue'. Ethics, therefore, is grounded in a keen, moment-to-moment attentiveness to one's fluctuating states of mind, demanding not mere adherence to rules and vows, but careful psychological self-discipline.

This does not imply an inner self-mortification, a deliberate suppression of any non-*bodhicitta*-like thought or feeling. When such impulses arise, they are to be calmly accepted for what they are (Shantideva is nothing if not aware of his own lusts and hatreds) but not followed upon and acted out. States of mind, however seductive or distasteful, are essentially transient and, if one does not identify with them, powerless. *Bodhicitta* empowers one with profound self-confidence, so that 'like a lion among jackals' one remains unmoved by the insistent howling of one's afflicted nature.

And not only unmoved. Such confidence enables the *bodhicitta* to grow and mature. Paradoxically, the cultivation of this selfless, compassionate, other-centred resolve requires withdrawal from the subversive lure of the world to a place of solitude, 'in forests, among deer, birds and trees, that say nothing disagreeable, a delight to associate with'. Here one can get to grips with the 'mad elephant of the mind', taming its unruly habits, finding at last the calm and clarity to discover the extent of one's connectedness with life.

The depth and intensity of love are founded on the depth and intensity of one's identification with others. 'In the same way as hands and legs are regarded as parts of the body,' Shantideva asks, 'why are embodied creatures not regarded as limbs of life?' Just as the uninjured hand automatically reaches out to soothe the pain of the foot, why do I not empathetically reach out to soothe the pain of others? When I understand that my sense of being a disconnected ego is a fiction, and that what I am comes into being because of the myriad relationships I bear and have borne with what is not-me, then surely such selfless compassion should be my response to suffering. It makes no sense to concern myself with merely the ending of my own anguish. For the deeper I understand the nature of the suffering 'me', the more I realize the *selflessness* of that which suffers. Such experiential insight opens me to the non-separateness and interconnectedness of all life — as though the entirety of life were indeed a single organism. Such transformation of attitude, realized in the loneliness of solitary meditation, inspires Shantideva to ever-heightened raptures of metaphor:

> Out of love to quell the pain of others,
> The person who is used to this,
> Plunges into deepest hell
> As a swan into a lotus-pool.

Yet before returning to the world (the poem mirroring the life of its author), Shantideva declares that everything he has said so far was to guide one to wisdom, for, no matter how great one's compassion, without wisdom the pain of others cannot be fully quelled.

Shantideva is concerned with wisdom rather than knowledge: 'the ultimate', he says, 'is not something that can be known.' The ultimate is also not something entirely transcendent, concealed behind and beyond the world, waiting to be discovered, nor is it sheer absence or negation of the world. It cannot be meaningfully said to be either 'something' or 'nothing'. In the words of the Dalai Lama, from his tent in Dordogne, it is nothing one can put one's finger on. No matter how hard we look into something, be it ourself or a chair, it is impossible to find anything that corresponds to the 'thingness' we instinctively imagine to reside therein.

The ultimate truth of things is 'transparency', the absence of any thingness in things. The wisdom that plunges into this infinite unfindability liberates the mind from its instinctive attachment to 'nuggets' of substance at the core of things, disclosing instead Nirvana — not a remote state apart from the world, but the immanent openness of being.

Such wisdom is called ultimate *bodhicitta* — in contrast to the altruistic resolve, called relative *bodhicitta*. These two ways of speaking about *bodhicitta* point to the unity of wisdom and compassion. Understanding transparency lies at the heart of compassion. For dissolving the nugget of self-centredness opens up the interconnectedness with the whole of life. The natural response to the suffering of those with whom one is not separate (like that of the hand to the pain of the foot) is compassionate concern. And the culmination of such concern is to guide others by whatever means to the ending of their suffering, which is realized through the wisdom of transparency. The two dimensions of *bodhicitta* set in perpetual motion an engagement with the suffering world grounded in the understanding that the suffering world is not anything one can put one's finger on.

6

PADMASAMBHAVA:
THE NYINGMA TRADITION

Nourished in the climate of Shantideva's Buddhism, but threatened by the political disintegration of the times, the Dharma began to weave its way across the Himalayas into Tibet. Shantideva lived midway between the reigns of the two Tibetan kings responsible for establishing Buddhism in the country. The first, Songtsen Gampo, is credited with the unification of the conflicting factions on the Tibetan plateau, creating for the first time a self-conscious Tibetan nation. As part of this process he married a Chinese and Nepalese princess, both of whom brought statues of the Buddha to Lhasa. He also appointed his minister Tönmi Sambhota with the task of creating a written script in order to translate the Buddhist scriptures into Tibetan. The second king, Trisong Detsen, built upon the achievements of his predecessor both politically, by extending the territory of Tibet (even occupying for a time parts of China and India), and spiritually, by establishing Buddhism as the state religion. To achieve the latter goal, he invited one of the last great figures of Nalanda, the abbot and philosopher Shantarakshita, to found a monastery on the banks of the Brahmaputra at Samyé and ordain the first Tibetan monks. This Shantarakshita achieved, but only with the help of the Indian tantric adept Padmasambhava.

While 770 CE is reckoned to be the year when Padmasambhava set foot in Tibet, his life before and after that time is incapable of being pinned down to any precise historical or geographical setting. His biography, the *Padma Tang Yig*, is the account of a mythic figure — part monk, part shaman, part yogin, part scholar — who represents, through a series of charged symbolic episodes, an ideal of enlightenment both comprehensible and endearing to the Tibetans of the 8th century.

To say that Padmasambhava was 'born' is already problematic. He is said to have first appeared in the land of Uddiyana, a place sometimes identified as the Swat Valley in modern Pakistan (part of the former kingdom of Menander), and sometimes as a quasi-divine, quasi-terrestrial realm. At an unspecified time in the past, the Bodhisattva Avalokiteshvara, upon seeing that Uddiyana was suffering severe famine and drought, appealed to the Buddha Amitabha for help. Amitabha spontaneously projected a beam of red light from his tongue, which struck a lake from whence a lotus blossom unfurled. He then projected the mystic syllable HRI from his heart which appeared as a golden *vajra* or sceptre in the centre of the lotus, which then transformed into an eight-year-old boy enveloped in a haze of rainbow light. Thus Padmasambhava, the 'Lotus Arisen One', came into the world. Rain cascaded down and the drought and famine of Uddiyana were dispelled.

The next sequence in Padmasambhava's legend follows the archetypal pattern of the Buddha's own life. The king of Uddiyana adopted the boy, groomed him for the kingship and arranged for him to marry a princess. But the young man, already weary of the glories of the world, chose to renounce his home and kingdom. As he was preparing to depart, however, he was accused of killing the wife and son of a minister and banished from Uddiyana. This peculiar twist to the renunciation story gives the first intimation of Padmasambhava's wrathful interactions with society, a quality that distinguishes him from Gautama and heralds his role as a tantric adept who uses force to counteract the unstable conditions of his time.

Padmasambhava wandered throughout India, meditating in

cemeteries, studying everything from philosophy to astrology, from healing to poetics. He mastered the Buddhist canonical texts and was initiated into the secret doctrines of the tantras. Outwardly he appeared as a shaven-headed, yellow-robed *bhikshu*, but inwardly he dwelt in radiant tantric mandalas, consorting with *dakinis*.

After many years he returned to Uddiyana accompanied by his disciple Princess Mandarava. He was soon recognized by the king and ministers and condemned to be burned alive. For three weeks smoke could be seen wafting from the pyre. When the king went to inspect the site he beheld not a smouldering fire but a vast lake, with Padmasambhava and Mandarava dancing in union upon a giant lotus flower, haloed in shimmering rainbows. The king implored Padmasambhava for spiritual instruction. Padmasambhava agreed and stayed in Uddiyana for thirteen years, after which he resumed his itinerant existence, travelling throughout India, Nepal, South-East Asia, even, according to some sources, as far as China, Russia, Persia and Egypt. He finally settled near Bodh Gaya, the place of Gautama's enlightenment.

By this time the abbot Shantarakshita was in Tibet, struggling to build the first monastery and thereby establish Buddhism. Not only was he meeting resistance from the priests and shamans of the pre-Buddhist Bön religion, but was also being hampered by the local spirits. King Trisong Detsen sought the advice of Shantarakshita. 'I have endeavoured to perfect the spirit of a Bodhisattva', replied the abbot.

If gentleness cannot prevail, we must rely upon one . . . before whom all negative forces tremble and become powerless. At this moment, the Doctor from Uddiyana, Padmasambhava, resides near [Bodh Gaya] in India. All your hopes for Tibet will materialize if you invite this incarnate Buddha.

Padmasambhava accepted the invitation and for many months travelled through Tibet, subduing the local spirits, then binding them by oath to protect and serve the Dharma. Each encounter is described as a magical battle with demonic figures, who emerge from glaciers, mountains and valleys only to be effortlessly tamed by Padmasambhava. These stories represent how the Tibetans' attachment to the local spirits of their former culture is not severed by Padmasambhava but transmuted into an aspiration for the higher truths of Buddhism.

When Padmasambhava meets King Trisong Detsen on the banks of the Brahmaputra, the mighty king is reluctant to pay obeisance. So Padmasambhava 'turned his hands and, springing up from his finger a miraculous flame seared the king's garments. King, ministers, courtiers could not withstand him. Bowing in unison, they gave greeting as though swept by a scythe.' In principle, at least, this recalls the encounter between Gautama and the five ascetics in Sarnath, and symbolizes Tibet's conversion from a powerful war-like state to a buddhocracy.

Padmasambhava made swift work of the spirits who were holding up work on Samye Monastery, even co-opting them as night-time labourers on the project. Once the monastery was finished in 779, Shantarakshita proceeded to ordain the 'Seven Examined Men' as the first indigenous *bhikshu*s in Tibet, thus establishing a monastic *sangha*. Then both Padmasambhava and Shantarakshita oversaw the beginnings of the immense task of translating the entire Buddhist canon from Sanskrit and Chinese into Tibetan.

Although Padmasambhava transmitted many tantric teachings to the disciples that flocked to him, he realized that people were not yet ready for some of the more advanced doctrines and practices. He is then said to have inscribed texts in a terse encoded script, which were concealed in temples, caves and mountain crevices, and predicted that his disciples of that time would later reappear to reveal these hidden teachings when the circumstances for their dissemination were ripe. These concealed teachings were called *terma* (treasures) and those who were to later disclose them *terton* (treasure revealers).

Padmasambhava's life at the Tibetan court was not without controversy. Shortly after his arrival, King Trisong Detsen presented him with his wife of two years, Yeshé Tsogyel, an act of generosity that so outraged the ministers still faithful to the Bön religion that the couple had to flee to Tidrom, a cave north-east of Lhasa, until the controversy died down. When the time came for Padmasambhava to leave the country, he was escorted to the border by a great throng of disciples. Having exhorted them to devote themselves to the Dharma, he 'mounted a winged horse which appeared from out of the sky, and, rising upwards in a mist of rainbow radiance, he vanished on the rays of the sun'.

Shantarakshita and Padmasambhava are still regarded as exemplary models for a Buddhist life, particularly among followers of the Nyingma school of Tibetan Buddhism, which traces its original inspiration to this period. Erudition and philosophical rigour cultivated within a monastic context, as well as a transforming and engaged life in the world formed the twin ideals of the early Buddhist community in Tibet. One of the most notable recent embodiments of these ideals was a lama called Kangyur Rinpoché, who, during the final years of his life as a refugee in Darjeeling, provided the initial impetus behind the creation of the Tibetan Buddhist enclave along the Côte de Jor in Dordogne.

Kangyur Rinpoché was born in the province of Kham in eastern Tibet around the turn of the century. He entered the local monastery of Riwoché as a young boy where he studied with

Jedrong Rinpoché, a disciple of the renowned 19th-century lama Jamyang Khyentsé Wangpo. While still a boy he went to pay homage to the ageing Mipham Gyatso, another major figure of the previous century, who was living in a cave-hermitage nearby. 'Who is this boy?' asked Mipham, pointing to Kangyur Rinpoché. 'Just a youngster from the village', replied the monks. Mipham commented: 'Youngsters become great teachers.'

Upon completing his formal studies in the monastery, Kangyur Rinpoché went into meditation retreat for nine years in remote parts of Kham. He then travelled many months on foot until he reached Talung Monastery in Central Tibet. When the time of the summer 'rains' retreat arrived, the monks invited him formally to recite the *Kangyur*, the translations of the Buddha's discourses in 108 thick Tibetan volumes to the monks. Due to his skill in reciting and explaining these texts he came to be known as 'Kangyur' Rinpoché and during his lifetime formally recited the *Kangyur* thirteen times.

In his early forties he returned his monastic vows and devoted himself to the life of a married yogin. Such a move was entirely in keeping with the tradition, enabling him to live in closer contact with the world without compromising his role as a teacher. It was also during this time that he visited India on pilgrimage and was recognized as a *terton*, a revealer of treasures (*terma*) concealed by Padmasambhava. Some of his finds took place in India, including Bodh Gaya. Although hidden encoded texts may be discovered, the Nyingma tradition acknowledges that the true *terma* is an insight revealed within the depths of one's own mind, the conditions for which were laid in previous existences and only now have come to fruition. The discovery of writings and images buried in caves are the external corroboration of such spiritual revelations.

By 1955 Kangyur Rinpoché sensed the impending Chinese takeover of Tibet and chose to leave for India, bringing with him hundreds of volumes of religious books. These were packed on mules and he set off across the Himalayas with his wife and young children. In 1960 they settled in a two-room wooden shack in the village of Lebong near Darjeeling. The books effectively became a library for the large number of lamas who sought refuge in India after the Chinese seizure of power in Lhasa in March 1959.

Life was hard and uncertain for the Tibetan refugees. They suffered from the hot and humid Indian climate, the strange diet, lack of proper housing and medical care, and extreme poverty. Yet faith in their religious traditions provided a sense of inner security and well-being that impressed itself on the Europeans who encountered them. Among these was the French film-maker and writer Arnaud Desjardins, who went to India in 1966 to make a documentary on Tibetan Buddhism. With the support of the Dalai Lama he travelled to several refugee communities to meet and film the lamas, among them, Kangyur Rinpoché in his hut in Lebong.

Upon returning to France, Desjardins showed the rushes of his film to friends and spoke excitedly of the lamas he had encountered. This prompted a small stream of men and women to travel to Darjeeling, who formed a circle of European disciples around Kangyur Rinpoché in India and established the nucleus of a Tibetan Buddhist group in France.

While Kangyur Rinpoché would often say that the 'Injis' (Westerners) would one day be drawn to the Dharma, the Tibetans around him, including his family, initially found this hard to believe. In the early 1960s the only Injis they met were either representatives of aid agencies or missionaries, neither of whom showed much interest in Buddhism. Many of the missionaries were as perplexed as the Tibetans when cultured Europeans started arriving from Paris and London to study Buddhism with an unkempt old lama.

Yet what impressed these early Western students of Buddhism (as well as similar groups clustering around lamas throughout the

Himalayas at this time) was the simplicity, warmth, humour and wisdom of the Tibetans, who had lost everything of value in Western terms (land, wealth, status, etc.) while retaining a radiant spirituality. They came to the Tibetans with a sense of spiritual loss and confusion. One of them recalls a meeting with Kangyur Rinpoché:

> I remember one rainy day. The rain was dripping through the roof and Rinpoché had opened his large, multicoloured umbrella to protect the books he had saved from Tibet. And he was laughing under his umbrella, a great laughter wiping out my hesitations, doubts, all the silly thoughts rising in my mind.

Kangyur Rinpoché was renowned for being disarmingly blunt and straightforward. He had no time for social niceties or chit-chat. He would sometimes be found just sitting in the marketplace in Darjeeling, merging with the life around him.

It was not long before Kangyur Rinpoché's European disciples found a better house for the family. Retreat huts sprang up in the grounds and Rinpoché began teaching on a more regular basis to the growing number of students. When explaining Buddhism, Kangyur Rinpoché emphasized the need to be firmly grounded in the essentials, such as commitment to the Buddha, Dharma and Sangha and cultivation of the *bodhicitta*, before proceeding to the more advanced contemplations on the nature of reality, such as *mahamudra* and *dzogchen*. 'If you lack the altruistic resolve of *bodhicitta*,' he would say, 'then both your *mahamudra* and your *dzogchen* will be rotten.'

Kangyur Rinpoché was frequently asked to visit Europe and teach. He would always promise to go but then explain that the time was not yet right. And the time never came. In January 1975, he fell ill and died.

The Nyingma tradition had nonetheless begun to find its way into Europe. A key event was a visit by Düjom Rinpoché, the head of the Nyingma school, to England and France in the winter of 1972. Düjom Rinpoché was born in the Pemakö region of south-east Tibet in 1904 and became one of the foremost scholars, poets, and meditation masters of his generation. He and his family left Tibet for India in 1958, mindful of the prediction of his predecessor Düjom Lingpa that his lineage would spread throughout the world — in particular to the West. Although the various Nyingma lineages did not really have a 'supreme head' in Tibet, in India Düjom Rinpoché was appointed as such by the Dalai Lama, when a leader was felt necessary for the coherence of the school in exile. He was a *terton* who found and wrote commentaries upon numerous concealed 'treasures'. Despite ill health, he wrote, travelled and taught extensively into his old age. Before Düjom Rinpoché left on his first tour of Europe and America in 1972, Kangyur Rinpoché had sent his eldest son, Tulku Pema Wangyal, to request him to visit his (Kangyur Rinpoché's) disciples in France.

Düjom Rinpoché spent a week in the 16th-century Château de Chaban, then the home of Bernard Benson and his family, where he gave teachings and tantric initiations and blessed Chanteloube, an old farmhouse in the woods nearby. He also accepted Mr Benson's gift of a large tract of land within the extensive grounds of the castle. But nothing was formalized during this visit and Düjom Rinpoché returned to India.

After Kangyur Rinpoché's death, his disciples turned to another leading Nyingma lama, Dilgo Khyentsé Rinpoché, to guide them. Khyentsé Rinpoché was born in eastern Tibet in 1910 to an aristocratic family descended from the early Tibetan king Trisong Detsen. He was recognized as an incarnate lama by Mipham Gyatso, entered Shechen Monastery in Kham at the age of eleven, and spent many years studying and meditating. He was a huge man, 6ft 6in (2m) tall, with a presence which would have been intimidating if he hadn't radiated such kindness and simplicity. In addition to a full schedule, which allowed only four hours' sleep and included a whole morning of meditation practice, he composed a total of twenty thick Tibetan volumes of writing. As an old man, not in the best of health, he returned twice to Tibet. During the first visit he helped restore his teachers' monasteries in eastern Tibet. His second visit, in 1990, eighteen months before he died, was to reconsecrate Samye Monastery, symbolically reviving the original tradition founded by Shantarakshita and Padmasambhava. He was also a *terton*, a teacher of the Dalai Lama and spiritual advisor to the Bhutanese royal family.

After the cremation ceremonies for Kangyur Rinpoché, which Khyentsé Rinpoché conducted, he too was invited to visit the Dordogne. Knowing of Kangyur Rinpoché's vision of Buddhism spreading in Europe, he agreed to go. Thus in December 1975, Khyentsé Rinpoché with Tulku Pema Wangyal as translator, made his first visit to Europe. He travelled extensively in France, visiting Arnaud Desjardins in Auvergne and teaching in Chanteloube in Dordogne. He proceeded to tour Scandinavia, Britain and the United States. On his return to India he stopped in Paris, at which point Tulku Pema Wangyal left the party and remained in France.

By this time, the visits of these lamas, coupled with the growing interest among Europeans, provided a significant momentum behind the Nyingma tradition. Two years before Khyentsé Rinpoché's visit, a young lama, Sogyal Rinpoché, had opened Dzogchen Orgyen Chöling in London, where he taught in faltering English. The following year Düjom Rinpoché asked him to take care of his newly founded centre in Paris.

In Dordogne, meanwhile, Tulku Pema embarked on the construction of several hermitages, which formed the nucleus of the retreat centre that the students themselves began to build in 1978, clearing the land with bulldozers. Düjom Rinpoché returned in 1979 and laid the first stone of the temple in the compound. In March 1980 Khyentsé Rinpoché arrived to give instructions and initiations required by the prospective retreatants, a group of seventeen men and seven women from Europe and America. The same autumn further initiations and teaching were given by Düjom Rinpoché, this time inside the finished temple. Having appointed Tulku Pema and Nyoshul Khen Rinpoché as resident lamas for the retreat, in the first week of December, Düjom Rinpoché formally closed the doors of the compound. They were not to be opened again for three years, three months and three days.

This period is regarded by all Tibetan schools of Buddhism as the optimal timespan for engaging in the transformative practices of the Buddhist *tantras*. The curriculum followed in Dordogne is based on that devised by the great 19th-century scholar and advocate of non-sectarianism (Rimé), Jamgon Kongtrul. The *tantras*, as opposed to the more widely known Buddhist *sutras*, teach forms of meditation that include methods of transformative imagination, in which one learns to view oneself as an enlightened deity and the world as a mandala; the use of mantra; and yogic exercises that free psycho-physical obstructions. These methods are regarded as an effective and rapid means of attaining enlightenment.

As a preparation for such practices, the first year of the retreat was devoted largely to preliminaries such as performing 100,000 full-length prostrations combined with recitations of the refuge formula, 100,000 symbolic offerings of the universe, and so on, whose aim is to rid one of egotistical ambitions, to cultivate a spirit of selfless generosity, and to establish a heartfelt commitment to the practice. During the second and third years the time was spent actualizing the tantric practices themselves.

As for centuries in Tibet, each retreatant was provided with a bare cell, containing an altar, under which was a cupboard for storing clothes, a bookshelf, a small table, and a 'meditation box' raised from the floor, filled with cushions and blankets, where, supported sometimes by a backrest, one spent the bulk of one's time sitting cross-legged, wrapped, when cold, in a *dagam* (padded cloak). Many meditators forewent a bed and slept sitting-up in the 'box'. Anything else was considered a luxury and forbidden.

Each day began at 4 a.m. with a bell to mark the beginning of the first of the four daily sessions. At 6.30 the retreatants would gather in the small temple and chant together for an hour. After breakfast, a second session would last until 11.30. Lunch was followed by instruction given either by one of the resident or visiting lamas in the temple. The third session was from 3.30 to 5.30 p.m., after which more prayers were chanted together. A bowl of soup and a slice of bread for supper preceded the final session from 7.30 to 9.30. Much of the time was spent in silence.

Despite these austere conditions, when the retreat was over most of the participants decided not to plunge back into the delights of the world, but to keep going. Since the compound was already reserved for another batch of eager hermits, they converted a nearby farmhouse into a closed compound and started again. Such behaviour presumably reflected their having reaped the experiential fruits of such practice. By the mid-1980s more than seventy people were engaged in these retreats in Dordogne alone.

Several books have been published recently describing Tantric Buddhism, but those who undergo such retreats are advised to remain silent about their practice. This is not so much to hide something (even if told about such practices, they would be largely meaningless) but to create a sealed inner state of enclosure in which the practice is contained. The idea of containment is suggested by the Tibetan word for 'retreat': *mtshams*, which means 'boundary'. So instead of 'going into retreat', a Tibetan would 'enter into boundaries'. In its deeper sense, this means that not only does one not cross certain physical boundaries, one does not stray from an inner state of contemplation into habitual discursive thinking.

Although many tantric practices are complex and demanding, the retreat concluded with a form of meditation that, on the surface at least, seems disarmingly simple. This is *dzogchen*, literally the 'Great Perfection', considered by many Nyingma lamas as the essence and culmination of the Buddha's teachings. In one of the earliest writings of this tradition, the *dzogchen* adept Garab Dorjé, from whom Padmasambhava received instruction, describes the practice:

> The nature of the mind is Buddha from the beginning.
> Mind is like space, it has neither birth nor cessation.
> Having realised the pure and equal meaning of phenomena,
> To remain there without seeking is the meditation.

Dzogchen points to an underlying experience of reality, which demands to be realized rather than speculated about. 'Not *sutra*, not *tantra*,' writes Namkhai Norbu, a contemporary adept,

> *dzogchen* does not see itself as the highpoint of any hierarchy of levels, and is not a gradual path . . . . The principal practice of *dzogchen* is to enter directly into non-dual contemplation, and to remain in it.

Since the 'Primordial State' that *dzogchen* speaks of is immanent in each moment, it is something that can be fully actualized in each moment. In practical terms:

> Don't follow the past, don't anticipate the future, and don't follow illusory thoughts that arise in the present; but turning within oneself, one should observe one's own true condition and maintain awareness of it just as it is, beyond the conceptual limitations of past, present and future.

By the time the first three-year Nyingma retreat in Europe ended on 15 April 1984 the tradition was far better established than it had been when the retreat began. Düjom Rinpoché was now living in Dordogne, in 'La Pechardie', a house at the top of the Côte de Jor. Before retiring from public life, he gave a final public discourse in August of the same year. He died at home on 17 January 1987, at the age of 82, and was succeeded by his son Shenpen Dawa Rinpoché, who now directs Urgyen Samyé Choling, his centre in Dordogne.

Elsewhere, Sogyal Rinpoché created the Rigpa Fellowship in London in 1981, which is now an international organization with centres, communities and retreat facilities in many European countries. Sogyal Rinpoché was born in eastern Tibet in the late '40s and raised from a young age by Jamyang Khyentsé Chokyi Lodro, one of the leading Rimé lamas of his generation, who settled in Sikkim as teacher of the Maharaja in 1958. In addition to his training as a reincarnate lama (*tulku*), Sogyal received a Western education at Delhi University and Trinity College, Cambridge. He has successfully managed to present his understanding of Tibetan Buddhism within the language of contemporary Western thought and structured his organization to meet modern needs. In 1992 he published his acclaimed *The Tibetan Book of Living and Dying*, a skilful adaptation of traditional Tibetan teachings on death and rebirth. He is known for his sense of humour, indefatigable energy, forthrightness and periodic eccentricity.

In Italy, Namkhai Norbu Rinpoché, a *dzogchen* master who for twenty years had been quietly teaching Tibetan and Mongolian linguistics in the University of Naples, began attracting disciples whom he instructed in the practice of *dzogchen*. Norbu was born in eastern Tibet on 8 December 1938 and recognized as a *tulku* of three different teachers. Although groomed for a high monastic position, he grew disillusioned with the orthodoxy and was drawn to a simple and illiterate lay physician called Jangchub Dorjé, who introduced him to *dzogchen* as a practice that ignored learning and cultural sophistication to address the essential human condition alone. Forced to leave Tibet in 1958, Norbu settled in Sikkim. In 1960 he was invited by the orientalist Professor Giuseppe Tucci to work at his institute in Rome. In 1965 he transferred to Naples. He is married to an Italian and fluent in the language.

Namkhai Norbu is a complex figure who serves as one of the most articulate links to the little-known and endangered culture of the non-orthodox, non-monastic Tibetan lay religious culture. Here is a man who holds a professorship at an Italian university yet whose spiritual life is rooted in experiences that for many contemporary people would be incredible. He witnessed his uncle's discovery of a *terma*, in this case a 'luminous white orb, made of no material known to us, about the size of a large grapefruit', taken from the rockface of a mountain which had been perceived in a dream. He has likewise recounted the stories of lamas known to him who have vanished from this world in a 'rainbow body', leaving behind only clothing, fingernails and hair.

Somewhat of a maverick within the Nyingma tradition, Norbu Rinpoché advocates an interpretation of *dzogchen* that regards it not as an exclusively Buddhist teaching but one that is equally a part of the pre-Buddhist Bön religion of Tibet. In recent years his university work has taken second place to the teaching of *dzogchen* retreats throughout Europe and America in which 'intrinsic awareness' is developed within the framework of bodily exercises, song, ritual practices and *dzogchen* philosophy. To preserve these traditions Norbu Rinpoché has created a network of 'Dzogchen Communities', which are now established in many Western countries.

Uniting many of these teachers of the Nyingma tradition in Europe is the impetus of Rimé, the 19th-century synthetic movement founded by Jamyang Khyentsé Wangpo, Jamgon Kongtrul and their associates. These lamas were dismayed by the sectarian divisions that had set in between the different schools in Tibet of the time, and concerned that many lineages of teaching were in danger of dying out. To rectify the situation they joined together to emphasize the need for mutual harmony and understanding between the traditions and to gather the teachings of the endangered lineages. To this end they travelled throughout Tibet, studying with lamas from different traditions, thereby cementing a unity in diversity through their interest in the preservation of Buddhism. The two great Nyingma teachers of this century, Düjom Rinpoché and Dilgo Khyentsé Rinpoché, were recognized as the incarnations of the Rimé lamas Düjom Lingpa and Jamyang Khyentsé Wangpo respectively.

If this non-sectarian impulse is transmitted via these lamas and their followers to Europe, it may further extend to embrace the other non-Tibetan Buddhist traditions that are taking root. Indeed, the current flourishing of Buddhism in the West is unprecedented in that it is the first time in history that so many Buddhist schools have had such close contact with each other. Non-sectarianism does not mean, however, that all the schools and doctrines should be thrown together in a grand eclectic mixing pot. The Rimé lamas of the 19th century did not found any special Rimé monasteries; they remained within their own traditions, while embodying in their lives a deep respect for diversity.

WILLIAM OF RUBRUCK:
FIRST ENCOUNTERS

On 18 January 1975, His Holiness Rangjung Rigpai Dorjé, the 16th Karmapa, descended from the heavens by helicopter onto an open patch of ground on the Côte de Jor near the Château de Chabon in Dordogne. A stocky and forceful man of fifty-one, simultaneously smiling and severe, he stepped from the helicopter and surveyed the fields and forest around him. Suddenly a freak hailstorm erupted as though from nowhere, showering the small crowd gathered for the occasion. The Karmapa alone had the foresight to bring an umbrella.

In the spirit of the Rimé tradition, Bernard Benson offered the Karmapa a tract of land on the side of the road opposite the land already given to Düjom Rinpoché. The lama consecrated the site as the focal centre for the Tibetan Buddhist Kagyu school in Europe and the impromptu heliport as the location for a monastery.

Unknown to those in Dordogne, Kangyur Rinpoché had died a week earlier in Darjeeling. As soon as he heard the news, Benson raced after the Karmapa to Geneva and implored him to start a centre on the donated land. In response, the Karmapa sent his nephew, Lama Jigmé Tsewang, to Dordogne, who set to work converting a derelict old farm into 'Dagpo Kagyu Ling'. As for the monastery, a tall pole, fluttering with prayer flags, was erected at the site, waiting (as is still the case today) for planning permission.

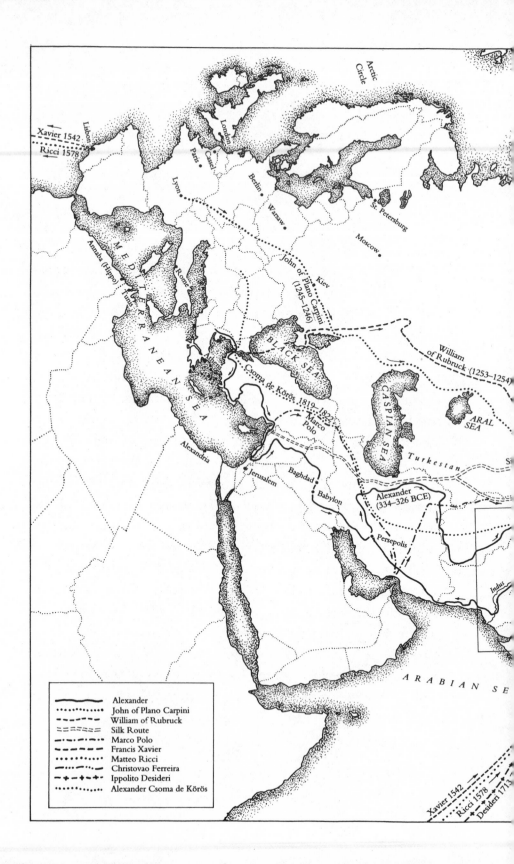

Xavier 1542
Ricci 1578

Lisbon

Arctic Circle

London

Paris

Cassel

Berlin

Warsaw

Lyon

St. Petersburg

Moscow

Kiev

John of Plano Carpini
(1245–1246)

M E D I T E R R A N E A N   S E A

Rome

Annaba (Hippo)
Tunis

BLACK SEA

William
of Rubruck (1253–1254)

Csoma de Körös 1819–1822

Marco
Polo

CASPIAN SEA

ARAL
SEA

Turkestan

S

Alexandria

Jerusalem

Baghdad

Babylon

Alexander
(334–326 BCE)

Persepolis

Indus

A R A B I A N   S E

Xavier 1542
Ricci 1578
Desideri 1713

	Alexander
	John of Plano Carpini
	William of Rubruck
	Silk Route
	Marco Polo
	Francis Xavier
	Matteo Ricci
	Christovao Ferreira
	Ippolito Desideri
	Alexander Csoma de Körös

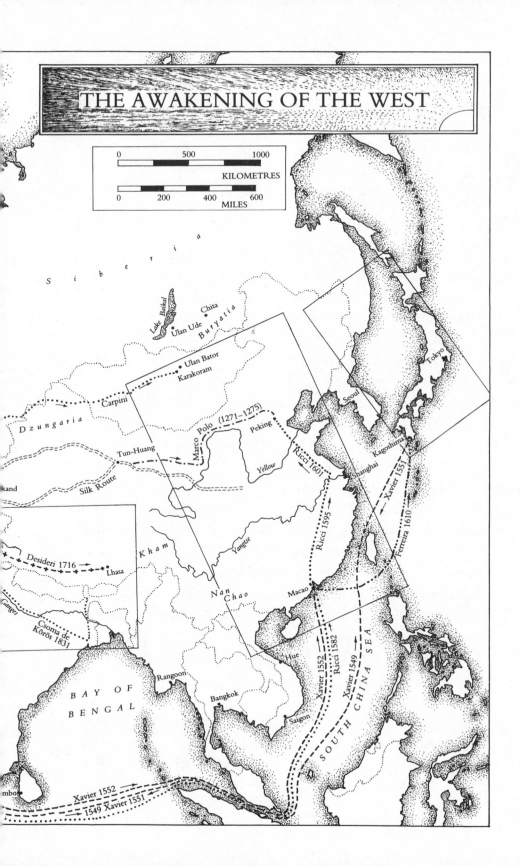

THE AWAKENING OF THE WEST

0   500   1000

KILOMETRES

0   200   400   600

MILES

S   i   b   e   r   i   a

Lake Baikal

Chita

Ulan Ude

B u r y a t i a

Ulan Bator

Karakoram

Carpini

D z u n g a r i a

Tun-Huang

Marco Polo (1271–1275)

Peking

Yellow

Ricci 1601

Tokyo

Seoul

Shanghai

Kagoshima

Xavier 1551

Ferreira 1610

Silk Route

kand

K h a m

Yangtse

Ricci 1595

Desideri 1716

Lhasa

Ganges

Nan Chao

Macao

Ricci 1552

Csoma de Körös 1831

Hue

Ricci 1582

Xavier 1549

BAY OF

Rangoon

BENGAL

Bangkok

Saigon

SOUTH CHINA SEA

mbo

Xavier 1552

1549 Xavier 1551

This enthusiastic implantation of Tibetan Buddhism in the heart of Europe would have horrified the Franciscan friar William of Rubruck who, during his stay in the Mongolian capital of Karakoram in 1254, became the first European to encounter Central Asian Buddhists. His first-hand account of his journey explains, among other things, the purpose of the pole:

> All the idol priests I have mentioned wear wide hoods of saffron. There are also hermits among them, so I learned, in the forests and mountains, leading lives that are extraordinarily ascetic . . . . The priests shave the head and beard completely, dress in saffron colour, and observe chastity from the time they shave their heads . . . . Wherever they go, they have constantly in their hands a string of beads, like the rosaries we carry, and keep repeating the words *On mani battam*, which mean 'God, you know' . . . . Over the gate [of their temples] they erect a tall pole, which if possible dominates the entire town: the pole enables one to recognise the house as an idol-temple.

If Friar William had not been expelled from the Mongolian court only eight months after his arrival but had stayed on for another year or so, he would have found himself face to face with Karma Pakshi, the second incarnation of the Karmapa, who reached Karakoram in 1256. Both Christian and Buddhist had similar motives for being there: to persuade Möngke Khan — at the time the world's most powerful man — to convert to their religion.

William of Rubruck lived during one of the most politically fraught and religiously fervent periods of history. The 13th century witnessed the lives of major religious figures both in the Christian West and the Buddhist East. In Europe St Francis of Assisi and St Dominic founded their respective orders. The Dominican Thomas of Aquinas laid the foundations of medieval theology through his Aristotelian interpretation of Christian doctrine, while later in the century, another Dominican, Meister Eckhart, was condemned for his mystical writings. In Asia, Muslim invasions effectively wiped out Buddhism in India. Shantideva's monastery, Nalanda, was sacked in 1197. In 1260 Kublai Khan established Tibet as a buddhocratic state. In Japan the Rinzai Zen tradition was introduced from China by Eisai and the Soto Zen tradition by Dogen, the Pure Land schools were founded by Honen and Shinran, and the radical prophet Nichiren established his order. It was during this period that the first eye-witness reports of Buddhism, such as Rubruck's and later Marco Polo's, reached Europe.

Europe in the 13th century was a culturally isolated collection of societies united by the all-pervasive and dominant Roman Catholic Church. During this time the Church, through the figurehead of the Pope, came to see itself as embodying total power, spiritual as well as temporal. Gregory IX declared that the Pope was the lord of the entire universe, governing not only humans but even inanimate things. His successor, Innocent IV, insisted that it was not Constantine who had given secular power to the Popes but that they had been endowed with it by Christ himself. With such authority, the Church mercilessly suppressed whatever it perceived as a threat to its own power. In the early years of the century, the Pope launched a concerted campaign against all forms of heresy, a move that became institutionalized as the Inquisition, which was to remain in force for the next 300 years.

The Church's intolerance likewise extended to other religions. While the pious Louis IX of France (later canonized as St Louis) was attending a theological debate between Christians and Jews at Cluny, one of the rabbis challenged the divinity of Christ and the immaculate conception. A knight in the audience jumped to his feet and broke open the rabbi's head with his sword. The abbot of Cluny protested, but King Louis declared that the best way for a Christian to defend his faith against non-believers was 'to thrust his sword into their entrails, as far as it would go'. When a Muslim emissary arrived in Europe in 1238 to seek support from the Church against the common threat of the Mongols, Peter des Roches, bishop of Westminster, remarked:

> Let us leave these dogs to devour one another, that they may all be consumed, and perish; and we, when we proceed against the enemies of Christ who remain, will slay them, and cleanse the face of the earth, so that all the world will be subject to the one Catholic Church, and there will be one shepherd and one fold.

Such attitudes found their strongest expression in the Crusades, periodically launched since the end of the 11th century, to try and wrest the Holy Land from the control of the Muslims. St Francis of Assisi joined the 5th Crusade in the hope of converting the Sultan of Egypt and thereby regaining the Holy Land without bloodshed. His attempt was unsuccessful, but it inspired his followers with a sense of mission to convert the heathens in the East through preaching and example. Thirty years later it made friars like William of Rubruck obvious candidates to perform the delicate task of negotiating with the Mongol Khans.

Europe was so preoccupied with internal conflicts and the fight against Islam, that when Mongol armies appeared on the horizon it found itself caught off guard. Rumours of a foreign army which had overthrown Muslims in Iran circulated among the soldiers of the 5th Crusade in Egypt. They assumed that any force hostile to Islam must be Christian and welcomed the news, imagining it to be of the legendary Prester John, commonly believed to rule a Christian kingdom in the East. In fact it was Genghis Khan, laying waste to the Muslim Khorezmian empire. The next hint came from the Queen of Georgia who wrote to the Pope of barbarous hordes attacking from the east — Genghis again. Even when renewed pleas from Eastern Europe for assistance were received after a fresh Mongol offensive in 1237, the Pope regarded the invasions as a providential act which would return the Eastern churches to the Catholic fold.

This serene indifference did not last long. Moscow fell to the Mongols in 1238 and Kiev, headquarters of the Orthodox Church, in 1240. On 9 April 1241, a combined force of Poles and Germans was massacred at Liegnitz in Silesia, after which the Mongols filled nine sacks with an ear sliced off each victim. Within a few weeks Hungary was occupied and by the spring of 1242 a Mongol detachment was within a few miles of Vienna. The Pope and the European rulers realized that an attack on their territory was imminent. They were saved, however, not by superior military might, but by the death of Ogödei, the Great Khan who had ordered the offensive. When his generals received the news, they called off the attack and raced back to Mongolia to attend to the succession of power.

Unknown to the Pope, these 'barbarians' were not just another wave of Huns or Magyars who in earlier centuries had invaded from the north-east and sacked Europe. By 1241, the Mongols controlled a highly efficient military and bureaucratic machine, staffed by Chinese, Indians, Arabs, Russians and others, ruling over a vast empire reaching from the East China Sea to Turkey, from Russia to the Persian Gulf. For the Mongols Europe was but an attractive pocket of farmland on the western edges of their Empire.

As the reality of the crisis sank in, doubts started to arise. Perhaps these Tartars were instruments of Divine Providence, appointed by God to punish Christendom for its sins? The Pope, for one, would not have been unaware of the corruption festering around him even in his own court. For some the Mongols were

85

the very 'Hammer of God'. The saintly Louis IX consoled his mother with the words: 'If these people, whom we call Tartars, should come upon us, either we will thrust them back into the regions of Tartarus [hell], whence they emanated, or else they shall send all of us to Heaven.' In practice, though, he realized that something had to be done. In June 1245 he oversaw a council convoked by Pope Innocent IV, one of the aims of which was to seek 'a remedy against the Tartars'. But by then the Pope had already taken matters into his own hands.

In March of the same year he had drafted two 'bulls' to the Emperor of the Tartars. The first outlined the Catholic credo and instructed the Khan to 'acknowledge Jesus Christ the very Son of God and worship His glorious name by practising the Christian religion'. The second adopted a more threatening tone. He explained that although God sometimes 'refrains from chastising the proud in this world for a moment,'

> if they neglect to humble themselves of their own accord He may not only no longer put off the punishment of their wickedness in this life but may also take greater vengeance in the world to come.

The letters were entrusted to a disciple of St Francis, an elderly friar called John of Plano Carpini, 'a kind, genial and heavily built man', who set out from Lyon (then the seat of the papacy) for Mongolia on Easter Sunday, 16 April 1245.

John was the first known European ever to have travelled so far to the east. The Asia into which he ventured was an unknown and mysterious place. During the so-called 'Dark Ages', Europe in its introverted isolation had pieced together a bizarre image of the East drawn from ancient Greek and Christian sources. John fully expected to encounter weird quasi-human monsters, based on the accounts of Herodotus and Megasthenes, more recently elaborated for popular consumption in the 'Alexander Romances', wildly imaginative legends then circulating as a fictional correspondence from Alexander to Aristotle. The biblical 'wise kings of the east', compounded with stories of St Thomas's mission in India, gave rise to the fantasy of a powerful Christian kingdom in the distant East, ruled by Prester John, who, once allied to his Catholic brethren in Europe, would join forces and unite the world under the Papal banner.

It took Friar John more than a year of arduous travel on horseback to reach his destination, Güyük Khan's vast tent city on the Mongolian steppes, whose enthronement as Great Khan he was to witness on 24 August 1246. Far from being a fabulous, magical kingdom, the country in which he arrived was 'large, but otherwise . . . it is more wretched than I can possibly say'.

The tent-city was a lavish encampment, host to a cosmopolitan throng of people from all over the Mongol Empire, who had gathered for the enthronement. John was duly brought before the Khan to whom he presented Innocent's letters. He received the Khan's reply on 13 November and left for home — six months on horseback across the frozen steppes until he reached Kiev, and then another six months back to Lyon. By the time he returned he had been gone two and a half years.

The Mongol Emperor was every bit as sure of his absolute authority as the Christian Pope. The Mongols had, by this time, adopted the Chinese political concept of the Mandate of Heaven and believed the Great Khan to possess it. For them anyone who did not offer them tribute was a rebel acting in defiance of Heaven. In their eyes they were as justified in waging war against such people, as the Christians felt justified in slaughtering heretics. 'How dost thou know', asked Güyük in reply to Innocent IV, 'that such words as thou speakest are with God's [Heaven's] sanction?'

From the rising of the sun to its setting, all the lands have been made subject to me. Who could do this contrary to the command of God? . . . Thou thyself, at the head of all the Princes, come at once to serve and wait upon us! At that time I shall recognise your submission. If you do not observe God's command, and if you ignore my command, I shall know you as my enemy. Likewise I shall make you understand. If you do otherwise, God knows what I know.

In fact, all this posturing came to nothing. Neither was the Mongol Khan struck down by a bolt of Christian lightning nor was Europe ravaged by Tartar hordes. Internal crises, combined with a prolonged military push against China, prevented the Mongols from ever renewing their European campaign. 'Negotiations' had reached a stalemate; the Pope neither responded nor sent further emissaries to the Khan.

William of Rubruck, from Cassal in French Flanders, was an elderly overweight friar like John of Plano Carpini. Having read John's account and heard reports of a colony of German slaves in Mongolia, he decided of his own accord to travel east to preach the gospel to the Khan and offer comfort to the slaves. He was, however, a confidant of Louis IX, who gave him official backing in the form of a letter requesting the Mongols to allow him to undertake his mission. And it was to Louis that William, on his return, made the report which contains the indelible account of his journey.

William arrived in the Mongol court on 27 December 1253. By this time Güyük had died and had been replaced as Great Khan by his cousin Möngke, described by William as 'snub-nosed, a man of medium build, and aged about forty-five'.

Since William's purpose was religious rather than diplomatic, he devotes considerable attention to the diverse religious groups at the court. Thus it is from him rather than John of Plano Carpini that Europe received its first account of Buddhist monks, their temples and practices. Although he paints a vivid picture of the religious controversies around the imperial throne, true to his missionary spirit, he makes no attempt to understand the different traditions. He seems to have been unaware of the difference between Buddhists and Taoists, both of whom he refers to as *tuin* (from the Chinese *tao-in*, 'man of the way') whom he peremptorily dismisses as 'belonging to the Manichaean heresy'.

Both John and William report the presence in the Mongol court of Nestorians, a breakaway Christian church, condemned as heretical in 431, whose missionaries travelled east and established their Church in Central Asia. Reluctantly, they found themselves relying upon these heretics both for company and information. While trying to convince them to return to the one true Church, the missionaries were also encouraged to learn from them that the Khan showed great sympathy to Christianity and was on the verge of joining the Nestorian Church. Nestorian hyperbole aside, such claims were not without foundation. Members of Güyük's family had been Nestorian, as were Möngke's mother and closest advisor. Despite initial optimism, however, William soon discovered that in dealing with the different religions of the empire, the Mongols subscribed to a notion quite alien to him: tolerance.

In Karakoram he found a multinational, pluralistic culture. People from all over the known world — including a French silversmith and an Englishman called Basil — worked in the employment of the Khan. They may not have been there by their own choice, but they were free to worship as they pleased. Having described the quarters of the city, William says: 'There are twelve idol [Buddhist] temples belonging to different peoples, two mosques where the religion of Mohamet is proclaimed, and one Christian church at the far end of town.'

Buddhism was the tradition in greatest evidence at the Mongol court. Ten years earlier, Güyük's brother and Möngke's cousin

Godan had become a patron of the Sakya school of Tibetan Buddhism. And only three years earlier Möngke too had appointed Buddhist monks to his entourage. Whatever his Buddhist leanings, Möngke had not yet committed himself to any one faith. (Persian records claim that he was on the verge of becoming a Muslim.) To help settle the matter, the Khan sent one of his secretaries to William:

> Here you are, Christians, Saracens and *tuins*, and each one of you claims that his religion is superior . . . The Khan would like you all to assemble together and hold a conference, . . . to enable him to learn the truth.

Thus the scene was set — on 31 May 1254 — for the world's first attempt at interfaith dialogue.

Putting their differences aside for the moment, William persuaded the Nestorians not to start by attacking the Muslims, as they would have liked, because they 'agree with us in saying that there is one God and therefore provide allies for us against the *tuins*'. He then proposed a rehearsal in which he would pretend to be a *tuin* and the Nestorians would challenge his views. But the Nestorians did not know how to argue and could only quote scripture. They agreed that William should open the debate.

Once the contestants were assembled in front of the Khan, William said to the *tuin*, in this case a Buddhist monk, chosen as his opponent:

> We firmly believe in our hearts and acknowledge with our lips that God exists, that there is only one God, and that He is one in a perfect unity. What do you believe?

The Buddhist replied:

It is fools who claim there is only one God. Wise men say that there are several. Are there not great rulers in your country, and is not Möngke Khan the chief lord here? It is the same with gods, inasmuch as there are different gods in different regions.

And so, largely at cross-purposes, the discussion continued. In William's one-sided account the Buddhist was finally silenced by superior Christian reasoning. William prides himself, in the retelling, on the strength of his arguments, but forlornly concludes:

> But for all that no one said, 'I believe, and wish to become a Christian.' When it was all over the Nestorians and Saracens alike sang in loud voices, while the *tuins* remained silent; and after that everyone drank heavily.

The next day William was summoned to an audience with Möngke Khan to hear the verdict: 'We Mongols believe', the Khan declared, 'that . . . just as God has given the hand several fingers, so he has given mankind several paths. To you God has given the Scriptures and you Christians do not observe them.' Despite the Khan's tolerant attitude, William's uncompromising approach was unwelcome. One wonders if he had got wind of the friar's private intentions, confessed in his report to Louis IX: 'for my own part I would, if permitted, preach war against them.' In any case, the Khan's decision was final: 'You have stayed here a long time,' he said, 'it is my wish that you go back.' Thus, on 16 August 1254, William of Rubruck was expelled from the Mongol court, having, in his eight-month stay, converted only six souls.

Faced with a similar threat of Mongol invasion, the Tibetans adopted a different tactic from the Pope — which (in the short term at least) proved more successful. As soon as news of Genghis Khan's subjugation of the Chinese population to the north-east of the country reached Tibet in 1207, a council was held, which decided to submit to the Khan and offer him tribute. This arrangement continued for twenty years, until Genghis's death in 1227. The lapse in payment, however, was treated as rebellion, and in 1240, Prince Godan, Genghis's grandson, invaded Tibet with 30,000 troops. Four years later, with Tibet firmly under his control, Godan wrote to Sakya Pandita Kunga Gyeltsen, one of the leading religious figures of the day:

> I, the most powerful and prosperous Prince Godan, wish to inform the Sakya Pandita, that we need a lama to advise my ignorant people on how to conduct themselves morally and spiritually . . . . I have decided that you are the only person suitable for the task. As you are the only lama I have chosen, I will not accept any excuse on account of your age or the rigours of the journey.

Unable to refuse, Sakya Pandita, accompanied by his young nephew Phagpa, set out for Godan's camp in his principality to the north-east of Tibet — at exactly the same time that John of Plano Carpine was making his way from Lyon to Karakoram. The lamas arrived in 1247.

Sakya Pandita made such an impression on Godan Khan that he was invested with temporal authority over the whole of Central Tibet. As Godan modified some of his more ruthless policies in accord with the precepts of Buddhism, so Sakya Pandita instructed his fellow countrymen not to resist the Mongols but to pay them regular tributes. This was the first time in the history of Buddhism that a monk was conferred with political power, and the beginning of the buddhocratic government of Tibet, which was to last, with interruptions, until 1959. With the backing of such a powerful Mongol prince, whose elder brother Güyük was Great Khan, Sakya Pandita realized that Tibetan Buddhist influence could now penetrate into the heart of the Mongol empire:

> The Prince has told me that if we Tibetans help the Mongols in matters of religion, they in turn will support us in temporal matters. In this way, we will be able to spread our religion far and wide . . . . If I stay longer, I am certain I can spread the faith of the Buddha beyond Tibet and, thus, help my country.

In 1251, four years after arriving at Godan's court, Sakya Pandita died, having named his nephew Phagpa as his successor.

This period was one of great internal struggle between the two main lines of succession within the Mongol ruling family. After the Great Khan Güyük died in 1248, he was succeeded, as we have seen, not by one of his own sons or brothers, but by his cousin Möngke, and his brother Godan's territory was taken over by Kublai, Möngke's younger brother. The link with the Sakya tradition of Tibet continued nonetheless. In 1253, Kublai invited the nineteen-year-old Phagpa to his court and accepted him as his religious teacher.

Although this shift of allegiance from one branch of the family to the other worked well in the Sakya monks' favour, Phagpa's good fortune was not greeted with unanimous approval in Tibet itself. The other contenders for power in Tibet were the lamas of the Kagyu school, principal among whom was the 2nd Karmapa, Karma Pakshi.

Both the Sakya and Kagyu traditions emerged in Tibet during the 11th century, when the second great wave of Buddhist teaching entered the country from India. During the 13th century they became the two most powerful forces in the land — and both vied for the support of the Mongols. At the same time Kublai invited Phagpa to his court, he also invited Karma Pakshi, who, being in Tibet rather than on Kublai's doorstep, took two years to reach the Khan, by which time Phagpa had been given supreme authority over Tibet. Karma Pakshi was greeted courteously at Kublai's court, but his presence gave rise to sectarian tensions and he soon decided to leave. On his way back to Tibet, he was intercepted by another envoy, offering an invitation he could not refuse: an audience with the Great Khan Möngke at his court in Karakoram.

By the time the Karmapa arrived, two years after the departure of William of Rubruck, Möngke had narrowed his choice of religions down to two: Buddhism and Taoism. A year after the 1254 debate, in which William had participated, Möngke held another, in which neither Christians nor Muslims were represented, to verify two Taoist texts that claimed the Buddha to be merely a barbarian disciple of Lao Tzu. The Buddhists won the debate. The texts in question were denounced as forgeries and ordered to be destroyed. But since these orders were not obeyed, a further debate had to be scheduled the following year (1256) to settle the matter. According to Tibetan records, this was when Karma Pakshi was at the court, where he 'invited many jealous Taoist masters to join him in debate. However, none were equal to it and they all accepted his teaching.' Chinese records confirm that the Taoists refused to appear and the Buddhists stated their case uncontested. The outcome was Möngke's conclusive opting for Buddhism:

> The literati say that Confucianism is the first of the doctrines; the Christians who honour the Messiah believe in celestial life; the Muslims pray to heaven and thank it for its blessings. If all these religions were carefully examined as to their origins, one will see that no one of them can be compared to Buddhism.

94

Then, returning to the same metaphor he had used with William of Rubruck, Möngke held up his hand and said: 'Just as the five fingers all project out from the palm, so Buddhism is the palm from which the others stem.'

Karma Pakshi, confident of the Great Khan's support, then set out for Tibet. During his stay at the court, the Karmapa revealed that in a previous life Möngke had been a disciple of the 1st Karmapa, Dusum Khyenpa, and had achieved a high degree of *mahamudra* insight. He also bestowed the tantric initiations of Chakrasamvara to his disciples at the court. In return he received the Mongolian title 'Pakshi', meaning *Acharya* ('Teacher'). As he was approaching Tibet, news reached him of Möngke's death in August 1259 during the campaign against the Southern Sung. A violent struggle broke out between Kublai and his younger brother Arigh Böke for the vacant throne, which Kublai won in 1260, thus making him Great Khan.

On such occasions, the Mongols had the habit of systematically killing all the influential figures of their predecessor's and contender's courts. The Karmapa was not only a favourite of Möngke but was also suspected of siding with Arigh Böke in the struggle for succession. Kublai Khan immediately dispatched a contingent of troops to arrest him. Somehow, Karma Pakshi escaped with his life.

> [The soldiers] wrapped him in a cloth and tried to tie him up, but his body was like a rainbow, with no substance and they found the task impossible. Then they forced him to drink poison, but far from having any effect, blinding rays of light began to stream from his body instead and the soldiers were very afraid. They took him to a high mountain and pushed him off, but he glided down, landed on a lake and travelled across the surface like a duck.

More prosaic accounts suggest that he was exiled in 'a deserted area near the ocean where there were few people to receive the Dharma'. He only returned to his home monastery of Tsurpu near Lhasa towards the end of his life.

Phagpa's influence, meanwhile, went from strength to strength. On three occasions he granted tantric initiations to twenty-five of Kublai's ministers. After each initiation he was granted authority over further regions of Tibet. In 1260, when Kublai became Great Khan, Phagpa was given the Chinese title 'Ti-shih' (Imperial Preceptor). In this role he was placed in charge of the *Tsung-chih-yüan*, the office created in 1264 to regulate all affairs connected with Buddhism throughout the Mongol empire.

Kublai Khan's personal allegiance to Phagpa and Tibetan Buddhism implied neither persecution of nor disinterest in the other religions of his realm. Like his predecessors he adopted a tolerant attitude to them all. Yet his reasons for adopting Tibetan Buddhism were motivated more by political expediency than spiritual yearning. By all accounts he was a ruthless warrior who drank and womanized heavily, the sort of man who was impressed more by the supposed magical feats of the Tibetan lamas than by their doctrinal subtleties. And when he finally conquered the whole of China and was declared Emperor in 1280, it only made sense for him as a foreign ruler to bring with him a foreign religion, and place its leading figure in charge of the indigenous Buddhist traditions of China.

Like many members of his family Kublai had a Nestorian Christian mother and wives. During an earlier period of his life, when he served as a chief minister for Güyük in Karakoram, he had appointed a Ch'an (Zen) Buddhist monk, Liu Ping-chung, as his chief advisor. And when he met Niccolo and Maffeo Polo (Marco's uncles) in his summer palace in 1265, he dispatched them as virtual ambassadors to the Roman pontiff, requesting that he be sent one hundred learned men versed in the liberal arts and some oil from the lamp burning at the Holy Sepulchre in Jerusalem. Ten years later, when the Polos returned with the young Marco, they brought the oil, but failed to provide the learned men, a lost opportunity that was deeply regretted in Europe. Two hundred years later, Christopher Columbus, sailing across the Atlantic in search of a short-cut to India, reminisces in his ship's log 'how on many occasions [the Khan] and his predecessors had sent to Rome to ask for doctors in our holy faith, so that they might instruct them in this, and that the Holy Father had never provided them, and so many peoples were lost, falling into idolatory'.

Kublai's pragmatic use of religion is further expressed in a passage of Marco's book, where he says to the Polo brothers:

> There are four prophets that are adored and revered by the whole world. The Christians declare their God to have been Jesus Christ, the Saracens Mohammed, the Jews Moses, the [Buddhists] Sagamoni Borcan [Shakyamuni Buddha] . . .; and I honour and revere all four.

This attitude allowed the wily Khan to keep visitors to the court guessing as to his personal preference. The Polos were convinced that he regarded 'the Christian faith as the most true' and only failed to convert because he was afraid of being harmed by the superhuman power of the lamas. Elsewhere, Marco Polo reflects:

> These Tartars do not care what god is worshipped in their lands. If only all are faithful to the lord Khan and give the appointed tribute, thou mayest do what pleaseth thee with thy soul . . . . They confess indeed in Tartary that Christ is Lord, but say that he is a proud Lord because he will not be with other gods but will be God above all the others in the world.

This passage was suppressed in the medieval editions of Marco's book for fear of being condemned by the Inquisition as blasphemous.

In many respects, Kublai Khan followed the example of Ashoka in according freedom of religion throughout his realm while personally being committed to Buddhism. Like Ashoka, his devotion to Buddhism increased the more his political ambitions were realized and he could turn his mind to matters other than war. Towards the end of his reign, the outward evidence of his allegiance to Buddhism became progressively pronounced. Its greatest public display occurred in 1288 when the Buddha's bowl, two teeth and a tuft of hair arrived in the capital from Ceylon. The entire population of Peking, including representatives of each religion, was required to attend the processional entry of the relics into the city. On this occasion Christians, Jews and Muslims agreed to participate with the 'idolators' in worshipping the relics.

Marco Polo, who served as a functionary in Kublai Khan's bureaucracy for nearly twenty years, provided Europe with a more detailed account of popular Buddhist practices than William of Rubruck, but hardly a more accurate one. Marco, a trader and adventurer with a knee-jerk faith in Catholicism, regarded the Buddha simply as the chief of all the idols he saw on his travels. His view was not substantially altered even after his visit to Ceylon in 1293, when he became the first European to learn both the outlines of the historical Buddha's life and the connection between Gautama and the 'idols' of Central and Eastern Asia. Impressed by the Buddha's sanctity, he commented, 'for a certainty, if he had been baptised a Christian he would have been a great saint before God'.

By the time Marco returned to Venice in 1295, relations between the European powers and the Mongol court had turned from very frosty to something approaching warmth. In 1263 Hülegü, brother of the deceased Möngke, sent a mission to Europe proposing a military alliance against the Muslims. The idea was enthusiastically taken up by Gregory X at the Council of Lyon in 1274. A sixteen-man Mongol mission arrived in Lyon for the council and left with an agreement on a joint strategy to reclaim the Holy Land. But internal disputes in Europe prevented the plan from being put into action.

The Council of Lyon also marked a highpoint in Christian missionary resolve. By this time the mendicant orders of the Dominicans and Franciscans had consolidated the faith in Europe and were actively spreading it abroad. A mission of five Franciscans, headed by John of Montecorvino, was dispatched to China by the Pope. John arrived shortly after Kublai's death in 1294 and was received by Kublai's grandson and successor Temür as a papal envoy. He tried but failed to convert Temür from Buddhism to Christianity. In 1313 he was appointed Archbishop of Khanbaliq [Peking] and Patriarch of the Orient, posts that continued to be filled until 1369, when, as the Mongol dynasty collapsed, the Christians were expelled from the city by Chinese nationalists.

Tibetan Buddhist influence in the Mongol court in China increased as the political strength of the dynasty declined. A Chinese official writing around 1300 estimated that half the annual income of the empire found its way into Buddhist monasteries (of which there were 42,318 in 1291). In 1309 an edict was issued declaring 'that anyone found guilty of striking a lama would have his hand cut off, and anyone insulting a lama would have his tongue removed'. Such was the power of the Tibetan Buddhist church that it fuelled Chinese resentment against the continuing Mongol rule of the country and became a factor in its downfall.

Another lama to reappear during the last years of the empire was Rangjung Dorjé, the 3rd Karmapa, successor of Karma Pakshi. It was he, rather than the Sakya hierarch, who ceremonially enthroned Toghan Temür, the last Mongol Emperor, on 19 July 1333, who, in return, gave Rangjung Dorjé the title: 'All Knower of Religion, the Buddha Karmapa.' Although Tibetan records lavish praise upon this great Dharma King, the French historian René Grousset describes Temür as

a weak, vacillating person, [finding] delight only in the company of his favourites and of Tibetan lamas. Dulled by debauchery, he took no interest in affairs of state and ignored the Chinese national rebellion now rumbling in the south.

And thus more than a century of Mongol domination came to a close.

KARMAPA:
THE KAGYU TRADITION

In 1974 the 16th Karmapa, Rangjung Rigpai Dorjé, set out from Rumtek Monastery in Sikkim on his first tour of the West. He travelled widely through America and Europe, establishing centres and conferring ordinations and initiations. Yet by far the greatest impact he made on the public was his performance of the Black Crown Ceremony.

Wherever the twenty-minute ceremony was held, the Karmapa would mount a luxuriously prepared throne, stand for a few moments surveying the audience and then, with a smile, drop abruptly to the seat. As *gyaling* (Tibetan oboe-like instruments) quivered in an eerie, slowly ascending pitch, he would remove his golden hat embroidered with pearls and reach for a red cloth bundle at his side. From it he would unwrap a solid and glistening midnight-blue crown, embossed at the front with a double *vajra*. Pulling himself upright, with an intently concentrated expression, he would raise the crown with his right hand and place it on his shaven head. Still holding the crown, with *gyaling* wailing in a sustained crescendo, he would turn the beads of a crystal rosary with the fingers of his left hand, while reciting the mantra of Avalokiteshvara one hundred and eight times. Then, the *gyaling* beginning to fade, he would remove the crown and return it to its cloth wrapping.

The first vision of the Karmapa wearing such a crown was beheld in the full moon early on the morning of 15 June 1339, by Toghan Temür, the last Mongol Emperor of China, as he looked out of his palace in Peking the day after the death of his teacher, the 3rd Karmapa. He summoned a craftsman to carve an image in the likeness of his vision. Many years later, in 1407, after the Mongol rulers had been replaced by the Chinese Ming dynasty, the Emperor Yung-lo invited the 5th Karmapa to his court. During a ceremony the Emperor saw a crown woven from the hairs of one hundred thousand *dakinis*, hovering above the Karmapa's head. He ordered a physical replica to be made. It is this crown that has been in the possession of the Karmapas ever since.

The Karmapas became figures of power, wealth and influence in Tibet, consorting with the emperors of China, but the origins of the Kagyu tradition they represent are humble, iconoclastic and austere.

The tradition traces its beginnings to the enigmatic Tilopa, who was born in India sometime during the latter part of the 10th century. Tilopa was initially employed as resident Buddhist teacher by the King of Vishnunagar. Finding this well-paid post meaningless, he tried in vain to resign. One night he discarded his monastic robes for rags and disappeared. He took up residence in a cremation ground, begged in the local town for his food and practised meditation. He became renowned as a *siddha* but only accepted one disciple, whom, in conventional terms, he treated appallingly. Tilopa's appearance alone would have put most people off: 'a dark man dressed in cotton trousers, his hair knotted in a tuft, and with protruding, blood-shot eyes.'

That one disciple was Naropa, a brilliant scholar with an aristocratic background who became abbot of Nalanda, still the greatest monastery in India, at the age of thirty-three. But in 1057, having held the post for eight years, he underwent a breakdown that forced him to resign. One morning, as Naropa was poring over a text on logic and epistemology, a terrifying shadow flickered across the page. He swung round to see an old crone, crippled and deformed, with a yellowing beard, who spluttered: 'What are you doing?' When he explained the content of the texts, she retorted: 'What do you understand, the words or the meaning?' When he said he understood the meaning, she broke into tears and wept, shaking her head and accusing him of lying. 'Then who understands the meaning?' asked Naropa in desperation. 'My brother,' she replied, 'Tilopa.'

Naropa's search for Tilopa reads like a nightmare. As he wanders through the countryside in search of his teacher, he finds himself in a series of situations that initially hold out the promise of a meeting but end in frustration. As he is about to slash his wrists with a razor, Tilopa appears and explains to him that throughout his breakdown the two of them had 'never been apart, but were like a body and its shadow', implying that life situations themselves, however distressing, are the true opportunities for insight. To seek a 'teacher' outside of them, with the belief that he will magically solve one's problems, is just another consoling delusion.

Nonetheless, Naropa stayed with Tilopa. But for the first year 'Tilopa sat motionless and stiff like a log, as if he had lost the power of movement'. Naropa waited devoutly on his catatonic teacher, circumambulating and beseeching him for instruction. When at last Tilopa responded, he told Naropa to accompany him to the roof of a temple. 'If I had had a disciple', he declared, 'he would have jumped down from here.' Naropa immediately leaped and lay immobile on the ground, overcome by pain. Only then, having soothed his disciple's injuries, did Tilopa teach him. This went on for twelve years, with Naropa undergoing another agonizing trial of his sincerity every twelve months, followed by the delivery of a set of pithy instructions in tantric practice.

In the end Naropa became a teacher in his own right, explaining and systemizing Tilopa's instructions. His synthesis of philosophical acuity and existential realization is today a guiding ideal of all schools of Tibetan Buddhism. The Kagyu tradition, which claims direct descent from Naropa, has produced through the centuries a number of figures who have embodied this ideal, the most prominent contemporary example being a reincarnate lama from eastern Tibet: Chögyam Trungpa, Rinpoché.

Trungpa was born in February 1939, recognized by the Karmapa as the 11th Trungpa Tulku and enthroned as the head of the Surmang Monasteries in the mountainous valleys of Kham, eastern Tibet. He had a precocious childhood, undergoing at least one major spiritual catharsis while still an adolescent. In 1959, shortly after completing his formal monastic education, he guided a large party of refugees out of Communist Chinese-controlled Tibet to the safety of India, where he was appointed by the Dalai Lama as an advisor to a school for young lamas in Dalhousie. Four years later he was awarded a Spaulding scholarship to Oxford University, where he studied comparative religion, philosophy and the fine arts, while refining his command of English. In 1968, together with his colleague Akong Rinpoché, he founded Samye Ling, the first Tibetan Buddhist centre in Europe, in the rolling hills of Dumfriesshire, Scotland.

Trungpa's brilliance as a scholar, poet and linguist drew an increasing number of Western students to the exposed and crumbling house in Scotland to hear him teach. His gifts as a teacher were only matched by his ability to attract controversy. Many of the students emerged from the anarchic restlessness of the 1960s, their interest in Buddhism fuelled by a rejection of society and a yearning for new values glimpsed in a haze of psychedelic intuitions. Trungpa embraced this counter-culture with a degree of openness that alienated his more conventionally minded students. In 1969 he returned his monastic vows and

Samye Ling developed a reputation in the local community for wild parties, free sex and the use of drugs. Late one night Trungpa crashed his car into the window of a practical joke shop. He was rushed to Newcastle General Hospital, to emerge many weeks later partially but incurably paralysed.

Trungpa evolved a style of teaching Buddhism that broke with the dry vocabulary of academia by employing colloquial terms and idioms with a poet's gift for metaphor. He was the first Asian Buddhist teacher to plunge into the existential plight of a Western culture and to articulate a way out of that dilemma in the language of those undergoing it. As the strife at Samye Ling over his behaviour was reaching its climax at the end of 1969, he wrote:

My journey to the overseas continent needs no
copyright,
For it has never been conducted in the same manner.
It is the fresh meeting of man,
The true meeting of living man.
It is the pilgrimage,
The great odyssey which I have never feared,
Since I have not hesitated to flow with the river's
current.

A few months later he shocked the community by marrying Diana Pybus, a young aristocratic English woman, severed his ties with Samye Ling and Akong Rinpoché, and flew to North America.

Chögyam Trungpa's startling seventeen-year encounter with the United States and Canada had a considerable impact on the development of Buddhism in Europe. Some of his followers established training centres in Germany, England and Holland along the efficient, stage-by-stage lines of his American organization, while two of his early British students, Michael and

Shenpen Hookham, created the Longchen Foundation in Oxford under his patronage. But his greatest influence in Europe was through his writings. Books such as *Cutting Through Spiritual Materialism* (1973) became landmarks in articulating Buddhist insights in a way that was both fresh and immediate. His meteoric ascent to fame and notoriety was followed with beguiled fascination from the other side of the Atlantic. Trungpa continued to impress and appal Europe with his 'Crazy Wisdom' antics, setting a model for a Buddhist life that was by turn eminently sane and disturbingly outrageous.

By 1974 he had established several rural retreat communities and a network of urban Buddhist study centres (called 'Dharmadhatus'); created Vajradhatu, a co-ordinating body to oversee the centres; the Naropa Institute, now an accredited liberal arts college; the Maitri Institute, a psychotherapeutic care facility; and had hosted the first visit of the 16th Karmapa to North America. In the United States Trungpa found an intelligent and eager audience, willing to help him realize his vision of establishing the Kagyu tradition within the matrix of American society, drawing upon ancient traditions while responding creatively to contemporary issues.

This shining achievement was accompanied, however, by an ever-lengthening shadow, the seeds of which were already visible in Scotland. Trungpa developed a reputation for heavy drinking and sexual promiscuity. As his organization grew in power, he formed the Dorje Kasung, initially a volunteer service organization that grew into a bodyguard and finally a khaki-uniformed, quasi-military corps. Trungpa's circle assumed eccentric regal trappings through his adaptation of the mythology of the *Kalachakra Tantra*, a complex Buddhist doctrine with millenarian overtones centred around the quasi-legendary realm of Shambhala. He became known as the 'Vidyadhara' ('Knowledge Holder', a title given to him by the Karmapa); his American successor Thomas Rich as the 'Vajra Regent Osel Tenzin', and his residence as the 'Kapala Court' — replete with courtiers and courtesans.

Trungpa Rinpoché died on 4 April 1987, in an intensive care unit in Halifax, Nova Scotia, his last years having been marked by alcohol-related illness and withdrawal from public life. In his final testament he exhorted the members of his community not to quarrel or create friction, to bring up their children in pure Buddhist fashion, and to focus on the expansion of his Vajradhatu organization. Three years later, in the wake of scandal and threats of litigation, the Vajra Regent died from AIDS, fracturing the community and raising serious questions about the ethics of tantric Buddhist teachers.

Behaviour that might have been acceptable among the *mahasiddhas* of medieval India and Tibet proved confusing and divisive in outwardly liberal but inwardly puritanical America. Trungpa's organization, now headed by his son, Sawang Osel Rangdrol Mukpo, seems solid and resourceful enough to survive these scandals. But the memory of Chögyam, the self-styled 'stray dog' who 'wanders around the world', is likely to remain an enigma.

Ambiguity also surrounds the recognition in January 1992 of a young boy in eastern Tibet as the 12th Trungpa Tulku. Before he died Chögyam Trungpa had warned his Western disciples that he would return only as a Japanese scientist or businessman. The young boy will be raised in Surmang Monastery, Trungpa's traditional seat in Kham.

Tilopa's instructions, systemized by Naropa, found their way into Tibet through Marpa the Translator, known as the 'Father of the Kagyu Lineage'. Marpa, depicted as a corpulent and imposing figure, came from a wealthy farming family in the Lhodrak area of southern Tibet. He was a married layman, who combined his practice of Buddhism with the running of the family estate. He lived during the 11th century, a period which marked the second major phase of Buddhism's dissemination from India to Tibet. Fresh translations of many Buddhist texts were undertaken at this time, giving rise to the term 'Sarma-pa', followers of the New Tradition, as opposed to the 'Nyingma-pa', followers of the Old. Marpa travelled to India three times and spent a total of twelve and a half years with Naropa, receiving from him the bulk of tantric instruction his teacher had been given by Tilopa.

The most famous of Marpa's many disciples was the yogin and poet Milarepa. The availability since the 1920s of Milarepa's dramatic biography in both French and English has made him one of the best-known exemplars of Buddhist values in Europe. He started life having been cruelly dispossessed by his paternal uncle and aunt upon the premature death of his father. At his mother's behest Mila became a black magician who caused the family home to collapse during a wedding feast, killing all the relatives who had cheated him. Instead of satisfaction at the death of his enemies, Mila experienced a crushing remorse that drove him to find a means to expiate his crime. This longing for a solution obsessed him: 'If I went out, I wanted to stay in. If I stayed in, I wanted to go out. At night sleep escaped me. I dared not confess my sadness or my longing for liberation.' In this frame of mind he was driven to seek out Marpa.

Far from welcoming Mila with open arms, Marpa treated him with scorn. Before imparting any teaching, he insisted that Mila build single-handedly a stone tower. Just as the tower was reaching completion, he would order him to dismantle it and start again. Marpa was unrelenting in the punishing tasks he set his disciple. As with Naropa, Mila was pushed by his teacher to the limits of his endurance to galvanize the resolve needed to enter the tantric path. The Buddhist *tantras* teach the possibility of Buddhahood in a single lifetime through a path that transforms the forces of self-destruction into those of enlightenment. In this respect, Mila — a criminal and sorcerer — was the perfect candidate.

Having given instructions, Marpa dispatched his disciple to remote mountain caves to meditate. And it is here that Milarepa comes into his own. Not only does he show superb proficiency in the tantric yogas and disciplines, but he blossoms as a creative individual, becoming the emblematic Buddhist saint of Tibet, a man who has risen from the depths of human evil to the heights of mystic exaltation, his transformation bursting forth in poetic song:

> I, whom you see, the man with a name,
> Am a son of the golden eagle;
> I grew wings and feathers in the egg.
> A child, I slept in my cradle;
> A youth, I watched the door;
> A man, I flew in the sky.
> Though the sky is high and wide, I do not fear;
> Though the way is steep and narrow, I am not afraid.

Mila spent the rest of his life in the solitude of high mountains. He neither became a monk, nor did he follow his teacher's example and become a married lama. He dressed in a simple white cotton cloth and kept warm through one of Naropa's yogic practices, the 'inner heat'. Tantric practice recognizes the complementarity of body and mind and its disciplines involve physical as well as spiritual practices. The 'inner heat', for example, is not merely a handy way of keeping warm in caves, but a means to disentangle subtle nervous obstructions, or 'knots', that keep us locked in a spasm of self-centred delusion.

Milarepa lived to the age of eighty-three. He founded no

monasteries or meditation centres; his disciples gathered around him in the mountains and outlying villages, recording his songs, and following his instructions. While venerated as a saint, he dismissed any pious interpretations of his life, proclaiming that he was an ordinary man who had reached his insights through his own endeavour. In the end he was poisoned by a jealous scholar.

Just as Naropa's qualities were embodied by Chögyam Trungpa, so, in modern Europe, were many aspects of Milarepa's life personified by another lama from eastern Tibet, Kalu Rinpoché. Through his radiant and deeply silent eyes, peering from a gaunt hermit's frame, Kalu Rinpoché epitomized for many who knew him the caring detachment of Mila.

Kalu Rinpoché was born to a physician-lama and his wife and at a young age recognized as an emanation of the 19th-century Rimé lama Jamgon Kongtrul. His parents were encouraged to send him to the nearby Nyingma Monastery of Dzogchen, but his father refused and chose to raise his son by himself. At the age of thirteen, he was ordained as a novice monk, and three years later, having completed his studies of Buddhist doctrine and medicine, entered his first three-year, three-month retreat in Pelpung Monastery. On completion of the retreat he left on an extensive pilgrimage to the historical Buddhist shrines of Central Tibet, returning to his homeland at the age of twenty-five to embark on twelve years of solitary retreat in the mountains. This period of solitude came to an end with his appointment as Practice Master of Pelpung, a post he occupied until the 1950s.

Some years before the Chinese usurpation of power, Kalu Rinpoché had been invited to Bhutan by the Karmapa on behalf of the royal family to renovate and revitalize Jangchub Chöling Monastery. The work completed, he headed to India to assist in the preservation of Buddhism among the Tibetan refugee community. He was offered a house in Sonada, a few kilometres from Darjeeling, where he settled in 1965. The house and land were consecrated as a monastery, and turned into a three-year retreat centre for monks and nuns. It was not long before he was discovered by curious Europeans and Americans, eager to study with such an eminent Tibetan yogin.

His first visit to the West was arranged by his foreign disciples in 1971. Most of the time was spent in North America, but he stopped over briefly in Rome, where he met Pope Paul VI. He returned in 1974, this time to found his first two centres in Europe: in Copenhagen and Paris. At the same time he sent his disciple Lama Sherab to take care of a group of Western students in the Château de Plaige, near Autun in Bourgogne. And it was here, on the evening of 5 December 1976, that he inaugurated the first three-year retreat to take place on European soil.

Seven men and six women of diverse nationalities had worked for months building two simple compounds in stone, wood and concrete. They had completed the necessary preliminary practices and learnt sufficient Tibetan to follow the meditation instructions. In 1980, Kalu Rinpoché returned to Plaige to greet the retreatants on their return to the world, consecrated a giant stupa in the grounds, and ushered another eleven men and eleven women into the next three-year retreat, thus initiating a cycle that has continued ever since.

Kalu Rinpoché continued travelling until shortly before his death at the age of eighty-five. It is estimated that he taught in over forty countries and established more than a hundred centres. He leaves behind him a network of study and retreat facilities in most European countries, directed by both his Tibetan and Western disciples. In France, where he has had the greatest impact, Lama Sherab oversees Kagyu Ling, the quaint old *château* of Plaige now overshadowed by a magnificent three-storey temple, while his oldest European disciple, Lama Denis Teundroup, directs Karma Ling, situated in the old Chartreuse monastery of St Hugon near the town of Pontcharra in Rhône-Alpes.

111

'Everything that I have accomplished', said Kalu Rinpoché towards the end of his life,

> whether in the secular or religious domain, has been done in the spirit of others' welfare. I have affixed to my actions the seals of profound dedication and prayer. Without exception I have given all good things I have had in my possession to the Dharma.

On 17 September 1990, a son was born to Kalu Rinpoché's nephew and personal attendant, Lama Gyaltsen Ratak, and his wife Drolkar. A year later the boy was recognized as the reincarnation of Kalu Rinpoché.

It was not, however, through Milarepa that the mainstream of the Kagyu tradition has come down to us but through his disciple Gampopa. Gampopa, the son of a Tibetan physician, was trained by his father in medicine. At the age of twenty-six, after the death of his wife, he received full monastic ordination. Initially he studied with teachers from the newly founded Kadam school, who emphasized the need for a firm basis in Buddhist ethics, doctrine and philosophy before proceeding to tantric practices. When he was thirty-two, he heard of Milarepa from some beggars and was inspired to seek him out. After much hardship, he found Mila at a place called Drin and stayed with him for thirteen months. He went into retreat for twelve years. On his return journey to Drin he received news of Mila's death.

For the rest of his long life, Gampopa became a widely respected teacher, noted for the way he unified the philosophical and monastic traditions of the Kadam teachers with the yogic doctrines of Naropa, Marpa and Milarepa, thus laying the foundations for the Kagyu school we know today. Two contemporary teachers who exemplify this unified approach of Gampopa are Thrangu Rinpoché and Khenpo Tsultrim Gyamtso, both of whom serve as instructors and preceptors at Rumtek Monastery in Sikkim, and teach widely in Kagyu centres in Europe and America.

One of Gampopa's chief disciples was a monk called Dusum Khyenpa, subsequently known as the 1st Karmapa. Dusum Khyenpa became a novice monk at the age of sixteen and devoted himself, as Gampopa before him, to doctrinal study in the Kadam tradition. He was thirty when he met his teacher, who initiated him into the tantric path. After many years in retreat, he spent the rest of his life teaching and founding monasteries both in eastern and central Tibet, the most famous of which was Tsurpu, near Lhasa, which, served as the official seat of the Karmapa.

Gampopa and other lamas of the day believed that Dusum Khyenpa had been prophesied by the Buddha as the 'man of action' (Karma-pa) who would spread the Dharma through a series of successive incarnations. As a fulfilment of this prophecy, shortly before Dusum Khyenpa died he left instructions as to the whereabouts of his next incarnation, thus inaugurating the system of recognized reincarnate lamas (*tulkus*), which became a common practice throughout Tibet. The young boy recognized as his successor was Karma Pakshi, the rival of Phagpa who was invited to the courts of Kublai and Möngke Khan.

The Karmapas have been noted throughout history for their charismatic zeal, both as religious teachers and political rulers. Twice they aspired for supreme leadership of Tibet, and twice they were thwarted, in both cases by a lama from another tradition with powerful Mongolian backing. The first time was when the Sakya lama Phagpa achieved control of the country under Kublai Khan, the second when the 5th Dalai Lama of the reformed Geluk order was enthroned by Gushri Khan in 1642. This might help explain the extraordinary determination of the Karma Kagyu in establishing themselves at the forefront of Tibetan Buddhism in the West.

Among Buddhist leaders in Tibet, the 16th Karmapa was one of the first to realize and act upon a sense of the impending fate of his country. He and Kalu Rinpoché had already forged ties with supporters in Bhutan and Sikkim before the Chinese clampdown in March 1959. The Karmapa was also one of the first to recognize the potential for the spread of Buddhism in the West. Unlike the Dalai Lama's Geluk order, which was implicated in the failure to secure the independence of Tibet, he could act from an uncompromised position, confident of the strengths of his tradition. In fact the Kagyu were the *only* major tradition not to have held political authority over the entire country: the Nyingma could look back with satisfaction to the days of Trisong Detsen in the 8th century and the Sakya to the Mongol dynasty of the 13th and 14th. The encounter with the world at large, imposed upon the Tibetans in 1959, was an opportunity for the Karma Kagyu tradition to realize its historical ambitions. 'There was one thought uppermost in Karmapa's mind', reads a biography, 'that, though in exile, he should not rest but must take full responsibility for rekindling and revitalising the torch of the Dharma, with the material and spiritual co-operation of the many Buddhists throughout the world.'

This sense of mission has borne fruit in a network of organizations throughout the world. The Karmapa's European centre is Dagpo Kagyu Ling, on the Côte de Jor in Dordogne. Attached to Dagpo Kagyu Ling is Kundreul Ling, in Le Bost, Auvergne, formerly the home of Arnaud Desjardins, now a retreat centre headed by Lama Gendun, a monk who has spent more than thirty years in secluded meditation. At present about ninety Western monks and nuns live in Le Bost, most of them engaged in three-year retreats. At any one time in Europe today up to three hundred people will be undergoing the traditional Kagyu meditation training. A similar programme is followed in Samye Ling, Scotland, which Akong Rinpoché has steadily developed since Chögyam Trungpa's departure. It now includes a golden-roofed Tibetan-style temple and in April 1992 purchased 'Holy Island' off the Western coast of Scotland with plans to convert it into an interdenominational retreat complex.

One of the Karmapa's most effective, albeit controversial, agents in Europe is the Danish teacher Ole Nydahl, who for the past fifteen years has travelled ceaselessly to promote the Karmapa's vision. A powerfully built, sun-tanned Viking of a man in jeans and T-shirt, Ole Nydahl projects an ecstatic, sensuous version of Tantric Buddhism. He has established more than fifty centres and communities, primarily in Germany and Poland, and is now expanding further into Eastern Europe and Russia. While emphasizing concrete experience over abstract belief, Ole Nydahl's approach nonetheless has fundamentalist and sectarian overtones. Nydahl suspects he is the emanation of a Buddhist protector-deity with a mission to create 'a lay and yogic organization built on friendship rather than hierarchy, held together by a common trust in the Karmapa, capable of bringing Buddhism into the 21st century as a living transmission'.

The 16th Karmapa died in a hospital in Zion, Illinois, on 5 November 1981 at the age of fifty-eight. Four senior *tulkus* — Tai Situ Rinpoché, Shamar Rinpoché, Goshir Gyaltsap Rinpoché and Jamgon Kongtrul Rinpoché — were appointed as a collective regency to oversee the transition and find the next incarnation. It was commonly believed that the 16th Karmapa had left the traditional letter containing details of his future rebirth. But no such letter was found until 1989, when Situ Rinpoché announced that he had discovered one, with precise instructions, concealed inside a talisman given to him by the Karmapa. This was not shown to the other regents until March 1992. Shamar Rinpoché, however, expressed doubt concerning its authenticity.

From this point on, events moved rapidly and dramatically. On 26 April Jamgon Kongtrul, who had been delegated to find the new incarnation in Tibet, was killed in a car crash near Siliguri, India. By this time a boy, as described in the letter, had been discovered in eastern Tibet and was soon to leave for Tsurpu, the traditional seat of the Karmapa. On 12 June Shamar arrived in Rumtek Monastery with an Indian army bodyguard to meet with Situ and Gyaltsab to discuss his reservations, but the presence of troops caused a violent clash between different monastic factions and the discussion was abandoned. Three days later the boy arrived at Tsurpu. On 29 June, Peking acknowledged the boy as a 'Living Buddha' — the first time a *tulku* has been recognized by the Chinese government since 1959. On 3 July, the Tibetan government-in-exile announced the Dalai Lama's recognition of the boy. On 27 September, in Tsurpu Monastery, the official enthronement of eight-year-old Ugyen Tinley, the 17th Karmapa, took place. Shamar Rinpoché, however, did not attend. In refusing to recognize the boy, he effectively broke with the other two regents. The true incarnation, he maintained, was yet to be found.

Central to the Kagyu — indeed all the Tibetan schools — is the key role of the spiritual teacher (Skt. *guru*; Tib. *lama*). The lama is seen as the very embodiment of the Buddha, without whose direct compassionate assistance, progress along the path to enlightenment is impossible. In Tantric Buddhism, the student is required to surrender completely to the teacher and follow his advice unhesitatingly. However unconventional the lama's behaviour may be, the student must regard it as the enlightened activity of a Buddha. Hence a disciple would tend not to judge Chögyam Trungpa's alcoholism and sexual profligacy by the standards of ordinary mortals, for she would have been taught to regard them as a display of a *mahasiddha*'s transcendent realization. Such was the impact of Vajrayana Buddhism in Tibet, that lamas like the Karmapa quickly assumed political responsibilities in addition to their religious functions, thus infusing secular power with spiritual purpose while also exposing spiritual detachment to secular corruption.

To what extent is this devotional Buddhism with feudal overtones adaptable to contemporary Europe and America? On the positive side, surrender to a lama's authority can serve to undermine egoistic obsessions and open one to a more enlightened perspective on life. If the lama is able to direct the student to spiritual freedom and understanding, then the relationship can result in the recovery and enhancement of one's own inner authority. But, as the Tibetan texts emphasize, utmost care and discretion must precede such an intimate commitment. If not, at best confusion and at worst exploitation will result. Today, when high-ranking lamas fly around the world, settling for a few days to lecture and confer initiations to huge audiences, how feasible is such an intimate relationship?

The Kagyu teachings culminate, however, in the eminently apolitical and direct instructions of *mahamudra* (the 'Great Symbol'). 'In meditation practice,' said Chögyam Trungpa,

> there is always some sense of going and not-going, some process of thinking and not-thinking taking place. But beyond that process of thinking and not-thinking, there is some basis of nonthought, nonconceptualisation. No matter how confused we might be, there is a dancing ground of experience that is common to everyone, . . . a basic state of mind that is clear and pure and natural. The realisation of that basic state of mind is what is known as *mahamudra*.

Teachers of the Kagyu tradition return inexorably to this expression of one's fundamental human experience. In the words of the 3rd Karmapa, 'the view of *mahamudra* is to add nothing to mind's nature. Being mindful of this view, without distraction, is the essence of practice.' Having received initiation in *mahamudra* from a lama, the meditator proceeds by following instructions to realize the key qualities of equilibrium, relaxation and naturalness, reminding herself that

> Since in the view of *mahamudra*
> Analysis does not apply,
> Cast mind-made knowledge far away.
> Since in the meditation of *mahamudra*
> There is no way of fixating on a thought,
> Abandon deliberate meditation.
> Since in the action of *mahamudra*
> There is no reference point for any action,
> Be free from the intention to act or not.
> Since in the fruition of *mahamudra*
> There is no attainment to newly acquire,
> Cast hopes, fears and desires far away.

9

DOGEN:
THE SOTO ZEN TRADITION

A meditation with marked similarities to *mahamudra* is practised every morning (except Mondays) not in enclosed three-year retreats in the French or Scottish countryside, but just down the road from the Place de la Bastille, in the heart of Paris.

As the city stirs groggily to life and a lone refuse truck empties a groaning skip into its maw, a steady trickle of men and women step off the deserted pavement into the 'Dojo Zen de Paris'. They weave past the Japanese knick-knacks and Buddhist books of the 'Boutique Zen' into a cramped back room, lined with shelves packed with *zafus* (round black cushions), and change their jackets and coats for simple black cotton gowns. A narrow corridor leads them into a pale spacious room, its walls sparely decorated with scrolls of cursive Chinese characters and black-and-white photos of a stern Japanese monk, and in the centre an altar and a drum. They seat themselves in rows facing the walls, adjust their posture so that the back is erect and taut, the chin pulled in, the head pressed upwards, the knees pressed down against the floor.

A bell is struck and the room becomes perfectly still. Twenty minutes later a voice thunders: '*Kyosaku!*' And the swish of a robed figure nimbly rising from the floor, bowing, then bare feet padding stealthily through the room are heard. Out of the corner of an eye a seated figure bows, then leans to one side, and a wooden stick cracks on to one shoulder, then the other, then another bow, and the padding continues . . . . Twenty minutes pass, the voice booms: '*Kinhin!*' Everyone rises, leans their *zafu* against the wall, and stands in line, walking slowly, elbows jutting uniformly outwards, right hand enclosing left fist at the heart. They sit again and the voice delivers an edifyingly enigmatic instruction on Zen, pausing for each phrase to pierce the alert stillness. Then drums, then chanting — both deep and roaring — then they stand and bow and the voice (its owner revealed as a shaven-headed Frenchman holding a lacquered brown stick), with mischievous lightness says, 'Bonjour!'

This practice of *zazen* ('seated meditation'), as transmitted through the Soto tradition of Japanese Zen Buddhism, is, according to Taisen Deshimaru (the stern monk of the photos), 'the process of becoming intimate with oneself'.

> One does not look outside oneself. During *zazen* it is necessary to concentrate on your posture, but you must forget about the body . . . . We must observe our minds . . . . In *zazen* your mind becomes like a mirror. So when [thoughts] appear, let them pass, like in a mirror.
>
> Zen is not a particular state but the normal state: silent, peaceful, unagitated. In *zazen* neither intention, analysis, specific effort nor imagination take place. It's enough just to be without hypocrisy, dogmatism, arrogance — embracing all opposites.

Taisen Deshimaru arrived via the Trans-Siberian Railway in the Gare du Nord of Paris in July 1967. He was fifty-three years old, penniless, unable to speak a word of French and owned only three things: his *zafu*, his monk's robe and the notebook of his teacher Kodo Sawaki. He had a mission: to establish in Europe what he passionately understood to be 'True Zen'. Twenty-four years later the 'Mission de Maître Taisen Deshimaru' has two hundred *dojos* (practice centres) and groups world-wide, ninety of which are in France, the rest spread mainly through Europe but extending as far as Uruguay and Cameroon.

Yasuo Deshimaru was born into an old Samurai family on 29 November 1914 in a small village at the southernmost tip of Japan near the city of Saga. His childhood was marked by intense experiences of loneliness, the cruelty of humans to other forms of life, and the poignant tragedy of impermanence – highlighted by the death of his grandmother. In each instance his mother's Pure Land faith inspired him towards a religious outlook on life. At the age of twenty he left the provinces and entered the University of Yokohama in Tokyo to study economics and English.

Outside his formal studies Deshimaru devoted himself to religious questions, studying Hinduism, Christianity and European philosophy in addition to Buddhism. Disillusioned with doctrinal and philosophical responses to the human dilemma, he turned to Zen. In 1936, after a disappointing retreat, he sought out Kodo Sawaki, a master he had known briefly while a student, who at the time was retreat-master of Sojiji (one of the two great Soto Zen monasteries). When Kodo Sawaki left his room in the monastery to lecture to the monks, he gave Deshimaru his notebook to read. 'He who walks alone', read the young man

goes forward alone. A man travels alone. A holy man needs nothing. One who has reached his true self strides quickly ahead. No one is above him. He feels himself one with the universe.

Why do I do *zazen*? For no purpose at all.

Profoundly impressed by these remarks, Deshimaru requested to be Kodo Sawaki's disciple and was accepted. His teacher then produced a bottle of distilled plum spirits and the two of them proceeded to get drunk.

Four years later, the Japanese attacked Pearl Harbour and the country was at war with the United States. Due to poor eyesight, Deshimaru was not conscripted, but sent instead to Indonesia to oversee a mine. He soon found himself practising *zazen* under torpedo attack on board 'The Supreme Law of the Buddha', an unarmed freighter loaded with a cargo of dynamite. The next ship he boarded was struck by fighter planes and he was cast adrift for a day and a night in the ocean with nothing but a lifejacket and his teacher's *rakusu* (token monk's robe). He nearly died from malaria, was imprisoned and sentenced to death for sympathizing with native rebels, and ended up in a prisoner of war camp in Singapore.

Upon returning to Japan he resumed his formal Zen training and went into business until 1965, the year of his teacher's death. In November of that year, while Kodo Sawaki lay dying, he summoned Deshimaru and agreed at last to his request to be ordained as a monk. After ordaining him as Mokudo Taisen, he said:

In India during the time of Bodhidharma, Buddhism was in a state of decadence. So Bodhidharma's teacher told him to take the Dharma to the East. Likewise in Japan, Buddhism is now dead. And so you, my Dharma heir, who know the true teachings of the Buddha, take them to the West so that Buddhism may again flourish.

Kodo Sawaki died in December. After burying his skull, Deshimaru sat in *zazen* for forty-nine days. Some months later he was invited by a French macrobiotic group to France.

He immediately concentrated on teaching *zazen*. For the next five years he built up a steady following, moving to ever larger apartments to accommodate the ever-growing number of students. In 1970 he founded the Association Zen d'Europe; in March 1972 he moved into a more stable *dojo* and later that year conducted his first big *sesshin* (meditation retreat) at Zinal, at which four hundred people participated. In 1980 his organization purchased La Gendronnière, a *château* in the Loire Valley, which became the focus for his Zen Mission. During the winter and summer retreats that followed more than fifteen hundred people attended to hear him teach.

While he continued to be critical of the formalism of Zen in Japan, his success in Europe led to recognition and respect in his homeland, and he was given the official title of 'Kaikyosokan' (missionary) by the Soto Zen Order. His life came to an abrupt end in 1982. He fell ill in February of that year and gave his final lecture on 15 April. The next day he flew from Paris to Tokyo, where he was admitted to hospital for an operation on 26 April. He died four days later. His last words to his students were: 'Please, continue *zazen*.'

In the spring of 1223 a young monk called Eihei Dogen, the originator of Deshimaru's form of Zen Buddhism, left the Japanese port of Hakata aboard a merchant ship for Southern Sung China in search of the 'True Dharma', which he had despaired of finding in the troubled Japan of his day. After 'sailing many miles, entrusting our ephemeral existence to the roaring waves', Dogen and his three companions crossed the East China Sea and docked off the coast of Ch'ing-yüan.

Zen Buddhism had recently been imported from China to Japan by a monk called Eisai, whom Dogen had met as a teenager. But Eisai's teachings had failed to answer the question that had consumed Dogen since the age of fourteen: 'If all beings originally possess the nature of Buddha, why does one need to arouse the *bodhicitta* and engage in practices to realise it?' Since China was the place where Buddhism, and Zen in particular, originated, it was there that Dogen was driven to resolve his perplexity.

At Dogen's time China had been home to Buddhism for more than a thousand years. The Dharma had made its way into the country from India via the trading routes of Central Asia shortly after the time of Jesus. For many Chinese, Buddhism offered a path of individual salvation that offered consolation in the wake of the collapse of the Confucianist Han dynasty in 220 CE. Five hundred years later it had become the predominant ideology of the land, its doctrines disseminated through a variety of indigenous schools. Largely because of its success, in particular its increasing economic power, factions within the government turned against it as a corrupting foreign influence and began a process of persecution which culminated in the crippling imperial decree of 845. From then on, Buddhism was eclipsed by Neo-Confucianism as the dominant way of thinking in China.

Two forms of Buddhism remained largely unscathed by this persecution: the devotional school of Pure Land and the contemplative tradition of Ch'an (Zen), the former because of its widespread appeal among the people; the latter because of the rural self-sufficiency of its monks and nuns.

Ch'an started as an obscure movement that emphasized meditation experience over doctrinal knowledge, tracing its origins back to Gautama via Bodhidharma, an Indian monk who taught in China in the 6th century. It crystallized into a distinctively Chinese form through the figure of Hui-neng, the Sixth Patriarch of the school, who had a huge influence on T'ang dynasty Buddhism through his simple yet pithy teachings that challenged the doctrinal preoccupations of the scholar-monks. For several generations after Hui-neng, the Ch'an tradition was strengthened by a succession of outstanding teachers, reaching a peak around the time of the 845 persecution — another factor in its ability to weather the storm.

By the time Dogen arrived in Southern Sung China in 1223, the Ch'an school had recaptured much of the influence that Buddhism had lost. The country in which it flourished, though, was an endangered bastion of Chinese civilization. A century earlier, in 1127, Sung China had been overrun from the north by the Jurchen, a non–Chinese tribe from Manchuria, who forced the Sung rulers south and established the Chin dynasty in the north. In 1215, eight years before Dogen's arrival, the armies of Genghis Khan burst down from the steppes and captured Yen-ching (modern Peking), squeezing the Chin rulers into a narrow strip of territory above the Southern Sung border. The Tibetan territories to the west had also submitted to Genghis, leaving the Southern Sung as a vulnerable oasis in which the historic culture of China struggled to retain its dignity and independence.

As a response to this crisis, the ruling gentry turned for inspiration to the Ch'an monks. The most notable of these was Ta-hui Tsung-kao, who had witnessed the Jurchen invasions of 1127 and fled south with the Sung court. Ta-hui was closely involved with the ruling circles, alternately sought for his advice and banished for his criticisms. During his lifetime Ch'an came to exert an unparalleled influence upon the lives of the Chinese.

Dogen immediately made his way to the monasteries of Ta-hui's disciples. But after two years of study and meditation, he found himself no nearer to solving his existential crisis than when he arrived. Ta-hui's approach involved intense inquiry into an often paradoxical question (Ch. *kung-an*; Jap. *koan*) that undermined all habitual and rational ways of problem-solving. The aim of such practice was to trigger an insight (*kensho*) which gave fresh and liberating insight to one's dilemma. The school of Ch'an Ta-hui followed traced its origins to the 9th-century Ch'an master Lin-chi (Rinzai), which had evolved into the most influential trend in

Chinese Ch'an Buddhism, and was the one which Eisai had already introduced into Japan.

Yet Dogen's dissatisfaction lay not so much with the form of meditation but with his inability to find an 'authentic teacher'. No matter how hard he 'gnawed on the iron stake' (to use Ta-hui's expression) of his dilemma, he was unable to resolve it because the teachers with whom he studied failed to embody the Dharma for him. On the verge of returning to Japan in despair, he heard of Ju-ching, the abbot of a monastery on Mt. T'ien-tung, whose approach, it was said, differed greatly from that of the others. As soon as he met Ju-ching, Dogen realized that this was the man who could help him.

Although Ju-ching abhorred the sectarian divisions in Buddhism, his tradition differed from that of Ta-hui in tracing its origins not to Lin-chi (Rinzai) but to two other 9th-century Chinese monks Ts'ao-shan and Tung-shan. This lineage came to be known as the Ts'ao-tung (Jap. Soto) school. As a follower of this line, Ju-ching gave less emphasis to *koan* meditation and recommended *zazen* alone. 'To study meditation under a master', he said,

> is to drop the body and mind; it is single-minded intense sitting (Jap. *shikan taza*) without burning incense, worshipping, reciting, practising repentance or reading sutras.

The commitment to such practice was personified by Ju-ching himself who, throughout Dogen's two-year stay, 'sat in meditation past eleven o'clock at night and got up at two-thirty or three and started it again'. Enlightenment finally came to Dogen during one of these late night sessions when Ju-ching yelled at the monk sitting next to Dogen: 'When you study under a master, you must drop the body and mind! What use is single-minded intense sleeping?' On hearing these words, Dogen grasped what it meant to 'drop the body and mind' and his dilemma was resolved.

He then went back to Japan to teach, in his own words, 'empty-handed', knowing nothing more than 'the eyes are horizontal and the nose is vertical', but, nonetheless, 'with a heavy burden on my shoulders.'

The Japan to which Dogen returned was a land that had been recently beset both with natural calamities and political upheavals. In 1185, fifteen years before Dogen's birth, the Minamoto Samurai family wrested power from the aristocratic court at Kyoto, thus ushering in the Kamakura Shogunate. Dogen, himself an aristocrat, would have keenly felt his elders' sense of loss and insecurity. The country was now ruled by the ambitious military class, the emperor reduced to a marginal and ineffective figure in Kyoto, far from the centre of government in Kamakura.

The tremendous political and social shift that inaugurated the Kamakura period demanded a comparable spiritual revolution: forms of religion that catered not to the aristocracy but responded directly to the concrete concerns of the warriors, the peasants and the city-dwellers.

The first of such movements were already underway when Dogen returned from China in 1227. These were the Jodo and Jodo Shin 'Pure Land' schools, founded respectively by Honen and his disciple Shinran, which taught the salvific power of the Buddha Amitabha, through faithfully reciting whose name rebirth in the Western Paradise of Sukhavati was ensured. In contrast to the earlier forms of Buddhism which emphasized liberation through one's own efforts, Honen and Shinran taught that salvation was only possible through abandoning self-centred spiritual ambition and opening oneself to the grace of Amitabha. Such teachings had immense popular appeal.

A Buddhist doctrine widely accepted at this time was that of the degeneration of the Dharma (*mappo*). Many sutras predicted that the teachings of the Buddha would pass through three phases (those of the True, the Semblant and the Degenerate Dharma) before disappearing altogether. In Japan it was believed that the world had entered the third phase in 1052. Justification for this view seemed widespread and the doctrine provided a convincing explanation for the calamities of the time. For many, it meant that the philosophical studies and meditation disciplines of earlier ages were no longer effective. Simple, faith-based practices were all that would work. The best one could hope for was to be reborn in a better world in order to achieve enlightenment there.

For Dogen this was unacceptable. Although he utilized the concept of degeneration to account for the disasters of the age, he rejected that it had anything to do with a parallel degradation of human capacity. Enlightenment through one's own resolve (as he had experienced himself) was possible regardless of the time and place in which one was born. Whether people were noble or base was determined not by the state of the world, but by the way they responded to it.

Dogen nonetheless followed the Pure Land schools in proposing a form of Buddhism that crystallized around a single practice, in his case *zazen*. He likewise attracted the wrath of the conservative Buddhist orthodoxy and it was not long before he was forced to leave Kyoto and settle in the outlying countryside.

Here, away from the intrigues and tensions of the city, Dogen was able to concentrate on what was closest to his heart: the practice of *zazen* and the training of monks. Although he occasionally made deprecating remarks about other approaches, his attitude was essentially non-sectarian:

In the Buddha's house we do not discuss superiority or inferiority of the teaching; nor do we concern ourselves with the depth and shallowness of the Dharma, but only with genuineness or falseness of practice.

In this he followed his teacher Ju-ching who deplored the very idea of dividing Buddhism into schools. For Ju-ching even the notion of 'Zen Buddhism' was anathema.

For Dogen, authentic practice was *zazen*, the utterly simple act of sitting still in a balanced posture, just as the Buddha himself had demonstrated beneath the Bodhi Tree. *Zazen* is not a technique which one practises now to help one reach the goal of enlightenment at some future date. For *zazen* transcends the dichotomy between 'practice' and 'enlightenment':

> To practice the Way single-heartedly is, in itself, enlightenment. There is no gap between practice and enlightenment or *zazen* and daily life.

Such emphasis on *zazen* expresses the solution to Dogen's own dilemma that drove him to China: 'If all beings originally possess the nature of Buddha, why does one need to arouse the *bodhicitta* and engage in practices to realise it?' The way he had phrased the question was at fault. In assuming that enlightenment ('the nature of Buddha') and 'practices' were different, Dogen had locked himself into a false dilemma of his own making. As long as that assumption remained intact, no matter how hard he practised, he remained stuck. It took the shock of Ju-ching's admonition to undermine his fixation.

A key notion in Dogen's understanding of *zazen* is that of 'non-thinking' (*hishiryo*). *Zazen* is beyond the dualism of either thinking (*shiryo*) or not-thinking (*fushiryo*). It neither involves being dispersed in trains of thought nor sinking into a dull state of mental inactivity. Non-thinking does not deny either thinking or not-thinking but transcends them in a higher unity.

Above all, *zazen* is something you sit down and do. 'You should stop pursuing words and letters', he says, 'and learn to withdraw and reflect on yourself. When you do so, your body and mind will

naturally fall away, and your original Buddha-nature will appear.'
Buddha-nature is not, as some Buddhist philosophy suggests, a
transcendent reality. For Dogen, it is the undistorted fact of
one's temporal existence. Nor is it something uniquely spiritual:
for Dogen, even 'the mountains and waters of the immediate
present are the manifestation of the path of the ancient Buddhas'.
Sitting in the posture of *zazen*, the mind freed in non-thinking,
the Buddha that you are and have always been is manifest.
In short:

> Studying the Buddha Way is studying oneself. Studying
> oneself is forgetting oneself. Forgetting oneself is being
> enlightened by all things.

Dogen initially shunned involvement with the ruling powers in
Japan, but his growing reputation attracted the attention of the
government. In 1247 he accepted an official invitation to the new
capital and taught there for seven months, and in 1250 received
a purple robe (the highest State honour for a monk).

A major part of his work was his writing. During his life he
composed the ninety-five fascicles of the *Treasury of the True
Dharma Eye* (*Shobogenzo*). The work broke with tradition in being
written in Japanese rather than classical Chinese. Yet for nearly
seven hundred years after Dogen's death it remained an obscure
document of the Soto school and was only published in 1816. Not
until the 1920s was it recognized as a masterpiece of Japanese
literature and philosophy and Dogen elevated to the stature of
major writer and thinker.

Dogen's health began to decline in 1250. In the summer of 1253,
he appointed his disciple Ejo as the head of Eiheiji, the monastery
he had founded in 1246 (now the headquarters of the Soto Order),
and reluctantly returned to Kyoto for medical treatment. He died
on 28 August, at the age of fifty-three, while seated in *zazen*.

On 5 October 1962, in the garden of Sojiji, a Japanese Zen trainee placed a praying mantis on the shaven head of an Englishwoman in order to frighten her. 'I carefully took it from my head', she wrote in her diary that night, 'and admired the golden glory that surrounded its body and placed it on a weed that had the same glory on its fronds. How simple and exquisite is this world in which we live . . . .' Unbeknown to her fellow trainees, earlier that day she had experienced *kensho*, 'the great flash of deep understanding'. It had been triggered by intense frustration with her treatment at the hands of one of the temple officers, who now appeared to her as gleaming with light from head to foot and towards whom she felt nothing but gratitude.

Peggy Kennett was born in England in 1924. After studying medicine, she turned to music and won a fellowship from Trinity College of Music, London. Although her initial interest in Buddhism, which began as a young woman, was towards the Theravada tradition, it shifted towards Zen. She was inspired by D.T. Suzuki, whom she met at the Buddhist Society in London, where she both studied and lectured. More significant, though, was her encounter with Koho Keido Chisan Zenji, the chief abbot of Sojiji, who visited London and invited her to come to Japan as his disciple. She set out by ship towards the end of 1961.

Her first stop was Malaysia, where, on 21 January 1962, she was ordained as a *bhikshuni* in the Chinese Lin-chi Ch'an tradition by Ven. Seck Kim Seng, receiving the name Tsu-yu. On 13 April she docked at Yokohama, was admitted to Sojiji, and given the Japanese equivalent of her Chinese name: Jiyu. From the outset she was subject to the enmity of the temple officers, who made her life as difficult as possible on account of her being both a foreigner and a woman.

131

On 28 May 1963, Koho Zenji formally gave her transmission, thereby acknowledging the validity of her *kensho* and confirming her as 'his true descendant' within the Soto Zen lineage. The following May she was installed as abbess of a small temple called Unpukuji in a village in Mie Prefecture. This gave her a degree of independence and, at the age of forty, she started training her first Western disciples.

Meanwhile, Koho Zenji had also appointed her as Soto Zen Bishop of London, in anticipation of her return to Britain, where he wanted her to introduce Soto Zen. The response from London was not encouraging. Christmas Humphreys, the founder and president of the Buddhist Society, wanted a 'real' Zen Master. Koho Zenji instructed a Japanese disciple to 'write to this man in England and tell him he obviously understands nothing whatsoever about true Zen'. Although this was phrased more diplomatically, it sealed Jiyu-Kennett's fate with the British Buddhist establishment.

The temple officers of Sojiji continued to complain bitterly about her presence. To placate them, the now-ailing Koho Zenji instructed her to go and see 'the greatest living saint of our school' so that he could confirm or deny the validity of her *kensho*. This was Kodo Sawaki, the teacher of Deshimaru, who was then lying terminally ill in a small temple outside Kyoto. She visited him on 5 October 1965. 'The old man looked at me for a long, long time', she recalled. 'His eyes looked straight through me and all through me.' Finally, he said to his assistant: 'Write to [Koho] Zenji, "I have seen. I am happy."' The following month Kodo Sawaki ordained Deshimaru. In December he died.

With her own teacher Koho Zenji's death on 1 November 1967, Jiyu-Kennett lost the only real support she had in Sojiji and Japan. Two years later, on 3 November 1969, she flew from Tokyo to California. She went on to England but was shunned by the Buddhist Society. She returned to the United States and in

132

November 1970 founded the Zen Mission Society at Shasta Abbey in Northern California. Three years later a small group of British disciples established Throssel Hole Priory near Hexham in Northumberland. The founders left to be trained in Shasta Abbey and for ten years Throssel Hole was run as a retreat centre under the leadership of a rotating abbotship appointed from California.

Illnesses of various kinds had beset Jiyu-Kennett during her stay in Japan and she returned in poor health. In 1975 she again fell ill and by April of the following year was too incapacitated to continue her duties as abbess. Doctors warned her that she may only have months to live. Then the disciple whom she considered her spiritual heir declared that he was unable to continue the training and left. At the same time an oriental physician diagnosed her illness as being due to the misguided nature of her teaching and way of life. She resigned as abbess of Shasta and decided to entrust herself to deep and sustained meditation.

As she began the retreat in a small room in Oakland, California, her new attendant, Daizui McPhillamy, experienced *kensho* by her bedside and she conferred transmission upon him. Shortly afterwards, the first of a series of forty-three visions began.

'I had no idea that I would experience this', she wrote later. 'All I knew was that, if I were going to die, I was going to do the finest job of it I possibly could; that I did not die happens to be a bonus; that I experienced this is an absolute joy for which my gratitude knows no bounds.' The visions lasted for nine months, until 26 January 1977, the first twelve occurring in Oakland, the rest at Shasta, where she returned on 25 October. Each vision unfolded as a dream-like episode, charged with Western and Buddhist religious symbolism, superimposing itself on whatever she saw around her. She compared the series of visions to an elaborated contemporary version of the classical Zen images of the ten 'ox-herding' pictures. By the time the final vision faded, she was cured.

She interpreted the experience as that of a 'third *kensho*'. Her first *kensho*, which she underwent in Japan, was followed in the intervening years by what she called an 'on-going' *kensho*. In London, D.T. Suzuki had told her: 'Once or twice I have had the great experience but a million times the little moments that make one dance.' These 'little moments', she believed, describe the process of gradual maturation between the first shock of *kensho* and the deeper and longer *kensho* she had now experienced through the unusual form of a sequence of visions. When asked why this experience had befallen her, she replied:

> We choose Heaven; Heaven does not choose us. When we are willing to pay the price that the Lord of the House demands for entrance, the gateless gate opens automatically. There is nothing special about me; I am neither holy nor unholy, enlightened nor unenlightened. I was born Peg Kennett and I will die Peg Kennett.

In the Pali Canon's account of the Buddha's renunciation, Gautama asks himself: 'Why, being myself subject to birth, ageing, ailment, death, sorrow and defilement, do I seek what is also subject to these things? Suppose, being myself subject to these things, I sought after the unborn, unageing, unailing, deathless, sorrowless, undefiled supreme surcease of bondage, Nirvana?' This famous passage is central to Jiyu-Kennett's understanding of Zen. But, for her, the 'Unborn' is more than just a negation of birth, ageing, ailment etc.; it is equivalent to the Absolute Mind, Buddha-nature, the Cosmic Buddha, the True Self, the Lord of the House, the Eternal, the Truth, God. This 'state of mind', she comments, 'has perhaps best been described by Meister Eckhart in the words, "And a man shall be free, and as pure as the day prior to his entry into his mother's womb, when he has nothing, wants

134

nothing and knows nothing. Such a one has true spiritual poverty."'

Such positive interpretations of Nirvana find their classic expression in the 16th chapter of the *Lotus Sutra*, an early Indian Mahayana Buddhist text, which appeared in written form around the 1st century CE. Compared to the stark realism of the Pali Canon, the *Lotus Sutra* is only notionally set in conventional time and space. The text abounds in mystic and mythic metaphor, presenting the Buddha not as a mere human mortal but as a shimmering display in historical time of Eternal Buddhahood. It claims that the different paths taught by Gautama inevitably culminate in this same Cosmic Buddhahood, which is both the underlying reality and ultimate destiny of all living beings.

Awakening to this cosmic reality can, for Jiyu-Kennett, 'only be achieved by *zazen* and the intuitive understanding which the teacher is always exhibiting to the pupil'. All theories, ideas, concepts and beliefs have to be discarded. In their place one 'must have absolute faith in the Buddhanature of the teacher'. Therefore, she concludes, 'Zen is an intuitive RELIGION and not a philosophy or way of life.' She deplores how for centuries Buddhism has been denied as a religion: 'this was because [people] feared saying the Truth lest they set up a god to be worshipped. The Lord is not a god and He is not not a god.'

Such language has aroused concern about the influence of Christianity on Jiyu-Kennett's presentation of Zen. These doubts are hardly allayed by encountering some of the forms she has chosen in which to present Soto Zen to the West. Members of her 'Order of Buddhist Contemplatives' live in 'Abbeys' and 'Priories', replete with 'sacristies' and 'vespers'. Buddhist texts are chanted in English to the accompaniment of an organ in medieval plainsong. The monks tend to be given old English names, such as Edmund and Gifford, rather than traditional Japanese or Buddhist names. Even her visions are more reminiscent of the experiences of Christian saints than Zen Masters.

Yet while comparisons can justifiably be made with the mysticism of Eckhart, the Christian associations are otherwise more apparent than real. The concept of a personal or creator God is absent, as is any reference to Christ or the Bible. To use aspects of traditional Christian monasticism and liturgy is seen as an expedient means to adapt the culturally alien forms of Japanese Buddhism to the West.

Since her return from Japan, Jiyu-Kennett has returned to a more traditional form of celibate monasticism instead of the system of married priests current in Japan — and among the followers of Deshimaru in France. Her 'third *kensho*' has convinced her that such experiences are impossible unless one is celibate. Likewise, following Dogen's insistence on the equality of men and women in the practice of *zazen*, the Order of Buddhist Contemplatives makes no distinction between monks and nuns: ordained men and women alike are, for want of a better term, 'monks'.

The Order's European centre is Throssel Hole Priory, a cluster of stone buildings on the vast windswept moors of Northumberland. Thirty-two ordained monastics live there under the direction of the forty-one-year-old British abbot Rev. Daishin Morgan. After a man or woman is ordained as a monk, they will serve at least five years as a novice before receiving full monastic transmission. In a further two years, they may be appointed as a teacher. Those whose *kensho* is certified may subsequently become a 'Reverend Master', i.e. a *Roshi* or Zen Master. Twelve members of the Order bear this title. It is estimated that the congregation in Britain is around a thousand. In addition to a small Priory at Reading, thirty lay meditation groups affiliated to the Order operate throughout the country, with one such group in Holland.

Apart from two brief visits to Throssel Hole in the early 1970s, Rev. Master Jiyu-Kennett has remained in California. Her struggles with the Soto Zen Order in Japan continue. The Japanese are reluctant either to endorse her Order or register her disciples (as is also the case with the disciples of Deshimaru in France). In recent years, she has strengthened ties with the Chinese Lin-chi Ch'an tradition that ordained her in Malaysia.

NICHIREN:

THE NICHIREN TRADITION

On 21 September 1980, a ceremony took place on the outskirts of the newly built rural city of Milton Keynes, north of London, to inaugurate the first Peace Pagoda to be erected in the Western Hemisphere by the monks and nuns of the Japanese Nipponzan Myohoji Buddhist order. Two years earlier the city had given its approval for the construction of a pagoda on the green-belt area overlooking the bird sanctuary of Willen Lake. Now, rising from a swarth of gently sloping meadow, stood a gleaming 50 ft (15m) structure, its bulbous base capped with a delicately lifting Japanese roof, from which rose a seven-layered spire crowned with a golden pinnacle. Conducting the ceremony was a ninety-five-year-old Japanese monk with vigorous white eyebrows, seated in a wheelchair, hammering a simple tennis-racket-like drum, while chanting in utmost earnest the words *Nam-myoho-renge-kyo*!

Nichidatsu Fujii was born on 6 August 1885 at the foot of Mt Aso in Japan. He was ordained in 1903 and the following year enrolled in the Nichiren Sect University. Prompted by a dream, he embarked, five years later, on a life-long commitment to world peace, which, he believed, could only be realized by chanting *Nam-myoho-renge-kyo* and wherever possible erecting pagodas as physical manifestations of that formula. In 1919 he inaugurated his first pagoda at Ta-lien in Manchuria. This was followed by several others in northern China and, in 1924,

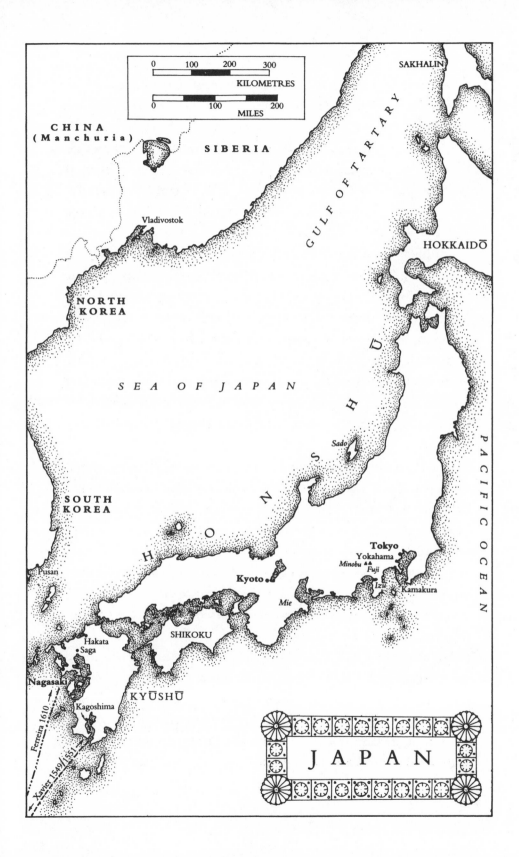

CHINA
(Manchuria)

SIBERIA

SAKHALIN

GULF OF TARTARY

Vladivostok

HOKKAIDŌ

NORTH
KOREA

SEA OF JAPAN

H
O
N
S
H
Ū

Sado

SOUTH
KOREA

Pusan

H
O
N
S
H
Ū

Tokyo
Yokahama
Minobu ▲▲ Fuji
Izu
Kamakura

Kyoto

Mie

PACIFIC OCEAN

SHIKOKU

Hakata
Saga

Nagasaki

Kagoshima

KYŪSHŪ

Ferreira 1610

Xavier 1549/1551

0   100   200   300
KILOMETRES
0   100   200
MILES

JAPAN

by the first Japanese pagoda in the town of Tagonoura.

In the autumn of 1930 he departed for India, convinced that the time had come for Buddhism, having set, as it were, in Japan, to rise again and spread westwards to its country of origin and beyond. Within three years he had met Gandhi at his ashram at Wardha, and when Gandhi beat the drum and chanted *Nam-myoho-renge-kyo*, Nichidatsu ecstatically declared that the 'independence of India was assured in the near future'.

On Nichidatsu Fujii's sixtieth birthday the atom bomb fell on Hiroshima. This event lent an additional urgency to his resolve. In the following years he and his monks travelled through Japan, China, India, Russia and America, urging governments to abandon their atomic weapons. This smiling little monk endlessly beating his drum became one of the symbolic figureheads of peace movements world-wide, his image beamed around the world by satellite almost each time a major demonstration was reported. He was received by kings, prime ministers, religious leaders and the Secretary General of the U.N.

The danger of nuclear war was just the most obvious symptom of a world that had lost its bearings. For Nichidatsu, Western civilization was to blame for this crisis, whose solution, he believed, lay solely in chanting *Nam-myoho-renge-kyo*. For 'except in Japan', he announced on 15 February 1976, 'there is no longer a religion that ascribes to the belief of eliminating Western civilization and leading humanity in the reverse direction . . . . The world is now completely ready to be annihilated on the basis of science as well as the social structure.' He challenged the idea that religious practice was a personal affair and need not be organized on a world-wide scale to tackle issues of social and political injustice. For only 'when humanity becomes one under a good religion, a religion of peace, then for the first time peace will be brought to the entire world'. To this end he and his followers have since erected a Peace Pagoda in London's Battersea Park and another in Vienna. Plans are afoot to build one near the cruise-missile base of Comiso in Sicily as well as in the town of Auschwitz. Nichidatsu's religion of peace is not simply Buddhism, however, but Buddhism as interpreted by a 13th-century Japanese priest called Nichiren.

Nichiren was born in the small fishing village of Kominato to the east of modern Tokyo on 16 February 1222. Unlike his older contemporary Dogen, his family was poor and simple, yet his parents recognized their son's unusual intelligence and spiritual aspiration and, when he was eleven, sent him to the local Tendai temple of Seicho-ji.

Four years later he was ordained as a novice monk and moved to Kamakura, the seat of the military dictatorship, to further his studies, and for the next five years absorbed himself in the teachings of the officially favoured schools of Pure Land and Rinzai Zen. Since childhood he had been driven by an intense longing to solve the 'eternal mystery' of human life. Neither Pure Land nor Zen teachings, however, were able to quench this thirst for insight, so he left for Mt Hiei, near modern Kyoto, to return to the earlier teachings of the Tendai (T'ien-t'ai) tradition into which he (as Dogen before him) had been ordained. Intent on unearthing what he called 'true Buddhism', he immersed himself in Tendai doctrine for ten years. At one point, like Dogen, he despaired of ever finding true Buddhism in Japan and explored the idea of going to China, but decided against it on the advice of a Chinese monk who convinced him of the equally sad condition of the Dharma there.

Yet his fifteen years of study were not in vain. In April 1253 (the year of Dogen's death) he returned to his home temple. After a few days of solitude he walked to the top of a hill overlooking the ocean. He placed his palms together and, to the rising orb of the sun, for the first time solemnly declared the quintessential outcome of his search: *Nam-myoho-renge-kyo* — 'Homage to the Mystic Law of the *Lotus Sutra*!' Later that morning he gave his first sermon in the small temple, which so outraged his audience that his teacher expelled him from the order. By August he had returned to Kamakura, the very centre of the political and religious establishment, to preach his controversial message.

Nichiren's studies had convinced him that of all the Buddhist teachings, that of the *Lotus Sutra* was supreme. The supremacy of the *Lotus Sutra* was a central doctrine of the Tendai school, a syncretic tradition founded in 6th-century China that arranged the bewildering array of translated Buddhist texts into a coherent chronology. According to this school, the Buddha spent the last eight years of his life teaching the *Lotus Sutra*, in which he revealed the true purpose of his life. All earlier teachings were considered as only provisionally true.

Nichiren refined this principle of Tendai Buddhism even further. '*Myoho-renge-kyo* (the *Lotus Sutra*'s full title in Sino-Japanese)', he declared in a letter written two years after arriving in Kamakura, 'is the king of sutras, flawless in both letter and principle.'

> Its words are the reality of life, and the reality of life is the Mystic Law (*myoho*). It is called the Mystic Law because it explains the mutually inclusive relationship of life and all phenomena .... Chanting *Myoho-renge-kyo* will therefore enable you to grasp the mystic truth within you.

He assured his correspondent that 'if you have deep faith in this truth and chant *Myoho-renge-kyo*, you are certain to attain Buddhahood in this lifetime'.

Nichiren's philosophy taps a current of Chinese Buddhist thought whose source is the *Avatamsaka (Hua-yen) Sutra*'s doctrine of the 'mutual interpenetration of all phenomena'. Buddhahood, according to this doctrine, is not separate from oneself as the distant culmination of life to which one ultimately aspires, but is immanent within each moment of life. This idea likewise underpinned the philosophy of Zen. But whereas for Dogen, the immanent truth of enlightenment could be immediately manifested only through *zazen*, Nichiren insisted that it could only be achieved through chanting *Nam-myoho-renge-kyo*.

In 1256, three years after he settled in the capital, a series of violent storms, droughts, earthquakes and epidemics beset Japan. In 1257 a severe earthquake struck Kamakura itself. In 1259 and 1260 famine and plague scoured the outlying countryside. Such calamities were believed to reflect the displeasure of the gods. Nichiren retreated to a temple to seek an answer in the Buddhist canon. He returned two years later and, on 16 July 1260, presented the government with a treatise entitled *The Security of the Land through the Propagation of True Buddhism*.

In some of the more prophetic Mahayana Sutras Nichiren had found passages which described the kind of disasters that appear when the rulers and people of a country turn against the true Dharma. Most of these calamities were alarmingly evident in Japan at that time. 'Only two have yet to appear', declared Nichiren, 'the "calamity of invasion from foreign lands" and the "calamity of revolt within one's own domain".' The reason for this state of affairs was obvious:

If people favour perverse doctrines and forget what is correct, can the benevolent deities be anything but angry? If people cast aside doctrines that are all-encompassing and take up those that are incomplete, can the world escape the plots of demons?

As for the solution:

It seems to me that prohibiting those who slander the Dharma and paying respect to monks who follow the Correct Way is the best means to assure stability within the nation and peace in the world at large.

For Nichiren 'those who slander the Dharma' were the followers of Pure Land Buddhism and the 'Correct Way' was that of the *Lotus Sutra*.

The government ignored him. But when word of his document reached the Pure Land Buddhists, a band of irate followers reacted by storming Nichiren's cottage. He managed to escape and within a few months returned to Kamakura. Official charges were brought against him, however, and he was banished for nine months to the remote Izu Peninsula.

In January 1268 Nichiren's sense of mission received a timely boost from the arrival in Kyushu of two Mongol officials to inform the Japanese of the accession of Kublai Khan to the throne of China. Referring to the Japanese emperor as the 'king of a little country', the Mongolians indicated that Japan was expected to pay tribute. The Samurai rulers were doubtless aware that Kublai Khan's armies, then tied down in a campaign to conquer the Southern Sung, would have insufficient resources to mount an attack on Japan. They ignored the demands and sent the embassy back to Korea.

For Nichiren this was a godsend. 'Now, nine years after I presented my work to the authorities', he wrote in April of the same year, 'this letter has arrived from the Mongols. The events that have occurred match the predictions made in my work as exactly as do the two halves of a tally.' The arrival of Kublai's envoys reinforced his conviction that Japan had turned from the true Dharma to embrace the false doctrines not only of the Pure Land but also of Zen, both of whose founders 'were possessed by devils'.

144

Henceforth, Nichiren's attacks on the other schools of Buddhism became more vehement and the sense of his own importance increased. On 10 September 1271 he was summoned by the deputy chief of military police to answer charges that he had pronounced two late officials of the ruling family to have been reborn in hell. He denied the offence, but used the opportunity to inform the tribunal of his views. 'Nichiren', he declared, 'is the pillar and beam of Japan. If you lose me, you will be toppling the pillar of Japan! Immediately we will face the disaster of "internal strife" and also "foreign invasion".' Since a second Mongol envoy was in Japan at this very time again demanding fealty, talk of 'foreign invasion' struck an inflammatory note. To prevent such calamity, Nichiren told the court that

> all the [Pure Land] and Zen temples . . . should be burned to the ground and their priests taken to Yui beach to have their heads cut off! If this is not done, then Japan is certain to be destroyed.

He later regarded this speech as one of the great moments of his life, but denied having personally made the pronouncements. 'Rather it was in all cases the spirit of Shakyamuni Buddha that had entered into my body.'

The deputy chief of military police saw otherwise and two days later had Nichiren arrested and taken to the execution ground of Tatsunokuchi to be beheaded. But, according to Nichiren's account, just as the sword was to fall, a brilliant object appeared in the sky, which so terrified the officials that they immediately called off the execution. Instead, as winter approached, Nichiren was banished to the desolate island of Sado.

Conditions in Sado were bleak. 'In the yard around my hut', recalled Nichiren, 'the snow piled deeper and deeper. No one came to see me; my only visitor was the piercing wind . . . . The *Lotus*

Sutra lay open before my eyes and *Nam-myoho-renge-kyo* flowed from my lips.' He devoted himself to understanding the deeper significance of the *Lotus Sutra*, not only for Japan but the world at large. Increasingly, he saw the *Lotus Sutra* as a blueprint for human history in which he played a pivotal role.

In defining the heart of the *Lotus Sutra*, Nichiren declared that only the second half of the 15th chapter, the whole of the 16th and the first half of the 17th were revelatory. Everything else the Buddha taught was 'Hinayana in nature and heretical'. Here, concealed in the heart of this 'one chapter and two halves' he claimed to find the characters of *Nam-myoho-renge-kyo*, which Gautama did not transmit to the disciples of his time, but entrusted to the myriad 'Bodhisattvas of the Earth', who were destined to surge forth as soon as the Dharma entered its period of degeneration. The task of these Bodhisattvas was to usher in an era of world-wide Buddhism.

According to the *Lotus Sutra*, the Bodhisattvas of the Earth first appeared during the 'Ceremony in Space', when a 'treasure tower' magically crystallized in the sky. Inside was the former Buddha Prabhutaratna, by whose side Gautama sat to announce the transmission of his deepest teaching to the Bodhisattva Visistacaritra (Jogyo). According to Nichiren, it was to this Bodhisattva that Gautama (presumably breaking into Sino-Japanese) first revealed *Nam-myoho-renge-kyo*. Since Nichiren saw himself as the sole person to propagate this truth in the Latter Day of the Law, he came to identify himself as a Bodhisattva of the Earth, the 'envoy of Bodhisattva Jogyo' and the 'votary of the *Lotus Sutra*'.

Nichiren emphasizes that even the Buddha realized how difficult it would be for people to believe and understand these teachings of the *Lotus Sutra*. The only reason that people of this degenerate age could believe in them at all was 'due to the fact that the world of Buddhahood is present in the human realm'. The

146

teaching of Gautama, he declared, 'is the Buddhism of the harvest', whereas that of the Bodhisattvas of the Earth is the 'Buddhism of the sowing'. Whereas Gautama revealed the fruits of Buddhahood, Nichiren revealed its cause: *Nam-myoho-renge-kyo*, the mystic law of life by resonating with which Buddhahood is manifested here and now.

Nichiren thus established a doctrinal basis for his views and found justification for the persecution he was suffering. Just as the *Lotus Sutra* predicts how in the latter 'frightful and evil age' its votaries will be 'reviled with foul mouths or attacked with knives and staves', so was Nichiren being abused in 13th-century Japan. Persecution only reinforced his conviction that he was indeed a Bodhisattva of the Earth.

In February, 1274 Nichiren received a pardon from the government. He was fifty-three. On 8 April, he was again summoned before a military tribunal in Kamakura, but this time for his advice. More convinced than ever of his predictions, he declared that the Mongols would invade by the end of the year. Such was his sense of inevitability, that he no longer remonstrated with the officials or insisted they follow him. On 12 May, he retired to the foothills of Mt Minobu, where he devoted himself to teaching, writing and counselling his friends and disciples.

Sure enough, in November of the same year, Kublai Khan attacked Japan with a fleet of seven hundred vessels from Happ'o (near modern Pusan in Korea). After overrunning two off-shore islands, the Mongol army landed at the Japanese port of Hakata (whence fifty years earlier Dogen had sailed for China) and inflicted heavy casualties. That night a sudden storm blew up and, fearful of their ships being dashed to pieces against the shore, the army retreated to the open seas. But the storm was of such severity that most of the fleet was shattered and sunk by the wind and waves. Thus Japan, for the time being at least, was saved from the 'calamity of foreign invasion'.

Six months later Nichiren concluded that the reason for the Mongol attacks was because 'from the ruler on down to the common people, all treat me with enmity'. As long as they continued treating him in this way, no matter how many soldiers were amassed to defend Japan, 'it will do no good. The people of Japan are certain to encounter the calamity of war.' He gleefully anticipates Japan's inevitable fate and his consequent vindication:

> Just see how it will be! When tens of thousands of armed ships from the great kingdom of the Mongols come over the sea to attack Japan, everyone . . . will turn their backs on all the Buddhist temples and all the shrines of the gods and will raise their voices in chorus, crying *Nam-myoho-renge-kyo, Nam-myoho-renge-kyo!* They will press their palms and say, 'Priest Nichiren, Priest Nichiren, save us!'

Although bitterly disappointed by the failure of his Japanese invasion, Kublai was in no position to fulfill Nichiren's prophecy. Since his cousin Kaidu was threatening his control of Central Asia and the campaign against the Southern Sung was still unconcluded, he was forced to direct his attentions elsewhere. Instead of rebuilding the fleet, Kublai sent yet another envoy to demand the Shogun's submission. Confident that the gods were on their side, the military government had the Mongol emissaries beheaded.

Nichiren, however, came to see the imminent defeat of Japan as a painful necessity. For 'if the invasion does not happen, the Japanese people will slander the *Lotus Sutra* more than ever . . . . The nation may be devastated by the superior strength of the Mongols, but slander of Buddhism will cease almost entirely.' Just as thirty years earlier Christian Europe had perceived the Mongols as the 'Hammer of God', so Nichiren saw them as 'a messenger from heaven sent to punish those hostile to the votary of the *Lotus Sutra*'.

It took Kublai five years before he was again ready to attack Japan. The rebellion in Central Asia had been quashed and the Southern Sung defeated. After making a final offer to the Shogun, who treated the envoys as spies and executed them, Kublai mounted a massive retaliatory expedition. In June 1280 a two-pronged multi-national naval invasion was launched: 40,000 seaborne troops from north China were to link up on the Japanese mainland with 100,000 forces from South China. Although the armies succeeded in establishing bases in Japan, they made little headway. On 15 August a typhoon blew up off the east coast of Kyushu. Again the armies attempted to flee to the safety of the open seas, and again were decimated in the attempt.

The Shogun felt utterly vindicated in his reliance upon the Buddhist and Shinto priests he had backed. Nichiren, however, remained undaunted. When challenged by opponents, he encouraged his followers to 'just ask them if they took the head of the Mongol king'. Indeed, Kublai immediately embarked on plans for another invasion. It took some time for the full extent of the humiliation of the military debacle to sink in. Not only had it shattered the Mongols' image of invincibility, but had severely depleted the State Treasury. Six years later Kublai abandoned the idea of ever conquering Japan.

Nichiren was succumbing to age and ill-health. While still convinced of his own significance, he recognized his human frailty. 'All the sufferings that befall my fellow human beings', he reflected, 'are, after all, my own sufferings.' Without ever mollifying his radical position, his feelings turned to the everyday condition of others. 'Just chant Nam-myoho-renge-kyo', he advised a soldier threatened with persecution for his beliefs:

> and when you drink saké, stay at home with your wife. Suffer what there is to suffer, enjoy what there is to enjoy. Regard both suffering and joy as facts of life and continue chanting

Nam-myoho-renge-kyo, no matter what happens. Then you will experience boundless joy from the Law.

Nichiren died at a friend's home on 13 October 1282, while en route to a curative hot spring in Hitachi.

Buckfastleigh is a sleepy rural town on the edge of Dartmoor, a few miles from Plymouth on the south coast of England. In February 1992, the monthly meeting of the local Nichiren Shoshu group took place in a semi-detached house on a council estate above the town centre. After a vigorous session of chanting *Nam-myoho-renge-kyo*, the group of ten men and women gathered downstairs in the living room and listened to a member read 'This Month's *Gosho*' from the organization's magazine *UK Express*. The *Gosho*, or sacred text of Nichiren, was one of his letters warning of imminent Mongol invasion. The central theme was *Itai Doshin*, 'many in body, one in mind', a plea for the unity essential to achieving *Kosen-rufu*, the organization's goal of securing 'lasting peace and happiness for all mankind through the propagation of true (i.e. Nichiren's) Buddhism'. Unity, or rather disunity, was the theme to which the group returned in the earnest discussion that followed over coffee and cigarettes. For only three months earlier, on 28 November 1991, Soka Gakkai, the lay society to which they and 20 million fellow members world-wide belonged, had been excommunicated by High Priest Nikken of Nichiren Shoshu's head temple in Japan.

Until the Second World War, Nichiren Shoshu was one of the smallest sects among those that propagated Nichiren's teachings. It was controlled by a handful of priests in seventy-five temples, and supported by a congregation of less than 90,000 — less than 3 per cent of Nichiren Buddhists in Japan. Doctrinally, it distinguished itself from the other orders by considering Nichiren rather than Gautama to be the true Buddha of this age and that only his writings were to be taken as authoritative. The difference between Nichiren's writings and all the preceding texts of Buddhism was similar to the difference between the New and Old Testaments of Christianity, with Nichiren (like Jesus) emerging as a fulfilment of the predictions contained in the earlier canon.

At the time of Nichiren's death, his prophecies of the 'calamity of invasion from foreign lands' and the 'calamity of revolt within one's own domain', had failed to materialize. After the failure of the second Mongol invasion, the Kamakura Shogunate seemed invincible to either internal or external threats. Nichiren's followers were forced to reinterpret his predictions as referring to future events. Ironically, though, the Mongol attacks did precipitate the collapse of the Kamakura government. Once victory was gained, the Shogunate lavished donations on the Buddhist temples in thanks for their successful intercession with the gods. The economically exhausted regime collapsed in 1333, plunging Japan into a horrific three-hundred-year period of civil war. Thus, claimed Nichiren's followers, the prophecy of 'revolt within one's own domain' had come true. The 'calamity of foreign invasion' was to take longer: until 2 September 1945, when Japan surrendered to the Allied Forces, allowing the first foreign army in Japanese history to occupy the country.

Shortly afterwards a businessman called Josei Toda was released from gaol, where he had been incarcerated since 1943 for his refusal to co-operate with Japanese government measures demanding religious unity among the Buddhist sects. Toda had joined Nichiren Shoshu in 1928, following the example of his friend, a controversial educator called Tsunesaburo Makiguchi. Two years later Makiguchi published a volume of his writings under the imprint of Soka Kyoiku Gakkai (Value-Creating Educational Society) and in 1937 formally established the Society as a lay religious organization under the aegis of the Nichiren Shoshu priesthood. Makiguchi's emphasis on individual 'Value Creation', combined with typical Nichirenesque intransigence, ran counter to the prevailing insistence on nationalist conformity. Although the Nichiren Shoshu priesthood was prepared to compromise with the State, Makiguchi was not. So the government suppressed the Society and threw both Makiguchi and his faithful ally Toda into gaol, where Makiguchi died in 1944.

After the war Toda used his business skills and preaching abilities to reorganize Makiguchi's Society. He shortened the name to Soka Gakkai and delivered a simple but compelling message to his humiliated and impoverished compatriots: by chanting *Nammyoho-renge-kyo* you will be able to achieve whatever you want. It will enable you, he promised, 'to have the cause of becoming a millionaire even though you had not made such a cause in your past existence'. Nichiren's predictions were used to make sense of Japan's defeat and people found a renewed sense of worth through their role in Soka Gakkai's highly structured and dynamic organization.

In addition to their daily practice of chanting, members were encouraged to convert their friends to Soka Gakkai by means of *shakubuku*, i.e. aggressive proselytizing, a policy which eventually had to be toned down because of the negative effect it was having on the organization's public image. Many found that chanting actually produced the benefits that Toda claimed for it, and were naturally enthusiastic in promoting the practice to others. By the time Toda died in 1958, the Society had grown from a handful of founders to a membership of nearly a million families. His funeral was attended by 250,000 people, including the prime minister.

Toda was succeeded by his devoted lieutenant, Daisaku Ikeda, who within ten years had increased membership to seven million. Ikeda's stated goal was to convert a third of the nation to Nichiren Shoshu Buddhism and gain the sympathy of another third, thus achieving a sufficient majority to influence the course of Japanese life. In 1965 he launched a political party called 'Komeito' ('Clean Government') which, within ten years, occupied seventy-five seats in the Japanese Parliament. Constitutionally, Komeito has had to separate itself from Soka Gakkai, but in many respects it remains the political arm of the religious movement.

Symbolically, Ikeda's greatest achievement has been the construction, on 12 October 1972, of the enormous Sho Hondo at Taiseki-ji, to serve as the sanctuary for the *Dai Gohonzon*, a mandala-like inscription of *Nam-myoho-renge-kyo* said to have been written by Nichiren on a wooden plank on 12 October 1279. Nichiren Shoshu now declared that the world-wide dominance of Nichiren's Buddhism was inevitable. For, Nichiren's prophecies having been fulfilled, the spread of his doctrine could now centre around his 'Three Great Secret Laws': the chanting of *Nam-myoho-renge-kyo*; the presence of the *Gohonzon*; and the presence of the sanctuary where the *Gohonzon* is enshrined. Due to Soka Gakkai's determination and fund-raising skills, this sanctuary, the largest religious edifice in the world, was at last in place.

In 1979 Ikeda resigned as president of Soka Gakkai, partly to smooth over tensions that had grown between himself and the Nichiren Shoshu high priest, and partly to concentrate his efforts on expanding Soka Gakkai outside Japan. He appointed himself president of the newly formed Soka Gakkai International. Largely through his efforts Soka Gakkai has grown into the largest lay religious organization in the world, with twenty million members in 115 countries.

Outside Japan the largest branch of Soka Gakkai is in the United States. Soka Gakkai Europe, under the chairmanship of Dr Eiichi Yamazaki, is based in Paris with a training centre at Trets, near Aix-en-Provence. The British headquarters is located in the sumptuous £3 million stately home of Taplow Court, near Maidenhead; the Italian headquarters is in Florence, and the

German in Frankfurt. Offices are also found in Amsterdam, Madrid and Stockholm, with the possibility of one opening soon in Moscow. The combined membership of Britain, Italy, France and Germany alone is approximately 26,000 people. Compared to Japan, however, the numbers are trifling; Soka Gakkai has a membership of over sixteen million, i.e. one in eight of all Japanese.

Why then, in the face of such success, did the Nichiren Shoshu priesthood choose to excommunicate the Soka Gakkai, the very organization that had transformed the order from an insignificant Japanese sect to a world religion in less than fifty years? According to the priests, the trouble began in November 1990, with 'Mr. Ikeda's ignorant and contemptuous public outbursts toward the High Priest and the priesthood'. A year later the High Priest issued a 'recommendation to disband'. The document stated that 'the Soka Gakkai, forgetting their own role and from a self-righteous perspective, has modified the traditional Nichiren Shoshu methods of teaching . . . . As a result, they have exhibited qualities of a completely different religion.' The priests pointed out that the order of expulsion referred only to the organization, not to its individual members, who were exhorted to join another Nichiren Shoshu lay association, Hokke-ko, as soon as possible. Very few, however, heeded this advice.

The heart of the dispute lies in a power struggle between High Priest Nikken and President Ikeda, which in turn reflects an underlying tension between traditionalism and modernism. The priests insist that Nichiren's chosen method of the transmission of his doctrine was through an unbroken priestly line, which they alone, of all the Nichiren schools, maintain. Ikeda, however, seeks to democratize the sect, to make each individual's practice the source of their decisions and actions, rather than dependence upon on the authority of a priest. The priests are concerned about the extraordinary prominence of Ikeda, a man whose every public speech is broadcast simultaneously in community centres all over Japan and who is received by leading statesmen throughout the world. Moreover, they suspect that leading figures in Soka Gakkai were planning to break away and take over the sanctuary enshrining the *Dai Gohonzon*, a move they preempted with the expulsion order. Since only a priest can give *gohonzon*s to new members of Soka Gakkai, Ikeda's organization is effectively prevented from growing. As the stalemate continues, the level of mudslinging increases to the detriment of both parties. Whether in the end the High Priest will be forced to resign or whether Soka Gakkai will declare itself as an independent 'protestant' sect remains to be seen.

To some outside observers, the dispute is part of a wider power-game in which Soka Gakkai plays a role in a campaign of co-ordinated Japanese economic and religious domination. Although 'democracy' is a word much favoured by President Ikeda in his speeches, there is no evidence of its application in his organization, in which all decisions descend from above. Following the same hierarchic model found all over the world, the 'Group' which chose to meet in Buckfastleigh is part of a 'District', (South Devon), which is part of a 'Chapter', (Devon Coast to Coast), which is subordinate to a 'Headquarters', (Devon and Cornwall), which is controlled by a 'National Office' (Taplow Court), which is part of 'Soka Gakkai International — Europe', whose director is appointed by President Ikeda.

In one of his last writings, Nichiren compared the passage of Gautama's Buddhism, which arose in the West (India) and set in the East (Japan), to that of the moon. In contrast, he compared his own Buddhism, which arose in Japan and would set in the West, to the sun. While the association may be lost to Westerners, it is evident to Japanese that the character for 'sun' forms both the name of their country 'Nippon' ('Rising Sun') and the name of 'Nichiren' ('Sun Lotus') — and also the name of the Peace Pagoda founder

'Nichidatsu', and his order 'Nipponzan Myohoji'. Nichiren insisted that he was the very 'soul' and 'eyes' of Japan. His teaching, which is justly considered as the only uniquely Japanese form of Buddhism, makes no secret of its world-wide mission. And this, in Nichiren's interpretation of aggressive proselytizing, is an end that can justify any means. In one of his major writings he approvingly quotes a passage from the *Nirvana Sutra*:

> Defenders of the True Law need not observe the five precepts or practice the rules of proper behaviour. Rather they should carry knives and swords, bows and arrows.

One has to square Soka Gakkai's declared intention of promoting 'education, culture and peace' with statements endorsed by the 'only Buddha of this age' which implicitly encourage killing, lying and stealing as means to attain the higher purpose of *kosen rufu*. Soka Gakkai eagerly looks forward to the 21st century as the age in which world-wide *kosen rufu* (when one third of the world will be converted to Nichiren's Buddhism and one third will be sympathetic) will be realized. One of President Ikeda's new year poems for 1992 promises that

> Immortality
> Is yours, dear comrades
> Striving for world *kosen rufu*,
> For you are the sun
> Of humanity.

The brutal eruption of Mongol military power at the beginning of the 13th century was one of the most catastrophic events of the

Middle Ages, but it also created the occasion for the first encounter since the time of ancient Greece between Buddhism and Western Culture. Although the meeting was brief, tentative and inconclusive, it was under those same conditions that the seeds were sown for the forms of Buddhism that were to expand most effectively throughout Europe in the second half of the 20th century. For during the tumultuous 13th century, the Karma Kagyu, Soto Zen and Nichiren traditions — the most prolific and energetic schools in Europe today — took root in Asia. Yet at the time none of them achieved prominence. Over the ensuing centuries all three traditions were eclipsed by more powerful rivals: the Karma Kagyu by the Sakya and Geluk schools, Soto Zen and Nichiren by the Rinzai Zen and Pure Land traditions. Today the situation is reversed. Although Sakya, Rinzai Zen and Pure Land teachers have established centres in Europe, they have comparatively small followings. The Geluk tradition, as we shall see, is in a stronger position, but it too has suffered a loss of eminence through association with the failed ancien régime of Tibet.

As the Mongol threat declined and disappeared, Christian Europe and Buddhist Asia, both shaken by the experience, returned to an inward-looking conservativism and for the next two hundred years had no significant contact with each other. This self-absorbed idyll was broken by Europe's rediscovery of its classical Greek heritage, which catalysed its momentous thrust to world domination.

THREE

JESUITS,
TULKUS
AND KOANS

FRANCIS XAVIER:
THE JESUITS

T o choose, in the middle of the 16th century, to sail from Lisbon to Goa via the Cape of Good Hope (then less optimistically called the 'Cape of Storms') in a creaking carrack of the yearly Portuguese Indian fleet presupposed an excessive zeal for one of two things: money or God. For these precarious high-pooped ships were guided as much by luck as navigational skill, were overcrowded both with desperate people and perilously stacked crates, tossed by high seas and sudden storms, threatened equally by jagged rocks and privateers, ridden with disease, understocked with food and water, and were so foul below deck that unwary passengers could faint or vomit just on descending there. Even on a fair-weather journey — a year's sailing if you were lucky — it was not unknown for half the ship's complement to perish.

Francis Xavier was a man of God, drawn to Lisbon in 1541 by the devout King John III of Portugal's plea for missionaries to evangelize the newly acquired territories of south India. He was thirty-five years old, of a cheerful and vivacious disposition, the scion of a noble Spanish family from Navarre, a teacher of philosophy and theology at the University of Paris, yet first and foremost an apostle of Christ committed to poverty and the Greater Glory of God. For the past eight years he had been a disciple of Ignatius Loyola, and only the previous year their Society of Jesus had been canonically established in Rome.

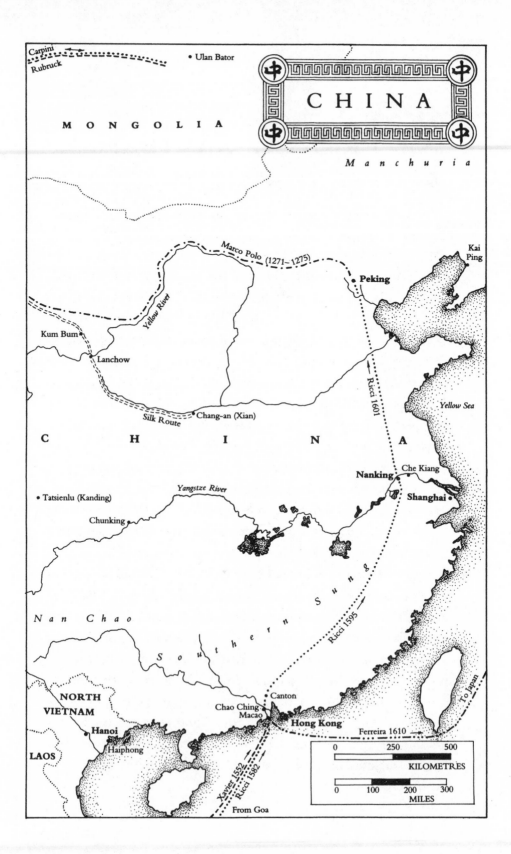

Carpini
Rubruck

• Ulan Bator

MONGOLIA

CHINA

Manchuria

Marco Polo (1271–1275)

Kai
Ping

• Peking

Yellow River

Kum Bum •

Lanchow

Ricci 1601

Silk Route

Chang-an (Xian)

Yellow Sea

C   H   I   N   A

• Tatsienlu (Kanding)

Yangstze River

Nanking

Che Kiang

Chunking

Shanghai

S o u t h e r n   S u n g

N a n   C h a o

Ricci 1595

To Japan

NORTH
VIETNAM

Canton

Chao Ching
Macao

Hanoi

Hong Kong

Ferreira 1610

Haiphong

LAOS

Xavier 1552
Ricci 1582

0	250	500

KILOMETRES

0	100	200	300

MILES

From Goa

As the boat groaned and heaved into the Atlantic swell and Francis Xavier watched the Iberian coastline recede and disappear forever, he left behind him a Europe in the grip of upheaval. Through its voyages of exploration, its rediscovery of classical humanism in Italy and the radical redefinition of Christianity underway in Germany, the continent was changing from a cluster of feudal medieval states, more or less united under the Catholic Church, into the embryo of the modern community of secular states.

In 1506, the year of Xavier's birth, Leonardo da Vinci finished the Mona Lisa and Michelangelo was commissioned to decorate the Sistine Chapel. This flourishing of art, philosophy and natural science was Europe's first reaction against the long–dominant ideas and strictures of medieval Christendom. The Renaissance initiated a comprehensive movement of individual emancipation, reasserting the rights of reason and the senses. Yet this European pride in the achievements of human knowledge and skill also fuelled the ambitions of popes and kings alike to extend their dominion beyond their borders over peoples of other lands.

In the late 15th and early 16th centuries this expansion was the preserve of the two great maritime powers, Spain and Portugal. On 7 June 1494, following a decree of Pope Alexander VI, the treaty of Tordesillas split the world along a straight line between the poles, 370 leagues west of Cape Verde in the Atlantic. Henceforth, all lands discovered to the west of this mathematical divide would be the property of Spain, all lands to the east that of Portugal. Unbeknown to them, the Buddhist countries of Asia were designated to await the arrival of their divinely appointed Portuguese masters.

Again in the year of Xavier's birth, the Portuguese established the first trading posts in Ceylon. Four years later, they conquered Goa and spread through much of southern India. By 1517 they had been to Canton and opened trade with China. And in 1543,

163

a year after Xavier docked in Goa, they accidentally discovered Japan.

The other great upheaval of the time, which galvanized the Catholic resolve of Loyola and Xavier, was the Reformation. On 31 October 1517, when Xavier was a boy of eleven, Martin Luther nailed his ninety-five theses to the door of the church in Wittenberg. By condemning the sale of papal indulgences, he fanned the widespread discontent with Rome and triggered the movement that was to break Rome's monopoly on religious authority in Europe. In 1521 Luther was condemned as a heretic and excommunicated.

Six years later Xavier left Navarre for the University of Paris where he met Ignatius Loyola. The small group that formed around them became the kernel of the Society of Jesus, which shunned the subversive movement in Germany and pledged its undying loyalty to Rome. Their eagerness was quickly seized upon by the pope, who saw in the Jesuits a finely honed instrument of reaction against the Reformation. Loyola and his followers had declared their aim as the salvation and perfection of humankind. To this end they devoted themselves to two activities: education and missionary work. Their role as the bright young shock-troops of Rome in the 16th century mirrored that of the Franciscans and Dominicans in the 13th. As Europe once more put out its feelers to the rest of the world, now offensively initiating the colonial era instead of defensively reacting to the Mongols, the task of confronting the idolators of Asia inevitably fell to the Jesuits.

To be fair, the Reformation had a sobering effect on Rome. As Xavier rounded the Cape of Storms on his way to Goa plans were already underfoot to pursue a process of reform. In 1545, while Xavier was converting breathtaking numbers of Indians in Malabar and Travancore, the Council of Trent held the first of its twenty-five sessions, the outcome of which was to inaugurate what came to be known as the Counter-Reformation.

On 24 June 1549, Francis Xavier set out for Japan, an unknown country as yet untouched by Christianity. He was accompanied by two fellow Spaniards — a priest and a lay-brother — and a Japanese convert called Yajirô. It was from Yajirô, formerly a lay follower of the Shingon school, that Xavier received his first impressions of Buddhism. Two days before his departure from Goa he wrote to his colleagues in Europe of something he had learnt from Yajirô 'which consoled me much':

and what he told me is that in the monasteries of his land, where there are many *frades* and a school, they have among them a practice of meditating which is as follows: He who has charge of the house, their superior, who is the most learned, calls them all together and addresses them in the manner of a sermon; and then he says to each one of them that they should meditate for the space of an hour on the following: When a man is dying and cannot speak, since the soul is being separated from the body, if it could then speak in such a separation and withdrawal of the soul, what things would the soul say to the body? ... After the hour had passed, the superior of the house examines each one of them on what he experienced during the hour when he meditated.

Thus Europeans received their first knowledge of Japanese Buddhism. Apart from its groping presentation of the *koan*, Xavier's description is a recognizable account of training in a Zen monastery.

The Jesuits landed at the port of Kagoshima on the island of Kyushu on 15 August 1549. Nichiren's 'calamity of internal strife' was in full swing. Since the collapse of the Kamakura Shogunate in 1333, central government control had all but collapsed and local feudal lords were perpetually at war, no one capable of gaining sufficient prominence to unify the land. Buddhist institutions had

165

likewise succumbed to this disarray and standards had fallen alarmingly from the enthusiastic days of the 13th century. The Rinzai Zen sect had risen to eminence through the support of the samurai, and its monks served as administrators and advisors to the fighting warlords. Nearly three centuries after their founders' deaths, the traditions of both Dogen and Nichiren had little influence.

Although no indigenous accounts of Xavier and his two friends survive, a contemporary description of Portuguese traders suggests the kind of impression they might have made:

The [foreigners] understand to a certain degree the distinction between Superior and Inferior but I do not know if they have a proper system of ceremonial etiquette. They eat with their fingers instead of with chopsticks such as we use. They show their feelings without any self control. They cannot understand the meaning of written characters. They are people who spend their lives roving hither and yon. They have no fixed abode . . . but withal they are a harmless sort of people.

Over the following years, as the Jesuits settled in the country, the Japanese would often be appalled by the habits of the Europeans. Xavier was keen enough to Japanese sensitivities to remark that 'in their culture, their social usage, and their mores they surpass the Spaniards so greatly that one must be ashamed to say so'.

Just as the Spaniards' etiquette dismayed the Japanese, the morals of the Buddhist monks and lay-people shocked the Jesuits. The most striking element in Xavier's sermons in Japan is his insistent moralizing. He would directly accuse gatherings of startled Buddhist monks to whose monasteries he had been invited of 'the abominable vice of Sodom which reigned amongst them', and implore them to change their ways. He likewise abhorred the

Buddhist denial of a personal God and an eternal soul. But in spite of these shortcomings, he declared that 'the people we have met so far is the best that has until now been discovered; and it seems to me that among the heathen peoples no other will be found to surpass the Japanese'.

When the Buddhist monks heard that Xavier had come from India, they assumed that he practised a form of Buddhism as yet unknown in Japan. Likewise, Xavier initially thought that Buddhism was a modified form of Christianity. These misperceptions allowed a brief period of comradeship between the Jesuits and some Shingon priests. But when Xavier broached the topic of the Holy Trinity one day, they merely laughed at him, whereupon he realized that 'the Shingon sect, like all the others, was a fraudulent law and an invention of the Devil'. From then on the Buddhists deliberately mispronounced the Latin word 'Deus' — that Xavier used for God — as 'Daiuso', meaning 'Great Lie'.

The Jesuits saw their task in Japan as similar to the work of the early Church in Europe. Part of the initial plan was to win over the Buddhist establishment to Christianity. By converting the pagan priesthood to God, the populace, it was assumed, would meekly follow. Xavier drew up a step-by-step procedure to undermine Buddhism. The missionaries were first instructed to prove the existence of a Creator God and a personal soul, then refute the potential convert's Buddhist beliefs. Only then were the more mythological and fantastic aspects of Christian faith to be introduced. To this end they were to befriend Buddhist priests with the hope of persuading them to join their cause.

In less than three months after his arrival, Xavier could write back to his brethren in Goa of his friendship with the esteemed abbot of Fukushoji, a Soto Zen Monastery in Kagoshima:

His name is Ninshitsu, which in Japanese signifies 'Heart of Truth'. He is among them as a bishop, and if his name is appropriate, he is indeed a blessed man. In the many conversations I had with him, I found him doubtful and uncertain as to whether our soul is immortal or dies with the body. Frequently he would say 'Yes', but again, he would say 'No.' I fear that other learned monks are like him. But it is a marvel how good a friend this man is to me.

Xavier poignantly conveys the contrast between the inflexible convictions of the Jesuit and the open, 'non-thinking' attitude of the aged disciple of Dogen. It is warming to see how, in spite of their differences, a mutual human respect could grow. The pair would often stroll together through the monastery grounds. On one occasion they came to the *zendo* (meditation hall) and Xavier asked what the monks were doing. Ninshitsu laughed and said:

Some are calculating the contributions received from their followers during the past months. Others think on how they might obtain better clothing and personal care. Still others think of holidays and pastimes. In short, no one thinks of anything of any importance.

Such candid remarks must have encouraged Xavier. But in the end he failed to convert Ninshitsu.

With others the Jesuits were more successful. Many monks were drawn to the missionaries out of curiosity, but found themselves impressed with their unshakable certainty and enthusiasm, qualities in short supply in Japan at the time. The greatest shock to the Buddhist community came with the conversion of the Zen master Kesshu, whose awakening had been confirmed by two leading authorities.

Christianity exercised a double attraction on the Japanese. For the rulers beset by internecine strife, it promised the resurrection of absolute authority whereby the wounds of the land might be healed. The moral injunctions of missionaries were likewise seen to fit well with the unambiguous samurai codes of value. As for the masses, the new religion offered a possibility of salvation from the horrors of the time, which the local gods and Buddhas had notably failed to deliver.

Having laid the foundations of a Jesuit mission, which fifty years later would have more than 200,000 souls in its care, Francis Xavier returned to Goa in November 1551, twenty-seven months after setting foot in Japan. The following April, his sights now set on the enormous untapped potential of China, he set sail again. But the Chinese authorities denied him entry to the mainland and he languished on the desolate island of Sancian off the coast of Canton, where he fell ill and died on 3 December 1552. His uncorrupted body was returned to Goa, where it still remains, displayed in public once every ten years for the Indian Catholics to adore and the sun-drenched, drug-befuddled European tourists to puzzle over.

On 6 October 1552, as Xavier waited for the mandarins to change their minds, a boy was born in the papal domain of Macerata, Italy, who was to succeed where his predecessor had failed. Educated from the age of nine in Jesuit schools and colleges, Matteo Ricci exemplified what the Society of Jesus stood for: immense erudition in the arts and sciences, total obedience to papal command, and sufficient physical stamina to cope with the ordeals of 16th-century sea travel. On 24 March 1578 he departed from Lisbon to Goa and on 7 August 1582 docked at the newly acquired Portuguese settlement of Macao. By September of the following year he was living in the town of Chao-ch'ing, south-west of Canton, in southern China.

The China Ricci came to know so well in the remaining twenty-seven years of his life was that of the Ming, a native Chinese dynasty that had seized power more than two hundred years earlier when it overthrew the last Mongol Khan in 1368. The first emperor, Chu Yüan-chang, was a former Buddhist monk who coined the term 'Ming' ('Light') to suggest the coming of an enlightened age connected with the future Buddha Maitreya. At Ricci's time, although Neo-Confucianism was the dominant ideology of the ruling classes, Buddhism was still the best organized religion of the land.

The predominant Buddhist schools of the period were, as in Japan, those of Lin-chi Ch'an (Rinzai Zen) and Pure Land. But unlike in Japan, where the religious sects competed for the patronage of the conflicting warlords, Chinese Buddhism was characterized by syncretism. This movement was spearheaded by the monk Chu-hung, a contemporary of Ricci, who not only advocated the identity of Zen and Pure Land thought, but accommodated Taoist and Confucian elements as well. Chu-hung was a keen monastic reformer who sought to reinstate the original monks' rule (*vinaya*), which over the preceding centuries had become severely corrupted, bringing the ordained Buddhist *sangha* into disrepute. At the same time he inaugurated a lay Buddhist movement, which attracted people from all walks of life and led to the revitalization of Buddhist thought and practice outside the monastery walls.

So ubiquitous were Buddhist monks and nuns that Ricci chose to imitate their dress, crop his hair and shave his beard in order to be esteemed as a religious. It took him several years to understand that because of the ambiguous standing of the Buddhist clergy, to be identified with them was of questionable advantage in gaining the sympathies of the ruling classes, whose conversion he had made a priority. In a letter of 1592, Ricci describes himself as an aspiring Confucian gentleman:

To gain greater status we do not walk along the streets on foot, but have ourselves carried in sedan chairs, on men's shoulders, as men of rank are accustomed to do . . . . We need this and other similar devices to show them that we are not priests as vile as their own.

By this time Ricci had learned to read and speak Chinese. He studied the Confucian classics, which he admired, finding in them 'nothing contrary to the essence of the Catholic faith'. Such a moral philosophy, he believed, would present no obstacles to the Chinese becoming good Christians. The main stumbling block to their conversion was Buddhism, which he dismissed as 'a Babylon of doctrines so intricate that no one can understand it properly, or describe it'. Not that he made any effort to do so. The Jesuits considered Buddhism to be a vulgar idolatry inspired by the Devil and would have nothing to do with it. When challenged by a Buddhist monk as to why he condemned the Dharma without having even read the sutras, Ricci haughtily replied: 'Since entering China, I have learned of only Yao, Shun, the Duke of Chou and Confucius and I do not intend to change.'

In his Chinese writings, Ricci ridiculed both the Buddhist belief in rebirth and the prohibition against the killing of animals. Upon hearing of the doctrines of non-self and transparency, he concluded that Buddhism was nihilistic and devoid of positive values. His Eurocentric bias led him to believe that the Buddhists were displaced Pythagoreans, whose doctrines had spread from Greece to India and thence to China.

Ricci's objections to Buddhism were not exclusively theological. Their well-established religious organizations, charitable bodies — of which several were operating during his stay in Peking — and, ironically, similarities in dress, ritual and even doctrine, presented a practical obstacle to be overcome. While in Macao the Jesuits had no hesitation in denouncing Buddhas and Bodhisattvas as devils, in China itself they were more circumspect. Nonetheless, when Buddhists converted, they would be encouraged to destroy all images, symbols and texts of their former faith. If this offended their families, then the Jesuits themselves would smash the Buddha statues, keeping only the more impressive ones to send back to Macao as, in Ricci's words, 'battle prizes'.

The military metaphor was disturbingly apt. One of the most passionately argued moral debates among churchmen of the time was whether an armed invasion of China would be a 'just war'. After the conclusion of the Council of Trent in 1563, the Counter-Reformation, in line with the policies of colonial expansion in Europe, became increasingly aggressive. Several of Ricci's detailed descriptions of China could well have served a military purpose. For Ricci shared the bellicose attitudes of his time. The Chinese appeared to him as weak and effeminate. 'Amongst us', he wrote home, 'it is held to be a fine thing to see an armed man,'

> but to them it seems evil, and they have a fear of seeing anything so horrible .... They consider that the most honourable man is he who flees and does not wish to harm another .... Whereas amongst our people the noblest and bravest become soldiers, in China it is the vilest and most cowardly who attend to matters of war.

Although he could write in such a vein for his Western readers, for the Greater Glory of God he was not above portraying Europe in a way that would appeal to the peace-loving Chinese. Having described the negative influence of Buddhism on their social and political life, he says:

> In contrast, on the whole and so far as one can see — for I should not dare to exaggerate — ever since 1,600 years ago, when our countries became Christian, in the more than 30

172

kingdoms which adjoin one another, over more than 10,000 square li, there has not been a single change of dynasty, not a war, not the slightest dispute.

Such staggering economy with the truth would have reinforced the positive impressions the Chinese had of Europe in the late 16th century on account of what they knew of recent developments in science. Ricci was fully aware that the many Chinese who came to see him did not do so out of a longing to be baptised. They sought him out for three main reasons: a conviction that the Jesuits could turn mercury into silver, an interest in Western mathematics, and a fascination with his 'Memory Palace' system of memorization. In accordance with Jesuit conversion procedure, Ricci encouraged them. He drew an immensely popular map of the world with place-names in Chinese; he showed them clocks and prisms; he translated a collection of homilies by the Stoic philosopher Epictetus and Euclid's *Elements of Geometry*; and he even wrote a cycle of eight short popular songs. Ricci thereby hoped to create a suitable cultural and moral framework within which to nourish the seeds of Christian faith.

So immersed did Ricci become both with teaching Renaissance arts and sciences and learning the Confucian classics, that soon he appeared as much Chinese as European. Around 1600, the great Confucian scholar Li-chi met Ricci and described him as 'an altogether remarkable man'.

> Although personally he is extremely refined, his manner is as simple as can be. In a noisy and confused gathering of several dozen people, with everybody speaking at once, the arguments that he follows do not disturb him at all. Among all the people I have ever seen, there is not his equal.

The act of dissemblance was now all but complete. 'I have now met him three times', continues a puzzled Li-chi, 'and I still do not know what he is here for. I think it would be much too stupid for him to want to substitute his own teaching for that of the Duke of Chou and Confucius. So that is surely not the reason.'

It was not long before the Chinese became aware of the Jesuits' intentions. One Wang Ch'i-yüan remarked:

> The barbarians began by attacking Buddhism. Next, they attacked Taoism, next the later Confucianism. If they have not yet attacked Confucius, that is because they wish to remain on good terms with the literate elite and the mandarins, in order to spread their doctrine. But they are simply chafing at the bit in secret, and have not yet declared themselves.

This was not the first time Christians had tried to implant their religion in Chinese soil. But neither the Jesuits nor the Chinese were aware of the fact. Even as he lay dying in Peking Ricci remained unaware that merely two and a half centuries before, the city had been the see of a Roman Catholic Archbishop. Not a trace of the 13th-century missions had survived. Shortly before his death he discovered that medieval Cathay was in fact China and that Khanbaliq was Peking, but he dismissed as fanciful the notion that a Christian community had ever lived there.

Despite his moments of optimism, Ricci was aware of how hard it was to convince the cultured Chinese of his faith. The Jesuits made a point of never mentioning the lawful execution of Jesus or displaying images of the crucified Christ, which they knew the Chinese would find offensive. When a eunuch at the court chanced upon Ricci's late 16th-century blood-dripping, hyper-realistic crucifix, he suspected black magic and screamed: 'This is a wicked thing you have made, to kill our king!' Instead, the missionaries promoted Christianity through the image of the virgin and child, which appealed to the Chinese because of its similarity to Kwan-yin, the feminine form of the Bodhisattva of Compassion. Such a clear instance of Satanic deception led the Jesuits to burn images of Kwan-yin with especial ardour. In the refutations of Christianity written by Chu-hung, the Christian God was identified with the deva who ruled the Tushita Heaven, a lowly celestial in the Buddhist pantheon.

Ricci records how he and his colleagues were warmly welcomed by the Buddhist monks they first encountered in China. But this reception cooled as the Buddhists realized that the Jesuits were not prepared to discuss religion or philosophy as equals. For a monk called Total Enlightenment this had to do with the failure of the missionaries to understand the principles of transparency and relativity:

> They cling to the idea that the Master of Heaven (i.e. God) is the Master of Heaven, that the Buddha is the Buddha, that beings are beings . . . they resort to distinctions between the self and others, this and that, yes and no. That is their fundamental error . . . . If they were not so attached to the idea of a Master of Heaven, they would not be attached to the idea of a Buddha either nor to the idea of beings, and then they would begin to understand the profound thought of our Buddhism and the meaning of the expression 'to save all beings'. Seeking to refute Buddhism as they do, while at the same time being attached to false ideas, they in effect attack themselves, destroy themselves, refute themselves. It is as the sutra says: 'Heretics are intelligent but they have no wisdom.'

For the Christians there could be no question of any dialogue with Buddhists as equals for the simple reason that truth could never be balanced against error. Reciprocity was inconceivable. Whenever Buddhist monks tried to initiate discussions with the missionaries, they were usually received with scorn and indifference.

175

The Chinese soon learnt to distinguish between the scientific learning of the missionaries, which they valued, and their religious beliefs, which they found absurd. The Neo-Confucian scholar Fang I-chih observed how the 'Westerners were clever at examining and fathoming things, but incapable of penetrating the innermost workings of the universe.' For all their rigour and intelligence in scientific matters, when it came to religion the Christians lapsed, according to a Buddhist scholar, into 'empty words and illusions'. The dualistic attitude of the missionaries reflected the absolute division between secular and religious life which was axiomatic to the Catholicism of the Counter-Reformation. But it was incomprehensible for the Buddhists of Ming China for whom relative and ultimate truth were two aspects of a single reality.

What amazed the Chinese about these educated Europeans was their arrogant self-assurance. While unquestioningly assuming their right to settle in China and preach the Gospel, the missionaries were incapable of acknowledging either the tolerant Buddhist attitude which allowed them to stay or that such rights existed for others. More than a century after Ricci's death, the Manchu emperor Yung-cheng bluntly told the Jesuits: 'If I were to send Buddhist monks into your European provinces, your princes would not permit it.' Even in the 18th century of the Enlightenment it is impossible to imagine the presence of Buddhists from Asia explaining their doctrines of impermanence, transparency, *bodhicitta* and awakening in Europe.

In the evening of 11 May 1610, Matteo Ricci, now a respected figure at the Chinese imperial court and an esteemed author, died peacefully in Peking, confident that the seeds of Christianity he had planted would, with the efforts of his successors, bear fruit. The emperor showed his rare appreciation by granting a burial place on the outskirts of the city. A tomb was dug, an 'idol' from an old pagoda broken up and crushed for cement, and Ricci laid to rest.

During the same year that Matteo Ricci died in Peking, Christovao Ferreira, a thirty-year-old Jesuit priest from Portugal, set sail from Macao to join the prospering mission in Japan. Many years later he recalled:

> I did not deem the thousands and tens of thousands of miles too far a distance. When I reached the Realm of the Sun, for years on end I endured hunger and cold, labour and privation, and that without complaint: it was all for the sake of preaching the [Christian] doctrine to every creature.

Within three years Ferreira was appointed assistant superior of the Jesuit residence in Kyoto. Seven years later, his command of Japanese fluent and his skills widely praised, he was designated *Procurator* of the Society of Jesus in Japan.

The Japan in which Ferreira arrived was very different from that of Francis Xavier. The long period of bitter factional wars had come to an end through the emergence of two powerful shoguns who had succeeded in uniting the country under a single rule. Hideyoshi achieved supremacy in 1590, and in 1603 his successor Ieyasu established the Tokugawa Shogunate, which was to remain in power until well into the 19th century. When Ferreira landed in 1610, this newly achieved unity was in the process of being consolidated. Under the authoritarian political framework of the Tokugawa regime, the regional *daimyo* (governors) were forced to submit to central policy, religious sectarianism was stamped out, Buddhist temples brought under greater state control, and the intentions of the European traders and priests examined with more suspicion than ever.

In the warring period, Christianity had flourished under the protection of sympathetic *daimyo*, culminating in the accession of the city port of Nagasaki to the Society of Jesus in 1580. But seven years later a decree was issued restricting the practice of the religion and expelling the missionaries. Although this was never enforced, it marked the first step in a successive wave of persecutions. Christianity was increasingly perceived as a potentially subversive movement, which shifted the loyalties of the people from the Emperor to God, and from the Shogun to the Pope.

The cause of the Jesuits was not helped by a dispute between Portugal and Spain over their claims to Japan. When, a century earlier, the Pope had divided the world into two by a line through the Atlantic, he had omitted to draw a line through the other side of the globe to show where the respective territories ended. Thus it was unclear whether Japan was the easternmost province of Portugal or the westernmost province of Spain. In 1593 the Portuguese-backed Jesuit monopoly on Japan was broken by the arrival of Spanish-backed Franciscans. The less urbane followers of St Francis scorned the Jesuits for wearing Buddhist-style robes and disseminating the secular sciences of the Renaissance. The Jesuits in turn found the Franciscans crudely evangelistic and insensitive to Japanese mores. The Buddhists, meanwhile, sat back and relished the display of Christian rancour. Tragically, this quarrel exacerbated a conflict that arose out of a Spanish shipwreck off the Japanese coast in 1596, which ended in the first Christian executions by the Japanese as twenty-six men and women were crucified in February the following year on a hilltop outside Nagasaki.

Things had settled down by the time Christovao Ferreira arrived. The Society of Jesus claimed nearly a quarter of a million Japanese followers. But four years later, on 1 February 1614, the Shogun Ieyasu issued an expulsion order that this time was carried out. The Jesuits who remained were driven underground. Ferreira chose to stay, and for the next fourteen years lived a shadowy existence, smuggled from one covert Christian enclave to another, administering the sacraments, hearing confessions, walking the beaches at night to evade detection, and smuggling reports to his superiors in Macao describing the heroic feats of martyrdom suffered by the captured priests and laity.

When he was finally arrested on 24 September 1633, Ferreira had risen to the post of Vice-Provincial of the Society in Japan and administrator of the Japanese Diocese.

By this time the Tokugawa authorities had realized that in crucifying Christians or burning them at the stake, they automatically created martyrs and thereby strengthened the faith of the underground Church. They now sought to force Christians to apostatize, issue a formal denunciation of their faith, and convert to Buddhism. In this way, especially if the apostate was a priest, the confidence of the Church would be undermined. Persuasion started softly with reasoned argument and, if that failed, proceeded to torture, the most feared of which was the *ana-tsurushi*. This entailed suspending the tightly bound victim upside down in a pit filled with excrement. To prolong the ordeal the temple was slit to prevent cerebral haemorrhage and the obnoxious fumes were such to induce partial anaesthesia, thus maximizing pain while delaying death. One hand was left unbound to allow the victim to signal apostasy.

Many leading Buddhist figures of the day were involved in the persecutions. The Zen monk Soden of Nanzenji Monastery in Kyoto rose to power under the Shogun Ieyasu and helped draft the expulsion order of 1614. Even the renowned Zen Master Takuan became enmeshed in politics. Takuan is best known for the invention of a pickled radish and his treatises on swordsmanship, in which he applied Zen Buddhist principles to the art of war. 'While killing', he wrote, there is no thought of killing; while giving life there is no thought of giving life; for in killing or in the giving of life, no self is asserted . . . . One who has attained this freedom cannot be interfered with by anybody on earth. He stands absolutely by himself.

Such notions lent a moral legitimacy to the cruelty of Takuan's patron, the third Tokugawa Shogun Iemitsu, who when he acceded to power in 1623 immediately had fifty Christians burnt to death to show his resolve to carry out the expulsion edict (a report of which 'with a view to eventual canonisation' was sent to Macao by Ferreira). In the summer of 1639 Takuan is recorded as being present at the interrogation of three priests, who were subsequently subjected to suspension in the pit, two of whom apostatized and one who hung there unregenerate until he died. Although earlier in his life Takuan had resigned as abbot of the influential Daitokuji Monastery after only three days in the post, he was unable to resist the supplications of the Shogun and spent the last twelve years of his life in the capital. Moments before he died, he picked up a brush and wrote the single character 'dream'.

At the time of Ferreira's arrest, not a single priest had yet denounced his faith. Most died after two or three days of agony; although one young woman endured the punishment for two weeks before expiring. Less than a month after his capture, Ferreira was subjected to the pit. After a mere six hours the Vice-Provincial raised his free hand and apostatized.

This was a devastating blow to the Christian community in Japan and the Jesuits in Macao and Europe. Worse still, Ferreira agreed to co-operate with his torturers in eradicating Christianity. He assumed a Japanese name, Sawano Chuan, and signed himself:

the resident of the country of Portugal,
Chief Bateren (priest) of Japan and Macao,
Christovao Ferreira,
reformed in religion and turned
an adherent of Zen.

The extent to which the first European Zen Buddhist understood or practised his newly acquired faith is hard to ascertain. The opening passage of his anti-Christian tract *Deceit Disclosed* (1636) has a marked Neo-Confucian and Taoist ring to its stilted celebration of the 'working of the shaping forces' in nature and the traditional Chinese virtues of 'Goodness, Propriety, Ritual and Knowledge'. He goes on to recall how he had 'wandered in delusion along a perverse path';

> for I knew not the True Way. I was quite like the man who walks bearing a plank on one shoulder, like one who does not know his right from his left . . . . Yet when I saw the customs of Japan, when I heard the truths of Confucianism and Buddhism, though I understood but the thousandth part of their meaning, I repented of my delusion and I reformed. And therefore I cast off the Kirishitan religion and settled my heart on the teachings of Lord Shaka [i.e. Shakyamuni].

Is Ferreira speaking his mind, or is he a broken man blindly following orders of the Japanese inquisitors? The rest of *Deceit Disclosed* is a point by point condemnation of Christian doctrine and offers no further clues as to his feelings about Buddhism. Little is known about the rest of his life. While some Christian sources claim that he repented of his apostasy and finally died a martyr's death in the pit, there is nothing to corroborate this. He died in 1650, almost exactly a century after Francis Xavier set foot in the country. Eleven years earlier, in 1639, Shogun Iemitsu had issued the Sakoku edict whereby Japan closed its doors to all traffic, commercial or otherwise, with Catholic lands. Ferreira's tomb can still be seen in Nagasaki, but since the record of his burial was destroyed in the atomic holocaust of 1945, the exact circumstances of his last days remain unknown.

As part of the Tokugawa policy of suppressing Christianity, a comprehensive catalogue of all Buddhist temples and shrines was drawn up, the schools and sects were strictly classified and defined, and every family was forced to register with a Buddhist group. Predictably, the followers of Nichiren put up the greatest resistance to this move towards religious unification and, just as predictably, were persecuted. The 1608 edicts outlawing their doctrines were only lifted through the last-minute intercession of one of Shogun Ieyasu's concubines. As Buddhism became the established religion of the land, the bureaucratic restrictions and controls stifled the once creative and turbulent traditions of the 13th century and, although the religion prospered materially, its spiritual vitality was weakened. The vestiges of the Christian Church were forced underground, but small pockets managed to survive, in increasingly garbled forms, until the re-opening of the country to the West in the middle of the 19th century. Buddhist statues were then found, inside which were secret compartments concealing miniature Christian altars.

The Jesuits in China also suffered decline. Matteo Ricci's policy of tolerating Confucian practices among Chinese Christians was forbidden by Rome in 1704. The missionaries who now arrived from Europe antagonized the Manchu emperors with their inflexibility and open disdain for Chinese values. Spanish Franciscans also appeared and did not hesitate to proclaim that the ancient line of the Sons of Heaven were burning in hell. In 1773 the Society of Jesus was suppressed. As Christianity waned, crucifixes were burned before statues of the Buddha. Matteo Ricci, the first European to introduce clocks that chimed the hour, nonetheless continued to be revered in China — not for his imitation of Christ but as the patron deity of the Shanghai guild of clockmakers.

TSONGKHAPA:
THE GELUK TRADITION

O n 12 February 1985, 444 years after the Iberian coastline slipped from Francis Xavier's view, a boy was born to Paco and Maria Torres amidst the cold technological gleam of the state hospital of Granada, Spain. 'He's so serene,' said the father, 'his face is full of light.' They decided to call him 'Osel' (Tibetan for 'Luminosity').

For Paco and Maria were disciples of Lama Thubten Yeshé, a charismatic and zany Tibetan Buddhist teacher who had died of heart disease in a Californian hospital on 3 March the previous year at the age of forty-eight. Since attending a two-week meditation course in 1977 on the island of Ibiza, the couple had, in spite of a growing family and little money, devoted themselves to establishing a branch of Lama Yeshé's world-wide Buddhist network in Spain. High in the Alpujarra mountains they created a retreat centre, which, according to the wish of Lama Yeshé, 'should be open to people of all religions who wanted time, space and peace to develop their interior life'. For six years they toiled by hand, building isolated cabins, a house, even the access road. When it was finished, the Dalai Lama, after celebrating mass with the village priest, came to bless the site. He named it 'Osel Ling' ('Place of Luminosity').

Meanwhile, Lama Yeshé's disciple Lama Thubten Zopa was enquiring into the whereabouts of his deceased teacher. One night he saw in a dream 'a small child with bright, penetrating eyes,

crawling on the floor of a meditation room'. The boy had
European features. When he visited Osel Ling in the autumn of
1985 he was startled to find the child of his dream crawling on
the floor of the shrine room. It was the six-month-old Osel. He
lifted him onto the teaching throne with him and asked Maria
about the circumstances of his conception and birth. She
remembered a video of Lama Yeshé's last visit to Osel Ling. They
played it and heard the fuzzy televisual image of Lama Yeshé say
to Maria and Paco:

> I know how much you have done for the centre, how
> dedicated you have been . . . . Even if I die I shall never forget
> you. We have much business, much karma business between
> us.

Six months later Osel went to Dharamsala, India, to be formally
examined. Lama Zopa laid four rosaries on a table, one of which
belonged to Lama Yeshé. 'Give me your *mala* (rosary) from your
past life', he commanded:

> Osel turned his head away as if bored. Then he whipped it
> back again and without hesitation went straight for the
> correct *mala*, which he grabbed with both hands, raising it
> above his head, grinning, in a triumphant victory salute.

Having passed this and other tests, Osel was officially recognized
by the Dalai Lama as the reincarnation of Lama Thubten Yeshé,
and in March, 1987, ceremonially enthroned.

The Geluk tradition of Tibetan Buddhism, to which Lama Yeshé
belonged, was founded on the teachings of a monk called

Tsongkhapa, whose painless birth in eastern Tibet in 1357 was likewise accompanied by auspicious portents and prophetic dreams. From an early age Tsongkhapa was recognized as a religious genius. He received the precepts of a lay Buddhist from the 4th Karmapa at the precocious age of three and left his remote homeland on the Chinese border for the spiritual heartland of Central Tibet when he was sixteen. He spent the remaining forty-six years of his life wandering through this area, studying with the greatest lamas of the day, writing treatises, debating, retreating to caves for prolonged meditations, and founding monasteries. He achieved a visionary synthesis of the diverse Buddhist traditions of his time, articulating them with rare lucidity in his writings and actualizing them through relentless yogic practice.

The year after Tsongkhapa's birth, Mongol hegemony over Tibet came to an end with the murder of the last ruling Sakya lama. Power in central Tibet returned to local control under the leadership of the influential Pamotrupa family. And when Tsongkhapa was eleven (1368), the declining Mongol dynasty of China was overthrown and the Ming dynasty established. Thus the yoke of Mongol rule, which had dominated Asia for 150 years came to an end and so began a period of optimistic independence both in China and Tibet. Tsongkhapa's spiritual vitality contributed in a timely way to this process of national renewal. Here was a man whose intellectual breadth embraced all the traditions — Sakya, Kadam, Kagyu and Nyingma — thus honouring each while forging them into a united whole. His life coincided with an era of almost unprecedented peace and prosperity in which Dharma flourished again as it had during the times of Padmasambhava and Milarepa.

As Tibet was redefining herself politically, Tsongkhapa embarked on a series of religious reforms. To the monks he emphasized the importance of adherence to the rule (*vinaya*), which in many monasteries had become lax. Through his writings he stressed how the basic doctrines of the Buddhist sutras were an indispensable prerequisite for the more advanced practices of the tantras. In philosophy he criticized those who relegated the status of the relative world to that of mere illusion, only through dispelling which the ultimate truth would shine forth. Like Dogen, he was a 'mystic realist', who saw the essential identity of the myriad phenomena of the world with their ultimate truth. 'When you understand how transparency appears as the process of cause and effect,' he wrote to a disciple, 'then you can no longer be a victim of philosophical error.' In other words, you will miss the point of Buddhism as long as you imagine the relative world to be somehow apart from its ultimate reality.

A relationship of mutual respect grew up between Tibet and China, with the Ming emperors regularly inviting the leading lamas to Peking. In 1407 the 5th Karmapa was received at the imperial court and given his famous black crown. The following year an invitation was issued to Tsongkhapa, who refused on the grounds of advancing age (he was fifty-one) and his wish to stay in retreat. In his place he sent his disciple Jamchen Chöjé, who reached Peking in 1409.

More compelling reasons for his refusal are found in his plans to institute a yearly Prayer Festival (Mönlam) in Lhasa, the first of which took place as Jamchen Chöjé approached Peking, and to found his own monastery (called Ganden) on a hilltop to the east of Lhasa, work on which started later the same year. The remaining ten years of Tsongkhapa's life were characterized by extensive teaching and the building of monasteries. In 1416 work began on Drepung to the west of Lhasa; in 1417 the main temple at Ganden was consecrated; and in 1419, the year of Tsongkhapa's death, Jamchen Chöjé started constructing Sera (where Lama Yeshé would later study) to the north of Lhasa. These three monasteries grew into the largest such institutions in the world, resembling small towns, with a combined population of more than 20,000 monks.

It is unclear whether or not Tsongkhapa wished to found a new religious order in Tibet. Towards the end of his life, with his immense following and the frantic building work in progress, he must have realized that it was inevitable. He may well have envisioned a renewed Buddhism, uniting the glorious achievements of the past, highlighted in an independent Tibet by his syncretic teachings and grand monasteries. It is unlikely that he would have foreseen the factionalism and power struggles that ensued in his name over the next two and a half centuries, which ended once more in Mongol intervention.

In 1434, a mere sixteen years after Tsongkhapa's death, the peaceful but short-lived Pamotrupa dynasty collapsed and the country entered a prolonged period of internal strife, which centred around the powerful families of Lhasa and Central Tibet, on one side, and those of Tsang, the province to the west, on the other. Both parties aligned themselves with different religious orders: the former with Tsongkhapa's Geluk school, as it came to be known, the latter with the Kagyu tradition of the Karmapa. The period was marked by years of uneasy truce, followed by outbursts of violence, in which neither side succeeded in unifying the fractured land.

The event which augured the end of this stalemate occurred in the summer of 1578 (the year in which Matteo Ricci sailed from Lisbon) when Sonam Gyatso, the most prominent Geluk lama of the day, arrived, at the invitation of Altan Khan, in a nomadic outpost on the Mongolian steppes. Sonam Gyatso was recognized as the third incarnation of Gendun Trup, a nephew and prominent disciple of Tsongkhapa. Altan Khan was the leader of the Tumed tribe of Mongols and had political aspirations of the order of Genghis Khan. Recalling the encounter between Sakya Pandita and Godan Khan more than three hundred years before, the two men came to an understanding. In return for his teachings, Altan Khan bestowed on Sonam Gyatso the title 'Dalai Lama' ('Dalai' meaning 'Ocean' in Mongolian — as does 'Gyatso' in Tibetan). In return Sonam Gyatso gave Altan Khan the title 'Religious King, Brahma of the Gods' and concluded with the ominous prophecy that within eighty years the khan's descendants would dominate Eastern and Central Asia.

He was not far off. Sixty-four years later (1642) Gushri Khan, leader of the Qoshot Mongols and head of an alliance of Mongol tribes, invaded Tibet, defeated the rulers of Tsang, displaced the Karmapa, and installed Ngawang Losang Gyatso, the 5th Dalai Lama, as ruler of the land. Two years later (1644) the Manchus toppled the fragile Ming dynasty and seized power in Peking.

The 1640s marked a turning-point in Buddhist East Asia. Regimes were now in place in Tibet, China and Japan that would, in the face of European expansion, become increasingly conservative, until their late medieval isolation was forcefully interrupted by the Western-dominated modern world. In the 19th and early 20th centuries, trading treaties were forced upon all three countries by Britain and America. Their 17th-century regimes collapsed under external economic or ideological pressure in 1868 (Japan), 1911 (China) and 1959 (Tibet).

Once Gushri Khan had placed the 5th Dalai Lama in power, he withdrew to the background, enabling the lama to consolidate his realm. Although followers of the Karmapa understandably resented the Dalai Lama's rule and the dominance of the Geluk school, the populace benefited from the stability and prestige of a powerful ruler. Still jittery about Sonam Gyatso's prediction, and desirous of the Dalai Lama's pacific influence over his irascible Mongol supporters, the Manchu emperor Shun-chih invited the Tibetan leader to Peking, where he was received with great pageantry in 1653.

Things began to fall apart after the Dalai Lama's death in 1682. His chief minister, Sangye Gyatso, concealed the death for fourteen years, substituting a double on state occasions. This high-handedness upset everybody: the Mongols, the Chinese — not to mention the Tibetans. Although a teenage 6th Dalai Lama was hastily announced and enthroned, he turned out to be singularly lacking in a monastic vocation and soon renounced his novice vows. Gushri Khan's grandson, Lhazang Khan, then seized control of the deteriorating situation. In 1705 his troops ambushed and executed Sangye Gyatso; the following year he arrested the 6th Dalai Lama and sent him into exile. The young poet and libertine died, under suspicious circumstances, near Lake Kokonor on the Chinese border before reaching his destination, and Lhazang Khan ruled the country alone as King of Tibet.

At this point the Jesuits appeared on the scene in the form of a thirty-two-year-old Italian from the town of Pistoia in Tuscany called Ippolito Desideri, who over eighteen months had walked from Delhi via Ladakh and the wastes of western Tibet to arrive in Lhasa on 18 March 1716. The Society of Jesus was not new to Tibet. A mission had been established in Guge in the far west of the country nearly a century before but soon had to be abandoned. In 1628 two Jesuits managed to reach Shigatse, but were expelled on the advice of the 10th Karmapa, who suspected them of wanting to destroy Buddhism. Desideri, whose longing to work in Tibet had received the approval of Pope Clement XI, was the first to reach Lhasa. Upon arrival, he was interrogated by a Mongol army commander. 'As to my rank', he explained to the soldier, 'I am a priest, and by profession a Lama,'

> bound by my religion and office to guide others into the straight path to rescue them from error and to teach them our Holy Faith, by which alone they could attain Heaven and eternal salvation. This, I said, was my only business, for I saw

190

they were all immersed in error, and had no one to show them the fetters by which they were bound, or the precipices into which they would fall headlong and go to eternal perdition.

Far from irritating the Mongol court, Desideri was ushered in to see Lhazang Khan, who gave him permission to preach and encouraged him to learn the language. Desideri threw himself into the task. 'From that day until I left Thibet,' he recalled, 'I made it a rule to study from early morning till sundown, and for nearly six years took nothing during the day save *cia* (tea) to drink.' Nine months later he was able to present Lhazang Khan with an exposition of Christianity — written in Tibetan.

According to Desideri's memoir, the king read and reread the book, then asked him to hold a public debate with the lamas. To prepare for this he suggested that he study their doctrines, attend their debates and write down his refutations of Buddhism. He then gave him permission to be admitted to the monasteries to pursue his research. This is reminiscent of Möngke Khan's 13th-century search for a religious ideology by which to rule his empire. Lhazang Khan was familiar with the work of the Jesuits in China and India. He even told Desideri that he would convert to Christianity if he could be convinced of its doctrines. So was he seriously toying with the idea of embracing the foreign faith and exercising his dominion over Tibet with the help of a European-influenced administration? He gave the young Jesuit an impression of wholehearted support. 'I lost no time', wrote Desideri, 'in obeying the king's commands, which so perfectly agreed with my own desires.'

Desideri began a daily routine of studying the Buddhist canon. At first (from March until July, 1717) he went to Ramoché, a temple dating back to the 7th century. Here he pored over volumes of the *Kangyur*, Tibetan translations of the Buddha's sutras, in order, he says, 'to obtain a complete insight into that false religion.

I compared one book with another, made notes, and copied everything that might furnish me with weapons to fight the enemy. I also held frequent disputations about these matters.'

In August of the same year he moved to Sera Monastery, where he was not only given a good house but allowed to construct a chapel and celebrate mass. Here he turned his attention to the *Tengyur*, the Tibetan translations of the major Indian Buddhist commentaries. 'Above all', he explains, 'I applied myself to . . . understand those most abstruse, subtle and intricate treatises [concerning] Tongbagni, or Vacuum (i.e. transparency).' Intellectually, he appears to have grasped the idea well. He succinctly notes that transparency means 'that nothing exists because nothing has any essence by itself, and therefore nothing exists which is not . . . unconnected, unfettered and without correlativity'.

As a good Catholic the notion appals him. 'Under the pretence of searching for the root', he reflects, the idea 'extirpates from the heart . . . the real and primary root of all things.' For its real aim is 'to exclude and absolutely deny the existence of any uncreated and independent Being and thus effectually to do away with any conception of God'. Such 'subtle artifice' could, of course, only be the work of the Devil, 'who has so adorned this monstrosity as to make it appear to [the Tibetans] of most sublime importance, the final step towards perfection, and the only path leading to eternal bliss'.

Not only was Desideri treading into an area where none of his confrères, even Ricci, had dared to go, he was penetrating an unknown philosophy more than a century before European scholarship would first 'discover' it — let alone understand it as well as he did. During his five years in Tibet, he not only mastered the spoken and written languages but composed four texts in Tibetan. Ironically, his memoirs remained lost in Pistoia until 1875 and were not published until 1904, nearly two hundred years after their composition. His Tibetan texts languished in the Jesuit archives in Rome and were first translated (into Italian) in the 1980s.

Another oddity is that Desideri never realized that what he was studying was Buddhism. Although he was dimly aware that the Tibetans' religion had originated in India but then fallen into obscurity, was familiar with Marco Polo's writings and had observed in Nepal worship of the 'False God' called 'Bod', he treats the Dharma as an obscure and unknown cult peculiar to Tibet. It would be another twenty years before the Jesuits connected the Buddhism of China and Tibet with that of ancient India.

Desideri does, however, see some good at work in the false religion of 'these blind pagans'. For while they 'absolutely deny the existence of a Divinity, confusedly, in practice, they do recognise it'. And although he considers the Dharma to be 'absolutely wrong and pestiferous',

> yet the rules and directions imposed on the will are not alien to the principles of sound reason; they seem to me worthy of admiration as they not only prescribe hatred of vice, inculcate battling against passions, but, what is more remarkable, lead man towards sublime and heroic perfection.

He is also amazed by the great 'esteem, veneration and respect' shown by the Tibetans (whom in this regard he compares favourably to European Catholics) not only for the lamas but even to Christianity:

> Many a time when telling them what the image of the Crucifix meant they would prostrate themselves, beat their breasts and beg to hold it in their hands, when they would kiss it and shed many tears on hearing that Jesus Christ had so suffered for the redemption of their souls.

Even in Sera 'many monks, doctors and influential persons' came to pray in his chapel, which he attributes not to a heartfelt appreciation of Jesus as a Bodhisattva (which was probably the case) but, with the casual arrogance of his age, to 'the esteem in which they held European missionaries'.

But while Desideri was busy poring over Buddhist texts in Sera in preparation for the great debate and, hopefully, the conversion of Lhazang Khan to Catholicism, trouble was brewing in Lhasa.

Discontent with the khan's autocratic manner had led Tibetan factions to conspire with another Mongol group, the Dzungars, to depose him and reinstate the newly found incarnation of the Dalai Lama. The Dzungar army reached Tibet in November, 1717. Lhasa fell in a single night of fighting and, four days later, Lhazang Khan was killed. The Dzungars did not, however, bring the Dalai Lama with them. Instead, the soldiers embarked on a savage frenzy of plunder, looting both the homes of the rich and the temples. Realizing their misjudgement of the Dzungars, the Tibetans appealed to the powerful Manchu Emperor of China, Kang-hsi, for help. In 1720 a Chinese army not only succeeded in routing the Mongols but also, to the delight of the Tibetans, reinstated the young 7th Dalai Lama in the Potala Palace.

This put paid to Desideri's plans. Although he stayed at Sera during the Dzungar attack on Lhasa, a few weeks later he escaped to Takpo province, just to the east of the capital, where he lived for the next three years. Ironically, his sojourn in Tibet was brought to an end not by an expulsion order from Lhasa, but by a letter from Rome in the early months of 1721, informing him that the Congregation for the Propaganda of the Faith had ruled that Tibet was to be the preserve of the Capuchins rather than the Jesuits. On 28 April he obediently but regretfully left for India. He returned to Rome in 1728, where he died suddenly on 14 April 1733.

By this time the Manchus had consolidated their control over Tibet. A military governor was installed in Lhasa with a garrison of two thousand troops, and a system of government established which would last with minor modifications until the collapse of the Manchu dynasty in 1911. The Dalai Lamas became the de facto rulers of the land under the secular protection of the Manchu court. The implications of this arrangement were summed up with alarming prescience by Desideri:

> After nigh twenty years of tumult and disaster . . . Thibet was thus subjugated by the Emperor of China in October, 1720, and here his descendants will probably continue to reign for many more centuries.

In 1912 the Tibetans succeeded in throwing off the Manchu yoke and entered a period of independence under the powerful 13th Dalai Lama. But they failed sufficiently to consolidate their sovereignty to prevent the newly victorious Chinese communists from invading and annexing the country in 1951. Eight years later, when they tried to shake off these more insidious descendants of the Sons of Heaven, they were brutally crushed.

Tamdin Rabten, at the time a monk at Sera, was so absorbed in his philosophical studies that he failed to notice the growing political storm, until the early morning of 19 March 1959, when 'after a day of normal debating', he recalls:

> I woke up at two or three o'clock to the sound of artillery fire. I looked out of my window towards Lhasa, and saw the city and surrounding area lit up like daytime with brilliant white flares. The sky was filled with dust from the intense bombardment . . . . After a while, I tried to eat something; but feeling such great sorrow, I could not swallow.

As the first rays of sunlight flooded the Lhasa valley, he heard to his relief that the young 14th Dalai Lama had slipped away two nights before. He then left the monastery, his home for the past twenty years, and set off on foot across the high mountain passes to India.

Tamdin Rabten was born in a prosperous farming family in the Tehor region of eastern Tibet (not far from where the 16th Karmapa and Kalu Rinpoché hailed) in 1920. At the age of nineteen, against his father's wishes, he ran off to Sera to become a monk. Far from home and deprived of any support, his initial years in the monastery were harsh and beset with ill health. But he was a determined student whose gifts were soon noted by his teachers and, as he graduated to the higher classes, a young reincarnate lama, Gonsar Rinpoché, was placed in his care.

India in 1959 had enough difficulties of its own to cope adequately with the 100,000 Tibetan refugees who poured over the Himalayas in the wake of the Chinese seizure of power. The Tibetans too were ill-prepared to cope with the sweltering heat of the lowlands. Yet Tamdin Rabten's first priority was 'to prevent the decline of the teachings of Lord Buddha'. He was assigned by the Dalai Lama to a community of 1,500 displaced monks in Buxadaur, an abandoned prison camp in the mountains of West Bengal, and immediately recommenced the training which he had been forced to interrupt in Sera. He taught and studied there until 1963, when he passed his final examinations to become a *lharampa* (first degree) *geshé* (doctor of buddhology) *angi-dangpo* (maxima cum laude).

Thus, at the age of forty-three, he reached the apex of scholastic achievement within Tsongkhapa's Geluk tradition, having passed through a course of more than twenty years' study. To become a *geshé* requires first of all a mastery of Buddhist logic and epistemology, then an in-depth knowledge of the entire range of Indian Buddhist doctrine and philosophy, followed by a meticulous analysis of phenomenology, cosmology and monastic discipline. Having committed the major texts to memory, one's understanding is honed through endless debate. The entire process is sustained by prayer, tantric ritual and other spiritual disciplines.

Geshé Rabten was invited to Dharamsala and appointed as a religious assistant (*tsenzhap*) to the Dalai Lama, with the responsibility of serving as the exiled ruler's debating partner. Shortly afterwards, he moved into a hut in the hills to begin an extended meditation retreat, coming down only occasionally to perform his official duties.

The purpose of this retreat was to realize experientially what he had mastered intellectually. In particular, his meditation focused on the meaning of transparency:

> When I examined this old monk who previously seemed so
> existent,
> He turned out to be just like the tracks of a bird in
> the sky.

He recorded his insights in a series of verses and later wrote a commentary upon them. His meditation unfolds as 'a battle between reason and appearance', in which, having logically critiqued the felt-sense of a 'real' self-identity, he absorbed himself in the resultant loss of that sense. Then:

> While absorbed in the sphere of the mind's
> transparency,
> I precisely examined the ways in which
> Merely nominal things were able to function.

Having exposed the fiction of a reified self and world, he analysed how self and world nonetheless function in a meaningful and value-ordered way. These reflections led him to realize that compassion is the spontaneous reflex of the understanding of transparency and interdependence. 'I became convinced', he wrote, 'that rather than making vast offerings at a temple it was better to give a bowlful of food to an unfortunate dog.'

In 1969, while still in retreat, the Dalai Lama asked Geshé Rabten to teach the first Westerners who were arriving in Dharamsala to study Buddhism. Over the following years a group of American and European disciples formed around him. In 1974 he flew to Switzerland and taught a month-long meditation course in Rolle, on Lake Geneva. The following year he was invited back as abbot of the Tibetan Monastic Institute in Rikon, near Zürich, the spiritual and cultural centre of the Swiss Tibetan refugee community. A number of his Western disciples followed him, and, on 6 January 1976, he gave lesson one in the first traditional course of *geshé* training to be undertaken in Europe.

The small group of students, most of whom were monks, settled in a nearby hamlet and walked daily to the monastery where Geshé Rabten would instruct them in the principles of logic. The texts he taught were committed to memory and debated. Apart from minimal oral translation, all of this was done in Tibetan. In April 1977, the group moved to the village of Le Mont Pèlerin, near Lausanne, where Geshé Rabten founded Tharpa Choeling, Centre of Higher Tibetan Studies. The older students began to teach the growing number of younger monks and nuns who came to join what was now the first fully fledged Tibetan Buddhist monastic community for Westerners in Europe.

Yet despite this promising beginning, within a couple of years the project began to show signs of strain. Some of the elder students (including the author of this book) returned to Asia. Geshé Rabten became increasingly involved in teaching elsewhere. Bit by bit, the community dissolved, and then, in 1984, Geshé Rabten's health began to fail.

What went wrong? The psychological demands of transplanting

what was effectively a branch of Sera Monastery to modern Switzerland proved unbearable. Geshé Rabten insisted on following a virtually unmodified programme of studies, pursued in an alien language. In addition to the linguistic burden, the content of much of what was taught seemed irrelevant. For in spite of the emphasis on analysis and debate, which attracted many students, certain key doctrines were treated as indisputable dogma. Moreover, relatively little time and emphasis was given to meditation. The blend was wrong. What may have been eminently suited to a Tibetan monk in Sera did not necessarily fit the spiritual needs and aspirations of a French or English monk in Europe.

In March 1986 Geshé Rabten died, leaving responsibility for his centres in Switzerland, Italy and Austria to his disciple Gonsar Rinpoché. The programme of *geshé* training he initiated has all but faded; Tharpa Choeling (now Rabten Choeling) continues as a monastery, but its main activity is serving the lay community in the area. In 1987 a Tibetan boy called Tenzin Rabgyé was born in India and three years later was enthroned as Geshé Rabten's reincarnation.

Adaptation of the Geluk teachings for Europeans has, however, been a primary concern of other Tibetan teachers, many of whom were disciples of Geshé Rabten. The foremost of these was Lama Thubten Yeshé.

Shortly after Thubten Yeshé was born in a village near Lhasa in May 1935, he was acknowledged by the nuns of a nearby nunnery as the reincarnation of their recently deceased abbess. At the age of six he was admitted to Sera Monastery and settled down to the discipline of study, prayer and debate. Like Geshé Rabten, he fled Tibet as soon as the Chinese bombardments began. He also ended up in Buxadaur, but, unlike the other monks, laid less store on gaining his *geshé* degree and included English in his curriculum. A young Sherpa *tulku* called Thubten Zopa, whose devout introversion served as a natural foil for Lama Yeshé's almost showmanlike extraversion, was entrusted to his care by Geshé Rabten and became a close disciple.

The first contact the two lamas had with Westerners was in 1965 while they were visiting Ghoom Monastery in Darjeeling. Zina Rachevsky, the thirty-four-year-old daughter of an exiled Russian aristocrat and an American heiress, a former socialite and beatnik whose interest in Theosophy and Tibet led her to the Himalayas, had arrived in Ghoom in search of another lama, Tomo Geshé Rinpoché. Because Lama Zopa was also known at the time as Tomo Rinpoché, she mistakenly thought he was the lama she sought. A strong friendship grew nonetheless and they spent the following year with the two lamas. In 1967 Zina was ordained as a nun by the Dalai Lama in Dharamsala, after which the three of them left for Nepal. Two years later they founded a small monastery on a hill near Kathmandu called Kopan.

Over the coming years Kopan became, for many Westerners, the next step after jubilation had turned to disillusion on reaching the terminus of the hippy trail. 'Hanging out with the lamas' was replaced by structured meditation courses, the first of which took place in November 1971. Zina Rachevsky went into retreat in the higher mountains. At this point she also began studying and practising Nyingma *dzogchen* meditation. She died suddenly and mysteriously in 1972 in a remote hermitage.

'As I saw more and more Westerners', recalled Lama Yeshé, 'I realised they were intellectually advanced. They easily understood the Buddha's teaching. What they lacked, however, was an experience of the teachings which they could only get from meditation.' He also realized that many of the traditional ways of presenting the Tibetan Buddhist teachings were anachronistic and poorly suited to the needs of modern men and women who required 'something more concrete, something they could relate to their own experience. I couldn't change the Buddha's teaching, but I had to find a way to get it across.'

The meditation courses were established on a yearly basis. They lasted a month and offered a comprehensive overview of Geluk-style Tibetan Buddhism, with Lama Zopa presenting the traditional teachings and Lama Yeshé unpacking them with wit and psychological insight. The courses were hugely successful. The resident community at Kopan grew to include a solid core of Western monks and nuns. Inevitably, with so many former students now back in their home countries, the lamas were invited to the West, their first trip being in 1974. Over the following years they travelled extensively through Australia, America and Europe, leaving a trail of embryonic centres and communities in their wake.

To co-ordinate these groups Lama Yeshé created the Foundation for the Preservation of the Mahayana Teachings (FPMT) in 1975, which served as an interlinking world-wide network of city centres, rural retreats and training institutes, businesses and publishing ventures. As soon as a major centre was established, Lama Yeshé would appoint a Tibetan *geshé* as its resident teacher, often assisted by a senior Western monk or nun. In addition the centre would host regular visits from himself and Lama Zopa as well as other Geluk lamas. The businesses (an import-export company in Kathmandu, a warehouse-shelving enterprise in Hong Kong, even a line of cocktail-dresses in New York) helped fund the centres; 'Wisdom Publications' disseminated the teachings; and Enlightenment Experience Celebrations (EEC) in India periodically brought the scattered communities together.

In 1974 Lama Yeshé was diagnosed as having a serious heart condition. But he put his trust in divinations rather than bypass surgery and for years astounded his doctors by repeatedly outliving their prognoses. In December 1983, after delivering a four-hour discourse on compassion in Kopan, he collapsed and had to be admitted to hospital in Delhi. In January he was well enough to fly to California for treatment. His heart finally gave up in the ultra-modern Cedars-Sinai Hospital in Los Angeles on 3 March.

His organizations and vision continue today under the direction of Lama Zopa. The FPMT now comprises more than fifty centres, including institutes in England, France, Germany, Holland, Italy and Spain. France is also home to Nalanda Monastery, south of Toulouse, which provides training for twenty or so Western monks (out of a total of about eighty monks and nuns world-wide).

The future, as well as considerable media attention, is focused on the development of Lama Osel, now seven years old and receiving a traditional education in the re-established Sera Monastery in south India. In April 1992, in an article in the FPMT's newsletter, Lama Zopa announced that a young French boy called Edouard had been recognized by Sakya Trizin, the head of the Sakya Tradition, as the incarnation of Zina Rachevsky, the first time a child has been acknowledged by Tibetans as the reincarnation of a Western Buddhist.

In 1982 a crisis erupted at the FPMT's English base, the Manjushri Institute. Five years earlier Lama Yeshé had invited his classmate Geshé Kelsang Gyatso to be spiritual director of the rambling Victorian folly on the Cumbrian coast, which had been bought (complete with galloping dry-rot) for a pittance in 1975. Under Geshé Kelsang's guidance it grew into a flourishing teaching centre. Predictably, perhaps, part of the resident community began to feel a stronger allegiance to the frail but charismatic Geshé Kelsang, with whom they studied daily, than Lamas Yeshé and Zopa, whom they saw only briefly once a year. Moreover, resentment grew at being subject to decisions about the Institute taken in distant Kathmandu. The community sought a greater say in the running of the centre. Negotiations failed to resolve the dispute and, much to Lama Yeshé's dismay, the

Manjushri Institute opted out of the FPMT network.

Geshé Kelsang Gyatso was born near Lhasa in 1932 and ordained at the age of eight. He studied in Sera and escaped from Tibet in 1959. But instead of joining the monastic community in Buxadaur, he withdrew to the Himalayan foothills and spent nearly twenty years in retreat. He then came straight to England.

Although Geshé Kelsang agreed with the FPMT that Buddhism had to be adapted to suit the requirements of the modern West, he had his own vision as to how this should be achieved. To this end he has written a total of eleven books in English that outline with considerable clarity the substance of his approach, which comprises three training programmes of different levels. This systematic way of teaching forms the framework in which his growing number of centres (mainly in England, but also in Spain and North America) operate.

In recent years, however, Geshé Kelsang and his followers have distanced themselves not only from the FPMT but also the Geluk tradition in India and even the Dalai Lama. One reason for this is their allegiance to a controversial protector deity called Dorjé Shukden, the practice of which the Dalai Lama has criticized on grounds of its sectarian and schismatic effects. Their clearest declaration of independence appeared in 1991 with the appearance of the 'New Kadampa Tradition', defined by Geshé Kelsang as 'a Mahayana Buddhist tradition that practises the pure Buddhadharma transmitted directly to Je Tsongkhapa by the Wisdom Buddha, Manjushri'. Although 'New Kadampa' was originally a synonym for 'Gelukpa', Geshé Kelsang uses the term to indicate a fresh approach in teaching Buddhism to Westerners based on the purity and simplicity of practice exemplified by the early Kadampa masters of Tibet.

It seems improbable that Geshé Rabten's dream of producing Western *geshés* in Europe will be fulfilled. Even his gifted disciple Geshé Thubten Ngawang, who has directed the Tibetisches Zentrum in Hamburg since 1979, has redesigned the traditional curriculum to meet contemporary needs. Geshé Thubten's approach combines the training of monks and nuns in the centre, a seven-year correspondence course in Buddhism in addition to lay residential courses, the support of Tibetan refugees in India, active promotion of Tibetan culture, and a commitment to inter-religious dialogue. Although FPMT literature still speaks of 'Geshé Training', in practice the emphasis, even at Nalanda Monastery, is on providing sufficient insight into Buddhist philosophy to support prolonged meditation practice and teaching work, but not the meticulous, encyclopaedic understanding required to become a *geshé*.

The one exception so far is Georges Dreyfus, a Swiss from Neuchâtel, who studied as a monk in Dharamsala and south India from the early 1970s to become the first European *geshé* in 1988. Although he has since disrobed and is now pursuing an academic career in the United States, two Westerners, an American and an Australian, are only a short distance away from completing their *geshé* degrees in south India. From the Tibetan side a new generation of monks raised in India are now becoming *geshés*. Among these is Geshé Thubten Jinpa, who has recently completed a degree in philosophy at Cambridge University, a sign perhaps that Buddhist and Western scholarship may one day converge.

13

HAKUIN:
THE RINZAI ZEN TRADITION

In the late afternoon of Sunday, 4 August 1991, a long, low table was placed at the front of the Bodhi Zendo in the Tiltenberg 'Grail Centre', in the village of Vogelenzang, near Amsterdam. A clean white cloth was laid along it upon which were placed two earthenware jugs filled with grape juice and two glazed clay dishes containing wafers. A.M.A. Samy, an Indian Jesuit priest, draped an ecclesiastical white strip of cloth over his yellow Japanese-style robe, smiled at the thirty men and women sitting cross-legged on *zafus* before him and said: 'In the name of the Father, and of the Son, and of the Holy Spirit.' The gathering murmured, 'Amen.' 'The grace of our Lord Jesus Christ and the love of God and the fellowship of the Holy Spirit be with you all', which elicited the concerted reply, 'And also with you.'

The occasion of this Eucharist mass was a five-day Zen retreat conducted by A.M.A. Samy (Gen-un-ken Roshi), who received a traditional Zen training in Japan under the Zen Master Koun Yamada. The same morning he had given a *teisho* (lecture) which focused on Case 41 of Wu-men's 13th-century collection of *koans*, *The Gateless Gate*:

Bodhidharma sat facing the wall. The second patriarch, standing in the snow, cut off his arm and said, 'Your disciple's mind is not yet at peace. I beg you, master, give it rest.' Bodhidharma said, 'Bring your mind to me and I will put it to rest.' The patriarch replied, 'I have searched for the mind but have never been able to find it.' Bodhidharma said, 'I have finished putting it to rest for you.'

This *koan* takes an episode from Buddhist history as a way of indicating a resolution to the dilemma one faces here and now. Like the dilemma, such a resolution is not rational but existential. It is achieved by breaking through the fixed patterns of conventional thinking with an 'intuition of what is essential' (*kensho*). Such an intuition may also be the only way to solve the 'koan' of this retreat: Why is a Jesuit priest teaching what Francis Xavier, Matteo Ricci and Ippolito Desideri denounced as the work of the Devil?

The systematic use of *koans* is most strongly associated with the Rinzai school of Zen Buddhism, founded in the 9th century by the fierce Chinese master Lin-chi (Rinzai in Japanese), defined and interpreted in the 12th century by Ta-hui of the Southern Sung, through whose followers it found its way into Kamakura Japan in the 13th and 14th centuries. It was Rinzai Zen rather than Dogen's Soto that captured the imagination of the Japanese ruling classes and received the patronage of the samurai government. It exerted the greatest influence on the Japanese arts of painting, landscaping, drama, flower arrangement and tea ceremony. Likewise, when the Tokugawa shogunate came to power after the warring period, Rinzai Zen monasteries played an important role not only in offering religious counsel but in serving as administrative centres for the State. Takuan, the master of swordsmanship, was of the Rinzai school.

Yet as the Tokugawa regime took hold, Buddhism, stifled by a narrow and authoritarian political framework, fell into decline.

By the middle of the Tokugawa era the vital sources of culture in Japan had all but evaporated and Buddhism, despite being the established religion, was largely reduced to formalities. It was in this atmosphere, in 1686 in a remote rural village, that Hakuin, the most important figure in Japanese Rinzai Zen Buddhism, was born.

Hakuin's mother was a devout follower of the Nichiren sect and it is from her that he received his first impressions of Buddhism. He was a sensitive child, who could be wrought with anguish upon the sight of rapidly shifting cloud formations above the sea. His terror was increased by the descriptions of hell recounted by the local Nichiren priest. At the age of fifteen his parents allowed him to follow his urge to renounce the world and become a monk. His spiritual quest was fraught with disappointment, doubts and a series of nervous breakdowns. Yet through reading Zen texts, seeking out the few isolated Zen masters, and applying himself remorselessly to *koan* practice, he achieved a total of thirteen major *kenshos*.

The first of these breakthroughs occurred when Hakuin was twenty-four. He had reached such a pitch of concentration that he lost the need to sleep and eat. Then suddenly:

> I was overcome by the Great Doubt. I felt as though freezing in an ice field extending thousands of miles. My bosom was filled with an extraordinary purity. I could neither advance nor retire. It was if I were out of my mind and only the word 'nothing' remained . . . . This continued for a number of days until one night while hearing the striking of the temple bell I experienced the transformation.

The 'Great Doubt' is an attitude of radical perplexity that permeates body and mind with such intensity that it feels, according to Wu-men, like 'a red-hot iron ball which you have gulped down and which you try to vomit up but cannot'. When this 'solid lump of doubt' finally exploded, Hakuin compared it to 'the smashing of a layer of ice, or the pulling down of a crystal tower . . . . All former uncertainties were fully dissolved like ice which melted away.'

Over the following years Hakuin wandered around the country, often mistaken for an ecstatic madman, deepening his insight through further *kensho*s. The emotional character of the experiences was gradually replaced by a profound serenity. Hakuin settled down in a dilapidated temple near the village of his birth and began to teach his growing circle of disciples and the local farmers and peasants. He wrote poetry and produced a series of remarkable brush paintings, many of them depicting himself, a mournful innocent peering mischievously from fathomless eyes.

Hakuin's concern was to revive the practice of Rinzai Zen in Japan. Towards the end of his long life he devised a *koan* which he felt to be singularly appropriate for his times:

If someone claps his hands, one hears a sound at once. Listen now to the sound of a single hand!

His intention was not to supersede the classic *koan* collections of China, but to awaken the Great Doubt. The key to *koan* practice is found not in the wording of the *koan*, but in the quality of perplexity that the *koan* is able to arouse. The depth and power of an intuitive breakthrough corresponds to the depth and power of the perplexity it resolves. Once gripped by Great Doubt, the verbal-form of the *koan* can be dropped. Nor does one then have to 'seek out a quiet place or avoid the places of activity in daily life'. Like Ta-hui and Dogen, Hakuin sought to bring Zen into the lives of ordinary people. Yet in doing so he neither oversimplified the practice nor underestimated its radical demand. 'The practice of Zen', he said, 'is by no means easy.'

Hakuin single-handedly moulded Rinzai Zen into the form it has today. He devised the system of 'koan study', a supervised training in which students pass from one *koan* to the next until the series is completed, at which point they may be authorized to teach. The emphasis in Rinzai is on abrupt *kensho* rather than sitting resolutely in *zazen*, which Hakuin, following Ta-hui, criticized as too passive.

Hakuin died in 1769 at the age of eighty-one. All teachers of the Rinzai tradition in Japan today trace their lineages back to him.

On 26 November 1953, Koun Yamada, a Japanese business executive in Kamakura, was returning home with his wife on a suburban train. He came across a passage in a Zen text in which the author declared: 'I came to realise clearly that Mind is no other than mountains and rivers and the great wide earth, the sun and the moon and the stars.' He broke into tears with the realization that after eight years of *zazen* he had finally grasped what this statement meant. After eating dinner, he went to bed. Half an hour later he abruptly woke up and the same passage flashed through his mind. He repeated it, then

> all at once I was struck as though by lightning, and the next instant heaven and earth crumbled and disappeared. Instantaneously, like surging waves, a tremendous delight welled up in me, a veritable hurricane of delight, as I laughed loudly and wildly: 'Ha, ha, ha, ha, ha, ha! There's no reasoning here, no reasoning at all! Ha, ha, ha.' The empty sky split in two, then opened its enormous mouth and began to laugh uproariously: 'Ha, ha, ha!'

The following morning he reported this experience to his teacher Yasutani Roshi, who confirmed it as a *kensho*.

Although Japan in the early 1950s was a very different place from that of Hakuin, the possibility of *kensho* still existed. The Tokugawa period came to an end almost exactly a century after Hakuin's death and with it ended the country's isolation from the rest of the world. This new period inaugurated not only a renewal of trading relations with the West, but also a renewed openness to European culture and religion. At the same time, Japan embarked on her own colonial ambitions. The increasing militarism of the government culminated in the invasions of China in the 1930s and ultimately the campaigns of the Second World War. While Buddhism was no longer the established religion, the spirit of samurai Zen still influenced the national ethos and *zazen* was used as a training exercise for kamikaze pilots. The humiliation of defeat ended the militarized phase of Japanese national ambition, which then turned towards the achievement of economic supremacy.

The life of Yasutani Roshi, Koun Yamada's teacher, spanned this entire period of transition. He was born in 1885 as the son of a pastry-shop owner in a small village, sent into the local monastery at the age of five and trained as a priest in the Soto Zen school. As was customary after the Meiji Restoration, on completion of his training he married and started to raise a family. Not having inherited a temple from his father, he took a position as an elementary-school teacher. Despite these responsibilities he continued his practice of *zazen* in the Soto style, but became frustrated with the tradition's non-committal attitude to *kensho*. At this point he met Harada Roshi, whose insistence on the primacy of intuitive breakthrough led him to quit his teaching post and dedicate himself once more to spiritual training. On the second *sesshin* with Harada Roshi, he experienced *kensho*.

At the height of the war (1943) Harada gave Yasutani the official seal of transmission and named him as his Dharma successor. For the remaining thirty years of his life, Yasutani devoted himself to

210

teaching Zen. In 1962 he travelled to the United States, where he helped lay the foundations for the 'Zen boom' of the late 1960s. He also lectured in England, France and Germany the following year. In Europe, however, his impact was more widely felt through the publication of Philip Kapleau's classic *The Three Pillars of Zen*, which contains the heart of his teaching. He was a simple man, indifferent to the status and finery that often encumber well-respected Zen masters. He died on 28 March 1973, toppling over painlessly just before taking breakfast.

After the breakthrough in November, 1953, Koun Yamada continued to study under Yasutani Roshi for a further seven years until he had passed more than six hundred *koans*. In 1961 he was appointed as Yasutani's Dharma successor. He never chose to become a priest but continued into old-age to combine an active public life with the teaching of Zen.

The approach of Harada and Yasutani is often described as an ecumenic synthesis of Soto and Rinzai Zen. More accurately, it is Soto radically reformed by Rinzai imperatives. In America this style of Zen has become widespread through such teachers as Philip Kapleau, Taizan Maezumi and Robert Aitken, all of whom are disciples of either Yasutani or Koun Yamada. Kapleau and Maezumi have both taught in Europe. Their American disciples Bodhin Kjolhede Sensei and Gempo Merzel Sensei, respectively, are actively carrying on their work in Sweden, Poland, Holland, England and France. And it is this tradition that is taught by the Jesuit Fathers such as A.M.A. Samy.

At the forefront of the Jesuit fascination with Zen was the German missionary and priest Hugo Enomiya-Lassalle. After the Meiji reforms, the Jesuits were able to continue the work of their 16th- and 17th-century predecessors. Born in 1898, Father Lassalle

211

arrived in Japan in 1929 where he founded a settlement in the Tokyo slums for the care of the destitute. In 1938 he moved to Hiroshima, where he stayed throughout the war and witnessed the dropping of the atom bomb. He then remained in Japan, becoming an advocate of world peace and, somewhat to his surprise, a student of Zen.

His interest in Zen began as an attempt to understand better the character of the Japanese people. This led him to appreciate the profound extent to which Japanese thought was influenced by Zen and to discover the value of Zen practice for his own spiritual life. Cautiously, he recommended its practice to Christians, arguing that the central experience of *kensho* is 'in itself neither Buddhist nor Christian nor necessarily connected with any religious confession.' He underwent the traditional *koan* training with Harada and in 1978 was himself acknowledged as a Roshi by Koun Yamada. During the last years of his very long life (he died in 1990) he travelled extensively, leading *sesshin*s in Europe, primarily for Christians. Those who knew him describe him as a quiet, transparent and unauthoritarian man.

The notion that Zen is somehow beyond all philosophical views and denominational affiliations has its origins in Zen Buddhism's classic definition of itself:

A special transmission outside the scriptures;
No dependence upon words and letters;
Direct pointing at the human heart;
Seeing into one's nature and the realisation of
Buddhahood.

As the tradition became increasingly identified as a 'single-practice' form of Buddhism both in Sung China and Kamakura Japan, the tendency to isolate Zen as an autonomous experience was reinforced. Despite their efforts to reintegrate Zen practice with Buddhist philosophy and doctrine, many of the greatest teachers (Ta-hui, Dogen etc.) were unable in the long run to counteract the popular demand for a form of Buddhism reduced to the simple act of sitting in *zazen* or puzzling over a *koan*. In the West, this attitude was given a virtual imprimatur through the enormously influential writings of D.T. Suzuki. 'Zen', he said, 'is neither monotheistic nor pantheistic. Zen defies all such designations. Hence there is no object in Zen upon which to fix the thought. Zen is a wafting cloud in the sky. No screw fastens it, no string holds it.'

The consequence of detaching Zen from its Buddhist matrix is to highlight a technique of meditation that can be appropriated and interpreted by different traditions and used to their own ends. Father Lassalle saw it as a remedy for the deeply engrained restlessness and despair of modern life. For him the practice of Zen was a means to recover the kind of inner repose and clarity needed in order to turn one's attention to God.

The teachings and practices of Buddhism have always been freely available to all who can benefit from them and it would be churlish to object to Christians or others using Zen meditation to revitalize their own traditions. One should not, however, assume that through their advocation of Zen, Father Lassalle and his colleagues are any more willing to encounter Buddhism on equal terms with Christianity than were their Jesuit forebears.

The theological device used to sustain the belief in the superiority of Christianity over Buddhism is the doctrine of 'revealed' as opposed to 'natural' truth. Father Lassalle can thus generously describe enlightenment (*kensho*) as 'perhaps the highest thing that man can achieve by his natural powers and efforts', only to conclude that 'enlightenment, sublime achievement as it is, cannot be identified with the mystical experience. Nor can it be guaranteed to lead to mystic experience.' For true mystical experience is a gift of God's supernatural grace and hence beyond the reach of either Buddhism or Zen.

213

How is enlightenment understood for a Christian like Father Lassalle? He describes it variously as 'the discovery and activation of a spiritual power which was not previously known or experienced, nor ever used; . . . a total view of all being; . . . a state of quietude, a true "coming to one's self;" . . . the most radical form of detachment from created things.' It is a refined psychological experience that affords a platform of clarity and calm in the midst of the turbulent world, which in itself neither affirms nor denies a Buddhist or Christian world-view, but provides a capacity to deepen one's understanding of either. For although neutral in itself, enlightenment is inevitably interpreted according to the world-view of the person who experiences it. The most Father Lassalle can say is that it 'leads us along the line that ends in the vision of God'.

While acknowledging that Buddhism has 'made much better use of the natural faculties of man than the Christian religion', and surpasses Christianity in having cultivated and preserved the experience of enlightenment, he qualifies this praise in explaining how 'the good that is in non-Christian religions can be seen as a substitute for the disadvantage they suffer from being so late in hearing of the revelation of God'. Furthermore, he believes that Buddhism is incapable of providing the kind of answers modern Japanese now expect from science and Western culture, because its philosophy is 'not suited for logical and dialectical reasoning'. He sees Buddhism as on the verge of collapse in Japan (a view shared by Kodo Sawaki and Koun Yamada) and asks:

I wonder whether in the long run Buddhism will be able to preserve these treasures [of Zen] for the Japanese people? It is not too late because the spirit of Zen is still alive in the character of the Japanese nation . . . . Is there not in all this a great task for the Christian mission? Should not Christianity take these values and fill them with a new life?

And would it not be easier for a Japanese to embrace Christianity if he should find therein something of his own?

Thus the circle, which began with Matteo Ricci's attempt to use Confucianism as a base for converting the Chinese to Catholicism more than three hundred years earlier, is complete. In the more liberal climate of Vatican II, with Ricci's view of acculturation now official Church policy, Father Lassalle is free to appropriate Zen as a convenient vehicle to achieve his self-declared missionary ends.

The Second Vatican Council (1962–5) articulated and authorized the significant shift in attitude within the Catholic Church that had arisen in the course of the 20th century. *Nostra Aetate*, one of the sixteen documents of the council, dealt specifically with the relationship of the Church to non-Christian religions and is endlessly cited to demonstrate the new spirit of tolerance. 'The Catholic Church', it declares,

> rejects nothing which is true and holy in these religions. She looks with sincere respect upon those ways of conduct and life, those rules and teachings which, though differing in many particulars from what she holds and sets forth, nevertheless often reflect a ray of the Truth which enlightens all men.

Thus Buddhism is no longer to be treated as a work of Satan, but as a pre-Christian reflection of God's saving grace, which culminated five hundred years later in the birth of Jesus. Christians are now exhorted to 'prudently and lovingly, through dialogue and collaboration with the followers of other religions, and in witness of Christian faith and life, acknowledge, preserve, and promote the spiritual and moral goods found among these men'.

This unequivocal endorsement of the work of Father Lassalle and others needs, however, to be seen in the light of the Council's decree *Ad Gentes*, which deals with missionary activity.

The Church, the document declares, 'is missionary by her very nature'. The purpose of mission is defined as 'evangelisation and the planting of the Church among those peoples and groups where she has not yet taken root'. Since there is only 'one Mediator between God and men, himself man, Christ Jesus', and 'neither is there salvation in any other', the text concludes: 'therefore, all must be converted to Him as He is made known by the Church's preaching. All must be incorporated into Him by baptism, and into the Church which is His body.'

The refreshingly tolerant notion of dialogue announced in *Nostra Aetate* is thus qualified by the same kind of intolerance that characterized the missions of Xavier and Ricci. Subsequently *Ad Gentes* urges seminary and college professors to 'teach young people the true state of the world and of the Church, so that the necessity of a more intense evangelisation of non-Christians will become clear to them and will nurture their zeal'. Laymen who work in secular institutions 'whose historical and scientific-religious research promotes knowledge of peoples and religions' are singled out for special praise. Since through their work 'they help the heralds of the gospel, and prepare for dialogue with non-Christians.' 'Dialogue' here is blatantly a euphemism for 'evangelisation'.

The tactics of the Church may have changed, but the goal remains the same. It would be paranoid, though, to suspect each and every Catholic as part of a Vatican plot to convert the world. Many, like A.M.A. Samy, would not share these views, and demonstrate through their words and actions a genuine pluralistic attitude. In the final years of his life Father Lassalle too became

216

increasingly open-minded and regretted the tone of some of his earlier writings. Yet anyone who calls him or herself a Christian somehow has to come to terms with the exclusivist and evangelical nature of the faith, as declared by the risen Jesus at the conclusion of the Gospel of Mark (16:15):

> Go into the whole world; preach the gospel to every creature. He who believes and is baptised shall be saved, but he who does not believe shall be condemned.

A resurgence of this imperative is apparent today through the Catholic and Anglican churches' common declaration of the 1990s as the 'Decade of Evangelisation'.

Many Christians today would follow Father Lassalle in admiring and even promoting the 'spiritual and moral goods' found in Zen Buddhism while subordinating the tradition to that of Christianity. This 'inclusivist position' might even allow that salvation can be found outside the Christian fold, because non-Christians are, unbeknown to themselves, mysteriously included in God's saving grace through Christ. Such an attitude has its roots in the writings of the 2nd-century apologist Justin Martyr, who believed all the truths of non-Christian religions to reflect the *Logos* of God. Even Socrates, for Justin, was a Christian. In the same vein the theologian Karl Rahner has coined the term 'anonymous Christians' to describe all Buddhists and others who are fortunate enough to meet Christian standards. The concept would be less patronizing were it applied reciprocally, but it is unlikely that Rahner considers himself an anonymous Zen Buddhist.

Pluralism, which acknowledges the independent validity of other spiritual paths, is intrinsically difficult for Christians. It has been described by a contemporary theologian as 'a monstrous shift indeed . . . a position quite new to the churches, even the liberal churches'. Yet pluralism is also problematic for Buddhists, who likewise tend either to write Christianity off as a massive delusion with a scattering of good intentions (exclusivism) or make Jesus into an honorary Bodhisattva and then co-opt his teachings into a Buddhist scheme of salvation (inclusivism). While pluralism is finding favour among some liberal Protestant thinkers, the Catholics who have contributed most towards the Christian encounter with Zen Buddhism have tended to adopt an inclusivist attitude. In addition to Father Lassalle, the Irish Jesuit William Johnston has also practised and written about Zen. He comes to a similar conclusion: 'From Zen, I can and will continue to learn many things. But I am convinced it is not the same as the Christian contemplation to which I am drawn.'

Such views have recently been given papal endorsement in a *Letter to the Bishops of the Catholic Church on some Aspects of Christian Meditation* issued on 15 October 1989 by the Congregation for the Doctrine of the Faith. This letter is a warning to the growing number of Christians drawn to Eastern forms of meditation not to fall prey to the dangers entailed in trying 'to fuse Christian meditation with that which is non-Christian'. It guarantees that consideration of the truths of Christian dogma will bring

> the wonderful discovery that all the aspirations which the prayer of other religions expresses are fulfilled in the reality of Christianity beyond all measure, without the personal self or the nature of a creature being dissolved or disappearing into the sea of the Absolute.

Until 1908, the inoffensive 'Congregation for the Doctrine of the Faith' was called the 'Holy, Catholic and Apostolic Inquisition', which makes the snowy-haired Cardinal Ratzinger, author of the letter and present head of this office, direct successor to the Grand Inquisitor of old.

There is, however, a much quieter movement within the Church working towards a closer understanding of Buddhism, that in the long term may bear the most fruit. This is the Commission for Interfaith Monastic Dialogue founded by Benedictine and Cistercian monastics in Belgium in 1978 'to make known to all monks and nuns of the order the existence of other monastic traditions, together with the spiritual values they enshrine'. Although the commission insists that it is not concerned with introducing oriental methods of meditation into Christian monasteries, it recognizes the value of encounter with other monks and nuns as a means of renewing its own contemplative traditions. Nonetheless, since the early 1970s formal *zazen* has been incorporated into the monastic routine of the Abdij Maria Toevlucht in Zundert, Holland. In Würtzburg, Germany, the Benedictine Williges Jäger has converted part of a monastery into a *zendo*, where regular, well-attended *sesshins* are held. And in 1979 a *zendo* was built at the Franciscan monastery in Dietfurt in southern Germany.

Such dialogue between people fully committed in every aspect of their existence to their religious faith operates at the deeper level of lived spiritual experience rather than that of doctrinal comparison. This allows the participants to open to a greater interpersonal trust and humility and to explore not only those elements on which they converge, but also those on which they diverge.

The realization of these ideals has been achieved through a series of 'Spiritual Exchanges' in which Christian and Buddhist monks have spent time living in each others' monasteries. Four such exchanges have taken place since 1978, the first three with Japanese Zen monks, the fourth with Tibetan Buddhist monks. Reflecting on the experience of staying in a Japanese Zen monastery in 1983, a Benedictine monk recalled:

The monastic ideal is a universal archetype. In all great religions we find men and women who seek to realise the unity of their persons and to reach the original simplicity . . . . As we bade farewell, we realised that we had taken part in a rediscovering of separated brethren. How is it that we ignored one another for so long?

Through such experiences of hospitality there emerges the possibility of a religion 'breaking through its particularity' (Tillich) and the beginnings of genuine pluralism.

One of the reasons Zen has been prone to inclusion within a Christian scheme of salvation is because of a tendency to distance itself from Buddhism. This could likewise be the fate of any tradition that reductively identifies itself with a form of meditation that somehow encapsulates its 'essence'. Despite the intention to make their traditions more accessible, those who promote either *vipassana* or *dzogchen*, for example, as forms of meditation that constitute the heart of Theravada or Nyingma Buddhism respectively, could unwittingly be taking the first steps on the path that has led Zen into its current predicament. Perhaps an even greater danger to the integrity of these traditions would be their appropriation as forms of psychotherapy. One only has to look at what has happened to 'Yoga', once an integral part of a spiritual tradition now often reduced to little more than a system of keep-fit.

The Buddha saw meditation as emerging out of a commitment both to a particular world-view and a set of corresponding ethical values. This model, which finds its clearest expression in the structure of the Noble Eightfold Path, is clearly at odds with the notion of Zen as a value-free experience interpreted according to one's religious or philosophic preference. Axiomatic to the Buddha's Dharma is the understanding that no matter how ineffable an experience enlightenment may be, it arises from a framework of thought and action with which it is profoundly interconnected. This perspective was shared by the theologian Rudolf Otto who, in 1925, wrote in the preface to the first German book on Zen Buddhism:

> No mysticism is merely a heavenly vault. Rather it rests on a foundation which it denies as far as it can, but from which it continuously receives its peculiar character, never identical with forms of mysticism developed elsewhere.

Among Rinzai Zen teachers in Europe today, Ven Myokyo-ni (Dr Irmgard Schloegl) of the Zen Centre in London makes a point of proclaiming the identity of Zen with Buddhism. 'The Zen Way', she writes unequivocally in the opening sentence of one of her books, 'is a Buddhist Way'.

She emphasizes the need for a grounding in a basic knowledge of the Buddhist world-view as an indispensable condition for Zen training. Her group also receives guidance from Soko Morinaga Roshi, a Rinzai Master from Daishu-in, Kyoto, who visits London regularly and ordained Myokyo-ni as a nun in 1984.

The Rinzai Zen tradition has failed to take root in the West as extensively as the Soto tradition, mirroring perhaps the historical eclipse of Rinzai by Soto in Japan itself. In spite of their strong Rinzai flavour, the teachers in the Harada-Yasutani line officially belong to the Soto school. There are only a scattering of small Rinzai groups throughout Europe. In Germany, for example, one finds the Berlin-based Mumon-kai Zen Centre of Dr Klaus Zernickow (Sotetsu Yuzen Sensei) with eight affiliated centres, and the Hakuin Zen Gemeinschaft in Munich, under the direction of Hozumi Gensho Roshi. Ven. Gesshin Myoko Prabhasadharma

Roshi, a German-born woman who holds both Japanese and Vietnamese Rinzai Zen lineages, likewise conducts *sesshins* in Germany and Holland.

The lesser-known Korean Zen tradition, however, is a form of Rinzai, although closer in approach to that of Ta-hui than of Hakuin, and has been spread in recent years largely by the Korean teacher Seung Sahn Sunim. Seung Sahn was born in North Korea in 1927 and received transmission in 1950. As an army-chaplain he rose to the rank of captain during the Korean war, after which he served as an abbot of a temple in Seoul. From 1962 he worked in Japan and Hong Kong and in 1971 departed for America. In 1983 he founded his own Kwan Um Zen School, whose style is consciously adapted to the needs of Westerners. From its base in America, the School has flourished primarily in Eastern Europe, with centres now in Warsaw, Budapest, Prague, Kaunus (Lithuania), Riga (Latvia), Tallin (Estonia), Kiev and Uljanovsk (Russia). On 11 October 1992, Seung Sahn gave transmission to Mu Deung Sunim (now Su Bong Soen Sa), an American of Chinese and Korean extraction.

In contrast to Seung Sahn's modified style of teaching, a more traditional Korean approach was taught by the late Kusan Sunim, who from 1975 to 1983 trained a small number of European monks and nuns in Songgwang Monastery in South Korea and, towards the end of his life, taught briefly in Denmark and Switzerland.

The Chinese Ch'an tradition is also finding its way into Europe through retreats given by Master Sheng-yen from the Institutes of Chung Hwa Buddhist Culture in Taipei and New York. These have been organized by the ethologist Dr John Crook as part of an on-going programme of Zen training based in Bristol and the Welsh hills.

The Jesuit encounter with Buddhism during the 16th and 17th centuries marked, in historical terms, the second and final attempt of a Christian-dominated Europe to come to terms with the Dharma based on an attitude of self-righteous rejection. While this attitude continues to prevail even today among some Christians, it has been largely supplanted over the last two hundred years by a secular approach rooted in the scientific and humanist ideas of the 18th-century Enlightenment. The next phase in Europe's attempt to understand Buddhism would be guided by rational and scientific knowledge, on the one hand, and romantic fantasy, on the other.

FOUR

REASON
AND
ROMANCE

14

EUGENE BURNOUF:
THE CONSTRUCTION
OF BUDDHISM

'. . . those who really know first consider the welfare of
sentient beings and then explain these things.' The foolish do
not understand this nor do they understand the characteristics of phenomena. The characteristics of all phenomena are
perfectly explained to be transparent . . .

Sutra on the Adherence to the Great Mantra

Peter the Great of Russia badly needed to believe that the
recently acquired territories of Siberia contained large
quantities of gold. In 1720 he dispatched Ivan Licharov to
check out rumours of a ruined city in Dzungaria. Near the source
of the river Irtych, Licharov found the ruins not of a fabulously
wealthy city, but of the Buddhist temple of Ablaikit, destroyed in
fighting between local Kalmyk Mongol warlords in 1671. Instead
of gold he brought back only a handful of small bronze statues
and a number of scattered loose-leaf pages in Tibetan.

The pages in this hitherto unknown script aroused the curiosity
of the Tsar. No one in St Petersburg, not even the imperial
librarian, could understand them. So in February 1721, a page was
dispatched to the German scholar J.B. Menke in Lipsial, who,
equally baffled, published a description of it the following year
in his *Acta eruditorum*. Still in the dark, in June 1722 Peter
forwarded the page to Abbé Bignon, who had been librarian to
King Louis XIV in Paris. Four years earlier Bignon had written

to the Jesuit missions in Asia to seek out oriental manuscripts for the Académie des Inscriptions. The page was identified as Tibetan and Etienne Fourmont, then absorbed in the tortuous task of cataloguing the academy's five thousand Chinese texts, was given the task of translating it. With the help of a small Tibetan–Latin dictionary compiled by Domenico da Fano, head of the Capuchin mission in Lhasa at the time of Desideri, Fourmont produced a Latin version of one side of the page, which in February 1724 was dispatched to Peter the Great.

The great Tsar wrote a letter of thanks to the *abbé* and was sufficiently impressed to order the collection of more such texts. Although Peter died the following year, and with him the imperial impetus for such knowledge, Russian scholars continued to be fascinated by this page of Tibetan. Ten years later a certain Müller took the page back to Siberia where a lama translated it for him into Mongolian. On his return to St Petersburg, Müller had this translated into Russian, on the basis of which he produced another Latin version in 1747. Twenty years later it was translated again, this time by an Augustine called Antoine-Augustin Giorgi in his *Alphabetum Tibetanum*: a voluminous compendium of facts, fables and curios about Tibet.

At the beginning of the 19th century the French sinologist Abel Rémusat studied these early efforts to decipher the text. 'I do not know', he remarked, 'how one can translate or correct a text that one is not even capable of reading. There is nothing to admire in all this; interpreters, commentators, champions and critics were all nearly equally unqualified — not just to understand a particular line but even to spell out a syllable of the passage on which they were commenting.' Not only did the translations bear little resemblance to the original page, they did not even make sense.

As it turned out, the Tibetan page was a fragment of a relatively obscure text, translated from a lost Sanskrit original, called the *Sutra on the Adherence to the Great Mantra*, a discourse by the Buddha

Vairocana on the use of mantras to reach enlightenment. The extract quoted at the head of this chapter is the opening line of the dislocated page.

This enigmatic episode encapsulates those seeds that would bear fruit, a little more than a century later, in Europe's full-fledged 'discovery' of Buddhism. In the colossal figure of Peter the Great stirred the essential forces of colonial domination: a volatile mix of expansiveness and ruthlessness, a passion for science and technology, unshakable conviction in the superiority of one's own beliefs yet an urgent need to know the ways of other people. While in Bignon, Fourmont, Giorgi and Rémusat we witness the beginnings of the crucially important task of collecting, cataloguing and deciphering texts — significantly in Paris, which was to become the intellectual centre of European orientalism.

The episode highlights the fragmentary nature of Europe's knowledge of Buddhism at the time. The very concept of 'Buddhism' did not yet exist. Although educated Europeans, mainly Jesuit missionaries, were now settled in Asian countries and sending back regular reports of Buddhist beliefs, they lacked a unifying idea to organize their scattered pieces of information into a coherent whole. While the diversity of non-Christian traditions was recognized, such differences that defined them were overshadowed by the error that united them.

Yet as early as 1664 the German Jesuit Heinrich Roth had composed a Sanskrit grammar, which he sent to his colleague Athanasius Kircher. But Kircher was preoccupied with deciphering Chinese and dismissed Sanskrit as 'absolutely barbarous' with no connection to either European languages or the 'primitive language' of Hebrew. Two years later, in a Latin biography of Francis Xavier, another Jesuit, Bartoli, wrote that it is in any case certain that Xaca (i.e. Shakya[muni]) was one of the most famous gymnosophists of India. His father was a king in the Gangetic basin and his surname 'Budda' means a wise or lettered person. He lived about a thousand years before Christ.

Such observations continued to trickle into Europe. In 1691 Simon de la Loubère, an envoy of Louis XIV, published his *Description du royaume de Siam*, in which he translated the life of Devadatta and some sections from the monastic rule. He was also the first European to note the existence of Pali and its resemblance to Sanskrit. Half a century later, the Jesuit Father Pons, writing from south India on 23 November 1740, observed that

the *bauddhistes*, among whom the view of metempsychosis has been universally accepted, are accused [by the *brahmans*] of atheism, and only regard the senses as principles of knowledge. Bouddha is the *foto* revered by the people of China, and the *bauddhistes* belong to the sects of the bonzes and lamas.

He even came up with a name for this religion: *bauddhamatham*, from Sanskrit, another grammar of which he had sent to Paris two years earlier. Then in 1767 Pons' colleague Father Couerdoux became the first European to recognize 'that Sanskrit belonged to the same family as the languages of Europe' — although this had already been intuited fifty years earlier by the philosopher Leibnitz.

And we only have to recall the writings of Ippolito Desideri languishing undiscovered during this entire period. These keys, which together could have unlocked the door to Buddhism, remained apart from each other. The door was to stay firmly closed until the middle of the 19th century.

Throughout the course of the 18th century three interconnected factors were gestating that would help give birth to what we know as 'Buddhism'. These were the emergence of the rationalist Enlightenment, the decline of religious authority and the consolidation of colonialism.

The rationalism of the Enlightenment sought to understand and order human affairs according to the principles of reason outlined by Descartes. Human reason rather than divine revelation became the primary authority for establishing truth and making moral and political choices. Although some of its most vociferous spokesmen, like Voltaire, were rabidly anti-clerical, its greatest contribution to religious thought and practice was its emphasis on tolerance. For once reason replaced revelation, then one set of beliefs could no longer be judged as *a priori* superior or inferior to another. Instead of relying on her dogmas, the Church had to justify herself in the higher court of reason. This detached rationality created the environment in which religions, including non-Christian traditions, could become objects of reasoned analysis and study.

This did not happen overnight. Despite the glorification of reason and science, Europe remained Christian in outlook. Nonetheless, an inordinate amount of rationalist hostility was directed at the Jesuits, in whose schools, ironically, many of the proponents of the Enlightenment, such as Descartes, had received their humanist and scientific education. Between 1759 and 1768 the Society of Jesus was expelled from Spain and Portugal and their overseas possessions, thereby cutting off the primary source of first-hand information about Buddhism. The Jesuits were subsequently outlawed in France and in 1773 Pope Clement XIV dissolved the Society by a decree that remained in effect until 1814.

In crushing the Jesuits, the advocates of rationalism and their allies succeeded in suppressing the most prominent symbol of Christian power and authority in Europe.

The 18th century was also one of unprecedented global expansion, with the British supplanting the Spanish and Portuguese as the pre-eminent nation of colonialists. In 1783 Sir William Jones, a poet, polyglot and renowned translator of Persian, appointed as a judge in the newly established British imperial regime in Bengal, arrived in Calcutta. In the figure of Jones rationalism and colonialism combined in just the right measure to propel oriental studies suddenly forward.

Within a few months of setting foot on Indian soil, Jones founded the Asiatick Society of Bengal, whose aim was to be the rational and systematic study of Asia. Its members were not academics but enthusiastic amateurs, most of whom were civil servants. Jones himself set out to learn Sanskrit in order to help him understand the traditional legal system of India. In November of the same year Charles Wilkins, under the auspices of the Society, published the *Bhagavad Gita*, the first Sanskrit text to appear in English. On 2 February 1786, in his address to mark the third anniversary of the Society, Jones declared that Sanskrit bore a stronger affinity to Latin and Greek,

> both in the roots of the verbs and in the forms of the grammar, than could possibly have been produced by accident; so strong, indeed, that no philologer could examine them all three, without believing them to have sprung from some common source.

Henceforth Europe was to receive a steady flow of translated Indian texts, which were to have a profound impact in challenging the West's sense of its own uniqueness.

Yet Jones and his colleagues remained ignorant of Buddhism.

Except in a few pockets in the Himalayas, for several centuries Buddhism had ceased to exist on the subcontinent. What knowledge remained was buried in the writings of Hinduism where it was dismissed as a nihilist aberration. With no Buddhists to consult, no Sanskrit Buddhist texts to read, and in a climate of brahmanical anti-Buddhist prejudice, these pioneers of Indian studies gave little attention to the obscure figure they knew as Boudh. Jones believed that Buddha was the teutonic god Wotan or Odin. The clan name 'Shakya' reminded him of that of the ancient Egyptian king Shishac. In the statues of the Buddha he noted strikingly Ethiopic features. The 'mild heresy of the ancient *Bauddhas*', he concluded, must have been imported to India from north Africa.

While the Royal Asiatic Society, as it became, was deciphering Sanskrit texts, the British regime in India was carefully mapping the land-mass of the subcontinent. Acquisition of precise geographic knowledge of its territories was crucial to Britain's sense of 'possessing' them. Geographic knowledge underlay and symbolized the other forms of knowledge which constituted Britain's dominance over India. As an instance of Francis Bacon's maxim 'knowledge is power', on 27 September 1909, the former Viceroy Lord Curzon declared to the House of Lords that

> our familiarity, not merely with the languages of the people of the East but with their customs, their feelings, their traditions, their history and religion, our capacity to understand what may be called the genius of the East, is the sole basis upon which we are likely to be able to maintain in the future the position we have won.

'Orientalism', the generic term for this kind of knowledge, has been defined by Edward Said as a 'system of knowledge about the Orient, an accepted grid for filtering through the Orient into Western consciousness'. Just as the surveyors painstakingly mapped out the physical lands, so the orientalists mapped out the inner geographies of the minds of the people who lived in those lands. In this way the colonial powers put to use the rational and scientific skills of the Enlightenment to enforce their superiority over the subject races.

This opposition between Europe and the Orient finds its roots in ancient Greece. Two Athenian plays, the *Persians* of Aeschylus and the *Bacchae* of Euripedes, the former dramatizing the victory of Greece over Persia and the latter centred around the orientalized figure of Dionysos, both concretize this division. The Orient, perceived as threatening and subversive, is defeated by the forces of superior power, reason and civilization. This hostile Greek attitude was inherited by the Romans. During the Christian Middle Ages the opposition was further stressed both by the Crusades and the Mongol invasions. The Oriental was now not merely a barbarian but an idolator and a heathen, one who was not simply ignorant of the truth but who corrupted and denied it.

In the European imagination Asia came to stand for something both unknown and distant yet also to be feared. As the colonizing powers came to identify themselves with order, reason and power, so the colonized East became perceived as chaotic, irrational and weak. In psychological terms, the East became a cipher for the Western unconscious, the repository of all that is dark, unacknowledged, feminine, sensual, repressed and liable to eruption. 'I content myself with noting', wrote another Imperialist, Lord Cromer, 'the fact that somehow or other the Oriental generally acts, speaks and thinks in a manner exactly opposite to the European.' Dionysos, the Greek god of frenzy who, according to mythology, had emigrated to India, now had

234

to be subjected to the Apollonian principles of reason that underpinned colonial rule.

Orientalism was and is not merely an obscure academic discipline. It is the means by which the West, for its own ends, constructs the East. The function of the East thus becomes that of helping the West define its own self-image. The task of the orientalist is to create a coherent set of concepts by which the East can be made familiar and thereby unthreatening to Western interests. One of these concepts, that we still use unthinkingly today, is 'Buddhism', a term for which there is no equivalent in Asia.

Two people who incarnated these attitudes were the Hungarian Alexander Csoma de Körös and the Englishman Brian Houghton Hodgson, both of whom worked at the task of collecting, cataloguing and analysing the texts which were to become the basis for Europe's construction of the concept 'Buddhism'.

Alexander Csoma de Körös was born in Transylvania on 4 April 1784. From a young age he became obsessed with a longing to discover the origins of the Hungarian people, which he believed to lie somewhere in Asia. On 1 November 1819 he left Transylvania and travelled eastward, arriving at Leh in Ladakh on 9 June 1822. Prevented by wars, travel prohibitions and lack of money from proceeding to his goal of Yarkand in Turkestan, Csoma was forced to abandon his journey. At this point he met William Moorcroft, an agent of the East India Company intent on securing British influence in Central Asia as a means of thwarting the southward advance of Imperial Russia. Turning Csoma's obsession to Britain's advantage, Moorcroft convinced the Hungarian that in the libraries of Lhasa he would find texts containing crucial information about the origins of his people.

235

Csoma spent the next nine years studying Tibetan at monasteries in Ladakh and Zanskar. Most of his time was spent poring over the Buddhist canon, meticulously collating materials for a Tibetan grammar and a Tibetan-English dictionary.

A certain Dr Gerard, who met Csoma in Zanskar in 1828, described him as 'like one of the sages of antiquity',

> living in the most frugal manner, and taking no interest in any object around him, except his literary avocations . . . . He has read through 44 volumes of one of the Tibetan works and he finds unceasing interest in their contents. He seems highly pleased with the prospects of unfolding to the world those vast mines of literary riches.

Gerard further describes him as 'scrupulously tenacious of correctness in everything relating to and said of him . . . frequently disconsolate as if he thought himself forlorn and neglected . . . full of vivacity, but this is often interrupted by the anxiety most natural to him, and he lapses into gloom without a visible cause'. While almost neurotically obliged to the British for their meagre support, he harboured the longing to make a lasting impression on the world which he felt disdained him. 'Mr Csoma has no selfish gratification', recalled Dr Gerard; 'the tribute of honest fame is his only ambition.'

To an extent, Csoma's wishes were fulfilled. In April 1831, he arrived in Calcutta to oversee the publication of the grammar and dictionary, which the Asiatic Society had managed to fund with government money on the grounds that it was a 'matter [of] national interest'. Six hundred copies of the texts were printed, establishing Csoma's reputation as the foremost expert on Tibetan of his time. He remained in Calcutta for eleven years, working as librarian for the Asiatic Society, responsible for cataloguing the Tibetan texts that arrived from his soul-brother in Nepal, Brian

Hodgson. In March 1842, at the age of fifty-eight, he left again on his travels, in pursuit of his childhood dream of finding the origin of his people. His first destination was Lhasa, where he hoped to delve into the riches of the monastic libraries. But he succumbed to fever in the Himalayan foothills and died on 11 April.

Despite the aura of romance surrounding Csoma de Körös, his twenty years of work for the British government point to his endorsement of the link between scientific knowledge and colonial power. Csoma's dictionary and grammar served as the philological equivalents of maps. Although he spent years in Buddhist monasteries and affirmed that 'the Tibetan faith . . . approaches nearer to the Christian religion than that of any Asiatic nation whatever', he remained aloof from the Dharma. He tended to dismiss much of the writings in Tibetan as 'wild metaphysical speculations', while affirming that they contained material of practical use, through acquaintance with which Europeans 'will excuse them in some degree for the extravagance in the dogmatical part of their religion'.

Yet within a century of his death, on 22 February 1933, Csoma was officially canonized as a Bodhisattva in the grand hall of the Taisho University in Tokyo and a statue of him in meditation posture, donated by the Hungarian Oriental Society, installed in the Japanese Imperial Museum. It seems that these were political gestures aimed at improving relations between Hungary and Japan rather than a joint celebration of the first Hungarian Buddhist. They would be curious accolades indeed for one who turned his linguistic skills to the translation of the Christian Liturgy, Psalms and Prayer-book into Tibetan as his contribution to the missionary endeavour.

What Csoma did for the study of Buddhism from Tibetan, Brian Houghton Hodgson did for its study from Sanskrit. Hodgson arrived in Calcutta in 1818 at the age of eighteen to serve as an administrator. In addition to his duties he also read for honours in Sanskrit. But he succumbed to the climate and was forced to take up a hill-appointment. His ambitions thwarted, in 1824 he settled in Kathmandu.

'I had been for several years a traveller in the Himalayas', he recalled later, 'before I could get rid of that tyranny of the senses which so strongly impresses all beholders of this stupendous scenery with the conviction that the mighty maze is quite without a plan'. Hodgson made it his life-long ambition to impose order on this chaos. He began by indulging his passion for collecting things: books, specimens, curios — anything that would help formulate a coherent plan of the culture around him. This, wrote his admiring biographer towards the end of the century, was in order to form 'part of a systematic scheme for bringing Nepal within the knowledge of the British Government'. Soon after his arrival in Kathmandu, Hodgson was drawn towards Buddhism via the Sanskrit and Tibetan texts he began to accumulate. Although Hodgson read these texts and wrote a series of essays outlining their doctrines, Buddhist ideas were of no more significance to him than a rare species of Himalayan insect. The aim of his studies was 'to seize and render intelligible the *leading* and *least* absurd of the opinions and practices of these religionists'. He insisted that he had 'no purpose to meddle with the interminable sheer absurdities of the Bauddha religion or philosophy'. Hodgson's contribution to Buddhist studies was not his scholarship; his importance lies in having provided the scholarly community with hitherto unknown Buddhist texts.

Ironically, the texts Hodgson sent to his Imperial masters in Calcutta, London and Oxford were stacked away on library shelves and ignored. It was only in Paris, where a collection of twenty-four Sanskrit volumes and manuscript copies of sixty-four others arrived from Hodgson in 1837, that the significance of his discoveries was realized by the man best equipped to make sense of them: the brilliant French philologist Eugène Burnouf.

Burnouf was born on 8 April 1801. His father was a renowned classicist who later helped teach him Sanskrit. After excelling at school and university, the young Burnouf devoted himself to furthering his knowledge of Sanskrit under the guidance of Léonard de Chézy. De Chézy had taught himself the language from the grammar compiled by Father Pons and became the holder of the first academic chair of Sanskrit in Europe, founded in 1814 at the Collège de France in Paris. After studying with him for two years, Burnouf and his colleague Christian Lassen published, in 1826, what they believed to be the first scholarly study of Pali. (Unbeknown to them, Benjamin Clough, a Wesleyan missionary, had published one in Colombo in 1824.) Six years later Burnouf succeeded de Chézy in the chair of Sanskrit.

His mastery of both Sanskrit and Pali, combined with an exacting philological intellect, made Burnouf the ideal person to construct from this fresh field of unexamined documents an intelligible scheme of ideas which would henceforth be the prototype of the European concept of Buddhism. Burnouf was motivated by the same kind of scientific enthusiasm and expectation that we find today among physicists searching for the ultimate constituents of matter or the origins of the universe. At the conclusion of his inaugural lecture at the Collège de France in 1833, he declared:

> We should not close our eyes to the most brilliant light that may ever have come from the Orient, and we shall attempt to comprehend the grand spectacle offered to our gaze . . . . It is more than India, gentlemen, it is a page from the origins

of the world, of the primitive history of the human spirit,
that we shall try to decipher together.

For the British such aspirations would have been unlikely to occur.
Knowledge of Sanskrit and Buddhism was of use to them only
insofar that it strengthened their knowledge of the subcontinent
over which they ruled. The French, having been thwarted in their
colonial ambitions over India, were free to aspire to nobler
achievements than the mere possession of territory.

Burnouf recognized that Hodgson's Sanskrit texts were the
originals from which the Chinese, Tibetans and Mongols had
made their translations, and his knowledge of Pali led him to
conclude that the Ceylonese texts in that language provided an
equally authoritative source. Soon after receiving Hodgson's
books, a complete edition of the Tibetan *Kangyur* (probably
collected by Hodgson and catalogued by Csoma) reached Paris.
Armed in addition with Csoma's grammar and dictionary,
Burnouf now possessed the materials from which he could
establish the Indian origins of Buddhism and, he hoped, settle the
issues of the Buddha's historicity and the development of
Buddhist doctrine.

Within weeks of receiving Hodgson's texts, he set to work on
translating the *Lotus Sutra*. But he soon realized that without a
comprehensive introduction, the text would make little sense even
to an academic audience. To this end he produced, in 1844, his
mammoth *L'Introduction à l'histoire du buddhisme indien*. In nearly six
hundred densely packed pages he offered Europe the first detailed
scientific survey of Indian Buddhist history, doctrines and texts.
The sheer scope of Burnouf's book, relying entirely on unknown
writings in Sanskrit and Tibetan, is awesome. Burnouf himself
was fully aware of the difficulties involved, describing the field
into which he entered as 'a completely new subject, with
innumerable schools, an immense metaphysical apparatus, an

endless mythology; everywhere disorder and a hopeless vagueness on questions of place and time'. He was the first to succeed in imposing rational order on this pervasive disorder, the basic form of which is upheld by scholars to this day.

Burnouf intended to complete this 'introduction' with two further studies, first an analogous survey of the Pali Canon, and second a comparison between the Pali and Sanskrit traditions. But his plan was prevented from achieving completion by his premature death at the age of fifty-one on 28 May 1852. His translation of the *Lotus Sutra* was published in October of the same year, making it the first full-length translation of a Buddhist sutra from Sanskrit into a European language. (The first sutra was a French translation of the *Diamond Sutra* by the Russian Isaak Jakob Schmidt from Tibetan that appeared in St Petersburg in 1837.)

In his writings, Burnouf rarely betrays his own feelings about Buddhism and refuses to speculate on its philosophic, religious and moral implications. One of the few glimpses we have of the man comes from the diary of the Sanskritist Max Müller, who recounts a visit he made to Burnouf in 1845. Having described him as 'spiritual, amiable and thoroughly French', he recalls how he was received 'in the most friendly way, [we] talked a great deal, and all that he said was valuable . . . "I am a Brahman, a Buddhist, a Zoroastrian; I hate the Jesuits" — that is the sort of man [he is]'.

Müller's impression has to be contrasted with the devout recollections of Burnouf's professional persona. Ernest Renan, a student of Burnouf who would later achieve fame through his historical accounts of the life of Jesus, addressing his teacher in 1849, recalled how 'in listening to your lectures, I have encountered the realization of that which previously I had only dreamt of: science becoming philosophy, and the highest results coming from the most scrupulous analysis of details'. In an obituary, another student, Jules Barthélemy-Saint-Hilaire, commented how 'among all the philologists of our time who have been struck down by death, there is perhaps no one that posterity will hold in greater esteem than him', a prophetic remark endorsed many decades later by the great French orientalist Sylvain Lévi: 'if philology has . . . its own peculiar form of genius, then it is in Burnouf that one should come to recognize and study it'.

Burnouf's greatest achievement was the construction of Buddhism as an object of European scientific knowledge. Burnouf regarded Hodgson's texts as providing Buddhist studies with 'their true and most solid base'. Despite their prejudices, the Jesuits at least recognized Buddhism to be a vital aspect of the cultures in which it was practised. Now the philologists had pinned down the truth about Buddhism on the hard evidence of its own writings. To know about Buddhism there was no longer any need to refer to its actual manifestations in the East. Indeed, when compared to these new revelations of scientific research, such manifestations were invariably discovered to be corrupt and inadequate reflections of the real thing.

In 1860 an article appeared in the French journal *Le Correspondant* by Abbé Auguste Deschamps who remarked:

> One has to admire with what speed, through its first contact with the spirit of investigation that characterises our age, Buddhism has emerged from its profound obscurity and its long silence.

The impact of Eugène Burnouf's work was not limited to orientalists but was felt throughout European and American society. It influenced an audience as diverse as the historian Michelet, the composer Wagner and the American transcendentalist Thoreau, spawning in its wake a flood of scholarly and popular books on the subject. Once Burnouf had drawn the outline, a mass of philologists, linguists, writers and poets rushed to fill in the details.

It is hard from our current perspective to appreciate the suddenness with which Buddhism first appeared in Europe. In 1835, two years before Hodgson's texts arrived in Paris, Cardinal Wiseman gave a series of lectures in Rome on the relation between science and religion. Although he treated Brahmanism and the philosophy of Lao-tzu, he failed even to mention Buddhism. Yet less than twenty years later, in November 1853, the French writer Felix Nève was able to describe Buddhism as 'the only moral adversary that Western civilisation will find in the Orient'.

This does not mean that Buddhism was entirely unknown until Burnouf. From the beginning of the 19th century Europe became aware of the extraordinary extent to which the teachings of the Buddha had spread through Asia, and periodically books appeared on the subject. But these were informed by speculation, romantic fantasy, Hindu prejudices and fads such as comparative mythology rather than knowledge of either Asian Buddhist practices or texts. This prompted Burnouf to comment in his *L'Introduction* how 'for certain people all questions relative to Buddhism have already been decided even though they have not even read a single line of the books I will be analysing here, indeed have not even suspected their existence'.

The appearance of Buddhism came at a time of tremendous cultural and political turmoil in Europe. Industrialization was marching forward at a seemingly unstoppable pace, creating the conditions for the revolutions that burst on to the streets in 1848 — the year of Marx's *Communist Manifesto*. Religious belief was under greater threat than ever from science, a landmark being the publication of Darwin's *On the Origin of Species* in 1859. 'The appearance of this little known religion on the terrain of science', wrote a nervous Abbé Paul de Broglie in 1886, 'has produced a profound surprise. It seems to destroy the entire basis of Christian apologetics, and even some of the proofs for the existence of God.' Until the 1840s the Buddha was vaguely conceived of as a mythic god in the Indian pantheon. Then, almost overnight, he was revealed as an historical figure, comparable in an alarming number of respects to Jesus. In addition to the crisis of home-grown unbelief surging all around it, the Church now had to contend with the emergence of a fully fledged rival from Asia.

No matter how noble a figure the Buddha appeared to be (as, for example, in the hugely popular portrayal by Sir Edwin Arnold in his poem *The Light of Asia*, published in 1879), the doctrines of Buddhism were perceived as disturbingly nihilistic. This perception, already current among the early missionaries, was reinforced by the Brahmanic views adopted by the first orientalists, further strengthened by the German philosopher Schopenhauer, and confirmed by Burnouf himself. The main difficulty lay in the concept of Nirvana, the meaning of which was to exercise the minds of numerous scholars and interpreters well into the 20th century — and arguably is yet to be settled. For theistic and positivist Europe, it was extremely puzzling why a religion which in other respects was so admirable should have as its *summum bonum* such an apparently negative aim.

Such distrust readily turned into the kind of loathing evident in the writings of two of the leading authorities to introduce Buddhism to the wider public: R. Spence Hardy and Jules Barthèlemy-Saint-Hilaire. Spence Hardy, a missionary in Ceylon who published, in 1853, *A Manual of Buddhism: In Its Modern Development*, was no advocate of Buddhism. In 1841 he had expressed the view that it was 'the bounden duty of the government of the country, from its possession of the Truth, to discountenance the system [Buddhism] by every legitimate means'. In the manner of a latter-day crusader, he saw the confrontation between Buddhism and Christianity as a 'prolonged and severe' contest which 'must end in the total discomfiture of those who have risen against the Lord and his Christ'.

In 1866 Barthèlemy-Saint-Hilaire published one of the most popular works on Buddhism, *Le Bouddha et sa religion*, with the intent of exposing 'this hideous system ... this narrow materialism ... worthy of disdain more than study'. Fourteen years later, in a letter to Abbé Deschamps, he concluded that 'Buddhism has nothing in common with Christianity, which stands above it just as the European societies stand above the societies of Asia.'

The scholars, meanwhile, were busy on a number of fronts. The primary task was to catalogue, edit and publish the canonical texts, thereby making them available for translation and interpretation. Considerable work was done in separating the historical facts of Gautama's life from mythical accretions, a task that mirrored a similar concern of the times regarding the life of Jesus. And much scholarly energy was taken up with a pervasive preoccupation of the 19th century: the quest for origins. This resulted by the 1870s in the Pali texts being widely accepted as earlier than the Sanskrit writings, which led to the assumption that they were therefore truer and more essential. Thus we observe a clear historic progression in the construction of Buddhism, working backwards, as it were, from the first missionary encounters with Buddhist monks, followed by the discovery of Sanskrit texts in Nepal, concluding with the recognition of the Pali canon as the most authoritative source — which neatly supported the belief that the later a particular manifestation of Buddhism was, the more corrupt it was liable to be.

The task of the European philological study of Buddhism was (and is) to make known in objective, scientific terms the content and meaning of this vast range of catalogued texts. In the late 19th and early 20th centuries a new generation of prodigious intellects set to work in translating, annotating and explicating many of the key works in Sanskrit, Pali, Tibetan and Chinese. The outstanding figures in this enterprise were T.W. and Caroline Rhys Davids, founders of the Pali Text Society in London; the French scholars Sylvain Lévi, Louis de la Vallée Poussin, Paul Demiéville and Msgr Etienne Lamotte; the Germans Erich Frauwallner and Edward Conze; the Russian Fyodor Stcherbatsky and the Italian Giuseppe Tucci.

Many scholars travelled to Asia to search through the libraries of remote Tibetan monasteries, explore deserted cave temples on the edge of the Gobi desert and tunnel underground to excavate the sites of former Buddhist centres in the Swat Valley and Afghanistan. Between 1900 and 1914 three British, four German, one French and three Russian expeditions set out to Central Asia, returning not merely with unknown texts in Sanskrit, Tibetan and Chinese, but also in the long lost languages of the vanished Buddhist cultures of Kuchea, Khotan and Sogdia. An entire sealed library of ancient Buddhist texts was discovered in Tun Huang in north-west China and its contents brought back to Europe to be deposited in the museums of London, Paris and St Petersburg. Likewise, numerous statues in metal and stone of Buddhas and Bodhisattvas, whole and in part, were acquired, great slabs of carved stone friezes were spirited away from disused monasteries, and frescos were peeled from the walls of temples. These raw materials for the rational construction of Buddhism were numbered, classified, documented, and exhibited in glass cabinets in humidity-controlled rooms.

Despite cutbacks, most major universities in Europe today have departments where Buddhist studies can be pursued. The towering figures of the earlier part of the century may no longer be alive, but their groundbreaking work is still being further corrected and refined. The present generation of European scholars find themselves drawn to finer and finer areas of specialization, digging out from the mass of texts minor works and fragments that have yet to be critically edited and analysed, tackling unresolved issues of interpretation, and reconstructing tiny periods of confused historical detail. Scholarly papers abound with titles such as:

The Relativity of the Concept of Orthodoxy in Chinese Buddhism: Chih-sheng's Indictment of Shih-li and the Proscription of the Dharma Mirror Sutra.
An Eleventh Century Buddhist Logic of 'Exists:' Ratnakirti's Ksanabhangasiddhih Vyatirekatmika.
Purport, Implicature, and Presupposition: Sanskrit abhipraya *and Tibetan* dgongs pa/dgongs gzhi *as Hermeneutical Concepts.*

This model of knowing Buddhism has established itself not only in Europe and America but has spread to Asian Buddhist countries as well. Much of the leading work in Buddhist scholarship is now done by Japanese philologists in Japanese universities — some of which are formally affiliated to traditional Buddhist orders. As part of their vocational training, novice monks and priests from Sri Lanka, Thailand, Korea and Japan today study Buddhism in Western-style university departments, train in textual criticism, and write Ph.D.s on specialist topics, their doctrinal understanding assessed by the standards of European scientific rationalism.

❧

It is a truism to speak of the globalization of European culture and civilization. Yet the seeds for this process were largely sown and cultivated by contemporaries of the 19th-century scholars who discovered Buddhism. While Csoma and Hodgson were painstakingly collecting their materials in Ladakh and Nepal, Hegel was declaring the aim of philosophy to be the acquisition of knowledge by means of a '*definite methodical procedure*, encompassing and ordering *detail!*' His system of intellectual engineering, combined with his doctrine of the irresistible historical advance of the 'world-spirit', influenced, among others, Karl Marx, whose ideas were to serve in the 20th century the single most devastating blow to Buddhism in Asia.

In *The Essence of Christianity* (published three years before Burnouf's *L'Introduction*) Ludwig Feuerbach argued that religious belief was merely a projection of unfulfilled human aspirations, idealizing in God the very attributes which humankind longed to achieve. This psychological interpretation of theism had a profound effect on Marx, who incorporated Feuerbach's views on religion into his own philosophy. But Marx criticized Feuerbach for failing to see that the human essence into which he dissolved the religious world was not 'an abstraction . . . in each individual', but 'the ensemble of social relations'. His critique culminated in the last of his famous *Theses on Feuerbach*: 'the philosophers have only *interpreted* the world in various ways; the point, however, is to *change* it.'

The Communist revolutions which engulfed Asia in the course of this present century succeeded in imposing a European quasi-religious ideology on those very countries where the Jesuits had so singularly failed to implant Christianity. Buddhism was perceived as a tool of oppression used by the ruling classes, and violently suppressed. The anti-Christian rhetoric was dogmatically applied to Buddhism, even though Feuerbach and Marx had given little thought to Buddhism in their critiques of religion. Starting with Stalin's persecutions of Buddhism in the Mongol republics of Russia in the 1930s, within twenty-five years Buddhists in China, Tibet, Vietnam, Laos, Cambodia and Korea had suffered a similarly gruesome fate.

Whether by means of colonialism, military defeat, communist revolution or the enticement of free-market capitalism, a version of 19th-century European rationalism has been firmly implanted in virtually every Buddhist country in Asia. (The sole exception is the little mountain kingdom of Bhutan.) Even if the days of the communist regimes are numbered, the pressures for formerly Marxist nations of Asia to be absorbed into the global consumerist economy will be immense. Whether the threat comes from oppressive dictatorships or planeloads of wealthy and libidinous tourists, traditional Buddhist societies find themselves culturally beleaguered and very much on the defensive.

15

ARTHUR
SCHOPENHAUER:
THE ORIENTAL RENAISSANCE

... Hurl into the water all the blank white men who arrive
with their little heads and their well-behaved minds. It is
necessary that these dogs hear us; we are not speaking of
ancient human ills. It is from needs other than those inherent
in life that our spirit suffers. We are suffering from a
corruption, the corruption of reason ....

Antonin Artaud

This tormented plea by the founder of the Theatre of the
Absurd appeared as part of a 'Letter to the Schools of the
Buddha' in the third issue of *La Révolution surréaliste*,
published on 15 April 1925 to commemorate the 'End of the
Christian Era'. The same issue carried addresses to the Pope and
the Dalai Lama, and letters to the rectors of the European
universities and the directors of the insane asylums. The gist of
the statements was that all the evils of the world could be traced
to Europe, while their solution lay among the Buddhists of Asia.

Such rejection of European rationalism had its origins in the
writings of Jean-Jacques Rousseau, the 18th-century opponent of
the belief in progress through rational knowledge and science.
Rousseau maintained that civilization was a corruption of human
nature; that a revolution in the human spirit rather than in the
structures of society was needed; that the heart and feelings were
closer to truth than reason. Such notions were at the root of the

Romantic movement that burst forth at the beginning of the 19th century in conscious revolt against the pre-eminence of rationalism.

Romanticism is more a frame of mind than a movement with clearly professed adherents. It is the shadow of the Enlightenment, and is as present in the proponents of rationalism as in its adversaries. Just as Eugène Burnouf looked *forward* to the conceptual ordering of Buddhism, at the same time he looked *back* to 'the origins of the world'. Although his reason declared a faith in human progress through science, his feelings revealed a nostalgic longing for a distant past. While science emphasized the objective and the real, the Romantics stressed the subjective and the ideal. As the world was being meticulously divided into types and species, Wordsworth was celebrating the 'quickening soul' of pebbles and daffodils. As industrialization imposed an increasing sense of predictability, monotony and repetition on the world, Byron, Baudelaire and others sought out the playful and passionate, a sense of child-like wonder, intoxication with a world never dulled or reduced to numbers.

Such clear contrasts with science and reason are less helpful in understanding the romantic attitude to religion. Many of the Romantics boldly rejected much of traditional Christianity. But having denounced the standard European framework of meaning, they found themselves desperately yearning for meaning. The secular alternative of scientific progress being equally anathema, many of them plunged into nihilistic despair. This produced a profound shock. As a remedy for their 'malady of the soul', some sought solace in a form of nature worship, some were drawn to artistic expression, and others, like Novalis, looked back to the pre-Renaissance age of Christian mysticism (itself a reaction against Aquinan scholasticism). As the yearning for spiritual experience grew stronger, this ushered in a revival of Catholicism and several leading Romantics returned to the Papal fold.

Questions of religion were given an additional twist by the appearance in Europe of the first translations of Indian sacred texts. Disillusioned both with Church and Reason, many Romantics turned to the East as a source of spiritual renewal. In 1800, Friedrich Schlegel, one of the leading figures of the movement, issued his clarion call: 'In the Orient we must seek the highest Romanticism.' India was perceived as the very cradle of humanity, an antiquity more profound and poetical than either Greece or Rome, whence a tired and jaded Europe would find regeneration. Both Schlegel and the poet Novalis were consumed with the idea that concealed in India was an original, universal religion that would unify and save humankind from the shallow materialism of Europe. Novalis imagined the Garden of Eden to be tucked away somewhere in the Himalayas.

This enthusiasm likewise affected the scholars. Abel Rémusat, for instance, encouraged his colleagues to seek in Asia

> a mine that is rich and untouched . . . let us endeavor to be allowed to gather what we may in the vast fields of the oriental imagination, to take anything that strikes our fancy, to leave behind everything considered unreasonable, and especially everything that seems too reasonable . . . . In this way there will be complete satisfaction: we will sail ahead on the ocean of Romanticism.

Suspicion that the roots of all wisdom lay in the distant Orient had already surfaced in the 18th century with Voltaire, who believed that 'our religion was hidden deep in India' and 'incontestably comes to us from the brahmans'.

The key to this Oriental Renaissance (a term first used by Schlegel in 1803) was the ability to translate and appreciate the sacred literature of Asia. For the first time in its history, Europe ignored the Greek prohibition against barbarism and overcame the Christian fear of idolatry to discover that there were other civilizations that had the power to question her. The publication in English, French and German of the *Bhagavad Gita* and the *Upanishads* in the final years of the 18th century dealt a stunning blow to Europe's sense of the uniqueness of her civilization. Within a few years an entire world that had been ignored for centuries abruptly appeared on the eastern horizon. Opinions were polarized between the colonial-rationalists, who dismissed the idea that anything of value could come from Asia, and the Romantics, who claimed that everything of value had its origins in Asia.

Instead of perceiving the East as something essentially 'other' than the West, the Romantics embraced the Orient in a reconciling vision of wholeness. The recognition of the common linguistic origins between Europe and India had the seismic effect of shifting their sense of Europe's origins beyond Greece and Palestine to India. In Schlegel's seminal *Über die Sprache und Weisheit der Indier* ('On the Language and Wisdom of the Indians'), published in 1808, he prayed:

> May Indic studies find as many disciples and protectors as Germany and Italy saw spring up in such great numbers for Greek studies in the 15th and 16th centuries, and may they be able to do as many things in as short a time.

This was no second Renaissance, but the logical culmination of the first. The divided world, so the Romantics hoped, would finally be made whole through the revelation of her most ancient archives.

'Whoever knows others as well as himself', wrote Goethe, 'must also recognise that East and West are now inseparable.' But he qualified this with a curious proviso: 'I admit that while dreaming between these two worlds one can waver, but such coming and going may be best done between going to bed and rising.' The image of dreaming is apt. While the rational mind ordered and dominated the East during Europe's waking hours, the East infiltrated Europe's unconscious as she slept. The historian Raymond Schwab has asked, 'was Romanticism itself anything other than an oriental irruption of the intellect?' It was no mere coincidence that orientalism and Romanticism arose at the same time in European history. Nor was this something new. Europe's loss of faith in her rational traditions in the 2nd century likewise ushered in a 'vogue of oriental prophets'(Jean Filliozat) with the rise of gnosticism. The Romanticism of the early 19th century, however, marked the inception of a self-doubt that could no longer be dismissed as an aberration. In the 20th century this malaise was to become virtually a way of life. And each time Europe was seized with another attack (1870s, 1920s, 1960s), it was invariably accompanied by a further wave of enthusiasm for the East.

The break-up of European consciousness into its rational and romantic components was crucial in determining the West's understanding of Asian traditions such as Buddhism. At the same time that Europeans were consciously constructing a map of oriental ideas to satisfy their rational intellects, they were unconsciously fashioning 'the contours of an imaginal landscape' that appealed to their romantic longings. No matter whether they detested or admired the East, a concern common to rationalists and romantics alike was how their images of the Orient could best serve their Eurocentric interests.

As a young man Arthur Schopenhauer was exposed to the genius of many of the key German Romantics of the Oriental Renaissance, many of whom frequented his mother's salon in

Weimar. Goethe (with whom Schopenhauer formed one of the few close friendships of his life), Friedrich Schlegel and his brother Auguste Wilhelm (a fellow student of de Chèzy with Burnouf, who later held the first chair in Sanskrit in Bonn), were familiar figures there. After a traumatic childhood, inheritance kept Schopenhauer from ever having to work for a living and he was free to turn his penetrating intellect towards the one thing that consumed him. 'Life is a wretched business', he announced. 'I've decided to spend it trying to understand it.'

At university in Berlin Schopenhauer attended the lectures of both Fichte and Schleiermacher, respectively the leading philosopher and theologian of the day, only to be deeply dissatisfied by what they taught. The ideas that had the greatest impact on him were those of Immanuael Kant. In 1818, at the age of thirty, he published his only major work: *The World as Will and Representation*. The book was ignored, but a second, two-volume edition in 1844, followed in 1851 by a collection of essays and aphorisms, established his reputation as one of the foremost thinkers of his age. He never married and spent the last twenty-seven years of his life in Frankfurt-am-Main. On the desk in his study stood a bust of Kant and a statue of the Buddha.

Schopenhauer was introduced to Indian thought at the age of twenty-five by the orientalist Friedrich Maier, who gave him a translation of fifty *Upanishads*, under the garbled title *Oupnek'hat*: a Latin translation by Anquetil-Duperron of a Persian translation of a Sanskrit original. The *Oupnek'hat* was nonetheless a revelation for the young Schopenhauer, who declared that any philosophy that did not agree with its doctrines was unacceptable. He began collecting translations and works on Asian thought in German, French and English. Five years later he confirmed that 'Sanskrit literature will be no less influential for our time than Greek literature was in the 15th century for the Renaissance'.

Publication of the first edition of *The World as Will and*

Representation coincided with the great wave of interest in Indian thought among the Romantics. But this enthusiasm for India either ignored Buddhism or uncritically subsumed it into Hinduism. Schopenhauer later acknowledged that 'till 1818, when my work appeared, there were to be found in Europe only a very few accounts of Buddhism, and those extremely incomplete and inadequate'. And even though the second volume of the enlarged edition of his magnum opus bristled with Indian ideas, Schopenhauer still had little access to Buddhist texts. Since he acknowledges his debt to the Russian scholar Isaak Jakob Schmidt, it is likely that he was familiar with the latter's *Diamond Sutra* — but this would have been the only canonical work available to him. Even in his collection of essays and aphorisms (published in 1851) Schopenhauer was still citing the 18th-century collection of travellers' and missionaries' tales, *Lettres édifiantes et curieuses*, as an authority on Buddhism.

The excitement about Buddhism that swept through Europe from the 1850s, in the wake of Burnouf's work, coincided with the last decade of Schopenhauer's life, when he finally won the acclaim he felt he deserved. During this period he wholeheartedly endorsed the newly revealed religion, seeing it as conclusive vindication for his views. 'You will arrive at Nirvana,' he declared, 'where you will no longer find these four things: birth, old age, sickness and death .... Never has myth come closer to the truth, nor will it.'

While Schopenhauer found inspiration in Indian and Buddhist sources, his notebooks show that he had already established the main outlines of his philosophy by the time he encountered the *Oupnek'hat*. In the second volume of his major work, having conceded to Buddhism 'pre-eminence' over all other religions, he remarks:

In any case, it must be a pleasure to me to see my doctrine in such close agreement with a religion that the majority of men on earth hold as their own . . . . And this agreement must be yet the more pleasing to me, inasmuch as in my philosophizing I have certainly not been under its influence.

Schopenhauer believed that by completing the revolutionary work of Kant, his system was the culmination of the Western philosophical tradition that began with Descartes. He was convinced that critical thinking had led him to the same conclusions that centuries before Indian and Buddhist teachers had intuited through allegory and mystical insight.

Schopenhauer was likewise convinced that the New Testament was of Indian origin, and speculated that Jesus had been brought up by Egyptian priests whose religion had originated in India. He nonetheless condemned the Christianity of his time for having been distorted by 'present-day Rationalists', whom he describes as 'honest but shallow people with no presentiment of the profound meaning of the New Testament myth'. In spite of colonialist efforts to export Christianity, he was convinced that it would never 'take root in India'. For 'the primitive wisdom of the human race will not allow itself to be diverted from its course by some escapade that occurred in Galilee'.

In extolling the wisdom of the Indian mystics, Schopenhauer did not endorse Hinduism or Buddhism as *religions*. He believed that humankind was 'growing out of religion as out of its childhood clothes'. Although such institutions were 'necessary for the people and an inestimable benefit to them', to require a Shakespeare or a Goethe (or a Schopenhauer) to believe in them would be like asking 'a giant to put on the shoes of a dwarf'.

Schopenhauer was the first European philosopher to challenge the assumption that this was the 'best of all possible worlds' where humankind was destined to ever-increasing progress and happiness. 'Our existence', he says, 'resembles the course of a man running down a mountain who would fall over if he tried to stop and can stay on his feet only by running on.' In such a transient, unstable world 'happiness is not so much as to be thought of'.

For Schopenhauer, as for Shantideva, the basis for morality is compassion, the capacity to identify with the other in such a way that 'the barrier between the ego and non-ego is for the moment abolished'. For only then do the other person's 'affairs, his need, distress and suffering directly become my own'. Schopenhauer's compassion extended equally to non-human life. He abhorred any cruelty to animals and was a vociferous opponent of vivisection. Even plants, he believed, were capable of feeling a degree of pain.

Above all Schopenhauer was convinced that the solution to the world's enigma lay in an understanding and acceptance of his philosophy. In brief, his improved version of Kantian thought asserted that the fundamental stuff of life was a blind and aimless energy that he termed 'will'. The will, as the noumenal 'thing-in-itself', was unknowable. All that could be known were the phenomena whose form the will assumed within experience. Such phenomena were necessarily represented within the dualistic framework of subject and object. Moreover, time and space were in-built structures of human consciousness that made things appear in a spatial location at a particular time. Not realizing this, people succumbed to an innate but deluded realism that drove them to achieve unattainable goals, such as happiness in this world. Schopenhauer believed that the purposeless striving of the will could, however, be suspended through contemplation of music and art and ultimately transcended through mystical intuition. 'It goes without saying', he concluded, 'that that which at present produces the phenomenon of the world must be capable of not doing so and consequently remaining inactive . . . . And this will be in its essence identical with the . . . Nirvana of the Buddhists.'

Schopenhauer describes the dilemma of human life, but unlike Buddhism offers little in the way of a practical solution. He speaks admiringly of mystical intuition, but says nothing about a path of spiritual discipline whereby it can be achieved. Although some of his contemporaries thought of him as a Buddhist, he preferred listening to music than sitting in meditation. His Buddhism was an intuitive sympathy with a way of life that he had neither the inclination nor opportunity to practise.

In the autumn of 1854 Richard Wagner, in exile in Switzerland, was immersed in composing the music for his opera *The Valkyrie*. While working on the second act he was given a copy of Schopenhauer's *The World as Will and Representation*, which he proceeded to read five times in the following nine months. In the words of Thomas Mann, this was 'the great event in Wagner's life .... It meant to him the deepest consolation, the highest self-confirmation; it meant release of mind and spirit.'

It also awoke in him an interest in Buddhism. In May 1856, while working on the orchestration for *The Valkyrie*, Wagner recalled how at that time

> Burnouf's *L'introduction à l'histoire du buddhisme indien* interested me most among my books, and I found material in it for a dramatic poem, which has stayed in my mind ever since, though only vaguely sketched. I may still perhaps work it out. I gave it the title *Die Sieger* (*The Victors*).

Five years later Wagner despaired of achieving a characterization of the Buddha. He kept revising *The Victors*, but remarked that 'the most difficult thing was to lend a dramatic, indeed even a musical form to that human being delivered from all his desires, the Buddha himself'.

The detachment of the Buddha, the release of Nirvana and the urgings of Schopenhauer to deny the will remained for the duration of Wagner's life as unattainable counterpoints to his restless creativity, passionate affairs and notorious egoism. 'Everything is strange to me', he wrote, 'and I often cast a nostalgic glance toward the country of Nirvana. But for me Nirvana again becomes, very quickly, Tristan.' He returned to work on *The Victors* in Venice in 1883, twenty-seven years after conceiving of the opera, and died while struggling with the dilemma it still posed him.

The growth of interest in Schopenhauer and Buddhism from the 1850s onward came to replace the more ebullient Romanticism and its accompanying fascination with Hinduism that characterized the earlier part of the century. This interest reflected the mounting uncertainty about the direction and pace of industrialized European civilization as well as concern about the challenges to traditional institutions. The combination of demands for political reform and the almost daily announcements of new scientific discoveries led to an era of spiritual doubt and social anxiety that cast a gloomy shadow over the 'best of all possible worlds'. The Churches became increasingly defensive. While many Protestants resigned themselves to revised versions of the life of Jesus and reinterpretations of articles of faith in the light of scientific, historical and philological insights, the Catholic Church took a stance of opposition. In 1864 Pope Pius IX produced the *Syllabus of Errors*, a document that ended by condemning any idea that the Pope 'can and ought to reconcile himself with progress, liberalism, and with modern civilisation'.

The tormented spirit of these times is captured in a diary entry of 16 August 1869, by the French writer Henri Frédéric Amiel. 'I am impressed, almost frightened', he wrote, by the depiction of Schopenhauer's idea of man. What I continue to appreciate in this misanthrope from Frankfurt is his antipathy toward everyday prejudices, toward European clichés, toward the hypocrises of Westerners, and toward superficial success. Schopenhauer is a great disillusioned thinker who professes Buddhism right in the middle of Germany, absolutely detached in the midst of the 19th century orgy.

In June of the following year he noted that although other religions had spoken of the evil and suffering of the world, 'Buddha alone provided the key to understanding it.' Similar sentiments appear in the journal of the Romantic poet Alfred de Vigny. '*J'ai l'esprit occupé de Bouddha*', he wrote ecstatically in March 1855. But four years later he described Buddhism as 'a religion too pure for the human race and too ideal for the common coarseness of the Celtic races'. Many writers preferred to concentrate on the similarity between the Buddhist and Christian emphasis on compassion and charity, about which the French historian Hippolyte Taine said: 'Of all the events in history, this concordance is the greatest.'

Buddhism also enjoyed considerable prestige in Britain. But whereas French intellectuals were fascinated by its doctrines, the British tended to be more impressed by the heroic stature of the Buddha himself. This admiration found its supreme expression in Sir Edwin Arnold's *The Light of Asia* (1879). This poetic retelling of the Buddha's life presented Gautama in such a way that satisfied the Victorians' romantic longing for spiritual fulfilment (but kept actual spiritual practice at a safe distance) while affirming the moral qualities of the ideal Victorian gentleman: personal detachment united with universal benevolence, uprightness, truthfulness, and perseverance. The positive impression of the Buddha was reinforced by his being perceived as an opponent of

Hinduism, like the many Victorians who found the customs of the Indians repellent. Moreover, the appearance of the Buddha coincided with a period of anti-Catholicism in Britain, a cause to which Gautama was also co-opted. He became the 'Hindu Luther' and his religion the 'Protestantism of the East'.

In 1888, while living in Arles, Vincent Van Gogh painted his *Self Portrait Dedicated to Paul Gauguin* in which he appears as a slant-eyed, shaven-headed Japanese Buddhist monk surrounded by a crude halo, in his own words 'a simple worshipper of the eternal Buddha'. Van Gogh's attraction to the image of the Buddha followed the breakdown of his Christian faith, his turning to art as a way of mystical insight and the inspiration he received from discovering Japanese art. In studying the woodblock prints of Hokusai and others that flooded into Europe at this time, Van Gogh observed:

> we see a man who is undoubtedly wise, philosophic and intelligent who spends his time doing what? In studying the distance between the earth and the moon? No. In studying Bismarck's policy? No. He studies a blade of grass.

As a true Romantic he pits the artist's concern for a concrete detail of nature against the allied foes of the rationalist measuring and mapping of the world and the imperialist desire to possess and control it. And at the root of this Japanese love of blades of grass he finds the Buddha with whom he struggles to identify. 'Isn't it almost a true religion which these simple Japanese teach us,' he wondered, 'who live in nature as though they themselves were flowers?' But Buddhism failed to save Van Gogh. In the year after painting the self-portrait he killed himself.

The 19th century abounded in attempts to prove what Voltaire and Schopenhauer had surmised: that Christianity originated in India. As early as 1834, N.A. Notovitch published the *Unknown*

Life of Jesus Christ, which, on the basis of a supposed Indian document, claimed that Jesus spent sixteen years in India being initiated by brahmins and Buddhist monks before returning home to teach — an unsubstantiated theory that continues to resurface today. In 1867 Adolf Hilgenfeld made Jesus an Essene and the Essenes Buddhists. In 1891 Karl Neumann published a book in which he placed sections from Buddhist sutras alongside passages from Meister Eckhart to show their identity.

Such writings were less works of detached scholarship than a fulfilment of Friedrich Schlegel's belief that the origins of all things would be found in the East. Ironically, Schlegel himself was the first to renege on his pledge. He converted to Catholicism in 1808 and twenty years later concluded that not only was 'the would-be similarity between Christianity and Buddhism not real, . . . it is like that between man and ape' — in the pre-Darwinian sense.

As the authority of the Churches weakened, it became common practice to use Buddhism as a means of discrediting Christianity. Some of the enthusiasm for Buddhism was more an aspect of anti-Christian rhetoric than a positive endorsement of the Buddha's teaching. Such is the case with Friedrich Nietzsche, in whom the Romantic movement both climaxed and (literally) broke down.

Nietzsche was born in Leipzig in 1844 — the year that saw the publication of both Burnouf's and Schopenhauer's completed masterpieces. At the age of twenty-one he stumbled across a copy of *The World as Will and Representation* in a second-hand bookshop. Reading Schopenhauer had the same liberating effect on Nietzsche's philosophy as it had on Wagner's music. Three years later Nietzsche began his friendship with the composer, which blossomed to a large extent because of their shared veneration for the philosopher.

Nietzsche soon broke both with Wagner as a friend and Schopenhauer as an educator to develop his own fiercely independent views. For him, not only was there no God or any kind of ordering principle, but no noumenon either. The world of phenomena, life itself, was not (pace Schopenhauer) an illusory and painful show, but a value to be passionately asserted. He endorsed Schopenhauer's primacy of the will, but reinterpreted it as the will to power, the evolutionary drive behind Darwin's survival of the fittest. So-called civilizing influences, like religion and morality, had, since the time of Socrates, been attempts to restrain and deny this will. Like Rousseau before him, Nietzsche inverted the hierarchy of Socrates and Plato which had placed reason above emotion and instinct. By returning to the pre-Socratic will to power, he went one step further than those Romantics who looked nostalgically back only to the Renaissance, medieval Christianity and ancient Rome and Greece. By confining himself to Europe, however, he was that much less radical than those who sought inspiration in Asia.

Nietzsche strongly identified with the pre-Socratic figure of Dionysos, the archetypal celebrant of will. Those calm Apollonian teachers who taught renunciation and detachment were no more than 'preachers of death', among whom Nietzsche included the Buddha. In *Thus Spoke Zarathustra* (1883–5) he derided those who 'encounter an invalid or an old man or a corpse and straightway they say "life is refuted." But only they are refuted, they and their eye that sees only one aspect of existence.' Buddhist dispassion was swept away in the same breath as Schopenhauerian pessimism, and in their place stood an entirely new and superior kind of human being: the *Übermensch*.

In the latter half of 1888 Nietszche wrote *The Anti-Christ*, his fiercest attack on Christianity, a religion which he scorned as 'active sympathy for the ill-constituted and weak'. Having spurned compassion as well as detachment, one would hardly expect much enthusiasm for Buddhism. Yet while acknowledging that both Buddhism and Christianity 'belong together as nihilistic religions', Nietzsche adds that 'they are distinguished from one another in the most remarkable way'.

> Buddhism is a hundred times more realistic than Christianity — it has the heritage of a cool and objective posing of problems in its composition, it arrives *after* a philosophical movement lasting hundreds of years; the concept 'God' is already abolished by the time it arrives. Buddhism is the only really *positivistic* religion history has to show us . . ., it no longer speaks of 'the struggle against *sin*,' but, quite in accordance with actuality, 'the struggle against *suffering*.' It already has ... the self-deception of moral concepts behind it — it stands, in my language, *beyond* good and evil.

In contrast, Nietzsche sees Christianity has having turned its awareness of suffering not towards personal liberation, but into 'an overwhelming desire to do harm, to discharge an inner tension in hostile actions and ideas', which historically found expression in the domination of heathens. Whereas Buddhism is 'a religion for *late* human beings',

> for races grown kindly, gentle, over intellectual who feel pain too easily (– Europe is not nearly ripe for it –): it leads them back to peace and cheerfulness, to an ordered diet in intellectual things, to a certain physical hardening . . . . Buddhism is a religion for the end and fatigue of a civilisation.

While Nietzsche had access to a far greater literature on Buddhism than Schopenhauer, his treatment is less tempered than his predecessor's. These passages reveal a volatile mix of opinionatedness with flashes of lucid intuition, an intimation, perhaps, of the inner conflicts that would lead to his irrevocable mental breakdown a few months later.

Nietzsche's madness is a chilling symbol for the kind of world that he himself foresaw: an age of great wars and revolutions and a spiralling descent into spiritual nihilism that would last for the next two hundred years. During the second half of the 19th century the Oriental Renaissance was drawn into a maelstrom of racist nationalism and spiritual fantasy, both of which played a role in the denouement of the Romantic movement.

The seeds of this outcome were already visible in the early enthusiasms of Schlegel, who not only made India the cradle of all humanity, culture and religion but also inferred a special relationship between India and Germany. He extolled the barbarian invasions of Europe and commented that Latin characters were unsuited to convey the purity of Hindu writings. By the middle of the century the term 'Aryan' had gained common currency, not merely to denote the new language group opened up through the discovery of Sanskrit, but as an ethnographic concept. These notions were crystallized in the notorious *On the Inequality of Human Races* written by the French orientalist Count Gobineau, who argued that the Aryans, whom he identified with the Teutons, formed a racial élite destined to rule over lesser peoples. Gobineau's theory was embraced by both Schopenhauer and Wagner.

Few could have suspected that the project of deciphering the ancient archives of humanity would be usurped to the cause of German nationalism. It gave the Germans an opportunity to counter the Latin bias of the Renaissance by claiming as their own an even earlier antiquity than that of Greece and Rome. Europe had been led to its current state of confusion because of its exclusive reliance on the Judaeo-Christian tradition. Henceforth, the way forward would come from Germany, a nation long despised and neglected by its neighbours, through the rediscovery of its Aryan ancestry. Although the Aryan spirit had been introduced into Europe, it had become corrupted by Semitic influences and, more recently, by rationalism and delusive notions of equality. Now was the time to purge it of its taints.

The attribution of Buddhist origins to Christianity removed the need to acknowledge any Jewish contribution to European religious life. Later in the century, Emile Burnouf (cousin of Eugène) claimed to have reconstituted the 'Aryan philosophy' inherited from the Buddhists by the Essenes and then passed to Jesus. In shifting the origin of spiritual and mythic truth to Asia, the Oriental Renaissance could thus sanction the centuries-old resentment against the Jews. Aryan supremacy, combined with the anti-Semitism of Gobineau and Nietzsche's concept of the *Übermensch*, all contributed to the 20th-century horrors of Fascism and Nazism. While it would be unjustified to lay the blame for such future atrocities at the feet of Romantic Orientalism, the movement unwittingly cleared the way for an unprecedented eruption of violence from within the European psyche.

At the same time a parallel but opposite trend culminated in a new religious movement that had a considerable impact towards the end of the 19th century. This was the Theosophical Society, founded in New York on 17 November 1875, by the American Colonel Henry Steel Olcott and the Russian noblewoman Helena Petrova Blavatsky. The declared aims of the society were to form the nucleus of a Universal Brotherhood of Humanity, without distinction of race, creed, sex, caste or colour; to study the ancient and modern religions, philosophies and sciences, . . .; and to investigate the unexplained laws of Nature and the psychical powers latent in man.

The movement soon spread to Europe and centres sprang up in most European capitals. In England the best-known convert to the cause was the feminist and socialist agitator, Annie Besant, who sensationally left the Fabian Society to join the Theosophists after reviewing Blavatsky's *Secret Doctrine* in 1889.

As a response to the weakening of Christian belief in the latter half of the century, the Theosophists drew on a number of alternative sources to construe a 'new' religion to replace the old. They claimed to have discovered an ancient wisdom tradition that underlay all particular manifestations of religion throughout the world. This tradition was preserved in a secret location in Tibet under the leadership of the 'Mahatmas', a group of spiritual masters organized into a body in the 14th century by Tsongkhapa. Through telepathetic communication Madame Blavatsky had received instruction from these masters, which she transcribed and explained in her own writings, notably *Isis Unveiled* (1877) and the *Secret Doctrine* (1888). Gautama and Jesus were seen as historical examples of such teachers who appear periodically in the world to restore this underlying wisdom of humankind.

The appeal of Theosophy lay in its skill in tapping a diverse range of contemporary beliefs and fantasies and moulding them into an internally coherent doctrine. Schlegel's call to find the 'highest Romanticism in the Orient' found its ultimate fulfilment in the discovery of the mystic Mahatmas concealed in Tibet. As one of the last remaining countries still to be explored and mapped by Europe, Tibet was the pre-eminent focus for romantic yearning, a spiritual paradise unsoiled by Imperial and materialist progress. The widespread vogue in spiritualism, with which both Olcott and Blavatsky were connected, lent credence to the possibility of telepathic messages being sent and received from Tibet. Yet what the Mahatmas taught were not the mundane dogmas of conventional religions but 'a science of the methodical development of certain internal faculties', a notion that catered to the pervasive and uncritical belief in science. Even the Darwinian theory of evolution, one of the greatest bugbears of Christianity, was turned to the Theosophists' advantage: just as human beings were the culmination of physical evolution, so the Mahatmas were the culmination of spiritual evolution. The Theosophists had found the key to the next and possibly final step in the evolutionary process.

Of all the religions extant in the world of her time, Blavatsky considered Buddhism 'even in its dead letter', as 'incomparably higher, more noble, more philosophical and more scientific than the teaching of any other church or religion', a view which dovetailed with the prestige the newly discovered religion was then enjoying. Blavatsky, however, took the unprecedented step of translating her words into action. On 25 May 1880, she and Olcott formally took refuge and received the five Buddhist lay precepts before a *bhikkhu* in a temple at Galle in Ceylon. She thus became the first European publicly to embrace Theravada Buddhism. For the Buddhists of Ceylon, this was an enormous boost for their traditional faith, which until then had suffered from unremitting Christian persecution. Olcott was so moved by the plight of the local Buddhists that he embarked on a campaign of reviving the tradition on the island. He studied the Dharma both from English and French scholarly works as well as with learned Ceylonese *bhikkhus*, and in 1882 produced his *Buddhist Catechism*, an immensely popular summary of Buddhist beliefs which not only helped fuel the revival in Ceylon but was translated and disseminated throughout Europe and America. Blavatsky and Olcott also inspired a young Singalese called Don David Hevavitarana, who, as Anagarika Dharmapala, became the leading Buddhist reformer of his time.

Despite the positive effect in Asia of Blavatsky's endorsement of Buddhism, the doctrines of Theosophy had little in common with Buddhism as it was understood and practised in the East. Blavatsky's knowledge of the Dharma was minimal. Yet through such publications as A.P. Sinnett's *Esoteric Buddhism* (1883), many Europeans came to believe that the occultist fantasies of Theosophy indeed represented the true teachings of Buddhism. Theosophy served as a romantic foil to the rationalism of the scholars, both of which were aspects of a common Eurocentricity.

The Theosophists believed that one of the aims of the Mahatmas was to prepare humankind for the advent of the future Buddha Maitreya. All Buddhist schools have taught that after the decline of Gautama's Dharma the world would enter into a dark period which would be regenerated by the appearance of another Buddha called Maitreya. Exactly when this would occur was sufficiently vague to allow the Theosophists to declare themselves as the vanguard of this future Buddha. In the spring of 1909 they recognized an impoverished young Indian boy called Krishnamurti as the incarnation of Maitreya. Krishnamurti was admitted into the Esoteric section of the Society, initiated on the Astral Plane by the Masters, and thus groomed to become the next World Teacher. (He rejected this role in 1929, with the declaration that 'truth was a pathless land', incapable of being organized into a collective system of belief, a view he promulgated tirelessly until his death sixty years later.)

However eccentric and dated the ideas of the Theosophical Society may appear today, in the first decades of its existence they attracted an enormous and respectable following. On 12 June 1911, Mrs Besant, accompanied by the sixteen-year-old

Krishanamurti, lectured at the Sorbonne on *Giordano Bruno: Theosophy's Apostle in the 16th Century*. The amphitheatre was packed with four thousand people, including the vice-rector, and hundreds more had to be turned away. Ten years later the University hosted the Society's first International Congress. Theosophical ideas also influenced leading figures in the world of music and art. The composer Schoenberg and the painters Kandinsky and Mondrian were all card-carrying Theosophists.

The same despair and irrationality that gave birth to Theosophy are also painfully visible in a plea from the playwright and poet Antonin Artaud to the Dalai Lama published in *La Révolution surréaliste* in 1925: 'O Great Lama!' he implores:

> We are your most faithful servants. Direct your lights to us in a language that our contaminated European spirits can understand and, if need be, transform our Spirit, make for us a spirit entirely turned towards those perfect summits where the Spirit of Man no longer suffers.

Such sentiments are manifestations of the undercurrent of feeling and emotion that for the most part lies concealed beneath the surface of Western civilization's advance. Europe has grown up in fear of these drives, whether they pour across her borders as invading hordes of Vandals or Mongols, or irrupt as revolutionary or counter-cultural forces within those borders. Today the fear of irrationality is more one of psychological and social breakdown than of external invasion. Instead of Theosophy, there is now the New Age, another resurgent Gnostic/Romantic fantasy that claims Buddhism as its own just as Mani did in the 3rd century and Mme Blavatsky in the 19th. But the Dharma will remain unheard as long its voice is drowned out by the clamour of these irrational and eclectic yearnings.

271

EVERYMAN:

THE AWAKENING OF THE WEST

... The scandal redoubled when Pécuchet declared how much he was attracted to Buddhism.

'Ha! ha! ha!' The priest broke into laughter — 'Buddhism!'

'Buddhism!' cried Madame de Noares, raising her arms.

'What? Buddhism?' repeated the count.

'You know all about it then?' said Pécuchet to M. Jeufroy, who looked muddled. 'Very well. It's superior to Christianity, and recognised long before it the vanity of earthly things. Its practices are austere, its faithful more numerous than all Christians together, and as for the incarnation, Vishnu didn't have one but nine. So, judge for yourselves.'

'Travellers' lies,' said Mme de Noares.

'A freemasons' conspiracy,' added the *curé*.

And everyone started speaking at once: 'Go on then, continue! — Lovely! — I find it funny myself. — Impossible!' So much so that Pécuchet, exasperated, declared that he would become a Buddhist.

'An insult to Christianity,' said the baron.

Mme de Noares sank into an armchair. The countess and Yolande stopped talking. The count rolled his eyes; Hurel waited for orders. The *abbé*, to console himself, read his breviary . . . .

Gustave Flaubert, Bouvard et Pécuchet, 1881

History is a selection of memories credibly arranged in chronological order. The episodes of which it is formed are, as Voltaire noted, but convenient fictions. Histories are written in order to assure both author and reader alike that things really did happen in the way they were described. Detailed scrutiny of evidence (inscriptions, coins, texts) strengthens the certainty that Menander invaded Pataliputra, William of Rubruck debated with Buddhists at the court of Möngke Khan, Matteo Ricci died in Peking and Arthur Schopenhauer had a bust of Kant on his desk. Yet each piece of evidence is merely a physical trace left by the inscrutable motives of the dead. The way the evidence is arranged into an episode as well as how the episodes are linked together result from the imagination and aims of the historian. 'It is a post-structuralist commonplace', writes the critic and novelist David Lodge, 'that language constructs the reality it seems merely to refer to; therefore, all texts are fictions (some more useful than others), whether they acknowledge it or not.'

A world that accepts the multiplicity of perception, the insubstantiality and contingency of reality, the disturbing, fragmented, elusive, indeterminate nature of the self, the pervasive confusion and anguish of human consciousness would seem to fit Buddhism like a glove. Yet this is nothing new. European advocates of Buddhism, from Schopenhauer onwards, have always been impressed by the compatibility of its doctrines with their own way of seeing the world. Kantians saw the views of Kant in Buddhism and Logical Positivists saw those of Bertrand Russell, just as today Deconstructionists behold the unravellings of Jacques Derrida. Within the last hundred years the teachings of Buddhism have confirmed the views of theosophists, behaviourists, fascists, environmentalists and quantum-physicists alike. Then is Buddhism just an exotic morass of incompatible ideas, a 'Babylon of doctrines', as Matteo Ricci suspected, which can be all things to all men? Or is this another illustration of the Buddha's parable of the blind men who variously interpret an elephant as a pillar, a wall, a rope or a tube depending on which bit of the animal's anatomy they clutch?

There are as many kinds of Buddhism as there are ways the fragmented and ever-changing European mind has to apprehend it. In each case 'Buddhism' denotes something else. For rationalists it means a philological object, something to be dissected and known. For romantics it is a fantasy object, where all is pure and good, a justification for one's disdain of the corrupt West. Yet while rationalists *think* they understand Buddhism and romantics *feel* they know — what is it really? The answer: nothing you can put your finger on. The Dharma is irreducible to 'this' or 'that'. To fix the elephant in either space or time is to kill her. The elephant breathes and moves — in ways one cannot foresee.

'The forms of Buddhism', writes the Vietnamese poet and monk Thich Nhat Hanh, 'must change so that the essence of Buddhism remains unchanged. This essence consists of living principles that cannot bear any specific formulation.' Accordingly, Buddhism cannot be said to be any of the following: a system of ethics, philosophy or psychology; a religion, a faith or a mystical experience; a devotional practice, a discipline of meditation or a psychotherapy. Yet it can involve all these things. The Buddhist attitude to life is neither rational nor non-rational; based neither on feeling, intuition nor sensation. Yet it includes them all.

Europe has entered a transitional phase in its relation to Buddhism. This is confusing. Information about Buddhism comes from a number of conflicting sources, many of which still reflect the rationalist fears and romantic yearnings of an earlier age. Even 'authentic sources' (which usually means 'ordained Asian males') can be blinkered by their own cultural and nationalist agendas which are not necessarily those of either Buddhism or the West. Buddhism is now something *practised* by Europeans in Europe, in relatively stable communities under the direction of teachers

274

trained in classical traditions. With a scattering of notable exceptions, this process began in earnest in the 1960s with the arrival of Theravada *bhikkhus*, Japanese *roshis* and Tibetan *lamas* in the West and the departure of young Europeans and Americans to Asia. In the last twenty-five years the number of Buddhist centres throughout Europe has expanded rapidly and profusely. This phase is nonetheless 'transitional' because, despite several attempts, Buddhism has yet to realize a distinctive European or Western identity.

Not only is the current practice of Buddhism in the West transitional, it is heretical. 'Heresy' is one of those highly charged terms, whose literal meaning is all but forgotten. Today it implies simply the rejection or denunciation of a tradition, whereas originally it meant 'to make a choice'. For during the Christian era in Europe to choose to think otherwise than the Church was to deny the Church. From the Church's point of view, rationalism and romanticism were but twin aspects of the heresy that exploded through Europe from the 18th century onwards. Yet the heretical breaking of the Church's stranglehold also ruptured the cohesion of the European soul, splitting it into its rational and romantic parts and pithing it of a spiritual core. Predictably, when Buddhism first appeared, the Dharma was either obscured by the grid of reason or twisted by the dreams of romanticism. It required two World Wars, Hitler and Stalin, the threat of nuclear war and environmental destruction and, in many cases, a hefty dose of LSD to render Europeans sufficiently humble to seek their lost spiritual centre elsewhere.

In its conventional sense, 'heresy' is negative: the denial of a tradition; whereas in its etymological sense it is positive: the making of a choice. To commit oneself to the Dharma of the Buddha is heretical on both counts. For it is a choice to practise something outside the Judaeo-Christian-Hellenic tradition. It is to choose as one's own what has historically been perceived as 'other'. Even in a traditional Buddhist country, to practise the Dharma is above all a choice. (It makes little sense to regard oneself as a Buddhist by birth.) Even when such a choice expresses itself as a life of faith, it is the choice rather than the faith that needs to be reaffirmed.

To choose the Dharma never has and never can occur outside a cultural context. For Europeans that culture is inseparable from the heritage of Christianity. While acknowledging that I encounter Buddhism within a framework of Christian (or 'post-Christian') values and even instinctively judge it by the standards of a Christian ethos, I also am conscious of rejecting Christian dogma. The idea of a God who breaks into history to save human beings from their sins through the death of his only Son makes no sense. From a Buddhist standpoint, such a God is to the cosmos what an independently existent self is to the mind–body complex: a consoling fiction. Just as the vision of the Buddha releases one from the need to believe in such a self, so does it free one from the need for such a God.

As a European, I cannot step outside the history of which I am a creature. To pretend otherwise is to succumb to the romantic fallacy. To practise the Dharma is not to reject reason or romance but to create a middle way between them. Just as I can respect and benefit from the clarity of rational textual analysis, so can I be nurtured by the depth and ardour of romantic feeling. But I no longer need to define the Dharma solely in rational or romantic terms. For I have opened myself to another source: an oral transmission of possibilities revealed through encounters with other people. More than anything else, this living, person-to-person transmission, as opposed to knowledge derived from texts, is the mark of the Dharma having penetrated the West.

So deeply engrained are the rational and romantic habits of mind, that even this encounter is expected to conform to certain stereotypes. The spiritual teacher is liable to be perceived either as a person possessed of boundless knowledge and authority (rationalism) or as an ideal father-figure or lover (romanticism). Yet to encounter the Dharma through another person requires such perceptions to be shattered. The Hassidic tradition tells of a rabbinical student who plans to visit a famous teacher — not in order to listen to his learned discourses, but to see how he ties his shoelaces. Contemporary accounts of Buddhist teachers in Europe and America abound with such anecdotes. For often a casual remark or gesture communicates the pulse of the Dharma far better than any explanation.

The forms Buddhism assumes as an institutional religion are always contingent upon historical conditions. Each Asian country in which Buddhism took root has produced its own distinct variant of the Dharma, often, as we have seen, in response to political and cultural forces. And if it is to take root in Europe, a similar pattern of adaptation will inevitably follow.

Exactly how this might happen is impossible to say. But has not Buddhism as an organized religion had its day? Have we not witnessed in the history of Asian Buddhist institutions the weakness inherent in investing so much authority in wealthy, hierarchic monasteries and churches, often morally compromised by links to governments and states? Could we not imagine an individuated form of the Dharma grounded in small autonomous communities of spiritual friendship? Could we not envision an existential, therapeutic, democratic, imaginative, anarchic, and *agnostic* Buddhism for the West?

Such transitions are bound to give rise to tensions. While an Asian Buddhist tradition may see its expansion into Europe as a means of self-preservation, its European adherents may be more motivated by a yearning to resolve their own spiritual crisis. Loyalties are liable to be torn between grateful allegiance to an Asian teacher and the urgent need to respond to the unprecedented demands of the current situation, which the Asian teacher may fail to understand. Such transitional periods are a fertile ground both for creative innovations as well as painful ruptures with tradition.

To say that Buddhism is transitory, insubstantial and conditional is merely to restate its own understanding of the nature of things. Yet its teachings endlessly warn of the deeply engrained tendency to overlook this reality. The danger of reification, i.e. to regard something as permanent, substantial and unconditional, is most liable to happen when that something is invested with an ultimate value. While the *locus classicus* of this error is the notion of self, the same mistake can just as easily be made with regard to Buddhism. Instead of seeing a particular manifestation of the Dharma as a living spiritual tradition of possibilities contingent upon historical and cultural circumstances, one reifies it into an independently existent, self-sufficient fact, resistant to change.

Living continuity requires both change *and* constancy. Just as in the course of a human life, a person changes from a child to an adolescent to an adult while retaining a recognizable identity (both internally through memory and externally through recurring physical and behavioural traits), so does a spiritual tradition change through the course of its history while retaining a recognizable identity through a continuous affirmation of its axiomatic values. Thus Buddhism will retain its identity as a tradition as long as its practitioners continue to centre their lives around the Buddha, Dharma and Sangha and affirm its basic tenets. But precisely how such commitment and affirmation are expressed in different times and places can differ wildly.

The survival of Buddhism today is dependent on its continuing ability to adapt. There is no inherent reason why a tradition that in the past has succeeded in travelling from India to Japan cannot make a similar transition to the countries of Europe. Europeans still like to think of the 'East' as a cultural monolith that contrasts with another such monolith: the 'West'. This colonialist bifurcation is strangely still in vogue. While such ideas may preserve Europe's sense of its inviolable uniqueness, they only create a barrier to the transmission of the Dharma. The differences between Indian and Japanese culture in the 13th century were as great (or as little) as those between, say, Italy and Thailand today.

For an organism to adapt to a new environment means that the organism is forced to change. Following this metaphor of adaptation, the practice of the Dharma is only meaningful if a significant transformation is effected within the practitioner. As long as the practitioner remains unaffected, the Dharma can be no more than a consolation, a diversion, a fascination or an obsession. A story from the 11th-century Kadam tradition of Tibet illustrates this well:

> One day an old man was circumambulating Reting Monastery. Geshé Drom said to him: 'Sir, I am happy to see you circumambulating, but wouldn't you rather be practising the Dharma?'
>
> Thinking this over, the old man felt it might be better to read some Buddhist scriptures. While he was reading in the temple courtyard, Geshé Drom said, 'I am happy to see you reciting scriptures, but wouldn't you rather be practising Dharma?'
>
> At this, the old man thought that perhaps he should meditate. He sat cross-legged on a cushion, with his eyes half-closed. Drom said again, 'I am so happy to see you meditating, but wouldn't it be better to practise the Dharma?'
>
> Now totally confused, the old man asked, 'Geshé-la, please tell me what I should do to practise the Dharma?'
>
> Drom replied, 'To practise means that there should be no distinction between the Dharma and your own mind.'

Drom was concerned to communicate the Dharma in a country where it was being reintroduced after a period of decline. His point is singularly relevant in the context of Buddhism in Europe today.

The primary concern of Buddhism is freedom from suffering. Such existential concern cannot treat suffering as something in any way *apart* from the person who suffers. Birth, sickness, ageing and death are not 'things' that I or you have, as though by chance. For it is you and I who are born, get sick, age and die. The tendency to distinguish between 'me', on the one hand, and 'my suffering', on the other, is rooted in the reification of 'I' and 'mine', which Buddhism recognizes as the very root of suffering. The same is true for the practice of the Dharma, the way that leads to the end of suffering. The person and the practice are not two different things.

For people raised in a technological culture, it might seem that Buddhism is concerned with solving the problem of suffering by correct application of certain spiritual techniques. This notion is merely another variant of the rationalist fallacy. Just as the scriptures of Buddhism were interpreted through the grid of philology, so now its practices are interpreted through the grid of technology. In addition to all the other things it is not, the Dharma is not a spiritual technology. This does not mean that it has no use for techniques, but it cannot be defined in technical terms.

As long as the Dharma is treated as 'other' it will not be understood. Hence historically Europeans have consistently failed to grasp what it is all about. Whether they rejected it as a heathen idolatry invented by the Devil, rationally interpreted it as a set of beliefs derived from a body of Asian texts, or romantically imagined it as an esoteric mystical system concealed in the Himalayas, in each case it remained stubbornly other. Even while all these attitudes continue to persist in the European psyche, a tidal change is occurring: the Dharma, in a rich variety of forms, is now being practised by Europeans. To practise it, as Drom suggested, means to make it one's own. But not in isolation: the practice of Buddhism can only flourish in *sangha* — spiritual community.

FIVE

SANGHA

BIDIYA DANDARON:
RUSSIAN CONNECTIONS

Sometime during the cold dark night of 22 February 1937, four trucks from the NKVD (Ministry of Internal Affairs) pulled up outside the nondescript boarding house next to the Tibetan Buddhist temple on Primorski Prospekt in the north of Leningrad. Four plain-clothed officers positioned themselves around the building while a gaggle of others marched inside to arrest Ostov Budhayev, a Buryat-Mongol lama. Budhayev was bundled into the back of a truck and ordered to squat on the floor. After rounding up the night's remaining quota of subversives, the trucks returned to the NKVD building on Liteinyi Prospekt and packed Budhayev into an underground cell.

On 29 August Ostov Budhayev was charged and convicted with offences under Article 58 of the Criminal Code, sub-sections 1a (*treason to the Motherland*), 8 (*terrorism*), 9 (*sabotage*) and 11 (*belonging to a criminal organization*). That night he was taken to a basement room sound-proofed with mattresses and shot at point-blank range in the back of the head. While his body lay in the morgue, his blood, merged with that of many others, was drained out of the building into the adjacent river. The following night the corpse was covered with sackcloth and packed into another truck, which trundled across the river, out of the city, to the suburb of Levashova, where it was tipped into a mass grave and concealed beneath lime and earth.

Although a Soviet citizen, Budhayev was ethnically a Mongolian from Buryatia, an area around Lake Baikal in Siberia. Buryatia submitted to the rule of the Tsar in 1689, during the relentless Russian drive eastwards, and was incorporated into Imperial Russia in 1728. Only fourteen years earlier it had received its first mission of Tibetan lamas, who converted most of the eastern part of the province from Shamanism to Buddhism. In 1741 two monasteries were founded and Empress Elizabeth Petrovna officially recognized a Russian Buddhist Church. (This was to be the last major movement of Buddhism from one country to another until modern times.)

In the same year that Stalin was systematically ridding Russia of its Buddhist monks, he also launched a wave of persecution against the orientalists in Moscow and Leningrad. More than five hundred specialists in Buddhism and other forms of Eastern culture were purged during this time, for the simple reason that they were engaged with forms of thinking that disagreed with Soviet Communism. Among them was a Buryat student of aeronautical engineering called Bidiya Dandaron, who was attending lectures at the Oriental Academy. Fortunately, Dandaron appeared too young and inexperienced even for the imaginative NKVD to charge him with crimes that demanded the death penalty. He received only ten years hard labour.

Bidiya Dandaron was born in December 1914 to the widow of a steppe lama called Bazarov Dandar and Dorje Gabzhi Badmaev, a Buryat poet, philosopher and yogin who was a disciple of one of the most prominent lamas of his day, Lobsan Sandan Tsedenov. Tsedenov had entered the local Kizhinginski Monastery as a young man, risen to the rank of *geshé* and was sufficiently esteemed to be included in an official Buryat Buddhist mission to St Petersburg and an audience with Tsar Alexander III in the 1880s. But having

284

been ushered into the palace Tsedenov refused to bow to the Tsar of all Russia. Not only was he evicted from the palace but also condemned by his fellow Buddhists. Scandalized, he forsook his monastic vows and retreated to a remote forest in Buryatia to begin a twenty-year contemplation of the tantric deity Vajrabhairava. By 1906, long hair and beard now replacing his shaven scalp, he declared himself a follower of the Nyingma tradition and began to accept disciples, among whom was Dandaron's father.

Shortly after his birth Dandaron was recognized as the reincarnation of Tsedenov's teacher, Hambo Lama Jayagsy Gegen, a former abbot of Kumbum Monastery in eastern Tibet. But when a delegation arrived from Tibet to take him back to Kumbum, Tsedenov refused to let him go. Then in 1917 came the revolution. The following year, taking the Bolshevik policy of land redistribution literally, Tsedenov was declared 'Dharmaraja' (Dharma-king) of a buddhocratic state of four hundred farmsteads in the Kizhinginski Valley. Such action was the policy of the Balagat (Nomadic) Movement of which Tsedenov was co-founder. One of the movement's aims was to remove the focus of spiritual authority from the monasteries by establishing Buddhist lay communities. The Bolsheviks, however, did not share their ideals and Tsedenov was imprisoned.

The community was forced underground. In July 1921 its members proclaimed the seven-year-old Dandaron as Tsedenov's successor. Tsedenov was released from prison in 1922, only to be banished from his homeland. He died on 16 March the following year. Dandaron, meanwhile, received his Buddhist education from his father and other lamas in the area. At the same time he entered the state education system, where he excelled at maths and science, which led to his studies of aeronautics in Leningrad.

Not all Buryat lamas agreed with the tantric, lay approach to Buddhism advocated by Tsedenov and later by Dandaron himself. Foremost among these was Agvan Dorzhiev, the founder of the St Petersburg temple, who devoted his life to preserving the monastic tradition and the Geluk system of rigorous Buddhist studies.

Dorzhiev was born in 1854 to a devout Buddhist couple in Khara Shibir, a mountainous district of Buryatia. A gifted scholar, he trained in the Gomang College of Drepung Monastery near Lhasa and achieved the rank of a *lharampa geshé*. He was appointed as a religious advisor (*tsenzhap*) to the 13th Dalai Lama, responsible for supervising the young leader's philosophical studies. It was not long before Dorzhiev assumed the additional role of lobbyist for the Russian cause. Convinced that the British were preparing to colonize Tibet, he explained to the head lamas how Russia was not only Britain's enemy but also a place where Tibetan Buddhism flourished. This political manoeuvring upset other factions in the government and the Dalai Lama advised Dorzhiev to take a three-year leave of absence.

Upon returning to Buryatia, Dorzhiev was summoned by Prince Ukhtomsky, an admirer of all things Asian and an influential figure at the court, to St Petersburg. This resulted in an audience with Tsar Nicholas II in 1898 when a possible Russian role in Tibet was discussed. On this note Dorzhiev left St Petersburg and made his way to Paris, where, in June of the same year, at a gathering of about four hundred people, he lectured on Buddhist doctrine and performed ceremonies in the Musée Guimet. In his memoirs he recalls meeting a 'lady called Alexandra'. This was most probably Alexandra David-Neel, who would later travel in Tibet and write at length on Buddhism.

The following year he was back in Tibet. As Dorzhiev saw it, the Tibetan government was split into three factions: those still loyal to the Manchu Emperor of China; those who feared the collapse of the Manchu dynasty and proposed closer ties with Britain; and those (like himself) who preferred an alliance with Russia. Seemingly persuaded by Dorzhiev's arguments, the Dalai Lama prepared an official letter and gifts for the Tsar and sent his tireless emissary once more on his way.

By this time Dorzhiev's involvement in the 'Great Game' had placed him firmly in the sights of British Intelligence, who failed to share his enthusiasm about a Russian presence along the north Indian border. Nonetheless, he travelled back to Russia via India, disguising himself as a pilgrim and somehow staying one step ahead of British informants. He met the Tsar at Yalta, presented him with the Dalai Lama's letters, then hurried back to Lhasa via Mongolia with the Tsar's reply. No sooner had he given the Dalai Lama the Tsar's letter than he was off again through India, this time overland to Ceylon, from where he took a boat to Odessa. His stature was such that he and his companions were escorted to St Petersburg as virtual ambassadors, ushered in to see the Tsar and handed replies written in gold.

This time Dorzhiev remained in Russia and embarked on the second great mission of his life: the reform of Buddhism both in his homeland Buryatia as well as Kalmykia, a region around the lower reaches of the Volga river near the city of Astrakhan, where the Kalmyk-Mongols were settled (it was also the birthplace of Mme Blavatsky).

After the breakup of the Yüan dynasty in 1368, the Mongol tribes had turned on each other in a struggle for political supremacy. In the early 17th century these ongoing conflicts and the need for new pastures drove the Kalmyks across the Urals onto the northern Caspian steppes. The Kalmyks had converted to Geluk Buddhism before they started on their migration and brought their religion with them, worshipping in mobile tent-temples and served by lamas trained in Tibet. Geographically to the west of the Urals, they became the first ethnic Buddhist community in Europe.

At the turn of the century, Dorzhiev found the standard of monastic life in serious decline. In trying to raise the calibre of the monks, he founded new monasteries, gave ordinations, encouraged the practice of philosophical debate and bestowed initiations. He also campaigned vigorously against the evangelism of the Russian Orthodox Church as well as the resurgence of indigenous Shamanism. His prestige as a religious advisor to the Dalai Lama, combined with his conviction and charisma, helped fuel a Buddhist revival.

By the time Dorzhiev returned to Tibet events had spun out of his control. Alarmed by Dorzhiev's manoeuvring, the Viceroy of India, Lord Curzon, had ordered Colonel Francis Younghusband to enter Tibet by force and demand a trade-agreement with the Dalai Lama. In April 1904 the British force reached Gyantse and was preparing to march on Lhasa. By July it was poised only twenty-five miles from the capital. On the state oracle's advice, the Dalai Lama, in the company of Dorzhiev, escaped from Lhasa and made his way to the safety of Urga (modern Ulan Bator), the capital of Mongolia.

Dorzhiev's fears of a British occupation of Tibet proved unfounded. As soon as the 'Anglo-Tibetan Convention' was signed, the British departed, leaving behind nothing more sinister than a couple of trading missions. The next time the Dalai Lama fled abroad, during the Chinese invasion of 1910, he turned not north but south — to the sanctuary of Darjeeling in British India.

Dorzhiev was only to see Tibet once more. In 1912, after the Chinese troops had been evicted and the Dalai Lama was returning in triumph to Lhasa, he travelled from Buryatia to meet his former ward in the southern Tibetan town of Phari. Although the reappearance of Dorzhiev sent tremors of apprehension through the British, he bore only a letter of good wishes from the Tsar. As a parting gift, the Dalai Lama gave him the equivalent of a fifty thousand rouble donation to the temple for which he had recently received permission to build in St Petersburg.

In spite of objections from the Orthodox Church, including threats from extremists on Dorzhiev's life, work on the temple had already begun in 1909 and was consecrated six years later in 1915. Dorzhiev acquired the services of one of the foremost architects of the day, Gavriil Vasilyevich Baranovsky, to actualize in European architectural terms his own ideas for a Tibeto-Mongolian style building. The painter and aspiring mystic Nicholas Roerich designed the stained glass for the skylight above the main hall and the building-committee included members of high society and prominent orientalists. Artists were brought from Buryatia to decorate the building in the traditional style. The temple was dedicated to the tantric deity Kalachakra. Sufficient monks were installed to conduct the bi-monthly monastic confessional and observe the yearly rains retreat, thus making it the first Buddhist monastery in a European capital.

St Petersburg at this time was a centre of spiritual and intellectual ferment. Theosophists, Anthroposophists and Gurdjieffians were all active in the city. Yet apart from a few European faces in group photographs taken on the steps of the temple, there is little evidence of European involvement in the practice of the Geluk Buddhism which would have been taught by Dorzhiev and his monks. The temple primarily served the religious needs of the sizeable Buryat and Kalmyk communities of the capital.

Then came the revolution. In the initial upheavals the temple was occupied by troops and desecrated. Dorzhiev was arrested by the Bolsheviks and incarcerated in the notorious Butyrki prison in Moscow. Only through the influence of his friends at the Academy was he released. Ironically, these inauspicious beginnings led not to further repression but to a period of Buddhist resurgence.

While the Bolsheviks immediately suppressed Christianity, it took them several years to work out a policy to Buddhism. Since the Marxist critique of religion was essentially a refutation of Christian theism, it was unclear exactly what a good party member should think of the Buddha's Dharma. The situation was compounded by the practical need to win the sympathy of the Buddhist populations of the nascent USSR to the Soviet system. Taking advantage of this ambivalence, Dorzhiev argued that Buddhism and Communism, with their common emphasis on a non-theistic, rational and altruistic philosophy of life, were perfectly compatible.

The 1920s were for the Buddhists of the Soviet Union a period of calm before the blunt instrument of Stalinist repression crushed them in the 1930s. The Leningrad temple was slowly restored and in 1926 became the 'Tibeto-Mongolian Mission', thereby falling under the protection of diplomatic immunity. Under Dorzhiev's leadership new monasteries were built in both Buryatia and Kalmykia. In January 1927 a 'Congress of Soviet Buddhists' was held in Moscow. Speakers emphasized the similarities between Buddhism and Communism and even sent a letter to the Dalai Lama praising Soviet policy. Some of Dorzhiev's more enthusiastic followers proclaimed that the spirit of the Buddha animated Lenin (himself a quarter Kalmyk) and that the Buddha rather than Marx was the true founder of Communism. The great German and Marxist literary critic Walter Benjamin, who happened to be staying in the same hotel, interpreted the proceedings somewhat differently. 'I was struck', he recalled, 'by the number of doors in the corridors that were always left ajar. What had at first seemed accidental began to be disturbing. I found out that in these rooms lived members of a sect who had sworn never to occupy closed rooms.'

The turning point came in 1929, when Stalin embarked on the repressions and purges which, by his death in 1953, were to have claimed the lives of as many as thirty to forty million people. Henceforth, Buddhism was viewed as just another tool of oppression, and anybody found still harbouring such beliefs was liable to be arrested. In addition to betraying the class-struggle, the lamas were charged of being either 'in the service of Japanese militarism' or engaged in 'fermenting pan-Mongolism'. The monasteries were systematically closed.

Following the assassination of Kirov in 1934, Stalin unleashed the full fury of his terror. Within the next three years most of the remaining lamas in Buryatia were arrested and either imprisoned or shot. Dorzhiev was banished from his homeland to a suburb of Leningrad, where he lived until his arrest in 1937, when he was transferred to a prison in Ulan Ude and died on 29 January 1938. Three months later the religious objects in the temple were transferred to the Museum of Religion and Atheism in Kazan Cathedral. Shortly afterwards the temple itself was rented to the Building Workers' Trade Union as a 'facility for physical culture'.

Until the Stalinist purges, Russia provided a direct and accessible overland route from Europe to a living source of Buddhist culture. In 1892 Karlis A.M. Tennisons, a nineteen-year-old Latvian, travelled from his homeland to Buryatia to seek out a Lithuanian aristocrat who was rumoured to live there as a Buddhist monk. Near the shores of Lake Baikal, in the Burkutchinsky Monastery, Tennisons discovered an eighty-five-year-old man with European features intoning a Tibetan text. Kunigaikshtis Gedyminas (Mahacharya Ratnavajra) had spent 'many decades' as a Buddhist monk, making him the first-known European since the Greek Dharmarakshita of Ashoka's India to have entered the monastic order. The following year, on 8 August 1893, with Gedyminas as preceptor, Tennisons was ordained.

The only records in English to mention Gedyminas are the unpublished and somewhat unreliable writings of Tennison's disciple and successor Friedrich V. Lustig. According to Lustig, Gedyminas told Tennisons that he had spent ten years in Ganden Monastery near Lhasa, presumably at some time in the middle of the 19th century. Other than this detail we learn nothing about Gedyminas' life.

After becoming a monk Tennisons travelled widely throughout Central Asia. During the First World War he served as a Buddhist chaplain in the Imperial Russian Army and then settled for a time at Dorzhiev's temple in Leningrad. In 1923, the 13th Dalai Lama granted Tennisons the title 'Buddhist Archbishop of Latvia, Head (Sangharaja) of Buddhists in the three Baltic Republics, Estonia, Latvia, and Lithuania'. On 27 November 1930 Tennisons ordained Lustig at the Imanta Buddhist Temple in Riga, Latvia, shortly after which teacher and disciple left the Soviet Union for Asia, where they stayed first in Thailand and, from September 1949, in Burma. Tennisons died on 9 May 1962, at the age of eighty-nine. On 12 May the Burmese newspaper *The Nation* reported that the body had, to the amazement of the hospital staff, shown no signs of decomposition. Thereafter, Lustig assumed Tennisons' titles and spent the rest of his days in a small room near the Shwedagon Pagoda in Rangoon. He died in May 1991.

Russia was also one of the first sources of scholastic knowledge about Buddhism. Some of the earliest information about Tibetan Buddhism was made available in Europe by Don. Benjamin Bergmann, who lived among the Kalmyk Mongols and published a study of their way of life as early as 1804. Isaak Jakob Schmidt, usually considered the founder of Mongolian and Tibetan studies in Russia and whose work was eagerly devoured by Schopenhauer, also stayed in Kalmyk communities and, between 1832 and 1837, wrote several articles on Mahayana Buddhism, the last of which included his translation of the *Diamond Sutra* from Tibetan.

The Buddhology which flourished in Russia during the early part of the 20th century was dominated by the towering figure of Fyodor Stcherbatsky and characterized by his attempt to combine the Western rationalist approach to Buddhism with the traditional methods of teaching preserved in India and Tibet. After completing his university training, Stcherbatsky studied with pandits in India and, as his interests turned more to Buddhism, sought out Tibetan lamas. On two occasions, in Urga in 1906 and Darjeeling in 1910, he met the exiled 13th Dalai Lama who agreed to his accompanying him back to Lhasa. For political reasons, Stcherbatsky was refused authorization for the journey. As a Russian, though, he had access to lamas in his own country. Through Dorzhiev he established contact with the monasteries in Buryatia and both he and his students (Obermiller, Vladimirtsov, Vostrikov) were able to study directly with *geshé*s.

Stcherbatsky was convinced that Buddhist philosophy was not an Asian cultural artefact but a coherent body of thought with affinities to Kantian and neo-Kantian ideas. He wrote his major works in English with the hope that they would attract the attention of modern thinkers. He even sent a copy of his books to Bertrand Russell (whose brother had become a self-declared Buddhist in the late 19th century). Russell's response was merely to comment on how greatly Indian thought had been influenced by the Greeks.

One of Stcherbatsky's great ambitions was to explore the monastic libraries of Tibet to unearth the lost Sanskrit originals of Buddhist texts. He was convinced that the Bolsheviks would be more sympathetic to this idea than the Tsarist regime had been. But once Stalin seized power, not only were Stcherbatsky's hopes of travelling to Tibet dashed for ever but publication of Buddhist texts became increasingly difficult.

During the 1930s Stcherbatsky was forced to witness the systematic destruction of his school of Buddhist studies. Although his foremost student Eugène Obermiller died of ill-health in 1935, most of the others were arrested and either killed or imprisoned.

As an internationally renowned scholar, Stcherbatsky was spared the fate of his colleagues and pupils. But his last years were marked by a gloomy introspection and inability to work. He died at the age of seventy-six on 18 March 1942, in Kazakstan, where he had been removed for safe-keeping during the war together with other ageing academicians whom the Soviet regime felt obliged to preserve.

When Bidiya Dandaron, the young Buryat *tulku* cum student of aeronautical engineering, arrived in Leningrad in 1936 he immediately sought access to Stcherbatsky's circle. Agvan Dorzhiev gave him a letter of introduction to Andrei Vostrikov, a scholar of Tibetan Buddhist logic, who welcomed him to his lectures at the Oriental Academy. When the NKVD arrested Vostrikov on charges of spying for Japan, they picked up Dandaron as well. Vostrikov was executed on 26 September 1937.

Following his arrest (together with that of his wife and two young children) Dandaron was transferred to a camp in Siberia. His wife was released but died a few months later from tuberculosis. Dandaron was tortured — the scars from a cavalry sabre remained until his death — and settled down to what was to be the first of his twenty-two years of imprisonment.

Dandaron would later refer to his time in the prison camps as 'nineteen years of Stalin's drudgery', but his time there was not wasted. After all, the best surviving minds in Russia were locked up together in Siberia. Dandaron brought to the camps a combination of yogic intuition, fluency in classical Mongolian and Tibetan, and a sharp scientific intellect. Against the oppressive backdrop of imprisonment, he deepened his practice of meditation, continued his Buddhist studies through discussions with other incarcerated lamas, and offered instruction to whomever sought insight or solace through the Buddha's teachings. For twenty years Buddhism in Russia hung on by the most tenuous of threads in the Gulag Archipelago.

In 1944 Dandaron was released from prison to the relative comfort of internal exile. But in 1947 he was again denounced, arrested and sentenced to a further ten years in the camps. Now in his mid-thirties, he assumed the role of teacher and counsellor, leading groups in Buddhist philosophy and meditation as well as writing articles and books. Finally, in 1955, he was released and rehabilitated in Buryatia, where he was appointed a research officer at the Buryat Institute of Social Sciences in Ulan Ude, responsible for cataloguing the huge number of Tibetan and Mongolian texts which had been deposited there on the closure of the monasteries.

Two years later the Buddhologist George N. Roerich (son of Nicholas the painter) returned from exile in India to Khrushchev's Russia. Roerich, a specialist in Tibetan and Mongolian studies, was appointed as the first director of the Buddhist branch of the Institute of Oriental Studies in Moscow, where his arrival stimulated a fresh wave of scholarly research. In 1958 Dandaron met Roerich and the two men began to collaborate. All of a sudden Buddhist texts started being translated again and articles appeared in journals discussing problems of Buddhist philosophy.

In 1960 Roerich decided to resurrect the Biblioteca Buddhica, a series which had published many of the seminal works of Russian Buddhologists but had come to an abrupt halt in 1937. He sought to reinaugurate the series with a Russian translation of the *Dhammapada* by his student Vladimir Tuporov. But while the book was rolling off the presses, the heavy hand of bureaucracy intervened and forbade its publication. In desperation Roerich turned to his friend G.P. Malalasekera, the founder of the World Fellowship of Buddhists and current Ceylonese ambassador to the USSR. Malalasekera organized an official reception in Moscow to celebrate the first publication into Russian of the revered *Dhammapada*. The book was rushed out. In spite of this success, the strain of the whole affair is widely believed to have led to the heart attack which prematurely ended Roerich's life on 21 May of the same year. He was fifty-eight.

Unlike other Westernized Buryat intellectuals Dandaron was not interested merely in providing information about his native culture and religion; he was a practising yogin and lama, concerned with passing on the Buddhist traditions of which he was one of the few surviving practitioners. By 1965 a circle of disciples had gathered around him, including an increasing number of European Russians who would travel many days by train across the Soviet Union to Ulan Ude to spend time in his company. He attracted a diverse group of men and women, united by a common despair about the materialism of the Soviet system.

Dandaron was no romantic who rejected the contemporary world in order to dream of a long-lost, idealized past. According to his disciple Alexander Piatigorsky, he worked

on the interpretation of the main propositions of Buddhist philosophy so as to enrich and develop modern scientific thought. At the same time he worked on an interpretation of a number of basic propositions of modern philosophical and scientific thinking so as to give them meaning in the context and spirit of Buddhism.

Dandaron combined this intellectual enquiry with traditional Tibetan Buddhist meditation training and, in particular, Vajrayana practice, engaging with his students, sometimes forcefully and eccentrically, to shock them out of their habitual attitudes. He used to say that 'it was not they who were coming to him in Ulan Ude, but Buddhism that was going West'.

The legacy of Stalinist intolerance still festered in the air. On

19 September 1972 Dandaron was arrested again, this time accused of founding an anti-Soviet Buddhist sect, which practised animal sacrifices and ritual sex and had ties with International Zionism. Shortly afterwards four of his European disciples in Buryatia (Butkus, Zheleznev, Montlevich and Lavrov) as well as numerous Buddhist scholars throughout the Soviet Union were arrested and interrogated on grounds of being implicated in his 'cult'. Charges against the scholars were dropped, but the four disciples were dispatched to psychiatric hospitals. Many others of his circle, including relatives, were declared 'morally unsuitable' and lost their jobs. Dandaron's writings were confiscated by the KGB and disappeared.

One might have expected these accusations to have rallied Dandaron's fellow Buryats around him, to have raised him up as an innocent victim of KGB oppression against persecuted minorities. But in fact it was Buryats (even his colleagues at the Institute) who denounced him and then testified against him. 'They hated him', recalled Piatagorsky, 'precisely because he belonged to *their* spiritual tradition, which they themselves had repudiated . . . . Dandaron, as it were, served as the living reminder of their apostasy from their former culture'. The local state-controlled newspaper, *Buryaad Unen*, commented:

If we look carefully at the members of Dandaron's group we can see that they are all as bad as each other — questionable, suspicious individuals. They have no conscience, no honour, . . . no notion of fatherland, of family, they are true vagrants, capable of anything to get money. In reality they do not believe in Buddhism, but are hiding their dark deeds behind religion.

In court Dandaron was portrayed as a drunken profligate and speculator in Buddhist antiquities, who cynically exploited the gullibilities of others in order to be worshipped by them. On 25 December 1972, he was found guilty on two counts: 'infringing the person and rights of a citizen under the guise of carrying out religious ceremonies' and 'swindling'. He was sentenced to five years' hard labour.

The treatment of Dandaron aroused considerable concern in the Buddhist world. The vice-president of the World Fellowship of Buddhists at the time, however, was a Buryat, S.D. Dylykov, who on 12 October 1973 wrote an account of the affair in a letter to the Secretary General of the Fellowship, which concluded:

> We, the Buddhists of the Soviet Union, do not doubt that the Soviet court has punished Dandaron for his crimes, rather than for his religious convictions.

Dylykov, a close relative of Agvan Dorzhiev, had lived in the boarding house next to the temple and witnessed the arrest of his fellow Buryats in 1937. In his will Dorzhiev had left all his property to Dylykov and entrusted the temple to his care.

Dandaron survived less than two years in the Vydrino corrective labour camp on the shores of Lake Baikal. He began to decline after being forced back to heavy physical work while injuries sustained in an accident had not fully healed. The official cause of death on 26 October 1974 was given as pneumonia and a brain tumour. He was buried near the camp. His relatives were not allowed to exhume the body.

Even as the ageing Dandaron languished in a Siberian camp, another movement was underway disseminating Buddhism in European Russia. This was the widespread *samizdat* publication of Buddhist writings, translated anonymously into Russian and circulated among a network of contacts in carbon and Xerox copies. These books began appearing in the late 1960s with the works of D.T. Suzuki and Alan Watts on Zen, and those of W.Y. Evans-Wentz, Alexandra David-Neel and Lama Govinda on Tibetan Buddhism. By the late 1970s interest and demand was such that only three to four months would elapse between publication of a Buddhist book in the West and its appearance in a Russian *samizdat* edition. One widely circulated title was Dandaron's *Thoughts of a Buddhist*, a presentation of Tibetan *lam.rim.* (stages of the path) teachings in modern Russian, concluding with an introduction to the Vajrayana.

Forbidden, unlike their counterparts in the West, from travelling to India or Japan to develop their interest in Buddhism, a few young Russians started making the long trek to Buryatia in the hope of finding lamas there. After the Second World War the authorities had allowed two monasteries — Ivolginski near Ulan Ude and Aginski near Chita — to open under the auspices of the communist-controlled Central Buddhist Board of the USSR. A handful of lamas who had survived the camps were permitted to live there and conduct ceremonies. This allowed the Soviet Union to present showcase monasteries to the outside world as well as to send representatives to international Buddhist conferences. By the time the first curious Russians arrived in the early 1970s, they were received by a handful of old monks, who, despite their age, agreed to teach them.

In 1985, with *glasnost* and *perestroika* in the air, the trickle of Russians travelling to Buryatia to study Buddhism increased dramatically. In 1987 the Dalai Lama stopped off in Leningrad en route to Mongolia. In 1989, Bakula Rinpoché, a senior lama from Ladakh, now serving as Indian ambassador to Mongolia, lectured in the city. The same year saw the first visit of the Danish Karma-Kagyu teacher Ole Nydahl, who raced around the country holding small informal groups wherever he found any interest.

Since then numerous contacts have been established with Buddhist groups in Western Europe and America, resulting in Buddhist teachers visiting Russia and Russians travelling to the West to study. Tibetans who have taught in Russia recently include the Kagyu Lama Tsechu Rinpoché, the Geluk Lama Geshé Thubten Ngawang and the Nyingma Lama Namkhai Norbu Rinpoché. Disciples of the Korean Zen teacher Seung Sahn from Poland have established a group in Uljanovsk. Links have been established with the Friends of the Western Buddhist Order both across the border in Helsinki as well as in England. The Vietnamese Zen monk, poet and activist Thich Nhat Hanh has also taught in Moscow.

In August 1992 the Dalai Lama visited Russia. In Buryatia and Kalmykia he gave novice vows to thirty young monks and full ordination to thirteen monks, taught and gave initiations to thousands of lay people, and blessed the sites of two proposed monasteries. He also visited the birthplace of Agvan Dorzhiev, a teacher of the Dalai Lama's previous incarnation, and performed the ritual of Offering to the Spiritual Master. The tour concluded with a lecture at Moscow university to a packed auditorium.

Dandaron's disciples have dispersed along various paths. After the trial, some left the country, such as Alexander Piatigorsky, who now holds a post at London University. Linnart Maell, another academic, settled in Tartu (Estonia) where he is now both president of the Estonian Oriental Society as well as vice-president of the Estonian National Party. He recently translated the *Dhammapada* and the *Bodhicaryavatara* into Estonian. Vladimir Montlevich, one of the four disciples declared insane, returned to Leningrad where he directs a small Dzogchen centre under the direction of Namkhai Norbu. Another of the four, Alexander Zheleznev, stayed in Buryatia. A loosely knit community of European Russians has grown up around him, comprised of more than a hundred people who have moved east to experiment with

300

a rural way of life based on Vajrayana teachings.

A new generation of Buddhist scholars is emerging in St Petersburg, several of whom are practising Buddhists. One of the most esteemed publications of late is Andrei Paribok's Russian translation from the Pali of *Menander's Questions* (1988).

Out of this chaos of divergent approaches, all bursting forth at a time of widespread social and political unrest and economic uncertainty, the future direction of Buddhism in Russia is impossible to surmise. In the wake of Communism's collapse, the Dharma offers an attractive alternative for a growing number of people. And given their historical connection with Tibetan Buddhism, it is no surprise that Russians feel the strongest kinship with that tradition.

Symbolically, the most significant recent event has been the return, in 1989, of Agvan Dorzhiev's temple in Leningrad to the Buddhist community of the city. During the 1960s the temple had been used as an Experimental Morphology Unit of the Leningrad Zoological Institute. In 1970, however, it was recognized as an important architectural monument and transferred to state ownership. In September 1990, Ven. Tenzin-Khetsun Samayev, a young Buryat lama was invited to serve as abbot. A month later the statute of the 'Datsan Kuntsechoney' — 'Dharma Place of Wisdom and Kindness', the name originally given to the temple by Agvan Dorzhiev — was officially registered.

Except for the spire missing from the top, the temple looks much as it did at the time of Dorzhiev and the boarding house where Ostov Budhayev was arrested in 1937 still stands next door. No longer an elegant avenue with horse-drawn carriages, Primorski Prospekt rumbles with the noise of trucks and buses. The view across the road, over the broad, still canal to the wooded park on Eliagin Island is largely unchanged from what Dorzhiev and his monks would have seen.

On entering the building one is struck by fragments of its

former grandeur: metalworked lotus leaves at the bases of the dark red marble columns in the portico, carved wooden lintels around the doors, painted motifs high and inaccessible at the tops of pillars . . .. Yet the overriding impression is one of disrepair and abandon. Crude scaffolding props up perilous ceilings. The bureaucratic grey and yellow paint, slapped over the vivid Tibetan colours, is blistered and peeling. In addition to Abbot Samayev, eighteen young Buryat novices, their bright red robes the only signs of warmth and comfort, live in bare rooms on the upper storeys. A poster on the wall proudly declares celebrations to mark 1991 as the 250th anniversary of Buddhism in Russia, but like everyone in St Petersburg today, the monks have barely enough to eat.

18

ALEXANDRA DAVID-NEEL: THE RAZOR'S EDGE

On the sun-drenched morning of 5 February 1921, a fifty-three-year-old Frenchwoman dressed as a Tibetan woman-lama, accompanied by Yongden, her adopted Sikkimese son, left Kum Bum Monastery in north-east Tibet intent on overcoming the geographical and bureaucratic obstacles that stood between her and Lhasa. Mme Alexandra David-Neel had assumed this disguise to conceal herself from the suspicious eyes of the British, who distrusted her just as they had earlier distrusted Dorzhiev, and to win the sympathy and help of the local officials and peasants. She later described herself as a 'reporter on the Orient', someone who at heart remained thoroughly critical and sceptical, while publicly divining the future and giving blessings to local people who perceived her as a *dakini*.

She confessed a helplessness, a homesickness for a foreign land, which she attributed in part to a distant Mongol ancestry through her mother: 'I can't tear myself away from Tibet', she admitted. 'I'm chained, nailed. I can't help it.' She was determined to the point of obstinacy, liable to act on impulse and prone to bouts of depression. 'Things seem to be strangely disintegrating around me and beneath my feet', she wrote to her estranged husband Philip in Tunis shortly before leaving. But such doubts rarely surfaced.

After wandering for two and a half years, she changed her lama's robes for rags. As humble pilgrims, she and Yongden headed for Lhasa, where they arrived on 24 February 1924. 'Just know', she wrote to Philip, 'that today I have arrived in Lhasa reduced to the state of a skeleton. When I pass my hand over my body, I find only a thin layer of skin covering my bones.' The first European woman to reach the city was not greatly impressed. 'I went there', she recalled, 'because it was on my route and this is just the sort of joke a Parisienne likes to play on those who have forbidden her access to somewhere.'

David-Neel's journey followed in the wake of a war that, in the words of the historian Alan Bullock, 'was so shattering in its impact, so far-reaching in its consequences, that it is profoundly difficult to recapture what preceded it'. The 20th-century break with tradition in the arts (Picasso, Matisse, Kandinsky), literature (Proust, Mann, Kafka, Joyce), psychology (Freud, Adler, Jung) and physics (Planck, Rutherford, Einstein, Bohr) was already underway before the outbreak of the Great War, but it took the brutal shock of millions dead and wounded in the heart of civilized Europe to force an awareness of the fragmented, uncertain and anxious world of today. The War sealed a rupture with the past every bit as irrevocable as that of the Renaissance, the Reformation, the Enlightenment, or Romanticism. Henceforth, the vacuous but pregnant term 'Modernism' came into its own.

For the German historian Oswald Spengler this war was more than just a bloody break with the past, or a regrettable precursor to another phase in the advance of Western culture. It was compelling evidence for the 'Decline of the West', the title of Spengler's *magnum opus* published in 1918. Despite the fact that civilizations fall as well as rise, Europe clung stubbornly to the idea of its inevitable progress, a belief W.B. Yeats called the 'last great Western heresy'. For Spengler, the soul of the West was doomed. 'A conversion to Theosophy or Freethinking', he wrote, is merely 'an alteration of words and notions, of the religious and intellectual surface, no more. None of our 'movements' have changed *man*.' And if, in our desperation, we '"go back to" Buddhism or paganism or Roman Catholicism', we will still 'feel the same'.

Such echoes of disintegration are as evident in the unsettling stories of Franz Kafka as in the grimly evocative *Waste Land* (1922) of T.S. Eliot, where the Buddha's *Fire Sermon* (blended with St Augustine) helps suggest a world consumed with despair. James Joyce's *Ulysses* was published in Paris the same year. The book employs images of cycles of time and reincarnation drawn from Theosophy — 'vegetable philosophy' as Joyce put it. The Irishman nonetheless kept his copy of Olcott's *Buddhist Catechism*.

Such condemnations of European tradition provoked a counter-reaction, a striking example being an essay by the French writer Henri Massis entitled 'Defence of the West' (1925). Massis argued that Western civilization was in imminent danger of destruction at the hands of the East. 'It is the soul of the West', he wrote, 'that the East wishes to attack',

> that soul, divided, uncertain of its principles, confusedly eager for spiritual liberation, and all the more ready to destroy itself, to allow itself to be broken up by Oriental anarchy, because it has of itself departed from its historical civilising order and its tradition .... Personality, unity, stability, authority, continuity — these are the root-ideas of the West. We are asked to break these to pieces for the sake of a doubtful Asiaticism in which all the forces of the human personality dissolve and return to nothingness.

Massis sees this 'powerfully organised, dark barbarism' at work in Germany, plotting her revenge on the Latin West that conquered her; in the claim of the Tokyo-based Oriental League: that the world would not find peace 'until Asia conquers the

Whites'; in the 'messengers' from Asia, such as Tagore and Gandhi; in the newly victorious Bolsheviks, heeding Lenin's cry to 'overcome the West by way of the East'; and in the 'pseudo-Orientalists', still yearning for the Romanticism of Rousseau. But this latest witness to Europe's ancient fear of the East can offer little in the way of a solution other than by stating that 'Western man has no more pressing need than the need for fresh definitions'.

Had it been published at the time, Massis would have found fuel for his thesis in W. Somerset Maugham's *The Razor's Edge*, a novel about a young American called Larry Darrell who, traumatized by the Great War, struggles to find meaning against the background of an affluent society rendered hollow and pointless.

After an unsatisfying spell in a Christian monastery, Larry finds work as a deckhand on a liner, jumps ship in Bombay and ends up at an ashram in a remote area of south India. During a retreat in a nearby forest, he sits beneath a tree at dawn and experiences enlightenment. 'I had a sense', he recalls,

> that a knowledge more than human possessed me, so that everything that had been confused was clear and everything that had perplexed me was explained. I was so happy that it was pain and I struggled to release myself from it, for I felt that if it lasted a moment longer I should die.

The final glimpse we have of Larry is as he prepares to board ship for America, where he plans to vanish among the crowds of New York as a cab-driver. 'My taxi', he explains, '[will] be merely the instrument of my labour .... an equivalent to the staff and begging-bowl of the wandering mendicant.'

Maugham's story works insofar that it reflects an actual phenomenon: Western engagement with Eastern traditions in the wake of the First World War. Larry's anonymous return to America likewise bears a prophetic ring, in prefiguring the return of young men and women from Asia many decades later to the resumption of ordinary lives in the West. But the novel fails in the author's inability to imagine spiritual experience as anything other than a prolonged mystical orgasm. The sincerity and urgency of Larry's quest is trivialized, and his final resolve fails to carry conviction.

The Europeans who travelled to Asia in search of another wisdom had to leave behind not only the security of their traditions but also the non-committal Romanticism of Somerset Maugham. For the first time in nearly two thousand years, they were preparing to embrace something else. This step was of another order than either the intellectual enthusiasms of a Schopenhauer or the muddled fantasies of a Blavatsky. It took two forms: the departure for Asia to train in Buddhist monasteries, and the creation of Buddhist centres in Europe.

Just as the first stirrings of Modernism began in the years before the War, so did the first departures of Western Europeans to study in the East. The story of Allan Bennett (Ananda Metteyya), ordained in Burma in 1901, has already been told in Chapter 4. Three years later a German, Anthon Gueth, entered the order.

From a young age, Gueth had been drawn to the religious life. At the age of ten he had expressed the wish to go to Africa as a missionary to convert the heathens. While his monastic vocation remained, his belief in Christianity faded and he turned to the study of Western philosophy. Like many of his generation, he became an enthusiastic student of Schopenhauer. In Frankfurt in 1899, at the age of twenty-one, a lecture on Theosophy convinced him he was a Buddhist. In May 1902 he renounced a promising musical career to go to India to study Buddhism. From Bombay he travelled to Colombo where he learnt of Bennett and went to

Burma to find him. In September 1903 he became a novice and in February 1904 a *bhikkhu* with the name Nyanatiloka.

Nyanatiloka plunged into the study of Pali and soon began work on his translation of the *Anguttara Nikaya*. He returned from Burma to Ceylon and in 1906 accepted his first European disciples. The same year, on a brief visit to Burma, he gave novice ordination to the Scotsman J.F. McKechnie (Silacara), an atheist who had been drawn to Asia by an appeal in Bennett's journal *Buddhism*. The year 1906 also saw the publication of Nyanatiloka's first book, *The Word of the Buddha*, which the following year was translated into English by Silacara and into Russian by Dorzhiev's followers in St Petersburg.

In 1910 Nyanatiloka returned to Europe to found a Buddhist monastery in Switzerland. His stay was brief; the time was not yet ripe. In Lausanne he ordained one novice, a German painter called Bartel Bauer (Kondanno) — the first time such an ordination had been given in Western Europe. The following year (1911) he settled in Ceylon with three disciples on a small island in a lagoon near the village of Dodanduwa. On 9 July, Nyanatiloka founded the monastery he had failed to open in Europe, naming it 'The Island Hermitage'. Two months to the day later (9 September) the German *bhikkhu* welcomed Alexandra David-Neel to the Island Hermitage to preside over a meeting of the Buddhist Theosophical Society.

Mme David-Neel had arrived in Ceylon from Marseilles aboard a Japanese freighter ten days earlier. She had established contact with Nyanatiloka during his stay in Switzerland the previous year when, from May to June, the *bhikkhu* had been a guest of the Neels in Tunis. Nyanatiloka had even explored the possibility of founding his monastery in north Africa.

As a child, Alexandra David-Neel had been fascinated by the idea of travel to faraway lands. This passion became interwoven with an interest in Gnosticism and Christian mysticism. At the age of nineteen she became an Anarchist. The following year (1888), as a freethinking and militant feminist, she went to London to improve her English and was drawn to the Theosophical Society, where Mme Blavatsky was teaching at the time. Although Alexandra was never initiated into the Society's inner circle, she thrived in the company of the Theosophists, many of whom, like her, were searching for radical political and spiritual alternatives.

Her understanding of Asian thought was deepened on her return to Paris by her studies with the Indologist Sylvain Lévi. She also attended courses with Edouard Foucaux, a student of Burnouf, who introduced her to Tibetan Buddhist texts. But her main interest was in Chinese; her first two books were to be studies of Chinese moral and political philosophers. For spiritual inspiration she visited the Musée Guimet, where the images housed in its vaults exerted for her a 'vibration' that neither the Theosophists nor the academics could provide.

After a visit to Ceylon and India in 1891, where she was initiated into the teachings of Vedanta, she returned to Europe and trained as an opera singer. It was through her musical work in Tunis that she met Philip Neel. Their relationship was passionate, stormy and ultimately unworkable. They married in August 1904 and a month later separated for the first time. On 27 September, she wrote to him: 'I warned you in advance: I am not pretty, I am not fun, *I am not a woman* . . . . Why did you persist? Were you deranged?'

They continued to be periodically reconciled, but she spent most of her time pursuing her interest in Buddhism. In London she befriended T.W. Rhys-Davids and his wife Caroline, two of the foremost translators of Pali texts. In 1907 D.T. Suzuki's *Outlines of Mahayana Buddhism* appeared and she embarked on a correspondence with him. Two years later her own first book on Buddhism was published in Paris.

The Buddhism of the Buddha and Buddhist Modernism presented a non-academic account of Buddhist practice for a cultured

European readership. By 'Buddhist Modernism' she referred to the approach of the Maha-Bodhi Society, founded in Calcutta in 1891 by Anagarika Dharmapala with the encouragement of Mme Blavatsky and Colonel Olcott. David-Neel espoused a reformed Theravada Buddhism, in which a return to the early teachings of the Pali canon was combined with a Protestant zeal to rid Buddhism of popular superstitions and clerical power. Buddhist Modernism, she claimed, was 'only a step away' from Socialism. (She was a friend of a militant socialist in Italy called Benito Mussolini.) Despite her connection with Suzuki, she ignored the Mahayana and distanced herself from Theosophical interpretations. Her approach was rigorous, austere and pragmatic.

When she arrived in Ceylon the following year, she was received at the Maha-Bodhi Society by Dharmapala and feted as a fellow missionary. Their combined resolve and sense of mission would have been reinforced by the founding of the first European branch of the Maha-Bodhi Society in Leipzig in May of that same year.

Yet the strange absence in so prolific a writer of any comment about Ceylon during her two-month visit suggests disappointment, even disillusion. In contrast, an effusive letter to her long-suffering husband, written two days after her departure from Colombo, describes her feelings on entering the Hindu temple of Madurai in Tuticorin:

Oh! How can I even describe the sight, that shiver that makes you tremble to the core of your being? One touches the very earth, that world of terrible and evil powers, the domain of the 'Other', as they said in the Middle Ages.

Instinctively, she knew that she 'had set out on a path which I will perhaps never rediscover if I ever turn back'.

She headed up the east coast of India to Calcutta, from whence she had planned to leave for Rangoon to pursue her studies of

Theravada Buddhism. But she changed her mind and headed instead for the Himalayan principality of Sikkim. The probable reason for this diversion was in order to meet the 13th Dalai Lama, currently in exile in Darjeeling. Upon being received on 14 April 1912 in Kalimpong, she became the first European woman to have an audience with a Dalai Lama. Although initially overawed, a second meeting in August prompted her to revert to her former self. 'I don't like popes', she wrote, 'I don't like the kind of Buddhist Catholicism over which he presides. Everything about him is affected, he is neither cordial nor kind.'

Her ambivalence about Tibetan Buddhism continued in Sikkim. On the one hand, she met a Nyingma lama — the Gomchen of Lachen — at a hermitage in the mountains, who, although 'truly ugly and dressed in filthy robes', overwhelmed her with his presence. On the other hand, she convinced her close friend Sidkeong, an Oxford-educated *tulku* and heir to the Maharaja, of the need to restore the degenerate Tibetan monasteries to the pure standards of the Theravada. Sidkeong was also abbot of Podang monastery, where, to the consternation of the monks, he allowed this foreign woman to preach her peculiar ideas.

In the summer of 1914 she received a visit from her friend Nyanatiloka, who, for unknown reasons, was trying to reach Tibet. Due to snow-blocked passes and a shortage of funds he was forced to return to Ceylon shortly before the outbreak of war. But he took with him two younger brothers of the Sikkimese scholar Kazi Dawasamdup, a friend of Sidkeong and David-Neel who later translated the *Tibetan Book of the Dead* with W.Y. Evans-Wentz (who, incidentally, had known Sidkeong at Oxford.) The younger of the brothers, as Bhikkhu Mahinda, became one of the foremost Singalese poets of this century. In September the Scottish *bhikkhu* Silacara arrived, but, after a long hike with Alexandra along the Tibetan border, also departed.

After this puzzling flurry of activity, Alexandra David-Neel set off alone to see the Nyingma lama. On 5 December, Sidkeong, who had been enthroned as the Maharaja in February, was found dead. Poisoning was suspected, possibly by those at the court who were scared by his plans for reform, possibly by his stepmother who wished her own son to have the throne. He was thirty-five.

As the situation in Europe deteriorated, Alexandra resolved to remove herself as far as possible from the conflagration. She built a hut next to the hermit's, which she named 'Great Peace', and spent the next two years in retreat, studying and practising Vajrayana Buddhism with the lama until the autumn of 1916, when she was expelled from Sikkim by the British political officer Charles Bell for having made an illegal visit to the Panchen Lama in Shigatse. Like Dorzhiev, David-Neel believed the British had plans to take over Tibet and, like Lord Curzon with Dorzhiev, Bell was suspicious of David-Neel's politics. So she and Yongden made their way to Japan, where they were hosted by D.T. Suzuki, and then to China. Now, if only to spite the British, she resolved to reach Lhasa.

As a national of an enemy state, Nyanatiloka (and four other German monks) was deported by the British authorities from Ceylon and interned in Australia. He appealed against this treatment on religious grounds, and was permitted to move to a neutral country. He settled in a Buddhist monastery in Chung-king, China, where he continued his work on his translation of the Pali *Anguttara Nikaya*.

During the first years of the Great War, a precocious teenager called Ernst Lothar Hoffmann embarked on a comparative study to decide whether he was a Christian, a Buddhist or a Muslim. He opted for Buddhism because of its emphasis on individual freedom, a principle that failed to help him avoid conscription into the German army in October 1916.

When the fighting was over, Hoffmann drifted south to an artist's colony in Capri to pursue his interest in painting,

Buddhism and archeology. In 1928 he took a boat to Ceylon with the intention to ordain. On the advice of Dharmapala, he chose to become an *anagarika* (a homeless layman) rather than a monk. He settled at the Island Hermitage and became a student of Nyanatiloka, who had returned two years earlier after spending five years teaching in universities in Japan. Nyanatiloka gave Hoffman the name Govinda. The same year they founded the 'International Buddhist Union', with Nyanatiloka as president and Govinda as general-secretary.

As with Alexandra David-Neel, Govinda originally intended to stay in Asia for a short period before returning to Europe to promote Buddhism there. He likewise considered the Theravada as the only authentic teaching of the Buddha and living in a small hermitage in Ceylon 'the fulfilment of all my dreams'. After travelling in Burma with Nyanatiloka, Govinda was invited to Darjeeling to participate in an international Buddhist conference. He looked forward to this 'opportunity to uphold the purity of the Buddha's teachings, as preserved in Ceylon, and to spread its message in a country where the Buddha-Dharma had degenerated into a system of demon-worship and weird beliefs'.

But, like David-Neel, he was overwhelmed by the spiritual riches he found in north India among the Tibetans. He met a lama called Tomo Geshé Rinpoché with whom he underwent a profound conversion, even though he spent only a few weeks in his company. The vivid and complex symbolism of Tibetan Buddhism appealed to his artistic and romantic spirit, which had little room for expression in Ceylon. In 1933 he travelled via Ladakh to western Tibet, where the open terrain and crystalline skies further inspired his poetic sense of the Dharma. In 1937 he visited Sikkim as the guest of the Maharaja and met Alexandra's teacher, the Gomchen of Lachen, then an old man, in his remote hermitage. He also stayed in Podang Monastery, where Alexandra had tried to reform the monks. His Sikkimese hosts convinced him, however, 'that if any religious reform was necessary in their country it could only spring from a reassessment of those cultural and traditional values upon which Tibetan Buddhism was based, but never through the introduction of alien ways of thinking, even though they might be closer to the historical sources of Buddhism'. Sidkeong and David-Neel's efforts at change evidently still rankled with the aristocracy more than twenty years later.

During this period Govinda was based at Rabindranath Tagore's university at Shantiniketan in Bengal, where he continued his studies and taught Buddhist philosophy and modern languages until the outbreak of the Second World War.

While Nyanatiloka, David-Neel and Govinda explored Buddhism in Asia, Europe saw the emergence of a number of lay societies whose interest was in 'producing Buddhists, unafraid to style themselves as such, rather than on making known the finer points of Buddhism'. The centre of Buddhism in Germany between the wars was *Das Buddhistische Haus* ('The Buddhist House') in Berlin, the first permanent Buddhist 'Centre' in Europe (it still functions today). The House was founded by Dr Paul Dahlke who, like many of the early Buddhists in Germany, became interested in the Dharma via Schopenhauer. He began his formal studies in 1900 during a visit to Ceylon, but found the monastic life there too severe and determined to develop a kind of 'lay monastery' in Germany where Buddhism could be seriously studied and practised. He began building his 'Buddhist House' in 1923; Anagarika Dharmapala stayed there briefly in 1925; and by 1926 the construction of a temple was completed. A renowned homeopathic physician, he sought to establish the compatibility of Buddhism and modern science. He wrote a total of twenty-two books, several of which were translated into English by Bhikkhu Silacara. He died in 1928.

At the other end of the country lived Georg Grimm, another Schopenhauer-inspired Buddhist, who co-founded the *Buddhistische Gemeinde für Deutschland* ('Buddhist Community for Germany') in Munich in 1921. Grimm came from a devout Catholic family who had hoped that their son would enter the priesthood. He learned Pali and published his major work *Die Lehre des Buddha* in 1915, translated by Silacara in 1926 as *The Doctrine of the Buddha: The Religion of Reason*. Grimm's approach was informed by the humanities rather than the sciences and his writings are infused with a warm, heartfelt commitment. The Buddhist Community was forbidden by the Nazis in 1933, and Grimm's book *Der Samsaro* was ordered to be burnt on publication in 1935. In the same year Grimm secretly formed the *Altbuddhistische Gemeinde* ('Old Buddhist Community') at his house in Utting, Upper Bavaria.

In the spring of 1932 Martin Steinke, a Berlin banker who ten years earlier had established a small Buddhist Society in the city, found himself galvanized by the discourses of a visiting teacher called Chao Kung, a Hungarian also known as Ignaz Trebitsch-Lincoln.

After a bewildering and chequered career, which included being a Christian missionary in Canada, the Liberal member of parliament for Darlington in England and a German spy during the Great War, Trebitsch-Lincoln ended up in China where a mystical experience drove him to a Buddhist monastery where he took the name Chao Kung. In December 1932, Steinke, with eleven other European aspirants to monkhood, accompanied Chao Kung back to China where, on 1 November 1933, they received ordination in Tsi-hia Shan Monastery near Nanking. Steinke (now 'Tao Chün') returned to Europe the following year with his teacher and fellow disciples to embark on a world-wide Buddhist missionary campaign. But, doubtful of Trebitsch-Lincoln's authenticity, he left the party in Liverpool and, having opened the European Buddhist Congress in London in September, went back to Berlin.

Steinke remained as the only native Buddhist monk in Europe. He lectured widely, published a magazine ('The Teaching of Freedom'), and in 1935 organized and conducted a Buddhist summer-school. The following year he built a wooden house in Potsdam, which served as a *vihara* in which lived a permanent Buddhist community.

Compared to Germany, Buddhist developments elsewhere in Europe during this period were meagre. In Britain the figure most comparable to Dahlke and Grimm was the barrister Christmas Humphreys. On 19 November 1924 the Theosophical Society in London agreed to the forming of a Buddhist Lodge under his presidency. The Lodge severed connections with the Theosophical Society less than two years later. Humphreys was a skilled organizer and writer of popular books on Buddhism, but he lacked the philosophical and linguistic skills of his German counterparts and retained a life-long commitment to the 'great principles' of Blavatsky. The Lodge became the central focus for Buddhism in Britain: publishing books, pamphlets and a journal, hosting visits of prominent Buddhists, and celebrating the yearly festival of Wesak.

In July 1926 Anagarika Dharmapala came to London and opened a branch of the Maha–Bodhi Society. His aim was to create not only a meeting place for lay Buddhists but a monastery for Buddhist monks. On 8 July 1928, with considerable fanfare, three *bhikkhus* arrived from Ceylon and settled at the Society. Despite initial enthusiasm, the cultural and psychological gulf between traditional Ceylonese Buddhists and modern Europeans soon made itself apparent, sparking debate about how or whether Buddhism should be adapted to contemporary needs.

Bhikkhu Silacara had returned to Britain in 1925, having disrobed on grounds of ill-health, and, as J.F. McKechnie again,

316

became involved with Dharmapala's work in London. The only British Buddhist monk in Asia at this time was Frederic Fletcher. Inspired by Arnold's *The Light of Asia*, Fletcher went to Ceylon in the 1890s, where he was introduced to Dharmapala. But he returned to England and entered the Army. In the War he rose to the rank of Major, but was so sickened by the slaughter that he resolved to become a Buddhist monk. In 1922 he joined an expedition to Tibet and was received by the Panchen Lama at Shigatse. He stayed there a year and became the first Western European to receive novice ordination in a Tibetan Buddhist tradition. In 1924 he returned to Ceylon, where he took higher ordination as a *bhikkhu*. His commitment to an ecumenical approach is reflected in his Pali-Tibetan-Sanskrit name: Bhikkhu Dorje Prajnananda. He made a brief visit to London in 1926.

The most notable events in Britain in the 1930s were the second European Buddhist Congress (the first was convened in Berlin in 1933), held at the Maha-Bodhi Society from 22–3 September 1934, followed, in July 1936, by the World Congress of Faiths, chaired by its founder, the man who had chased Dorzhiev out of Tibet, Sir Francis Younghusband. The Buddhist representatives at the latter meeting were D.T. Suzuki, who impressed everyone with his enigmatic Zen ways, and G.P. Malalasekera, who was to found the World Fellowship of Buddhists in 1950 and later get George Roerich out of a tight spot in Moscow. Also in 1936 the twenty-one-year-old Alan Watts published his first book, *The Spirit of Zen*, and became the editor of the Lodge's journal *Buddhism in England*. He had first contacted the Lodge in 1929 while still a schoolboy. He did not remain in Europe for long though; he left for America in 1938 with his young bride.

On 10 May 1925 Alexandra David-Neel and Yongden returned to France. As the first Western woman to reach Lhasa, she was received with enthusiasm and invited to lecture throughout Europe. She published several books in quick succession, in which she gave a detailed and sympathetic account of a culture and religion which were still barely known. In 1928 she settled in Digne in a house named 'Samten Dzong' ('Fortress of Meditation'). But she missed Asia. In 1936 she and Yongden boarded a train for Moscow. After being chaperoned around the city, probably unaware that Stalin's anti-Buddhist purges were in full swing, they took the Trans-Siberian to Peking where they arrived on 26 January 1937.

David-Neel was motivated more by a compulsive yearning to return to Asia than any definite plan. In July of the same year Japanese troops stormed Peking and by December occupied Shanghai and Nanking. Instead of accepting the offer of safe passage to Hong Kong, Alexandra and Yongden chose to escape the fighting by retreating west into the Chinese hinterland towards Tibet. She was sixty-nine.

The excitement Alexandra David-Neel aroused in France for the magic and mysteries of Tibetan Buddhism did not translate into a corresponding willingness to practise the Dharma. She accepted no disciples, preferring to give occasional lectures to large, awestruck audiences and then retreat to Digne. The year of her return coincided with the publication of Jacques Bacot's translation of the life of Milarepa, and it was through an extraordinary generation of orientalists (Lévi, de la Vallée Poussin, Demiéville, Grousset, Lamotte, Bacot, Pelliot, Finot, Toussaint) that the literate French public learned about Buddhism. Moreover, from 1919, in the Collège de France, where Burnouf had taught nearly a century before, a course on Zen was given by Masaharu Anesaki from the Imperial University of Tokyo — the first time in Europe that an Asian (albeit a very Westernized one) had taught Buddhism in such a sanctum of rational knowledge.

The only group of practising Buddhists in France during this period was that formed by Mlle Constant de Lounsbery in 1929, called *Les Amis du bouddhisme* ('Friends of Buddhism').

The founding of this group followed a visit to Europe in 1928 by the Chinese abbot Tai Hsü from Nanking, a key figure in the revival of Buddhism in China in the first years of the Republic. His wish was to create a non-sectarian 'International Institute of Buddhist Studies in Europe', with a committee in each capital city. In November he arrived in London where Christmas Humphreys agreed to form the London committee of his planned Institute. He then went to Germany and France, where Mlle de Lounsbery's group was established in Paris under his auspices. The aim of *Les Amis* was to distance Buddhism from the occultism of Theosophy by presenting it as 'the authentic and rational wisdom of the Orient'.

In Italy interest in Buddhism between the wars was limited. The outstanding figure was Giuseppe Tucci, a brilliant orientalist who had lived in India from 1925–30, where he taught in Tagore's university in Shantiniketan and conducted his first expedition to Tibet. In 1932 he became Professor of Indian and Far Eastern Studies in Rome and the following year founded his own Institute of Far Eastern Studies (ISMEO). Unlike many academics, Tucci had a shrine in his house and considered himself a practising Buddhist of the Kagyu school.

When war again broke out in Europe in 1939, the hopes of these first European Buddhists, both at home and in Asia, were temporarily shattered. The Germans suffered most. The Buddhist societies were suppressed and Buddhist books were either banned or could only be published with modifications approved by the Nazi censor. Steinke and a number of his followers were arrested by the Gestapo in 1941 and detained for several weeks. Another German Buddhist, Siegmund Feniger, who was Jewish, left for Ceylon in 1935 to escape the Nazi's final solution. He was ordained by Nyanatiloka as a novice in 1936 and the following year as a *bhikkhu*, with the name Nyanaponika.

British India and Ceylon were far from ideal sanctuaries.

Irrespective of their being Jewish, like Nyanaponika, or even naturalized British citizens, like Govinda, in 1941 all German-born monks and scholars were interned in a camp near Dehra Dun in the Himalayan foothills. While Nyanatiloka and Lama Govinda were in different sections and saw each other only occasionally, Nyanaponika formed a close friendship with Govinda.

In London the Maha-Bodhi Society closed down shortly after the outbreak of war. In 1940 the Buddhist Lodge lost almost their entire stock of literature to a German bomb. In April 1941 another bomb seriously damaged the house in which they met in Westminster. After the initial period of soul-searching as to whether a Buddhist should fight Nazism or be a conscientious objector, those who remained in the country worked hard to sustain the activities of the Lodge, which, in May 1943, became the 'Buddhist Society, London', and its magazine *The Middle Way*. One of those supporting the Society at this time was John Blofeld, a Buddhist who had lived in China before the war and translated a number of Zen texts.

Throughout the German occupation *Les Amis du Bouddhisme* continued, on a diminishing scale, to meet in Paris. Mme David-Neel and Yongden (now a naturalized Frenchman) remained immobilized in Tatsienlu (modern Kangding), on the border of eastern Tibet, and later in Chengdu until September 1945.

In 1943 Trebitsch-Lincoln died in Shanghai. Georg Grimm, 'The Mildest Judge in Bavaria', passed away three months after the War in Utting. The Ven. Tai Hsü died in 1947, his plans for an International Institute of Buddhist Studies in Europe unfulfilled. Bhikkhu Dorje Prajnananda (Fletcher) died in Burma in 1950, and J.F. McKechnie in the obscurity of a nursing home in Bury, England, the following year.

The scholarly studies of Buddhist texts, the philosophy of Schopenhauer, the syncretic visions of Theosophy and disenchantment with Christianity created the basis upon which this small group of cultured Europeans, most of whom knew each other, set out to explore and embrace the Dharma. They had to face disinterest and persecution, survive revolutions and wars. The tortured political struggles of Europe preoccupied the majority of those who otherwise may have been drawn to the Dharma. Conditions were not yet sufficient to galvanize a broader movement of interest.

'I am the prisoner of a dream', wrote Alexandra David-Neel upon arriving in Sikkim in 1912, 'of an attraction to I know not what.' The life of this Frenchwoman is an extreme example of the struggle between rational detachment and romantic fascination. She swung between these poles, presenting herself as a 'reporter on the Orient' one moment, a convert to the magic and mystery of Tibet the next. A similar but less extreme pattern can be detected in Lama Govinda. 'Some inexplicable force seemed to keep me back', he recalled when contemplating leaving the Himalayas in the early 1930s. 'The longer I stayed on in this magic world into which I had dropped . . ., the more I felt that a hitherto unknown form of reality was revealed to me . . . .' Much of his writing, however, presents methodical and ordered accounts of Buddhist doctrine replete with diagrams and charts: a striking contrast to his appearance as a luxuriously robed lama who believed himself to be the reincarnation of Novalis.

After the war, Alexandra David-Neel and Yongden returned from China via Calcutta, where they met Govinda for the first and only time. They returned to France and lived in Digne for the rest of their lives. She published another eleven books, but obstinately refused to take on the role of a teacher. On 7 November 1951, Lama Yongden died at the age of fifty-two, an alcoholic alienated from his own culture and smothered by the will of an indomitable mother-figure. Alexandra found herself alone. Those who knew her during this time describe a stubborn and temperamental misanthropist. Yet as she sat crippled by arthritis in Digne, yearning for Tibet, she regarded the Chinese communist invasion of 1951 as both inevitable and, for the majority of Tibetans, welcome. Again that poignant contrast between the nostalgic romantic and the hard-headed, left-wing French intellectual.

In July 1969 Arnaud Desjardins came to interview her for French television. 'Don't you think, *messieurs*,' she asked, 'that it is rather indecent to come and film the death of an old woman?' On 8 September she died. She was nearly one hundred and one years old.

19

SANGHARAKSHITA:
ADAPTATION

Friday, 3 July 1992. Seven young men with Sanskrit names emerge from a terrace house in Cambridge and climb into the back of a white Mercedes van. They drive out of the city against the early morning traffic, picking up others on the way, curve through the leafy lanes of the countryside, and pull to a halt in an industrial estate near the village of Fulbourn. In a storeroom–cum–office they sit in a circle and chant a verse in Tibetan to a bronze image of the Bodhisattva Tara. After reporting in, the work–schedule is consulted and jobs are allocated for the day. At just after 9 a.m. Windhorse Trading, listed as one of the hundred fastest-growing companies in Britain in 1992, gets underway.

Sangharakshita, the man whose vision lies at the root of this thriving economic activity, was born as Dennis Lingwood in south-west London to a working class family in 1925, only a few hundred yards from where Allan Bennett (Ananda Metteyya) had died two years earlier. A sickly child, he received little schooling and was for the most part self-taught. In the summer of 1940 he was evacuated to Devon, where he came across Mme Blavatsky's *Isis Unveiled* and, 'having read it straight through twice, realized I was not a Christian and never had been'. Back in London the following year he unearthed two Buddhist texts, the *Diamond Sutra* and the *Platform Sutra*, after reading which he knew 'that I was a Buddhist and always had been'. He made contact with the Buddhist Society, and took the three refuges and five precepts from the Burmese monk U Thittila.

Lingwood's passage to Asia was provided by the British army into which he had been conscripted in 1943. On 23 August the following year the Signals Unit to which he had been assigned was posted to Delhi. Finding little trace of Buddhism, he applied for a transfer to Colombo. But the Buddhist monks he met in Ceylon failed to inspire him. The nineteen-year-old soldier sought instead the guidance of swamis in the Ramakrishna Mission. What attracted him to these reformed Hindu swamis instead of the ceremonious *bhikkhu*s was that 'they demonstrated that the spiritual life, far from being practicable only in the remote past, could be, and in fact had been, lived in modern times'.

With the end of hostilities in 1945 Signalman Lingwood applied for a six-week leave. But instead of returning to his unit he disappeared into India. After a couple of years of moving from one religious organization to another, including a disappointing stint at the Maha–Bodhi Society in Calcutta, he concluded that 'far from being a help to spiritual development', such institutions 'were only a hindrance'. Together with an Indian friend, Rabindra Kumar Banerjee, they chose to follow the Buddha's own example of 'going forth' from home to homelessness, severing 'at one stroke our connection with an incorrigible world'.

On 18 August 1947, they gave away their belongings, dyed their clothes ochre and said goodbye to their friends. Their initial plan was to head south for Ceylon to receive ordination as Buddhist monks. In their ascetic zeal, however, they had renounced their identification papers and were refused permission to land. Instead they spent fifteen months taking care of a deserted ashram near the town of Muvattupuzha in Travancore. After nearly two years of Hindu ashrams and homelessness, the yearning to take ordination again took hold and they headed for Sarnath, the site of the Buddha's first sermon, to request the novice vows from the Singhalese monks who lived there. To their bitter disappointment they were refused. The monks, it seemed, were reluctant to take any responsibility for these vagrants.

They learned, however, of an elderly Burmese *bhikkhu* at Kusinara, the town where the Buddha died, who might be willing to ordain them and so set off in the intense April heat on foot to arrive, exhausted, ten days later. This time they were more fortunate. The monk, U Chandramani, ordained them as novices. Banerjee was given the name 'Buddharakshita', and Lingwood 'Sangharakshita'. Before they had been a week in the robe, their preceptor instructed them to go and teach his disciples in southern Nepal.

Unbeknown to Sangharakshita, on 24 April 1949, a mere eighteen days before his own ordination in Kusinara, two other Englishmen had been ordained as novices by Nyanatiloka, now an old man of seventy-one, in a glade at the Island Hermitage. These were Osbert Moore and Harold Musson, two former army officers whose interest in Buddhism had developed in Italy during the war upon reading *La Dottrina del Risveglio* ('The Doctrine of Awakening') by the Italian esotericist and fascist Julius Evola.

Moore and Musson were given the names Nanamoli and Nanavira, respectively, and the following year received full ordination as *bhikkhu*s in Colombo. Both men became accomplished Pali scholars. Nanamoli produced some of the finest English translations of Pali texts to have appeared, including the massive *Visuddhimagga* ('Path of Purity') of the venerated Theravada commentator Buddhaghosa. He died suddenly of a heart attack in 1960.

His friend Nanavira retreated to a remote hermitage in a forest near Matara in the south of the island. Prevented by chronic illness from pursuing intensive meditation, Nanavira turned his attention to understanding the Dharma as presented by the Buddha in the Pali Canon. He became increasingly radical and unorthodox in his views and ended his life in 1965, convinced that he had attained the first level of sainthood, that of Stream Entry (*srota-apanna*). A collection of his brilliant and controversial writings was published in 1987 under the title *Clearing the Path*.

The period from the end of the Second World War until the 1960s was one of the bleakest in terms of Western involvement with Buddhism. In addition to Sangharakshita, Nanamoli and Nanavira only a small handful of Europeans were to become Buddhist monks during this time. The Buddhist Societies that had been founded in Europe before the war continued to function with a slowly growing membership, but few new organizations or centres were created. Nyanatiloka, the longest-ordained European monk, died on 28 May 1957. His extraordinary life was acknowledged by his being given a state funeral attended both by the prime minister of Ceylon and the German ambassador.

In March 1950, the twenty-four-year-old Sangharakshita found himself alone in the Himalayan town of Kalimpong in north-east India. For the past seven months he had been studying Pali and Abhidharma with Bhikkhu Jagdish Kashyap, the disgruntled Bihari professor of Buddhist studies at Benares Hindu University. While visiting Kalimpong, Kashyap-ji decided to relinquish his university post and instructed his young English disciple to stay in the hill-station and work for the good of Buddhism. Sangharakshita was to remain there for the next fourteen years.

On 24 November he returned briefly to Sarnath to receive *bhikkhu* ordination from another senior Burmese monk, U Kawinda. While it is traditional for a newly ordained monk to remain with his preceptor for five to ten years, U Kawinda asked Sangharakshita formally to renounce this 'reliance' on him. Thus the need for self-reliance, which had characterized the young man's life from boyhood, was again required of him. Just as he had educated himself in the Western tradition, so he would largely educate himself in the Buddhist. By dint of circumstance and predisposition, he was forced to cultivate an independence of mind, which enabled him to arrive at an understanding of Buddhism that was not defined by the dogmas of any one school.

The one person with whom Sangharakshita discovered an affinity during his early years at Kalimpong was Lama Anagarika Govinda. After his release from internment, Govinda had married a former student Rati Petit, subsequently known as Li Gotami, and become a lama in the Kagyu school of Tibetan Buddhism. In 1948 the couple had undertaken their epic journey to the ruined city of Tsaparang in western Tibet, the record of which comprised Govinda's celebrated autobiography *The Way of the White Clouds*. When Sangharakshita first met the Govindas in October 1951, he was already familiar with the lama's thinking through a series of articles that had appeared in the Englishman's newly founded journal *Stepping-Stones*. Govinda's most recent contribution had confirmed Sangharakshita's own feelings that Buddhism was a living experience that could not be identified with any historical or cultural expression. 'It is far better', Govinda had stated, 'to approach all forms of Buddhism and of Buddhist life with an open and unprejudiced mind and to accept whatever leads towards the realization of Enlightenment. This is the only criterion of Buddhism.'

By this time Sangharakshita was acquainted with several European specialists on Buddhism. Living in Kalimpong were Marco Pallis, the English author of *Peaks and Lamas*, and George Roerich, the Russian Tibetologist. He had also met the Austrian scholar Herbert Guenther, who was then teaching in Lucknow.

327

Yet despite their erudition none of these men affected the English monk as did Lama Govinda. Of the twelve days they spent together that cloudless autumn, he wrote:

> my feeling that we were kindred spirits received more abundant confirmation than I had dared to hope, and I was left in no doubt whatever that despite the fact that he was a married lama and I was a celibate monk I had more in common with Lama Govinda than with any other Buddhist I had ever met.

One reason for this kinship was their shared passion for literature and the fine arts. Govinda was the first Buddhist Sangharakshita had known to declare openly the compatibility of art with the spiritual life. Until then, the young monk-poet had struggled with these apparently conflicting vocations to such a degree that on occasion his personality felt split into two. 'Sangharakshita I', he confessed,

> wanted to enjoy the beauty of nature, to read and write poetry, to listen to music, to look at paintings and sculpture, to experience emotion, to lie in bed and dream, to see places, to meet people,

while

> Sangharakshita II wanted to realize the truth, to read and write philosophy, to observe the precepts, to get up early and meditate, to mortify the flesh, to fast and pray.

Govinda encouraged him to pursue both sides together in the conviction that there was 'a deep inner connection between them'. He gave him a small book in which he had written:

Art and meditation are creative states of the human mind. Both are nourished by the same source, but it may seem that they are moving in different directions: art towards the realm of sense-impressions, meditation towards the overcoming of forms and sense-impressions. But the difference pertains only to accidentals, not to essentials.

Another aspect of Lama Govinda's influence was to encourage a greater sympathy for the Tibetan Vajrayana tradition. After a week together in Kalimpong, Sangharakshita accompanied the Govindas to their house in nearby Ghoom. It was here, twenty years earlier, that Govinda himself had turned to Tibetan Buddhism. As the iconography of Tibet had stimulated Govinda's artistic sense, so had the tantric teachings — of which the art was an outward expression — transformed his understanding of the spiritual path.

In his own way, Sangharakshita was undergoing a journey similar to that of David-Neel and Govinda before him. Although ordained as a Theravada monk, he was disillusioned with the dogmatism, formalism and nationalism of many of the Theravada monastics he encountered. Two years after meeting the Govindas, he began studying with the Geluk lama Dhardo Rinpoché. Several years later, in 1959, some of the greatest Tibetan teachers of the 20th century arrived in Kalimpong, having fled across the Himalayas from the Chinese. And from these, who included Jamyang Khyentsé Rinpoché, Düjom Rinpoché, and Dilgo Khyentsé Rinpoché, he received initiations and teachings in the Nyingma tradition.

Yet what distinguished the young English monk from the somewhat aloof figures of David-Neel and Govinda were his organizational skills. Within two months of arriving at Kalimpong he had formed the Young Mens' Buddhist Association (YMBA) and within another two months had launched the first issue of

Stepping-Stones. Although mornings were spent studying, afternoons and evenings were devoted to teaching (everything from English to Abhidharma), arranging activities for the young men of the town, editing and writing articles, haggling with printers and soliciting funds. He became enmeshed in the Byzantine social and political life of Kalimpong, cultivating friendships with influential merchants and exiled Greek princes alike, and incurring the disdain of Christian missionaries.

In September 1952 Sangharakshita accepted an invitation from the Maha-Bodhi Society to write a biographical sketch of the Society's founder, Anagarika Dharmapala. His discovery of the late 'Reviver of Buddhism' through his books, letters and journal-entries had an impact on him comparable to the encounter with Govinda the previous autumn. Dharmapala exemplified the Buddhist ideal to which Sangharakshita himself aspired. 'Far from being an activist and organiser in the more superficial sense', he wrote, 'he was an idealist and a man of vision, . . . beneath the dynamic activity of the selfless worker for Buddhism there lay the serenity and mindfulness of the yogi.'

The 'fervent admiration' he felt for Dharmapala also helped reconcile him to the organization his hero had founded. Henceforth he decided to help the Society in its work of reintroducing Buddhism to India. Through the discovery of Dharmapala he had glimpsed the 'vibrant, idealistic Buddhist organisation' that the Maha-Bodhi Society had once been.

The early 1950s were the crucial formative years for Sangharakshita in which his self-confidence as an organizer and self-understanding as a contemplative matured. In July 1954, at the age of twenty-nine, he was invited to give a series of lectures in Bangalore, south India. Their success encouraged him to write his panoramic study, *A Survey of Buddhism*, which was published in 1957 to coincide with the 2,500th anniversary of the Buddha's awakening. 'I was concerned', he recalled, 'to see Buddhism not only in its full breadth but also in its depth.' He felt that Western scholars as well as modern Asian monks largely failed on either or both of these counts and that consequently the presentations they gave of it were 'fragmentary, distorted, and often completely misleading'.

A Survey of Buddhism was the fruit of thirteen years' study and reflection. Yet apart from the seven months with Jagdish Kashyap and, since 1953, occasional sessions with Dhardo Rinpoché, Sangharakshita's knowledge of Buddhist doctrine was based on English translations of canonical texts and scholarly studies of the material. His knowledge of Pali and Sanskrit remained fairly rudimentary and he learned neither spoken nor written Tibetan. The overview that emerges from his meticulous prose testifies both to a capacity for synthesis and an innate power to grasp essentials.

The final catalyst in the formation of Sangharakshita in the 1950s was Dr Bhimrao Ramji Ambedkar, an Untouchable who had risen to become free India's first Law Minister. Ambedkar was interested in Buddhism as a way for millions of fellow Untouchables to escape from the repressive caste system of India, which, although outlawed by the very Constitution Ambedkar had himself helped devise, was in practice as entrenched as ever. The two men did not meet, however, until the end of 1952, when Ambedkar's political career was effectively over. Four years later, in Nagpur on 14 October 1956, Ambedkar formally converted to Buddhism by taking the refuges and precepts from U Chandramani. He then turned to the 380,000 Untouchables who had gathered for the occasion and administered the same refuges and precepts, plus twenty-two vows of his own devising. Six weeks later, before this movement of mass-conversion could get underway, Ambedkar died.

Sangharakshita continued Ambedkar's work by lecturing throughout central and western India to ex-Untouchables and was profoundly moved by the fervour of these poor, illiterate and disenfranchised people towards Buddhism. Thirty years later, on completing a book on Ambedkar's work, he found himself 'more convinced than ever that my approach to Buddhism was in line with that of the great Untouchable leader'.

October 1962 marked the closure of two important cycles in Sangharakshita's life. On the 12th of the month he received the Bodhisattva precepts from Dhardo Rinpoché, thus completing a circle that began twenty-one years earlier in his encounter with the two Mahayana Buddhist texts that convinced him he was a Buddhist. The second circle was completed nine days later when he received initiation into the practice of Padmasambhava from Khachu Rinpoché, thus formalizing the intuitive identification with the tamer of Tibetan demons that had been a part of him since his early days in the Himalayas. He was now prepared to undertake the mission to which he has dedicated his life.

❧

Sangharakshita returned to England in August 1964 at the invitation of the English Sangha Trust and settled in the Hampstead Buddhist Vihara. Because of his commitments in India he had only intended to stay for four to six months. The months grew into two years.

As he lectured throughout the country, he became aware of the state of Buddhism in the land he had left twenty years ago. The dominant figure at this time was Christmas Humphreys and the 'official church' the Buddhist Society he had founded forty years earlier. The trustees of the English Sangha Trust tended to be members of the Society who did not agree with its (i.e. Humphreys') lay approach, and had, as we have seen in Chapter 4, been trying unsuccessfully for the past nine years to establish an ordained community of Buddhist monks in Britain. The

English *bhikkhu* in Kalimpong seemed the ideal person for the task.

Sangharakshita recognized that in the early 1960s there was a tremendous potential for the Dharma in Britain. The English Sangha Trust, however, believed that the only acceptable form of *sangha* was the kind of traditional Theravada monasticism of which he had been so critical in India, while the Buddhist Society seemed to promote Buddhism as a kind of spiritual pastime rather than a fully committed engagement with the Dharma. While paying a farewell visit to India in 1966, Sangharakshita was informed that he would not be welcome back at the Hampstead Vihara. Some of his unconventional ideas and behaviour had proved unacceptable to the English Sangha Trust.

He returned to London nonetheless and set about creating an organization that would fulfill his own vision of what a contemporary Buddhist *sangha* could be. On 6 April 1967 he founded the Friends of the Western Buddhist Order (FWBO) and a year later ordained nine men and three women as the nucleus of the Western Buddhist Order.

Sangharakshita chose to adapt the traditional structures of Buddhism to suit contemporary needs rather than insist that Westerners adapt to the time-honoured forms of Buddhism in Asia. From the outset he had been inspired by individuals who had likewise sought reform: Mme Blavatsky; Ramakrishna; Lama Govinda; Anagarika Dharmapala; and Dr Ambedkar. His time in India had taught him that Buddhism was a comprehensive and practical philosophy of life unlimited by cultural and ethnic identities. It was a protean movement that throughout its history had proven how it could adapt to a wide range of changing conditions. Moreover, contrary to how it often appeared, Buddhism was not a private religious indulgence but a potential agent of social change.

His provocative stance against the British Buddhist establishment blended well with the counter-cultural enthusiasms of the late 1960s. He grew his hair and experimented with sex, attracting to his Order rebellious young men and women who sought a spirituality commensurate with the liberating ethos of the times. (A similar phenomenon was occurring at this time around Chögyam Trungpa in Scotland.) Sangharakshita's self-confessed 'erratic' process of discovery now reached a point where Sangharakshita I in particular found a sympathetic environment in which to flourish. He has compared his evolution to 'that of Yeats' butterfly',

> which flutters zig-zag fashion from flower to flower, and symbolizes the psyche or soul, rather than that of the hawk, which hurls itself straight on its prey, and symbolizes the logical mind.

But while confessing an intuitive, romantic impulse at the root of his actions, he was able to realize his vision because of his rational gifts as a synthesizer of ideas and organizer of people.

Central to the development of Sangharakshita's understanding of the Dharma was the emergence of Going for Refuge to the Buddha, Dharma and Sangha as the 'central and decisive, indeed the definitive, act of the Buddhist life'. Superficially, this seems an unremarkable observation, since Going for Refuge has always been regarded as that which defines someone as a Buddhist. Yet he noticed that the Going for Refuge among many Buddhists had degenerated over time into the pious repetition of formulae. Going for Refuge was likewise seen as a preliminary step to be superseded by the more 'serious' commitments of taking the monastic, Bodhisattva or tantric vows.

Since Going for Refuge refers to a reorientation of one's life away from mundane concerns to the values embodied in the Buddha, Dharma and Sangha, then *any* decisive act along the path must essentially be a Going for Refuge. Thus renunciation, receiving ordination as a monk or Bodhisattva, Stream Entry and the arising of *bodhicitta* are united in their being different levels of intensity in Going for Refuge. Sangharakshita sees the driving force of this act even in the process of biological evolution. 'Each form of life', he reflected, 'aspired to develop into a higher form or, so to speak, went for Refuge to that higher form.' Thus Going for Refuge is, at this level, neither a devotional act, a commitment nor a spiritually transformative experience, 'but the key to the mystery of existence'.

In the 1960s Sangharakshita developed his idea of Buddhism as the 'Path of the Higher Evolution', in contrast to that of biological, or 'Lower', evolution. While the latter was 'the process of development from amoeba to man, . . . the Higher Evolution was the process of development from man to Buddha'. The idea in itself was not new; it had been used by the Theosophists in the 19th century. Human beings stood midway between these two evolutionary processes and could either remain cycling meaninglessly in pursuit of transient comforts or follow a path which would lead them towards authentic individuality. When this choice occurred, then, and only then, did one truly Go for Refuge.

Thus ordination into the Western Buddhist Order is achieved by consciously and formally Going for Refuge. To become ordained no longer means receiving a particular set of monastic precepts. In this way the traditional division between monks and laity is dissolved and in its place emerges a *sangha* united not by a common form of lifestyle but by a common commitment. Upon receiving ordination, one is given the title 'Dharmachari' or 'Dharmacharini' (Farer in the Dharma).

Since 1967 over five hundred people world-wide have 'Gone for Refuge' and thus been ordained into the Western Buddhist Order. Prior to receiving ordination the aspirant is required to live as a 'Mitra' ('friend' in Sanskrit), a kind of novitiate period which occurs when one has decided to stop 'shopping around' among other spiritual groups (including Buddhist ones), maintain close contact with Order Members, do a daily meditation practice, and help with the activities of the FWBO. Only when the Order is satisfied with one's commitment and level of understanding and practice is one invited to attend the three-month retreat that culminates in ordination. Henceforth one will be known by the new name given at the ceremony and will be encouraged to devote oneself to the aims of the Order. One is neither required to be celibate nor to live in a community; one is free to assume whatever role in society one believes will best express one's commitment to the Three Jewels. The same procedures apply to both men and women.

The Western Buddhist Order has been described as 'a free association of aspiring individuals who come together voluntarily out of a common commitment to the development of individuality'. The Order is distinct from the FWBO, which is the wider 'positive group' of men and women for whom the Order serves as a nucleus of spiritual inspiration. The FWBO operates through three primary institutional forms: public Buddhist Centres, of which there are currently fifty-five, mostly in Britain and among ex-Untouchables in India; residential spiritual communities; and team-based Right Livelihood businesses such as Windhorse Trading near Cambridge, which now employs sixty people.

The FWBO distinguishes itself from most other Buddhist organizations by refusing to rely primarily on donations for support. It aspires to the creation of an economically self-reliant Buddhist community in which each aspect of one's existence — work, living arrangements, even cultural activities (FWBO Arts has recently produced a Buddhist play and an oratorio) — becomes an integral part of an all-embracing practice of the Dharma.

By seeking to adapt traditional Buddhism to the needs of modern society, the FWBO does not identify with a particular

Asian form of the Dharma. Its teachings are drawn from all Buddhist schools, although more from the Indo-Tibetan than the Sino-Japanese traditions. Yet despite this ecumenical approach, FWBO centres remain closed to all Buddhist teachers from outside the Order and Order Members rarely follow Sangharakshita's own example in exploring other living Buddhist schools. The organization's sole living link with tradition at present lies in the person of Sangharakshita. Consequently, the FWBO is often perceived by other Western Buddhists as a self-enclosed organization that, in spite of its claim to contemporary relevance, has limited interaction with the wider Buddhist community.

Adaptation is not so much an option as a matter of degree. Even the most conservative Tibetan lama or Sri Lankan *bhikkhu* tends over time to modify what he says and does simply in order to be understood in the modern West. Likewise, even the most radical interpreter of Buddhism needs to base her interpretations on canonical texts simply in order to be credible as a Buddhist. For cross-cultural communication to be meaningful, both partners in the dialogue need to be willing to relinquish attachments to certain conditioned beliefs. Wherever one stands, one cannot ignore the calls either of the past tradition or of the present situation. Faith in the past must combine with compassion for the present in order to ensure a continuity of value for the future.

At one end of this 'spectrum of adaptation' are those who see any change as a weakening of the pure tradition that has to be tolerated simply to survive in a hostile, un-Buddhist environment. At the other end are those who wish boldly to jettison all past forms of tradition as weighed down with cultural burdens that hinder the inner dynamism of the Dharma from bursting forth in fresh and vital ways. Most schools of Buddhism in the West would probably be clustered around the middle of the band, if anything leaning towards the 'traditional' pole. The FWBO, however, would be found considerably further towards the 'dynamic' pole.

Another school in the dynamic region of the spectrum would be the Arya Maitreya Mandala Order founded by Lama Govinda at the instigation of Tomo Geshé Rinpoché in 1932 — although not formally established until 1952. As a symbol for this future-oriented movement of spiritual renewal, Tomo Geshé chose the forthcoming Buddha Maitreya to serve, in Govinda's words, 'as a bridge that over and above all differences should join the essence of all traditions of the Buddhist Dharma with the present and the future'. Today there are eighty-four ordained members of this order, mainly in Germany, Hungary and Austria, all of whom have passed through a comprehensive series of stages in the teachings of all the Buddhist schools, culminating with initiation into the Vajrayana. Approximately four hundred people are receiving training in the tradition. Since Lama Govinda's death in 1985, the Order has been under the direction of Dr Karl Heinz Gottman (Advayavajra).

From the outset, the Arya Maitreya Mandala Order was to be 'a brotherhood of mind and heart, ready to help those who had been inspired by the teachings of the Buddha and who wanted to put it into practice as human beings of our time'. For Lama Govinda it was 'of no consequence' how many people joined the order. He saw the urge to proselytize as arising from a Nietzschean will to power and indicative of 'a weakening of the religious sense'. Neither did Lama Govinda spend time developing an organization in Europe. More than thirty years passed before he returned in 1961 to a Europe transformed beyond recognition from what he had known. Subsequent visits were rare, and in his final years of illness he chose to move from India to California, under the care of the San Francisco Zen Center, than settle in Europe. The wider influence of his work is still primarily through his writings.

In contrast to Govinda's approach, the FWBO's attitude to spreading the Dharma is one of heartfelt urgency. 'There are thousands of people almost on the doorstep who could benefit from contact with Buddhism as presented by the FWBO', Sangharakshita told a Men's Seminar in 1980. 'So why isn't one making it available to them?' Elsewhere, the organization's most articulate polemicist, Dharmachari Subhuti, has argued that criticism, in a spirit of friendship, 'is an essential part of the process of growth'. Moreover, the creation of the 'New Society' as envisioned by the FWBO is bound to meet with resistance. 'The enemies to be attacked are legion', writes Subhuti. In particular, the FWBO is critical of Christianity, which it holds responsible for many of the deep-seated guilt-feelings of Westerners, and has encouraged blasphemy as a means to free oneself from its sub-conscious grip. It likewise questions assumptions about family life, liberalism, romantic love and so on that Westerners continue to uphold uncritically even though they consider themselves Buddhists. For the FWBO, Western society as such needs to be subject to the unflinching scrutiny of Buddhist values.

Yet adaptation, in whatever form it takes, leads inevitably to a deeper engagement with European culture. Looking forward to the future task of the FWBO, Sangharakshita commented in 1975:

Then we [will] have to start linking up with other areas of thought, maybe salvaging whatever we can that is positive in Christianity, and studying people like Goethe and Blake to find out what there is in them that is compatible with what we are trying to do.

And on 10 January 1985, four days before he died in his wife's arms, Lama Govinda replied enthusiastically from America to the first letter he had received from the Englishman in several years.

I am a great admirer of Italian art, and like you, I always uphold the importance of European culture. Without knowing the roots of our own culture, how can we absorb the essence of Buddhist culture?

This question is one that has to be asked by all who sincerely practise Buddhism in the West today, irrespective of whether they follow a traditional Asian school or a modern movement such as the FWBO. If Buddhism is to survive in the West it has to avoid the twin dangers of excessive rigidity, which will lead to marginalization and irrelevance, and excessive flexibility, which will lead to absorption by other disciplines and a loss of distinctive identity.

20

SATIPATTHANA:
MINDFUL AWARENESS

Two hundred yards from the medieval grandeur of St Peter's Square and the forbidding walls of the Vatican City a group of Italians sit in cross-legged silence on the wooden floor of the Circolo 'L'Orfeo', a martial arts centre in a tiny back street. No one is dressed in robes; there are no religious images — not even a whiff of incense or a discreet candle. The people are of all ages and a wide range of backgrounds; there are rather more women than men. Before them, seated on a chair, is a slight, scholarly figure with a greying beard. Corrado Pensa is a professor of oriental religion and philosophy at the University of Rome and president of A.Me.Co., the *Associazione per la meditazione di consapevolezza* (Association for Awareness Meditation). He speaks of paying mindful attention to the simplest aspects of everyday life, of quietening the incessant chatter of the mind, of cultivating fresh and clear awareness, of extending loving kindness: i.e. Buddhist practice stripped down to bare essentials.

The origins of this practice are found in Gautama's own discourse on the 'Foundations of Mindfulness' (*Satipatthana Sutta*) in the Pali Canon. It has been described as 'the most important discourse ever given by the Buddha on mental development', and as such is highly revered in all Theravada Buddhist countries of Asia. The Buddha opened the discourse by declaring:

> There is, monks, this way that leads only to the purification of beings, to the overcoming of sorrow and distress, to the disappearance of pain and sadness, to the gaining of the right path, to the realisation of Nirvana: — that is to say the four foundations of mindfulness.

These four foundations are the four areas of life to which mindful awareness needs to be applied: body, feelings, mind and objects of mind. In other words, the totality of experience.

The Buddha recommends that a person retire to a forest, the root of a tree or a solitary place, sit cross-legged with body erect and then turn his or her attention to their breath. Then, 'mindfully he breathes in, mindfully he breathes out. Breathing in a long breath, he knows that he breathes in a long breath, and breathing out a long breath, he knows that he breathes out a long breath.' There is no attempt to control the breath or in any way interfere with the immediacy of experience as it unfolds. If the breath is long, one recognizes it to be long; if short, one recognizes it to be short.

Yet for many this seemingly straightforward exercise turns out to be remarkably tricky. One finds that no matter how sincere one's intention to be attentive and aware, the mind rebels against such instructions and races off to indulge in all manner of distractions, memories and fantasies. One is forced to confront the sobering truth that one is only notionally 'in charge' of one's psychological life. The comforting illusion of personal coherence and continuity is ripped away to expose only fragmentary islands of consciousness separated by yawning gulfs of unawareness. Similarly, the convenient fiction of a well-adjusted, consistent personality turns out to be merely a skilfully edited and censored version of a turbulent psyche. The first step in this practice of mindful awareness is radical self-acceptance.

Such self-acceptance, however, does not operate in an ethical vacuum, where no moral assessment is made of one's emotional states. The training in mindful awareness is part of a Buddhist path with values and goals. Emotional states are evaluated according to whether they increase or decrease the potential for suffering. If an emotion, such as hatred or envy, is judged to be destructive, then it is simply recognized as such. It is neither expressed through violent thoughts, words or deeds, nor is it suppressed or denied as incompatible with a 'spiritual' life. In seeing it for what it is — a transient emotional state — one mindfully observes it follow its own nature: to arise, abide for a while, and then pass away.

The Buddha described his teaching as 'going against the stream'. The unflinching light of mindful awareness reveals the extent to which we are tossed along in the stream of past conditioning and habit. The moment we decide to stop and look at what is going on (like a swimmer suddenly changing course to swim upstream instead of downstream), we find ourselves battered by powerful currents we had never even suspected — precisely because until that moment we were largely living at their command.

The practice of mindful awareness is a first step in the direction of inner freedom. Disciplining oneself to focus attention single-mindedly on the breath (for example) enables one to become progressively more quiet and concentrated. Such stillness, though, is not an end in itself. It serves as a platform from which to observe more clearly what is taking place within us. It allows the steady depth of awareness needed to understand the very origins of conditioning: namely, how delusion and craving are at the root of human suffering. Such meditative understanding is experiential rather than intellectual, therapeutic rather than dogmatic, liberating rather than merely convincing.

The aim of mindful awareness is the understanding that frees one from delusion and craving. In Pali, such understanding is called *vipassana* ('penetrative seeing'), and it is under this name that the traditional practice of mindful awareness is frequently presented in the West today. *Vipassana* is often translated as 'insight', and courses are offered on 'insight meditation'.

This usage has given rise to some confusion. It has led to the impression that some Buddhists practise *vipassana*, while others (such as practitioners of Zen or Tibetan Buddhism) do not. In fact, *vipassana* is central to *all* forms of Buddhist meditation practice. The distinctive goal of any Buddhist contemplative tradition is a state in which inner calm (*samatha*) is *unified* with insight (*vipassana*). Over the centuries, each tradition has developed its own methods for actualizing this state. And it is in these methods that the traditions differ, *not* in their end objective of unified calm and insight.

∽✿∾

While the Buddha's discourse on the Foundations of Mindfulness has always been highly revered in Asia, its instructions have not always been widely practised. Over the centuries there has been a tendency for such meditation training to be seen as the exclusive preserve of monastics. And even among monastics the majority have tended to function as clerics and priests rather than contemplatives. The systematic cultivation of mindful awareness was often restricted to a handful of hermits in the rural forest traditions. Such developments were blatantly at variance with the intention of the Buddha. Although his discourses were formally addressed to monks and nuns, they record many instances of lay men and women attaining meditative realization. The Burmese Buddhist revival at the beginning of this century was in large measure an attempt to return to this spirit of the original teachings.

Nor is it coincidental that this revival occurred simultaneously with that of Anagarika Dharmapala's in Ceylon. Both movements were in part reactions of the Buddhist community to continued colonial occupation and repression. The Buddhists were challenged to redefine themselves both in response to the invective of Christian missionaries as well as the claims of the secular, rational and scientific culture of Europe. Stimulated by these demands, a reinvigorated Buddhism emerged. Yet while challenging the claims of Christian dogma and European cultural supremacy, the movement nonetheless assumed a protestant, rationalist flavour. It is notable that in Thailand, a country that had evaded colonization, such a reform movement did not then occur.

Two of the prime movers in Burma were the monks Mingun Jetawan Sayadaw and Ledi Sayadaw. As a young man Mingun Sayadaw had set out to find a teacher who could give practical instructions on the means to realize what he had learnt in the scriptures. Finally he found a monk meditating in a cave in Upper Burma who directed him simply to follow the instructions on mindful awareness the Buddha gave in the *Satipatthana Sutta*. By practising in this way he became convinced that he had discovered the direct means to awakening taught by Gautama. This method was then disseminated by Mingun's disciple Mahasi Sayadaw.

After completing his doctrinal studies and meditation training with Mingun Sayadaw, Mahasi returned to his native village in 1941 at the age of thirty-seven and began teaching practical courses in mindful awareness to both monks and lay people. So successful were these courses that in 1949, U Nu, the first prime minister of independent Burma, invited Mahasi to teach in Rangoon. An estimated 45,000 students have since trained in the Rangoon centre alone, while up to 600,000 have practised in the network of centres elsewhere in the country. Mahasi continued teaching until his death in 1982, by which time many Americans and Europeans had undergone the training and were starting to teach in their own countries.

Ledi Sayadaw, the second great reformer, likewise sought to reinstate mindful awareness at the centre of Buddhist practice. While he himself was a monk, his approach has been mainly disseminated through a line of lay meditation teachers. The first of these was a wealthy farmer called Saya U Thet who in turn taught the remarkable Sayagyi U Ba Khin.

Born in 1899, U Ba Khin rose rapidly through the ranks of the British imperial civil service in Burma and, on independence in January 1948, was appointed Accountant General of the new state. He retired from this post in 1953, but was immediately drafted back into government service, heading up to three government departments simultaneously as well as chairing various boards and committees. He also raised a family of six children.

U Ba Khin began practising *vipassana* meditation in 1937 under Saya U Thet and by 1941 had started teaching others. As Accountant General he offered meditation classes to his staff, initially after work in his own office and, from 1952, in the International Meditation Centre he founded in Rangoon in order to offer intensive ten–day retreats. He died in 1971.

While Mahasi Sayadaw and U Ba Khin had much in common, their methods of instruction differ. Mahasi instructs the meditator to focus on the breath in the rise and fall of the abdomen, whereas U Ba Khin starts with the sensation of the breath as it passes over the upper lip. Mahasi then emphasizes mentally 'noting' whatever occurs in the field of awareness, whereas U Ba Khin teaches systematically 'sweeping' the body from head to toe to observe increasingly subtle layers of sensation. Both agree that the aim of the practice is to lead the meditator to an understanding of the characteristics of existence: impermanence, suffering and selflessness, and that such insight purifies the mind of confusion and disturbing emotions and leads ultimately to the unconditioned realm of Nirvana.

The impact of these Burmese reformers is directly or indirectly

346

felt today wherever courses on *vipassana* are held in the West. In addition, other forms and interpretations of mindful awareness meditation have filtered in from Thailand, Sri Lanka and Mahayana Buddhist traditions. In keeping with its emphasis on personal experience rather than adherence to orthodoxy, many *vipassana* teachers continue to explore ways to render the practice more intelligible and accessible to secular Western society. Others, however, insist on strict adherence to the norms of practice inherited from the founding figures.

Principal among these is Satya Narayan Goenka, whose role in disseminating the practise of *vipassana* world-wide is unparalleled. Born into a wealthy Indian family in Burma in 1924, Goenka became a highly successful businessman. Severe and apparently incurable migraines led him to attend a ten-day intensive retreat with U Ba Khin in 1955. Although curing the headaches, the retreat revealed to him the far greater significance of such meditation practice. For the next fourteen years he became a diligent student of U Ba Khin. In 1969 he moved to India with his teacher's blessing to teach *vipassana* in its land of origin.

In the 1970s a spiritual odyssey to India was incomplete without having done an obligatory 'Goenka course'. Goenka started by teaching Indians, but his audience soon came to include the varied Europeans, Americans and Australians who wandered through the subcontinent in search of religious experience. The disciplined and systematic ten-day meditation courses proved exceptionally well suited to the needs of these Westerners. In 1976 Goenka opened his own specially constructed retreat facility in Igatpuri, not far from Bombay. Around the same time he was invited to teach abroad by students who had returned home and established their own embryonic meditation groups. He led his first retreats in Europe in England and France during the summer of 1979.

Today there are networks of Goenka students and 'assistant-teachers' throughout the world. It is estimated that 19,000 people have been taught by Goenka in more than 250 courses around the world. In Europe approximately three thousand have attended retreats in England, France, Germany, Belgium, Spain, Switzerland, Italy, Portugal and Sweden. Permanent retreat centres have been established in England and France. The ten-day course format remains the same no matter where the retreats are held. When Goenka is not present, his lectures are played from a video-recorder. 'It is not necessary to call oneself a Buddhist in order to practise this teaching', he has said. He likewise professes no concern with Buddhism. 'I teach Dharma, that is, what the Buddha taught. He never taught any "ism" or sectarian doctrine. He taught something from which people of every background can benefit: an art of living.'

Despite this open-minded attitude, Goenka can be severely critical of other Buddhist practices, even other forms of *vipassana*, on the grounds that they are somehow 'impure'. To combine them with U Ba Khin's method will have a detrimental effect on one's meditation. Such exclusivist views have contributed to his students becoming isolated from the wider Buddhist community as well as to a souring of relations even with the other disciples of U Ba Khin currently teaching in the West.

In addition to Goenka, three other teachers who trained with U Ba Khin in Rangoon are active in Europe today. Mother Sayama, a Burmese lay woman, based at Splatts House near Calne in Wiltshire, offers two ten-day courses a month. John Coleman, an American-born former CIA agent in Thailand, now settled in England, leads retreats in his centre in Italy. And Ruth Denison, a German-born naturalized American, conducts courses every year in Germany.

Compared to the method of U Ba Khin (especially as presented by Goenka and Sayama), the practice of mindful awareness as taught by Mahasi Sayadaw has tended to become more diffused through the absorption of influences from outside his particular school. One of the first Europeans to train at Mahasi's centre in Rangoon was the German *bhikkhu* Vimalo (Walter Kulbarz) during the 1960s. After many years in the forests of Thailand, Vimalo returned to Europe in 1977 to the Haus der Stille, a retreat centre near Hamburg, to live and teach. Today his *vipassana* retreats are informed as much by his own extensive study of the Pali canon, the movement and breathing exercises of Ilse Mittendorf, and the writings of modern psychotherapy, as by the teachings of Mahasi. He disrobed in 1982, after twenty-five years as a monk, and currently lives in the Sharpham North Community in England.

The centre of the Mahasi tradition in the West is the Insight Meditation Society in Barre, Massachusetts, founded in 1976 by the Americans Joseph Goldstein, Jack Kornfield and Sharon Salzburg. The three-month retreats conducted there every winter offer the most systematic training in Mahasi-style *vipassana* available outside of Asia. Due to the lack of a comparable facility in Europe, many Europeans have attended these retreats. Several European teachers, such as Corrado Pensa and Vimalo, also conduct courses there. Goldstein and Kornfield's eloquent and non-sectarian presentation of mindful awareness practice has had a significant impact in Europe through their writings and the retreats they have conducted. Both have incorporated insights from other Buddhist and non-Buddhist traditions into their teachings and continue to explore ways in which to enhance the practice of *vipassana* in the West.

Fred von Allmen, a Swiss from Bern, spent four years in Barre and now teaches *vipassana* full-time throughout Europe (Switzerland, Germany, Sweden, Italy, Spain, England). His Buddhist background is likewise diverse, ranging from many years with Geshé Rabten and other Tibetan lamas, intensive retreats in India with Anagarika Munindra, a disciple of Mahasi Sayadaw, and Goenka. He is the most active teacher connected to the 'Dhamma Gruppe', a Theravada-inspired organization that schedules retreats throughout Switzerland.

In 1977 Christopher Titmuss and Christina Feldman returned from Asia and founded 'Gillets', in Kent, the first lay community dedicated to mindful awareness practice in Britain. Titmuss was ordained as a *bhikkhu* in 1970 in Thailand and trained under the guidance of the meditation teacher Ajahn Dhammadaro. In 1974 he visited India and trained briefly with Goenka before beginning to teach Westerners himself, first in India and Australia before returning to the U.K. Feldman had initially travelled to India in 1969 and studied with Geshé Rabten and others. She met Christopher Titmuss in 1974. Their teaching style emphasizes an uncompromising immediacy of spiritual experience and rapidly shed many of the traditional and doctrinal aspects of Buddhism. They became leading exponents of a more socially engaged form of spiritual practice, espousing political, environmentalist and feminist causes. In 1984 they founded Gaia House in south Devon, which serves as a silent year-round retreat centre offering courses on *vipassana* and related forms of Buddhist meditation.

Corrado Pensa, the leading Italian teacher of *vipassana*, was the last student of the great orientalist and explorer Giuseppe Tucci, under whose guidance he devoted himself to the study of Sanskrit Mahayana Buddhist texts. Dissatisfied with philology, his interest turned towards comparative religion. The stirring of a sense of inner adventure, however, led him to Jungian psychology. In the 1960s he was drawn to Zen Buddhism and studied in California with the Soto Zen teacher Shunryu Suzuki. He returned to California the following year to explore the new forms of therapy being developed at Esalen Institute, where, in 1975, he did his first *vipassana* course with Jack Kornfield. A year later he went to Barre to train more intensely.

While the practice of mindful awareness is at the core of what Pensa teaches, he provides a framework for it both by explaining Buddhist philosophy and psychology and often encouraging students to undergo psychotherapy. A.Me.Co., the association he has founded for this purpose, provides structured courses in meditation as well as a network of sitting groups that meet throughout the city. The association invites other teachers from elsewhere in Europe and organizes longer retreats at centres in the countryside.

'In Europe,' remarked the English *bhikkhu* Nanavira in 1963, 'intellectualism takes precedence over tradition; in the East, it is the reverse. In Dharma terms, the European has an excess of *panna* (intelligence) over *saddha* (faith), and he tends to reject what he cannot understand, even if it is true; the Oriental has an excess of *saddha* over *panna*, which leads him to accept anything ancient, even if it is false.'

The protestant nature of the Burmese and Ceylonese revivals at the turn of the century has tended to elevate immediate personal experience over faith in tradition; rational understanding over doctrinal conviction; and lay organization over monastic community. Many proponents of *vipassana* feel that such moves are a return to the original Dharma as envisioned by the Buddha. Some, such as S.N. Goenka and Christopher Titmuss, have questioned the use of the very term 'Buddhism' to describe what they are talking about. Others present *vipassana* as a kind of meta-psychotherapy, in which classical Buddhist concepts are redefined in modern psychological terms. By making the Dharma more widely accessible in the West, this process may well be a healthy contribution to the demystification of Buddhism. But it runs the risk of throwing the proverbial baby out with the bathwater, of losing sight of the originality, comprehensiveness and depth of the Buddha's vision in a dazzle of latter-day enthusiasms.

A valuable counterweight to such tendencies is the presence in Europe of Theravada monastics, with whom many of the lay *vipassana* teachers are involved in on-going dialogues. Arguably, the emphasis on technique in many *vipassana* groups, as well as the prevailing norm of intense bursts of meditation practice during week or ten-day retreats, reflect the needs of a secular society pressured by work and family commitments. In a monastic setting, the form of life itself, rather than proficiency in meditation technique, serves as the basis for mindful awareness.

It has also been argued that the emphasis on insight (*vipassana*) over inner calm and absorption (*samatha* and *jhana*) reflects a modern lay situation removed from the kind of monastic tranquillity required for the cultivation of deep meditative calm. This view has been challenged by the German nun Ayya Khema (Ilse Ledermann), based at Buddha Haus near Munich. While acknowledging that insight is the crucial factor in Buddhist enlightenment, she is critical of the disparaging attitude to absorption often found among *vipassana* meditators. She seeks to restore the practice of absorption as an effective way to the realization of insight. 'The first three [of the eight] meditative absorptions', she claims, 'are not difficult to achieve.' Through absorption one recovers the 'original purity' of the mind that leads to the joy and detachment conducive to the arising of insight.

Another dimension of meditation practice emphasized by Ayya Khema and many other *vipassana* teachers is the systematic cultivation of loving-kindness (*metta*). This too has its origins in the Pali Canon, where it is taught as one of the four 'divine abodes' (*brahma-vihara*) of compassion, loving-kindness, sympathetic joy and equanimity. Mahayana Buddhist teachings on *bodhicitta* and the Bodhisattva ideal have also influenced the practice of *vipassana*, resulting in what some of the teachers have called: 'Theravada practice with Mahayana motive.'

21

NHAT HANH:
ENGAGEMENT

1 *1 June 1963*. On Phan-dinh-Phung Street in Saigon an elderly Buddhist monk called Thich Quang Duc sits down cross-legged in meditation. He pours petrol over his body and lights a match, then remains calm and immobile as his body bursts into flames. As the Vietnam war intensifies, other monks and nuns follow his example. As these images appear on television screens around the world, they provoke incomprehension and horror. A monk seated like a Buddha being engulfed by fire in a country ravaged by war sears itself into the Western mind.

Three years later, in May 1966, a thirty-nine-year-old Vietnamese monk, Thich Nhat Hanh, arrives in America, ostensibly to lecture on 'The Renaissance of Vietnamese Buddhism' at Cornell University. The true purpose of his visit is to tell the American people of the sufferings of his fellow countrymen and women. The Christian-based Fellowship of Reconciliation has organized a three-week tour for him. But invitations keep coming, and the tour continues for three months, extending beyond the United States to Europe.

In America he meets with leading religious figures and politicians. Thomas Merton writes: 'I have far more in common with Nhat Hanh than I have with many Americans, and I do not hesitate to say it.' The Secretary of Defence Robert McNamara extends his appointment to listen more carefully to what he has to say. In a joint press conference, Martin Luther King identifies the struggle of blacks in America with that of the Buddhists in Vietnam, and the following year nominates Nhat Hanh for the Nobel Peace Prize. The visit to Europe culminates, on 16 July, in an audience with Pope Paul VI in which the Buddhist monk urges the Supreme Pontiff to encourage Catholics in Vietnam to join hands with Buddhists to end the war. Wherever he goes, audiences are humbled and moved by this slight, gentle monk who gives voice to the silenced masses of his tormented land.

Thich Nhat Hanh and his fellow Buddhist activists sided neither with the Communist north nor the anti-Communist south. Nor did they harbour any desire for political power themselves. They sought understanding instead of conflict. Above all they spoke for millions of peasants for whom the ideological differences were meaningless, for whom the war meant nothing but destruction, terror and death.

In June 1965 Nhat Hanh had written to Martin Luther King explaining that the self-immolations were neither desperate acts of suicide nor political protests. The monks' aim was solely that of 'moving the hearts of the oppressors, and at calling the attention of the world to the suffering endured by the Vietnamese . . . . To say something while experiencing this kind of pain is to say it with utmost courage, frankness, determination, and sincerity.' In Nhat Hanh's poetic vision, each burning monk or nun became Vietnam herself: 'a lotus in a sea of fire'.

The first Buddhists to set foot on Vietnamese soil were Indian missionaries travelling by sea to China in the 2nd century CE. Although the form of Buddhism that eventually emerged in Vietnam was Chinese, indigenous monks developed their own schools and literature. The monasteries tended to belong to one of the four Thien (Zen) schools founded in Vietnam between the

6th and 13th centuries, while the lay people largely practised Pure Land devotions combined with Confucianist ethics and popular Taoist rituals.

In 1284 and 1287 the Vietnamese succeeded in repelling the Mongol army of Kublai Khan that invaded from China. From the 14th century Theravada Buddhism was introduced in the south of the country from neighbouring Cambodia to serve the immigrant Khmer population. During the 15th and 16th centuries, Buddhism was suppressed first by Ming Chinese invaders and then by Neo-Confucianist governments. Early in the 18th century the monk Lieu Quan founded another Zen school, which dominated the central and southern parts of the country until modern times.

Catholicism was first introduced by missionaries in 1533, but had little impact until the arrival of the Jesuit Alexandre de Rhodes in 1625. By the end of the century nearly a million Vietnamese had converted. The strong missionary presence in the country was a crucial factor in paving the way for the French colonial conquest of Vietnam in middle of the 19th century.

As resistance to French occupation strengthened, Buddhism emerged as a central focus for national aspirations. From 1895 to 1898 Zen monks spearheaded an uprising against the French, which came to be known as 'The Monks' War'. In the 1930s, inspired by the Chinese abbot Tai Hsü's reforms in China, a revival movement started among the Buddhists of Vietnam. It was during this period that the concept of 'Engaged Buddhism' (*Nhap Gian Phat Giao*) began to be discussed. In the early 1940s this became linked with the idea of Buddhism as the true national religion of the land.

Such was the world into which Nguyen Xuan Bao was born in 1926. From a young age he felt drawn towards the monkhood and, in 1942, when he was sixteen, entered Tu Hieu monastery as a novice, receiving the name Thich Nhat Hanh. His teacher was a 41st generation successor of the Chinese Ch'an master Lin-chi

(Rinzai) and belonged to the Lieu Quan school of Vietnamese Zen. In 1945, while pursuing his studies, a popular revolution brought independence to the country under the leadership of Ho Chi Minh. While the revolution initially infused the young Buddhists with great hope, they grew alarmed at the way the Communists ruthlessly eliminated opposition. On 27 December 1946, an American-supported French fleet landed at Haiphong in an attempt to regain control of the land, which triggered the Indochina war.

Against this backdrop of fighting, Nhat Hanh received full ordination in 1949. The following year he co-founded An Quang Temple in Saigon, the first Buddhist seminary to include courses in the Western sciences and humanities. On 6 May 1951 the Buddhist National Congress at Hue agreed to unify all the Buddhist associations of the land into the 'All Vietnam Buddhist Association', one of whose aims was to promote National Buddhism as a vehicle of unity and salvation for the warring country. Two months after the defeat of the French at Dien Bien Phu in May 1954, a cease-fire agreement was signed in Geneva. The country was to be temporarily divided until free elections could be held in 1956 to reunify the land.

But the elections never took place. Instead, the southern half of the country fell under the control of the Catholic dictator Ngo Dinh Diem. America saw South Vietnam as a bastion against the spread of Communism and was prepared to back Diem no matter how corrupt and autocratic he became. The first U.S. advisers arrived as early as 1955. The following year the thirty-year-old Thich Nhat Hanh was appointed editor-in-chief of *Vietnamese Buddhism*, the periodical of the All Vietnam Buddhist Association. Under his editorship the journal criticized the Diem regime and its Catholic 'personalist' philosophy, promoted Buddhism as the national religion, and spoke of the pressing need for Buddhism both to modernize and become more engaged with social issues.

Diem, however, sought to create a Catholic state. In 1957 the government ordered the abolition of Wesak as a national holiday, a move that made the Buddhists celebrate it with even greater fervour, thereby forcing the government to reverse its decision. The confrontation highlighted the role of Buddhism as a base of popular opposition, which in turn made Diem increase his suppressive measures against it.

Diem's refusal to hold the agreed elections caused the Communists in the north to adopt a more aggressive stance, which led to the outbreak of hostilities in 1959. America increased its military support, which ultimately led to the sending of combat troops.

As President Kennedy's advisers were leaving America for Vietnam, Thich Nhat Hanh left Vietnam for America to study comparative religion and teach Buddhism at Columbia University in New York. During the three years he was abroad, Buddhist non-violent resistance to Diem grew in intensity, peaking in the critical year of 1963. In June, Thich Quang Duc immolated himself in Saigon; in September, the Vietnamese Buddhist Association sent a detailed document to the United Nations describing the suppression of Buddhists by the government; and on 1 November, a peaceful, Buddhist-inspired uprising toppled the Diem regime. Before the end of the year, a Buddhist National Congress succeeded in uniting the Mahayana and Theravada schools in Vietnam as the 'Unified Buddhist Church', the first time such a feat of reconciliation has ever been achieved.

When Nhat Hanh was summoned to return home in early 1964, the prestige of Buddhism was at an all-time high. It was widely identified as a focus for national feeling that offered a grass-roots alternative to the competing ideologies of Capitalism and Communism. But the Buddhist organizations were poorly equipped to translate this popular support into effective means for achieving social change and peace. Education was considered crucial. To this end Nhat Hanh helped found the Van Hanh Buddhist University in Saigon. And within the university he created the School of Youth for Social Service, whose aims were to 'train rural development cadres and to mobilize the latent resources of Buddhism to carry out the task of developing the rural areas'. As the carnage intensified, however, the school's work increasingly involved rebuilding communities and villages devastated in the wake of fighting.

After the fall of Diem, it became transparent that the true powerbrokers in South Vietnam lived in Washington. The Americans immediately installed another puppet regime, which was again peacefully brought down the following year. So they backed a strongman, General Nguyen Cao Ky, and increased his military clout, enabling him to survive the next Buddhist-led attempt to overthrow him in 1966.

In February 1964, the government had issued a decree declaring that anyone promoting 'neutralism' would be considered 'pro-Communist'. The following year Nhat Hanh published a collection of poems which deplored the war and yearned for peace. Four thousand copies were sold in the first week of publication. The government ordered it seized and denounced its 'neutralist' author as a Communist, while the North Vietnamese declared that 'his soul and body have obviously been entirely bought by the Pentagon and the White House'. Both sides began to intimidate his colleagues and students, many of whom were assassinated. He narrowly missed being killed when a curtain deflected a grenade thrown into his office. The same year he founded the Tiep Hien Order (Order of Interbeing), a reformed Buddhist movement that emphasized social responsibility and pacifism based on the practice of mindful awareness.

Had he not been asked to go abroad to speak in May of the following year, the chances of his avoiding either imprisonment or violent death would have been slim. By the time he completed his widely publicized tour in America and Europe they would have been nil. He settled in Paris. When the peace negotiations began in 1969, he established, at the request of the Unified Buddhist Church, a Buddhist Peace Delegation in the city. After the signing of the Peace Accords in 1973, he was refused permission to return to Vietnam. He moved to Fontvannes, a hundred miles south of Paris, and founded a small rural community called 'Sweet Potatoes', where he devoted himself to meditation, writing and gardening.

Buddhism is still widely perceived in the West as a world-forsaking, passive religion bent on personal enlightenment and Nirvana. By overlooking the enormous social, political and cultural contributions it has made throughout Asia over the past 2,500 years, a one-dimensional image of the Dharma is formed: Buddhism is at best a harmless mystical preoccupation, at worst a socially irresponsible indulgence. One can rest assured that it has nothing to do with toppling governments or seriously upsetting the status quo.

Just as Buddhism has produced its recluses, contemplatives, philosophers and saints so has it produced its reformers, social activists, artists and kings. A complete picture of the Dharma is impossible without taking these two interacting dimensions into account. Only then do Gautama, Ashoka, Nagarjuna, Shantideva, Padmasambhava, the Karmapa, Ta-hui, Dogen, Nichiren, Tsongkhapa, Hakuin, Dorzhiev, Dharmapala and others come alive as complex, engaged personalities. The present Dalai Lama serves as an effective ambassador for Buddhism precisely because he replaces the popular stereotype of the other-worldly Buddhist monk with a warm, humorous, politically involved yet at the same time detached, wise and saintly human being — who also happens to be a Buddhist monk.

As we have seen through the course of this book, all Buddhist traditions have played an active and transformative role in the social, artistic and political life of their respective cultures. It is also true that Buddhism has periodically declined and stagnated, resting on its past glories and falling under the sway of inert leaders. The historic course of Buddhism has been a rhythm of peaks and troughs rather than a steady growth or decay. Neither Marco Polo nor the Jesuits in Japan would for a moment have perceived Buddhism as an ineffectual, other-worldly religion. But when Europeans came to 'construct' Buddhism during the heyday of colonialism, it was no longer the force it had been. This was in part due to the isolationist and defensive policies adopted by many Asian countries in response to the military, technological and economic superiority of the West. These policies (which in most cases were strongly supported by Buddhist leaders) tended to make Buddhism conservative, introverted and increasingly powerless as a force for change.

It was no coincidence that the concept of Engaged Buddhism emerged in Vietnam in the 1930s on the rising tide of national self-confidence that fuelled the drive for independence from colonial oppression. A similar process was occurring simultaneously in China with Tai Hsü's reforms, in Japan with the Nichiren revivals, and in Burma with a strong Buddhist resistance to the British. At the beginning of the century Anagarika Dharmapala had initiated a comparable movement in Ceylon and India, as had Agvan Dorzhiev in the Buryat and Kalmyk areas of Russia. All of these movements could equally be regarded as Engaged Buddhism.

While many of these movements drew upon the values of ideologies that were not explicitly Buddhist (such as nationalism, democracy, liberalism, socialism), their roots lay in Buddhist traditions with long histories of social and political engagement. In this sense, Engaged Buddhism in Asia is merely the renewal of a dimension that had either lain dormant or been suppressed during the colonial period.

Likewise, in the West today, as the alienated and disaffected generations of the second half of the 20th century outgrow their romantic fascination with Buddhism, it is no surprise to find a growing concern among them for social, cultural and political issues. Whether or not one calls such concerns Engaged Buddhism is irrelevant. They are simply a sign of the Dharma's mature unfolding in Western culture. For this is the way the practice of Buddhism works: insight into the selfless and interconnected nature of life expresses itself in the world as appropriate compassionate action.

In Mahayana Buddhism in particular great emphasis is laid on realizing the union of wisdom and compassionate action. Human fulfilment is seen to lie in the *integration* of the inner and outer dimensions of life, *not* in transcendent wisdom or world-saving compassion alone.

As long as we remain delusively convinced of our egoic separation, then we remain cut off from the capacity to empathize fully with others. Such empathy is nothing other than the affective response to insight into the absence of egoic separation. For when the fiction of isolated selfhood is exposed, instead of a gaping mystical void we discover that our individual existence is rooted in relationship with the rest of life. For Thich Nhat Hanh, this is the realization of 'interbeing'; for the Dalai Lama that of 'universal responsibility': two ideas at the heart of contemporary Engaged Buddhism.

In the 20th century, the notion of interbeing (or interdependence) has assumed a meaning hitherto undeveloped in traditional Buddhist societies. The smaller the world becomes, the larger its population and the scarcer its resources, so are we made correspondingly aware of the effects our simplest actions (driving a car, eating a hamburger, owning a refrigerator) on the planet as a whole. The implications of this insight have led to the conclusion that the very 'poisons' of the mind (delusion, greed and hatred) to be uprooted through Buddhist practice have become *institutionalized* in the forms of the multinational corporations, consumerism, and the arms industry that increasingly dominate life on earth.

If one accepts this analysis, then one must question what it means to act compassionately in the world today. Many proponents of Engaged Buddhism would argue that it is no longer enough merely to aim at a transformation of consciousness; it is necessary to analyse, challenge and replace the very structures of society that institutionalize delusion, greed and hatred.

Visions of an ideal society have occurred repeatedly in Buddhist history. Professor Trevor Ling has argued that a major concern of Gautama himself was 'the gradual establishment of a universal republic, with the Buddhist sangha at its heart', an ideal that Ashoka subsequently sought to realize in India. Over the centuries, Chinese, Japanese and Tibetan kings have been identified as incarnations of Bodhisattvas and have spoken of creating a Pure Land on Earth. The Sakya and Geluk 'buddhocracies' of Tibet were probably the closest any society has come to realizing a state run on Buddhist lines, although their dependency on secular 'protectors' in both cases weakened their autonomy and contributed to their downfall. Today the only sizeable Buddhist country to have survived both colonial and communist domination is Thailand, but the role of the monastic *sangha* in the life of the state is largely ceremonial.

At the furthest extreme from engagement lie some of the detached, amoral views of Zen found in Japan. D.T. Suzuki remarked that 'as long as its intuitive teaching is not interfered with' Zen may be found 'wedded to anarchism or fascism, communism or democracy, atheism or idealism, or any political or economic dogmatism'. In other words, Buddhist practice need have no bearing at all on the kind of society one lives in.

However far-reaching the goals of nascent Buddhist societies have been, they have all recognized that for such a society to function it must be rooted in the spiritual practice of individuals. Such practice is not a way to evade other responsibilities but to provide a secure foundation upon which to face them. 'Our society is a difficult place to live in', comments Nhat Hanh. 'If we are not careful, we can become uprooted, and once uprooted, we cannot help change society to make it more livable. Meditation is a way of helping us to stay in society.' Engagement, like adaptation, is not an option but a matter of degree and needs to be measured along a spectrum. At one end are simple acts of kindness, in the middle organizations providing social services, and at the far end visions of another kind of society altogether.

For many Buddhists engagement with society involves the creation and running of urban centres and rural retreats where the study and practice of Buddhism can be pursued. This frequently involves the promulgation of Buddhist ideas through the publication of magazines and books. As more intelligible information about the Dharma becomes available and as more European Buddhists are able to explain it, this has generated a growing interest in Buddhism among philosophers, theologians and scientists. Studies have been published comparing Buddhist thought with that of philosophers such as Ludwig Wittgenstein, Martin Heidegger, A.N. Whitehead and Jacques Derrida. The Anglican theologian Don Cupitt has drawn on Buddhist ideas in his writings, and in July 1992 hosted a symposium 'Buddhism and Modern Western Thought' at Emmanuel College, Cambridge. The striking similarities between Buddhist descriptions of reality and some of the findings of quantum physics have been frequently noted, above all in Fritjof Capra's *The Tao of Physics*. The newly emerging field of cognitive science, however, might prove to be the most fertile soil for the inclusion of Buddhist ideas. The Paris-based Chilean biologist Francisco Varela, for example, argues for the use of Buddhist contemplative disciplines as tools in cognitive scientific research into the nature of mind.

An area with one of the strongest links to Buddhism in Europe is that of psychology and psychotherapy. Buddhism is becoming the 'religion of choice' for many therapists, who either are Buddhists, have practised Buddhist meditation, or incorporate Buddhist ideas into their work. The attraction of Buddhism lies not only in its analysis of human suffering in terms of deep-seated psychological error and disturbance, but also in its practical approaches to dealing with them. The only complete system so far to be founded on Buddhist principles, while integrating many of the insights and skills of other therapies, is that of Core-Process Psychotherapy, taught by Maura and Franklin Sills at the Karuna Institute in Devon, England. In Scotland, the Tara Trust, under the direction of Akong Rinpoché of Samye Ling, is developing a five-stage system of therapeutic training. While more closely aligned with traditional teaching and meditation methods, the system, as with Karuna's, is aimed at extending Buddhist principles of healing beyond the Buddhist community.

In the wider social sphere Buddhists are active as peace-campaigners, environmentalists, prison chaplains, hospice workers, educators and social workers. In Britain, for example, the Network of Engaged Buddhists (formerly the Buddhist Peace Fellowship) campaigns on a range of social, environmental and political issues, while also arranging meditation retreats. From the Forest Hermitage near Warwick the English *bhikkhu* Ajahn Khemadhammo directs Angulimala, an organization of Buddhist prison chaplains, who serve around fifty jails throughout the country. Elsewhere, the Buddhist Hospice Trust has created a network of people involved in work with the dying; the Dhamma School Project is preparing to found the first Buddhist school in the country; while the Rokpa charity of Samye Ling is feeding and clothing homeless people in the inner-city areas of Glasgow,

London, Barcelona and Brussels. In the last two general elections, the *vipassana* teacher Christopher Titmuss has stood for Parliament as a candidate for the Green Party.

In terms of the sheer number of people affected, the most extensive social action project undertaken by Buddhists in Europe is that of the Karuna Trust. Founded in 1980 by members of the Western Buddhist Order, its purpose is to continue the work started by Dr Ambedkar among the ex-Untouchable Buddhists in India. In addition to teaching Buddhism and creating Buddhist centres, much of the FWBO's work has been to help the ex-Untouchables raise their material standards of living. To fund this work, they have raised £3.75 million through door-to-door appeals in Britain. In India the FWBO goes under the name 'Trailokya Bauddha Maha Sangha' ('Great Buddhist Community of the Three Worlds'). Eighteen centres are now functioning and 124 ex-Untouchables have been ordained as Dharmacharis.

All these activities and projects are Buddhist responses to interests and needs within the kind of society we live in today. Ostensibly, they aim at no more than the furthering of understanding, the reforming of existing disciplines or the improving of social standards. At a deeper level, though, Buddhists engaged in these tasks may see their work as the first steps in the building of an alternative society founded on Buddhist principles. Many feel that modern secular societies need more than just a cosmetic overhaul to set them right. For whether societies are run along socialist or capitalist lines (or a mixture of the two), something fundamental is missing. They have lost sight of where they are heading and are driven by the ultimately destructive forces of delusion and craving. While some Buddhists maintain that this is simply the nature of the world, others insist that compassion demands that one tackle the root societal causes of this collective suffering. At this point engagement goes beyond mere reform and advocates radical social and political change.

Nowhere is this more explicit than in Sangharakshita's movement. 'The creation of a New Society', declares Subhuti, 'is the purpose of the FWBO.' Its aim is 'not to find a corner for Buddhists in the midst of the old society . . . . It wishes to change society — to turn the old society into the new.' The FWBO is under no illusions that this is about to happen overnight. Sangharakshita has described this process of change as one of 'aware growth' that will take place in a number of stages, probably over generations.

Another contemporary movement with designs to create a world-wide, Buddhist-inspired society is the Soka Gakkai (Chapter 10). Ken Jones, a leading exponent of Engaged Buddhism, however, has commented that Soka Gakkai's activities are only 'directed to reforming and morally toning up society and not to radical transformation of the existing industrial consumerism'. Indeed, Soka Gakkai values and encourages material success as an indicator of the power of chanting *Nam-myoho-renge-kyo*. Moreover, Nichiren doctrines such as *Itai Doshin* ('many in body, one in mind') seem to suggest that their ideal society might be totalitarian in nature.

One of the most potent myths to animate Tibetan Buddhist culture is that of Shambhala. According to the *Kalachakra Tantra*, Shambhala is a harmonious society ruled by a lineage of enlightened kings. The myth tells of how a peaceful army will one day rise forth from Shambhala to save the world from destruction and inaugurate a golden age of enlightened culture. Although versions of this myth fuelled both the shuttle-diplomacy of Dorzhiev as well as the millenarian fantasies of Mme Blavatsky and Nicholas Roerich, it makes more sense to see it as a psychological truth: that the Dharma, if practised sincerely and on a wide enough scale, could one day herald a revolution in human culture. The salvational dimension of Kalachakra is kept alive by the present Dalai Lama, who regularly gives the Kalachakra empowerment around the world. In the summer of 1985 he offered it for the first time in Europe, in Rikon, Switzerland, to about five thousand people, and dedicated it to world peace.

Since 1977 the Shambhala myth has been creatively re-interpreted by the Kagyu lama Chögyam Trungpa Rinpoché as the basis for a secular tradition aimed at establishing an enlightened society. 'The Shambhala teachings', explains Trungpa,

> are founded on the premise that there is a basic human wisdom that can help to solve the world's problems. This wisdom does not belong to any one culture or religion, nor does it come only from the West or the East. Rather, it is a tradition of human warriorship that has existed in many cultures at many times throughout history.

To cultivate such warriorship Trungpa instituted the Shambhala Training Programme. The training, which includes meditation, flower arrangement and the martial arts, aims at developing such qualities as awareness of basic goodness, fearlessness, an open and tender heart, regal dignity, elegance, precision, non–aggression: culminating in a warrior's 'authentic presence'. Approximately twelve hundred people have completed the training since it began in Europe in 1982.

In 1975 Thich Nhat Hanh returned to Asia for the first time to attend a conference in Thailand organized by the Thai Buddhist activist Sulak Sivaraksha, during the course of which the fall of Saigon occurred. The following year he went to Singapore in order to help the 'Boat People', who had fled the Communist regime in Vietnam in the hope of a better life elsewhere. Since the Singapore government refused the refugees permission to land,

Nhat Hanh and his colleagues used three boats to smuggle them ashore at night and provide those offshore with food and water. At two o'clock one morning the police raided their headquarters and gave them twenty-four hours to leave the country. 'At that time', recalled Nhat Hanh, 'we were caring for more than seven hundred people in two boats at sea . . . . What could we do in such a situation? We had to breathe mindfully. Otherwise we might have panicked or fought with our captors, done something violent in order to express our anger at the lack of humanity in people.' They had to leave. Thich Nhat Hanh was forced to return to France.

In 1982 his community settled at Plum Village, two derelict farming hamlets near the town of Sainte Foy la Grande in south-west France. From here he continued to help the growing number of Vietnamese refugees in camps in south-east Asia and Hong Kong as well as destitute families in Vietnam itself. The community sent material support and campaigned on behalf of those suffering persecution. Although his books were banned, they continued to be hand-copied and circulated clandestinely in Vietnam. Some of his writings were translated into French and English and he was invited to teach in America. In 1987 Arnold Kotler, a former Zen monk and peace-activist in California, produced an edited collection of his talks entitled *Being Peace*. Five years later a hundred thousand copies were in print in English and it had been translated into nine European languages.

As early as 1966 Nhat Hanh had become aware of how much anger, hatred and frustration were driving the peace movement. Many anti-war activists in America, he discovered, were interested not in reconciliation but in a Communist victory over America. Towards the end of his mission, he found himself shunned and marginalized by some within the peace movement because of his refusal to take sides. 'Peace work', he declared, 'means, first of all, being peace . . . . It is not by going out for a demonstration against nuclear missiles that we can bring about peace. It is with our capacity of smiling, breathing, and being peace that we can make peace.' If it were not for the example of Nhat Hanh and others, this could easily be misconstrued as a recipe for passive inaction. The same point is made by the Dalai Lama. In his acceptance speech for the Nobel Peace Prize in Oslo in 1989, he affirmed: 'Inner peace is the key':

> if you have inner peace, the external problems do not affect your deep sense of peace and tranquillity. In that state of mind you can deal with situations with calmness and reason, while keeping your inner happiness.

This is no idealistic moralizing from secluded monks, but responses from men who for the whole of their lives have had to deal with more suffering than most of us could imagine. They are examples of how meditative practice is the very ground upon which sane and loving engagement with the world is possible.

'Life is filled with suffering,' remarks Nhat Hanh, 'but it is also filled with many wonders, like the blue sky, the sunshine, the eyes of a baby.' The retreats and workshops given in Plum Village and elsewhere in Europe by Thich Nhat Hanh and members of his 'Order of Interbeing' emphasize simple awareness of these everyday wonders, the cultivation of kindness, the ability to breathe mindfully under all circumstances, the capacity to accord one's life with the basic ethical precepts: this is what Buddhism boils down to. 'How can we practise at the airport and in the market?' asks Nhat Hanh. 'That is Engaged Buddhism. Engaged Buddhism does not only mean to use Buddhism to solve social and political problems. First of all we have to bring Buddhism into our daily lives.'

EPILOGUE

Wednesday, 23 September 1992. I am sitting in an aeroplane bound from London to Berlin. Several thousand feet below me Europe is in a dither called 'Maastricht'. The continent is collectively biting its fingernails over its common future.

Buddhism has penetrated the pages of today's *Times* in two items: in a piece on Nirvana — the American 'grunge-rock' group — and in an editorial on the recent Chinese white-paper on Tibet, which is quoted as saying: 'The democratic reforms conducted in Tibet in 1959 abolished the decadent and extremely dark feudal serfdom and the serfs and slaves thus gained personal freedom.' The editorial is suitably indignant and proclaims its support for the Dalai Lama.

My friend Hans Gruber meets me at Tegel Airport. Later that afternoon we go to the Brandenburg Gate and the Reichstag. I plan to bring this story to a close at the Berlin Wall, ideally (if I can find it) at the spot where the Dalai Lama held the candle and prayed for peace. But there is not a trace of the wall left — unless you count the paint-sprayed chips of concrete being sold to tourists at 3 DM each by enterprising Turks. A taxi-driver directs us to Checkpoint Charlie, where he says a section still stands. So we follow the zig-zagging red line on Hans' old map that still shows the wall. But it can only be inferred by the patches of wasteland that once were its bleak and sinister no-man's land. We lose it altogether after Köthener Strasse, partly because of its sheer elusiveness and partly because of an argument we are having over a phrase scrawled on a wall opposite the Reichstag: *Ein Mensch ohne Geschichte ist wie ein Baum ohne Würzeln* ('A person without history is like a tree without roots'). I think it's true, Hans doesn't.

Thursday, 24 September. Berlin is a city obsessed with the erasure of its past. In the East, this is achieved not so much by removing an unpleasant reminder of the post-war division, but by erecting emblems of the West's victory. The squat functional buildings around Alexanderplatz scream from their rooftops: MAZDA, SANYO, PHILISHAVE, CASIO, PEPSI! Blot out the giant words with one's hand, and nothing is left to draw the eye: just a featureless expanse of urban conformity, reflecting a vision of human society where people were spared the delusive allure of consumerism but might well have wondered what they were living for.

Out in the suburbs, where Bernauer Strasse meets Acker Strasse, we at last find a hundred yards of wall, complete with no man's land and barbed wire fences. The wall is so badly chipped that rusty reinforcement rods protrude from the concrete like exposed innards.

Okay, the real reason I'm in Berlin is to attend the 1992 Congress of the European Buddhist Union, whose theme 'Unity in Diversity' seems a fitting conclusion for this book. When the conference was first announced, the Dalai Lama had agreed to attend, which would have served my authorial purposes only too well. I had fantasies of photographing him next to the non-existent wall. In the end he agreed to be the patron.

The conference is held in a sports-stadium in Prenzlauerberg in the East. We arrive for registration in the early evening. Outside the main gate a young man in Japanese Zen robes paces up and down the pavement with a placard demanding freedom for Tibet, while his equally earnest friend meditates cross-legged inside an open-doored Volkswagen van. These Zen Buddhists have also been given the job of door-keeping, a task oddly suited to their rather stiff demeanour. Inside the hall is a display of Zen archery and flower arrangement, put on by Trungpa's Shambhala Training people. The corridors around the hall are packed with stalls displaying the promotional literature and assorted Dharma-ware of a bewildering number of organizations from all over the continent.

Friday, 25 September. The Congress officially gets underway at 9 a.m. Twelve hundred Europeans take their seats in the hall. The opening preamble mentions how the first such Buddhist Congress took place in Berlin in September 1933. (I later learn that this is not much spoken of because the organizer, Dr Wolfgang Schumacher — a student of Dahlke — was a Nazi at the time.) This present meeting has been arranged by the German Buddhist Union under the aegis of the European Buddhist Union, an umbrella organization of the different national Unions founded in its present form in 1975 by the Frenchman Paul Arnold. The aim of these Unions is to promote friendship and co-operation among Buddhists both at a national and European level. Berlin was chosen as the site because of its being such a powerful symbol for the ending of war and the healing of divisions in Europe. On a more sombre note, a fax is read out from a Buddhist in what was Yugoslavia, imploring us not to forget the plight of his land.

Then the inevitable ceremonies: the disjunct rumbling in Pali of the Refuges by two Theravada *bhikkhus*; the agonizingly refined chanting in Sino-Japanese of the *Heart Sutra* by a German Zen nun; concluded with the rapid growling of prayers in Tibetan by a cluster of monks in burgundy robes. The portly Doboom Tulku from Delhi reads out the Dalai Lama's message to the Congress — 'inner peace is the key', a theme taken up by a nervous representative from the Berlin Senate, who emphasizes how sorely the Buddhist virtues of tolerance and openness are needed in his city at this time.

Then we're off. Sogyal Rinpoché speaks eloquently about the teachings of the Nyingma school, but weakens the impact by laughing a bit too forcefully at his own jokes. He stresses the importance of transmission from qualified masters and the need for better training facilities in Europe. He sees the strength of Buddhism lying in its diversity and believes there is no hurry to create a Western form. For if we practise sincerely, the 'blessings of the Buddhas and Bodhisattvas' will lead us to a synthesis of the traditions all in good time.

Daishin Morgan from Throssel Hole follows with a sincere, humble and moving reflection on death. As usual I am troubled by Roshi Kennett's quasi-theistic view of the Unborn. 'The aim of my life', he says (following Sir Edwin Arnold), 'is to become the dewdrop that becomes one with the shining sea — the Unborn, the Buddha-nature.' 'I hope that when I die', he confesses, 'I will be able to look the Unborn in the face.'

And so the day goes on. The afternoon finishes with a young Tibetan lama, Traleg Rinpoché, standing in for His Eminence the Shamarpa — too embroiled in the fiasco around the new Karmapa to spare time for Europe. After the talk (a lucid account of Tibetan Buddhist psychology), a woman asks: 'I have been going to Buddhist centres for some time and so far have met no enlightened beings. Why are they so rare?' The Rinpoché coolly replies: 'How are you enlightened enough to know there are no enlightened beings?' A spontaneous reflex of higher insight? Or nimble evasion of the question?

Saturday, 26 September. The best way to dampen enthusiasm about something is to attend an international conference on it. Hans and I concede that we had to force ourselves out of bed to be in time to make the long subway journey from Kreuzberg to the East. We seem driven by a primal, unconscious duty to be part of a mass affirmation of something.

We're late anyway. The besuited figure of Sangharakshita is

already standing on the platform reading a paper in his clipped, emphatic English. 'One last word', he concludes, raising his hand. 'I have spoken on the integration of Buddhism into Western society because that is what I was asked to speak on. But as my talk proceeded it will have become obvious to you that what we really have to do is integrate Western society into Buddhism.' The full text is available as a smart booklet from the FWBO stall immediately after the talk.

Prabhasadharma Roshi, the German Rinzai nun of the ceremony, gives a rambling, poetic, enigmatic, personal account of Zen. 'Why did the Dharma come to Berlin?' she asks, and has everyone slowly and rhythmically answer: 'The oak tree in the garden!' This, she claims, reveals the direct, unmediated experience of reality as opposed to the world we have learnt through description and language, i.e. the 'Deathless', a.k.a. the Unborn. She bows beautifully.

The afternoon opens with the resounding *Dong!* of Thich Nhat Hanh's 'mindfulness bell', calling everyone to stop and breathe for a few moments. Nhat Hanh invites Sister Phuong to sing 'Un Sourire', a wistful song about the fleeting beauty of a smile that redeems even the most painful situation. 'Peace is there', he assures us in his innocent, lisping way. 'We need only to touch it. In the practice of Buddhism one does not turn oneself into a battlefield, taking the side of good against evil.' The words have the quality of a lament. Then I notice Mahaghosananda, the diminutive, transparent and incredibly scruffy Supreme Patriarch of Buddhism in Cambodia, until recently a fellow exile from his land, his ancient, avuncular face beaming from the front row.

There is nothing wistful about Ayya Khema. The stocky little white-haired German nun knows exactly what she is talking about and delivers it with gusto. She speaks of perfect concentration, where the mind finds at last its true home in unconditional freedom, purity and peace. To realize this, she asserts, is our responsibility as Buddhists if we wish to fulfill not only the broader meaning of 'Unity in Diversity', but peace on Earth.

Before she finishes, I have to go. Arnie Kotler of Parallax Press has invited me to dine with Petra Kelly, co-founder of the German Green Party and active supporter of the Tibetan cause. She is attending a conference in the city on the effects of radiation and had come that afternoon to the Congress to hear Thich Nhat Hanh. We take the subway to Alexanderplatz, then a bus via the Brandenburg Gate to her hotel on the Kurfürstendamm.

By the time we cross the busy Kurfürstendamm to an open-air restaurant, dusk is falling and the glitzy electric lights of West Berlin are taking over. Petra is accompanied by her partner Gert Bastian, a gentle elderly man, formerly a major-general in the Bundeswehr, who renounced his military career in favour of Green politics. Until the recent elections when the Greens lost their seats in the Bundestag, they had both been members of the German parliament.

We sit at the one unoccupied table outside and order food. Petra talks incessantly on her current passions, with Gert injecting brief supportive comments in his softly caring voice. She predicts that the extreme-right will win seats in the Bundestag at the next election; she admires Sister Phuong's voice she had heard sing that afternoon; she bemoans the fact that the principles of Green politics seem incompatible with the holding of power. Her eyes are like animated emeralds, glittering from the dark brown pools that circle them.

As the evening grows late a chill breeze wafts up the Kurfürstendamm. I begin to doubt whether Petra will ever pause long enough for me to ask my question. For here is someone who might know about the Dalai Lama's stopover in Berlin in December 1989. I seize a rare gap in the rush of syllables.

Following the Dalai Lama's autobiography, I tell them of his standing by the wall, being given a candle by an old woman, praying for peace and so on, and ask if, by chance, they know where it took place. She laughs. At the time she and Gert were pressing the German government to take a more pro-Tibetan stance. It was they who had arranged the visit.

On this point, she says, the autobiography is both inaccurate and incomplete. Not only was the 'old woman' the middle-aged East German human rights activist Bärbel Bohley, the 'crowd' was a hand-holding circle of political radicals from both Germanies, including Gert and herself, and the location was unambiguously the *East* Berlin side of the wall.

Against all regulations, she had made a government car available for the Dalai Lama and his staff to cross into the Soviet Zone at Checkpoint Charlie. Having performed the ceremony at the wall by the checkpoint, they were escorted by the East German Secret Police (Stasi) to a meeting of the 'Round Table of the Citizen's Action Movement'.

By now I am scribbling Petra's words onto a paper napkin. This, she says, was the first time the Dalai Lama had encountered 'a genuinely revolutionary situation'. With the fall of Egon Kranz that day, the Communist Party had lost its grip on power. In the chaotic but potent vacuum that prevailed, the Citizen's Action Movement was confident that it would take over the government to create an independent, demilitarized, nuclear-free and environmentally aware East German state, which would subscribe neither to the capitalist nor communist dogmas. The Dalai Lama was assured that he would be the first official guest of the new rulers, who also promised to recognize the independence of Tibet.

Both the Dalai Lama and the aspiring government were deeply moved by the meeting. But she also remembers the nervousness of his staff, some of whom wanted to cut the meeting short and hasten back to the safety of the West.

The dreams of the Citizen's Action Movement were never to be realized. They had underestimated the power of the West German institutions to control the course of events. Within a matter of weeks the stage was set for reunification as defined by the Federal Republic.

Petra's respect for the Dalai Lama often clashes with her frustration with his political advisors, whom she considers reactionary and ill-informed. The autobiography's failure to mention the meeting with the Citizen's Action Movement might simply reflect a concern of the Dalai Lama's staff that His Holiness be associated with a failed political movement. History is a process of selection: its convenient fictions as much a reflection of what one chooses to omit as what one decides to include.

Sunday, 27 September. Hans and I are tempted to join a wild-haired man in the subway who is going to spend his Sunday in the countryside of former East Germany in search of the fish-eagle. The playful, religious intensity of his quest puts to shame the self-important spirituality of some of our fellow Buddhists. But loyalty to the cause prevails over the thrill of following such a treacherous whim.

The Congress, however, redeems itself in the closing podium discussion. Sogyal Rinpoché, Thich Nhat Hanh, Sangharakshita and Dr Rewata Dhamma are seated behind a long table. They not only pronounce on the topics put forward by the chair (wisdom and compassion, monastic versus lay Buddhism etc.), but seem called upon to qualify, endorse, refine, challenge each other's position. This lends a vitality to the discussion that turns it into a scrupulously deferential debate, the success of each speaker tacitly measured by the length and intensity of applause.

When the Congress concludes with the obligatory chanting and prayers I feel uplifted, my cynical reservations about conferences replaced by an inexplicable nostalgia for what has taken place. But it is over and I hurriedly make my farewells as the hall and the corridors urgently empty and the once proud stalls are interred in cardboard boxes and plastic bags. The sun is shining for a change.

I jump into a taxi with two friends and silently pull away just as the giant Buddha image is lowered by ropes from the front of the stadium.

They drop me not far from what used to be Checkpoint Charlie. This ultimate symbol of East-West hostility has been appropriated by the tourist industry. A twenty-yard fragment of wall together with the famous wooden sign YOU ARE LEAVING THE AMERICAN SECTOR are all that remain. The broad expanse of tarmac beyond them, where grim-faced security police once scrutinized those who dared to cross, serves as a parking lot for buses to disgorge clusters of camera-toting Japanese.

A fenced-off area behind the wall is preserved as a self-declared 'monument of human delusion', housing bits of barbed-wire fence, machine-gun posts, tank barriers, high-powered street lamps and a solitary watchtower — perhaps the one beneath whose gaze the Dalai Lama lit his candle and prayed for peace. Only six months later, on 22 June 1990, his prayer was answered when Checkpoint Charlie was 'solemnly dismounted' — as the tourist blurb recalls. And framed on the ground at the foot of the tower is a quotation from the Roman historian Livy:

> There are times, people and events on which and whom only history can pass final judgement — the only thing that remains to be done by the individual is to report on what he saw happening and what he heard.

Postscript

The Buddhist Retreat Centre, Ixopo, South Africa. Thursday, 31 December 1992. On this, the last day of my allotted timespan for this book, I am in another hemisphere from that in which the historical encounter between Buddhism and Western Culture has largely taken place. A hundred yards away through the heavy mist covering these hills of Natal is the first Buddhist stupa on the African continent, on a site chosen by Lama Govinda during his visit in 1972, overlooking the valleys, dirt roads and villages of Zululand.

Four days after having dinner with Petra Kelly and Gert Bastian in Berlin, both of them were lying dead in their house in Bonn from gunshot wounds. Shortly after returning home from Berlin, Gert shot Petra and then committed suicide. When their decomposed bodies were found three weeks later, no note or other indication was left offering a reason for their deaths. I find it incomprehensible that two such committed people should have ended their lives in such a way. I was so grateful to them for giving me that twist of history with which to conclude my story (even promising before we parted to send photos and check my text for accuracy). Their deaths have now given that twist a tragic, unsettling turn. History has broken into my story, upsetting its neat conclusion.

When, forty years ago, in 1952, the Jesuit scholar Henri de Lubac came to conclude his study of the encounter between Buddhism and the West, he wrote as though he were describing the closing chapter to an episode of purely historical interest. He had not the slightest inkling of the rapid expansion of Buddhism that would occur in the following decade. Perhaps the lesson to be drawn from Gert Bastian and Petra Kelly's deaths is that of the sheer unpredictability of human behaviour. Although, with hindsight, I can read Henri de Lubac's conclusions with a bemused chuckle, I can no more see the future now than he could then. It would be arrogant and foolish even to hazard a guess at the state of Buddhism in another decade, let alone forty years hence, in 2032.

GLOSSARY OF
TECHNICAL TERMS

Since this book is intended for a non-specialist readership I have omitted all diacritical marks on Sanskrit, Pali and Japanese terms. Likewise Tibetan terms have been transcribed phonetically rather than scholastically. For uniformity and simplicity, I have tended to use Sanskrit rather than the Pali equivalent – even when discussing Theravada Buddhism.

Ch. = Chinese
Jap. = Japanese
Skt. = Sanskrit
Tib. = Tibetan

Anagarika (Pali). Lit: 'homeless wanderer'. A Buddhist layperson who has taken vows including celibacy.

Anguttara Nikaya (Pali). Lit: 'collection of gradual sayings'. A section of the Pali Buddhist canon.

Arhat (Skt.). A person who has attained Nirvana through freeing himself from the origins of suffering, delusion and craving.

Avalokiteshvara (Skt.). The archetypal Bodhisattva who personifies compassion.

BCE. 'Before the Common Era'. A non-Christian alternative for 'BC'.

Bhikkhu (Pali). A fully ordained Buddhist monk.

Bhikshu (Skt.). See *Bhikkhu*.

Bodhicitta (Skt.). Lit: 'awakening mind'. The aspiration to attain Buddhahood for the sake of all living beings.

Bodhisattva (Skt.). Lit: 'awakening being'. A person who aspires to become a Buddha.

Buddha (Skt.). Lit: 'awakened one';. A person who has attained both Nirvana as well as the optimal capacity to benefit others.

Buddhanature (Skt. *buddha gotra*). The capacity within any living being to become a Buddha; the Buddhahood latent within any living being.

380

CE. 'Common Era'. A non–Christian alternative for 'AD'.

Ch'an (Ch.). See *Zen*.

Dakini (Skt.; Tib. *khandroma*). Lit: 'sky dancer'. An actual or archetypal woman who personifies the playful, dynamic aspect of enlightenment.

Dharma (Skt.). Lit: 'law'. (1) The teachings of a Buddha. (2) The truths referred to by the teachings of a Buddha. (3) The application of the teachings of a Buddha.

Dojo (Jap.). A centre for the practice of Zen meditation.

Dzogchen (Tib.; Skt. *maha ati*). Lit: 'great perfection'. Enlightenment; direct Vajrayana teachings aimed at activating primordial awareness.

Elders (Skt. *Sthavira*). An early Indian Buddhist school which revered the *arhat* as the optimal state of human attainment.

Enlightenment (Skt. *bodhi*). A state of consciousness in which the four noble truths are indisputably evident.

Geluk (Tib.). Lit: 'virtuous tradition'. One of the four schools of Tibetan Buddhism. Founded by Tsongkhapa in the 15th century. See Chapter 12.

Geshé (Tib.). Lit: 'spiritual friend'. A title given in the Geluk tradition of Tibetan Buddhism to denote a high degree of doctrinal learning.

Gohonzon (Jap.). A mandala–like inscription of *Nam-myoho-renge-kyo*, used as an object of worship in Nichiren Shoshu Buddhism.

Hinayana (Skt.). Lit: 'lesser vehicle'. A pejorative term given by followers of the Mahayana to the spiritual path of those who practise Buddhism for selfish motives.

Jewels, Three (Skt. *tri ratna*). The Buddha, the Dharma and the Sangha; the three central values to which a Buddhist commits his or her life by 'going for refuge'.

Kadam (Tib.). An early school of Tibetan Buddhism founded in the 11th century by Atisha, subsequently incorporated into the Geluk tradition.

Kagyu (Tib.). Lit: 'oral lineage'. One of the four schools of Tibetan Buddhism. Founded by Marpa in the 11th century. See Chapter 8.

Kangyur (Tib.). Lit: 'translation of the [Buddha's] word'. The Tibetan Buddhist canon of *sutras* and *tantras*.

Karuna (Pali and Skt.). Compassion.

Kensho (Jap.). A sudden experience of insight into the nature of reality.

Koan (Jap.; Ch. *kung-an*). Lit: 'public case'. A record of an encounter between a teacher and student in which an experience of enlightenment is triggered. Used as an object of meditation in Zen meditation.

Lam-rim (Tib.). Lit: 'stages on the path'. A systematic presentation of the path to enlightenment as found in Tibetan Buddhism.

Lharampa (Tib.). Lit: 'divine doctor'. The highest rank of *geshé*.

Madhyamaka (Skt.). Lit: 'the middle'. A system of Buddhist philosophy developed by Nagarjuna and his followers based on the principle of transparency.

Mahamudra (Skt.). Lit: 'great seal'. Transparency; direct Vajrayana instructions for realising the true nature of mind.

Mahasiddha (Skt.). Lit: 'great adept'. A person who has realised enlightenment through the Vajrayana.

Majority (Skt. *Mahasamghika*). An early Indian Buddhist school that sought a more democratic Buddhist community; the forerunners of the Mahayana.

Mahayana (Skt.). Lit: 'great vehicle'. The spiritual path of those who practise Buddhism for the sake of all living beings.

Maitreya (Skt.). Lit: 'the loving one'. The archetypal Bodhisattva who personifies loving kindness. According to all Buddhist schools, the next Buddha who will appear on this earth as a world-teacher.

Manjushri (Skt.). The archetypal Bodhisattva who personifies wisdom.

Mappo (Jap.). The degeneration of historical time; the period in which the Buddha's teachings fall into decline.

Metta (Pali; Skt. *maitri*). Loving kindness.

Nirvana (Skt.). The cessation of the origins of suffering, delusion and craving. In the Mahayana sometimes a metaphor for 'transparency'.

Noble Truths, Four (Skt. *catuharyasatya*). Suffering; the Origins of Suffering; the Cessation of the Origins of Suffering; the Way Leading to Cessation.

Nyingma (Tib.). Lit: 'ancients'. One of the four schools of Tibetan Buddhism. Founded by Padmasambhava in the 8th century. See Chapter 6.

Pali. The ancient mid-Indic language in which one of the earliest canons of Gautama's discourses is recorded.

Pure Land. In Mahayana Buddhism, a realm created by the compassion of a Bodhisattva or Buddha where beings may aspire to be born in order to complete the path to enlightenment under more propitious circumstances. Name of Chinese and Japanese schools of Buddhism based on such beliefs.

Rimé (Tib.). Lit: 'without bias'. A 19th-century reform movement in Tibet that sought to preserve endangered Buddhist teachings irrespective of their sectarian origins.

382

Rinpoché (Tib.). Lit: 'precious one'. A title of respect given to Tibetan lamas of high rank. See *Tulku*.

Rinzai (Jap.; Ch. *Lin-chi*). The Zen Buddhist line of transmission that traces its origins to the 9th-century Chinese Ch'an master of the same name. See Chapter 13.

Roshi (Jap.). Lit: 'old monk'. An authorised Zen Master.

Sakya (Tib.). Lit: 'grey earth'. One of the four schools of Tibetan Buddhism, named after the region in Southern Tibet where its founding teachers originated in the 11th century.

Samatha (Skt.). Lit: 'mental calm'. A concentrated, equanimous state of mind in which excitement and dullness are overcome.

Samsara (Skt.). The frustrating, repetitive cycle of birth and death; the opposite of Nirvana.

Sangha (Skt.). Lit: 'community'. The community of people committed to the practice of the Dharma. Sometimes used to refer exclusively to ordained monks and nuns.

Satipatthana (Pali). Lit: 'foundation of mindfulness'. The practice of mindful awareness meditation. See Chapter 20.

Selflessness (Skt. *anatman*). See *Transparency*.

Sesshin (Jap.). An intensive period of sitting meditation.

Shakyamuni (Skt.). Lit: 'Sage of the Shakya [Clan]'. An epithet of Gautama Buddha.

Shingon (Jap.). The tantric school of Japanese Buddhism.

Shramana (Skt.). A wandering ascetic.

Sima (Pali). A monastery's formal boundary within which monastic ordination can take place.

Soka Gakkai (Jap.). Lit: 'Value Creation Society'. A lay Buddhist organisation that follows the teaching of the 13th-century monk Nichiren. See Chapter 10.

Soto (Jap.; Ch. *Tsao-tung*). The Zen Buddhist line of transmission that traces its origins to the Chinese Ch'an masters Tsao-shan and Tung-shan. See Chapter 9.

Sutra (Skt.). A Buddhist discourse attributed to Gautama Buddha.

Tantra (Skt.). Lit: 'continuum'. A Buddhist text attributed to Gautama or another Buddha that describes an accelerated path to enlightenment by means of mantra, transformative imagination and yogic exercises.

Tendai (Jap.; Ch. *T'ien-t'ai*). A syncretic 6th-century school of Chinese Buddhism founded by Chih-i, which subsequently went to Japan.

Tengyur (Tib.). Lit: 'translation of the commentaries [to the Buddha's word]'. The Tibetan Buddhist canon of Indian and selected Tibetan commentarial literature.

Theravada (Pali).   The tradition of Buddhism prevalent in Sri Lanka, Thailand and Burma based on the teachings of the Pali canon.

Transparency (Skt. *sunyata*).   Lit: 'emptiness'. The absence of inherent self-existence in persons or things. Synonym of 'selflessness'.

Tulku (Tib.).   Lit: 'emanated presence'. A recognised reincarnate lama.

Universal Monarch (Skt. *chakravartin*).   An Indian mythological figure representing the ideal state of kingship; a model of unenlightened perfection.

Vajrabhairava (Skt.).   A deity of the higher yoga tantras. The wrathful aspect of Manjushri.

Vajrayana (Skt.).   Lit: 'diamond vehicle'. The path to enlightenment as described in the Buddhist *tantras*.

Vihara (Pali; Skt.).   Lit: 'secluded place'. A Buddhist monastery.

Vinaya (Skt.).   The rule followed by Buddhist monks and nuns; ethical discipline.

Vipassana (Pali; Skt. *vipasyana*.).   Lit: 'penetrative insight'. Understanding of the central truths of the Dharma by means of meditation practice.

Wesak (Pali).   The yearly celebration of the Buddha's birth, awakening and death that takes place on the full moon day of the fourth lunar month in Sri Lanka, South East Asia and Tibet.

Yamantaka (Skt.).   See *Vajrabhairava*.

Zafu (Jap.).   A round cushion used for sitting meditation.

Zazen (Jap.).   Lit: 'sitting meditation'. According to Hui Neng: 'where the mind has nowhere to abide'.

Zen (Jap.; Ch. *ch'an*).   Lit: 'meditation'. A contemplative form of Buddhism that originated in 6th-century China and spread to Korea and Japan.

Zendo (Jap.).   Lit: 'meditation hall'. A formal building in a monastery dedicated to the practice of Zen.

NOTES

'(Tr.)' *indicates that the passage has been translated from the original language by the author.*

Prologue

p. xv. 'With some emotion . . .': Gyatso, 290.
p. xvi. 'Gentle and full of honesty . . .': Gyatso, 290–1.

Chapter 1. Menander: Greeks in India

p. 5. 'I have just as much of the earth . . .': Sedlar, 72.
p. 7. 'are best esteemed . . .': McCrindle, 98–9
p. 7. 'live in the woods . . .': McCrindle, 102.
p. 8. 'Go forth, and walk . . .': Lamotte, 97.
p. 9. 'I do not call truth . . .': Lamotte, 233.
p. 13. 'As a lion captured . . .': Lamotte, 425.
p. 13. 'When Menander, who had ruled . . .': Lamotte, 421.

Chapter 2. Nagasena: The Dharma

p. 16. 'I am Nagasena, sir, . . .': Horner (2), 34–8 (adapted).
p. 20. 'What is the use of going forth . . .': Horner (2), 42 (adapted).
p. 20. 'When the flame . . .' and 'it is not possible to point . . .': Horner (2), 100 (adapted).
p. 21. 'He who sees the Dharma . . .': Horner (2), 97 (adapted).
p. 21. 'Nagasena, have you seen . . .': Horner (2), 97 (adapted).
p. 21. 'Nagasena, how would you define faith? . . .': Horner (2), 47–9 (adapted).

p. 22. 'Ethics is defined as the basis . . .': Horner (2), 45—6 (adapted).

p. 22. 'And just as rafters in a roof . . .': Horner (2), 52—3 (adapted).

p. 23. 'How many factors of awakening . . .': Horner (2), 115 (adapted).

p. 23. 'How would you define wisdom . . .': Horner (2), 53—4 and 44 (adapted).

p. 24. 'Venerable Nagasena, where does': Horner (2), 105 (adapted).

Chapter 3. Basilides: Gnostic Connections

p. 26. 'The world today speaks for itself . . .': Dodds, 12.

p. 27. 'flourished in antiquity . . .': Welbon, 5.

p. 28. 'had long been disposed . . .': D. Mackenzie, v.

p. 29. 'was Buddhist pure and simple . . .': Kennedy, 383.

p. 29. 'pain and fear are as inherent . . .': Kennedy, 388.

p. 29. 'the soul has previously sinned . . .': Kennedy, 390.

p. 29. 'the soul is not a single entity . . .': Kennedy, 391.

p. 29. 'primitive turmoil and confusion . . .': Kennedy, 395.

p. 30. 'Wisdom and deeds have always . . .': Lang, 25.

p. 35. 'people of whom we know little . . .': Rachewiltz, 21.

Chapter 4. Bhikkhu Sangha: The Order of Monks

p. 38. 'These monks only eat . . .': de Lubac, 46—7 (Tr.).

p. 40. 'He's American; he can't eat . . .': Sumedho, 45.

p. 41. 'the noblest and gentlest soul . . .': Wilson, 58.

p. 41. 'to carry to the lands . . .': Humphreys, 2.

p. 46. 'I know that you have had . . .': Ajahn Chah (1), 127.

p. 47. 'If you want to really see . . .': Ajahn Chah (1), 114.

p. 48. 'This mind, monks, is luminous, . . .': Nanananda, 58.

p. 48. 'About this mind . . .': Ajahn Chah (2), 1.

p. 48. 'the One Who Knows, . . .': Ajahn Chah (1), 8.

p. 49. 'There isn't anything . . .': Disciples of Ajahn Chah, 28.

Chapter 5. Shantideva: The Bodhisattva

p. 56. 'When neither something . . .': Shantideva (1), IX: 34.

p. 57. 'I am no butcher; I am a healer . . .': Dowman, 226.

p. 58. ' . . .will not harm others . . .': Watson, 100.

p. 58. 'So even when I have done . . .': Shantideva (1), VIII: 116.

p. 59. 'There are two aspects to *bodhicitta*: . . .': Shantideva (1),
   I: 15—16.
p. 59. 'A blindman who has chanced . . .': Shantideva (1), II: 28.
p. 59. 'The words of a lunatic . . .': Shantideva (1), III: 42.
p. 60. 'a watchman at the gateway . . .': Shantideva (1), V: 29.
p. 60. 'Thieves in search of an opportunity . . .': Shantideva (1),
   V: 28.
p. 60. 'Like a lion among jackals . . .': Shantideva (1), VII: 60.
p. 60. 'In forests, among deer . . ..': Shantideva (1), VIII: 25.
p. 60. 'Mad elephant of the mind . . ..': Shantideva (1), V: 3.
p. 60. 'In the same way as hands and legs . . .': Shantideva (1),
   VIII: 114.
p. 61. 'Out of love to quell . . .': Shantideva (1), VIII: 107.
p. 61. 'The ultimate is not something . . .': Shantideva (1), IX: 2.

Chapter 6. Padmasambhava: The Nyingma Tradition

p. 65. 'I have endeavoured to perfect . . .': Tarthang, 13.
p. 66. 'turned his hands and . . .': Tarthang, 28.
p. 67. 'Padma[sambhava] mounted a winged horse . . .': Tarthang, 32.
p. 70. 'I remember one rainy day . . .': Godet. *Memoir.*
p. 70. 'If you lack the altruistic resolve . . .': Shantideva (2), ii.
p. 75. 'The nature of the mind is Buddha . . ..': Tulku Thondup, 69.
p. 75. 'Not *sutra*, not *tantra* . . .': Namkhai Norbu, 34.
p. 75. 'Don't follow the past . . .': Namkhai Norbu, 142.
p. 77. 'luminous white orb . . .': Namkhai Norbu, 53.

Chapter 7. William of Rubruck: First Encounters

p. 82. 'All the idol priests . . .': Jackson, 163 and 153—4.
p. 84. 'to thrust his sword . . .': Olschki, 181.
p. 84. 'Let us leave these dogs . . .': Rachewiltz, 74—5.
p. 86. 'If these people, . . .': Rachewiltz, 80.
p. 86. 'acknowledge Jesus Christ . . .': Dawson, 75—6.
p. 87. 'large, but otherwise . . .': Dawson, 6.
p. 87. 'How dost thou know, . . .': Dawson, 86.
p. 88. 'snub-nosed, a man of medium build, . . .': Jackson, 178.
p. 89. 'belonging to the Manichaean heresy . . .': Jackson, 232.
p. 89. 'There are twelve idol [Buddhist] temples . . .': Jackson, 221.
p. 90. 'Here you are, Christians, . . .': Jackson, 229.

p. 90. 'agree with us in saying . . .': Jackson, 231.

p. 90. 'We firmly believe in our hearts . . .' (to end of debate): Jackson, 232–3.

p. 91. 'But for all that no one said, . . .': Jackson, 235.

p. 91. 'We Mongols believe, . . .': Jackson, 236–7.

p. 91. 'for my own part I would, . . .': Jackson, 173.

p. 92. 'I, the most powerful . . .': Shagapa, 61–2.

p. 93. 'The Prince has told me . . . .': Shagapa, 63.

p. 94. 'invited many jealous Taoist . . .': Thinley, 50.

p. 94. 'The literati say that Confucianism . . .': Ch'en, 423.

p. 95. '[The soldiers] wrapped him . . .': Douglas and White, 44.

p. 96. 'a deserted area near the ocean . . . .': Thinley, 51.

p. 97. 'how on many occasions [the Khan] . . .': Olschki, 190n.

p. 97. 'There are four prophets . . .': Olschki, 182.

p. 97. 'These Tartars do not care . . .': Olschki, 179.

p. 98. 'for a certainty, if he . . .': Olschki, 256.

p. 99. 'that anyone found guilty . . .': Ch'en, 420.

p. 100. 'All Knower of Religion . . .': Douglas and White, 49.

p. 100. 'Toghan Temür, a weak . . .': Grousset, 323.

Chapter 8. Karmapa: The Kagyu Tradition

p. 102. 'a dark man dressed in cotton . . . .': Guenther (2), 36–7.

p. 103. 'never been apart, but were . . .': Guenther (2), 37.

p. 103. 'Tilopa sat motionless . . .': Guenther (2), 43.

p. 105. 'My journey to the overseas . . .': Vajradhatu Sun, 10.

p. 108. 'If I went out, I wanted . . .': Lhalungpa (1), 41.

p. 109. 'I, whom you see . . .': Chang (1), 6.

p. 112. 'Everything that I have . . .': Sèngué and Tsomo, 49.

p. 114. 'There was one thought . . .': Douglas and White, 118.

p. 115. 'a lay and yogic organisation . . .': Ole Nydahl (interview, Leningrad, May 1991).

p. 117. 'In meditation practice, . . .': Lhalungpa (2), xv.

p. 118. 'the view of *mahamudra* . . .': Chang (2), 32.

p. 118. 'Since in the view of *mahamudra* . . .': Nalanda Translation Committee, 90.

Chapter 9. Dogen: The Soto Zen Tradition

p. 120. 'the process of becoming intimate . . .': Deshimaru (4), 19–20.

p. 120. 'Zen is not a particular state . . .': Deshimaru, quoted from 'Zen' a pamphlet published by the Dojo Zen de Paris.

p. 121. 'He who walks alone goes forward . . .': Crépon, 1.

p. 121. 'Why do I do *zazen*? . . .': Triet, 3.

p. 122. 'In India during the time of Bodhidharma, . . .': Deshimaru (4), xxviii.

p. 123. 'sailing many miles, . . .': Kodera, 117.

p. 126. 'To study meditation under a master, . . .': Kodera, 58.

p. 126. 'sat in meditation past eleven o'clock . . .': Kodera, 59.

p. 128. 'In the Buddha's house . . .': Tanahashi, 149.

p. 129. 'To practice the Way . . .': Yokoi, 46—7.

p. 129. 'You should stop pursuing words . . .': Yokoi, 46.

p. 130. 'the mountains and waters . . .': Cleary, 87.

p. 130. 'Studying the Buddha Way . . .': Cleary, 32.

p. 131. 'I carefully took it from my head . . .': Jiyu-Kennett (2), I: 68—9.

p. 131. 'the great flash of deep . . .': Jiyu-Kennett (3), 7.

p. 132. 'write to this man . . .': Jiyu-Kennett (2), II: 37. [The identification of Humphreys was communicated in an interview with Rev. Daishin Morgan, April 1993.]

p. 132. 'The old man looked at me . . .': Jiyu-Kennett (2), II, 87—8. [The identification of Kodo Sawaki was communicated in an interview with Rev. Daishin Morgan, April 1993.]

p. 133. 'I had no idea that I . . .': Jiyu-Kennett (3), 8.

p. 134. 'Once or twice I have had . . .': Jiyu-Kennett (3), 8.

p. 134. 'We choose Heaven . . .': Jiyu-Kennett (3), 257.

p. 134. 'Why, being myself subject . . .': Nanamoli, 10.

p. 134. 'state of mind has perhaps . . .': Jiyu-Kennett (1), 18—9.

p. 135. 'only be achieved by *zazen* . . .': Jiyu-Kennett (1), 53.

p. 135. 'must have absolute faith . . .': Jiyu-Kennett (1), 44.

p. 135. 'Zen is an intuitive . . .': Jiyu-Kennett (1), 13.

p. 135. 'this was because . . .': Jiyu-Kennett (3), 179.

Chapter 10. Nichiren: The Nichiren Tradition

p. 140. 'independence of India . . .': Fujii, 62.

p. 140. 'except in Japan there is no longer . . .': Fujii, 28.

p. 140. 'when humanity becomes one . . .': Fujii, 98.

p. 142. '*Myoho-renge-kyo* is the king . . .': Seikyo Times, 3.

p. 142. 'Buddhahood in this lifetime . . .': Seikyo Times, 5.

p. 143. 'Only two have yet to appear . . .': Yampolsky (1), 38.

p. 143. 'If people favour perverse doctrines . . .': Yampolsky (1), 25.

p. 144. 'It seems to me that prohibiting . . .': Yampolsky (1), 31.

p. 144. 'Now, nine years after I presented . . .': Yampolsky (1), 46.

p. 144. 'were possessed of devils . . .': Yampolsky (1), 45.

p. 145. 'Nichiren is the pillar and beam . . .': Yampolsky (1), 240.

p. 145. 'all the [Pure Land] and Zen temples . . .': Yampolsky (1), 240–1.

p. 145. 'Rather it was in all cases . . .': Yampolsky (1), 241.

p. 145. 'In the yard around my hut . . . .': Yampolsky (1), 330–1.

p. 147. 'is the Buddhism of the harvest . . .': Yampolsky (1), 171.

p. 148. 'from the ruler on down . . .': Yampolsky (1), 199.

p. 148. 'it will do no good . . .': Yampolsky (1), 200.

p. 148. 'Just see how it will be! . . .': Yampolsky (1), 239.

p. 148. 'if the invasion does not . . .': Yampolsky (1), 354.

p. 148. 'a messenger from heaven . . .': Yampolsky (1), 354.

p. 149. 'just ask them if they took . . . .': Montgomery, 142.

p. 149. 'All the sufferings that befall . . .': Montgomery, 142.

p. 149. 'Just chant *Nam-myoho-renge-kyo*, . . .': Seikyo Times, 161.

p. 152. 'to have the cause of becoming . . .': Montgomery, 185.

p. 154. 'Mr. Ikeda's ignorant and . . .': Myodo, 1.

p. 154. 'the Soka Gakkai, forgetting . . .': Myodo, 1.

p. 156. 'Defenders of the True Law . . .': Yampolsky (1), 144.

p. 156. 'Immortality/ Is yours . . .': NSUK Bulletin, 1.

Chapter 11. Francis Xavier: The Jesuits

p. 165. 'which consoled me much . . .': Shore, 3 (quoting Schurhammer).

p. 166. 'The [foreigners] understand to a certain degree . . .': Shore, 2.

p. 166. 'in their culture, their social usage, . . .': Dumoulin, 210.

p. 166. 'the abominable vice of Sodom . . .': Spence, 224–5.

p. 167. 'the people we have met so far . . .': Elison, 14.

p. 167. 'the Shingon sect, like all . . . .': Shore, 3.

p. 167. 'His name is Ninshitsu, . . .': Dumoulin, 200.

p. 168. 'Some are calculating . . .': Dumoulin, 200.

p. 171. 'To gain greater status . . .': Spence, 115.

p. 171. 'nothing contrary to the essence . . .': Spence, 210.

p. 171. 'a Babylon of doctrines . . .': Spence, 210.

p. 171. 'Since entering China, . . .': Gernet, 214.

p. 172. 'battle prizes': Spence, 249.

p. 172. 'Amongst us, it is held . . .': Spence, 44.

p. 172. 'In contrast, on the whole . . .': Gernet, 110.

p. 173. 'an altogether remarkable man . . .': Gernet, 19.

p. 174. 'The barbarians began by attacking . . . .': Gernet, 52.

p. 174. 'This is a wicked thing . . .': Spence, 247.

p. 175. 'They cling to the idea . . .': Gernet, 218.

p. 176. 'Westerners were clever at examining . . .': Gernet, 59.

p. 176. 'empty words and illusions . . .': Gernet, 121.

p. 177. 'I did not deem the thousands . . .': Elison, 297—8.

p. 179. 'While killing, there is no thought . . .': Suzuki, 166—7.

p. 181. 'the resident of the country of Portugal, . . .': Elison, 318.

p. 181. 'working of the shaping forces . . .': Elison, 295.

p. 181. 'wandered in delusion . . .': Elison, 295—6.

Chapter 12. Tsongkhapa: The Geluk Tradition

p. 184. 'He's so serene . . .': V. Mackenzie, 90.

p. 184. 'should be open to people . . .': V. Mackenzie, 92.

p. 184. 'a small child with bright . . .': V. Mackenzie, 96.

p. 185. 'I know how much you have done . . .': V. Mackenzie, 97—8.

p. 185. 'Give me your *mala* . . .': V. Mackenzie, 101.

p. 187. 'When you understand how transparency . . .': Tsongkhapa, *The Three Principal Aspects of the Path*, v.13. (Tr.)

p. 190. 'I am a priest, and by profession . . .': Filippi, 91.

p. 191. 'From that day until I left Thibet, . . .': Filippi, 94.

p. 191. 'I lost no time in obeying . . .': Filippi, 102.

p. 191. 'to obtain a complete insight . . . .': Filippi, 104.

p. 192. 'Above all I applied myself . . .': Filippi, 104.

p. 192. 'that nothing exists because . . .': Filippi, 249.

p. 192. 'Under the pretence of searching . . .': Filippi, 248.

p. 192. 'to exclude and absolutely deny . . .': Filippi, 105.

p. 192. 'who has so adorned this monstrosity . . .': Filippi, 245.

p. 193. 'absolutely deny the existence . . .': Filippi, 250.

p. 193. 'absolutely wrong and pestiferous . . .': Filippi, 300.

p. 193. 'Many a time when telling them . . .': Filippi, 177.

p. 194. 'the esteem in which they held . . .': Filippi, 177.

p. 195. 'After nigh twenty years . . .': Filippi, 170.

p. 195. 'after a day of normal debating, . . .': Wallace, 104.

p. 196. 'to prevent the decline . . .': Wallace, 106.

p. 197. 'When I examined this old monk . . .': Rabten, 25.

p. 197. 'While absorbed in the sphere . . .': Rabten, 35.

p. 198. 'I became convinced that rather . . .': Rabten, 75.

p. 200. 'As I saw more and more Westerners . . .': V. Mackenzie, 52.

p. 201. 'something more concrete . . .': V. Mackenzie, 53.

p. 203. 'a Mahayana Buddhist tradition . . .': New Kadampa Tradition promotional literature.

Chapter 13. Hakuin: The Rinzai Zen Tradition

p. 205. 'Bodhidharma sat facing the wall . . .': Yamada, 208.

p. 207. 'I was overcome by the Great Doubt . . .': Dumoulin, 249.

p. 207. 'a red-hot iron ball . . .': Yamada, 14.

p. 208. 'the smashing of a layer of ice, . . .': Dumoulin, 249.

p. 208. 'If someone claps his hands, . . .': Dumoulin, 257.

p. 208. 'seek out a quiet place . . .': Dumoulin, 258.

p. 208. 'The practice of Zen, . . .': Dumoulin, 254.

p. 209. 'All at once I was struck . . .': Kapleau, 216.

p. 212. 'in itself neither Buddhist . . .': Lassalle (1), 35.

p. 213. 'Zen is neither monotheistic . . .': Dumoulin, 270.

p. 213. 'perhaps the highest thing . . .': Lassalle (1), 63.

p. 213. 'enlightenment, sublime achievement . . .': Lassalle (1), 91.

p. 214. 'the discovery and activation . . .': Lassalle (1), 36.

p. 214. 'a total view of all being; . . .': Lassalle (1), 39.

p. 214. 'a state of quietude, . . .': Lassalle (1), 56.

p. 214. 'the most radical form . . .': Lassalle (1), 74.

p. 214. 'leads us along the line . . .': Lassalle (1), 74.

p. 214. 'made much better use . . .': Lassalle (1), 88.

p. 214. 'the good that is in . . .': Lassalle (1), 89.

p. 214. 'not suited for logical . . .': Lassalle (1), 67.

p. 214. 'I wonder whether in the long run . . .': Lassalle (1), 69–70.

p. 215. 'The Catholic Church rejects nothing . . .': Abbot, 662.

p. 215. 'prudently and lovingly . . .': Abbot, 663.

p. 216. 'is missionary by her very nature . . .': Abbot, 585.

p. 216. 'evangelisation and the planting . . .': Abbot, 591.

p. 216. 'one Mediator between God and men, . . .': Abbot, 593.

p. 216. 'teach young people the true state . . .': Abbot, 627.

p. 216. 'whose historical and scientific-religious . . .': Abbot, 629.

p. 217. 'a monstrous shift indeed . . .': Langdon Gilkey, in Hick and Knitter, viii.

p. 218. 'From Zen I can and will . . .': Johnston, 132.

p. 218. 'to fuse Christian meditation . . .': Ratzinger, 11.

p. 218. 'the wonderful discovery . . .': Ratzinger, 14.

p. 219. 'to make known to all monks . . .': de Béthune (1), 4.

p. 220. 'The monastic ideal is . . .': de Béthune (2), 3.

p. 221. 'No mysticism is merely . . .': Rudolf Otto, Dumoulin, 271.

p. 221. 'The Zen Way is a Buddhist Way . . .': Schloegl, 1.

Chapter 14. Eugène Burnouf: The Construction of Buddhism

p. 227. ' . . .those who really know first . . .': Vorobyova-Desyatovskaya, 38 (Tr.).

p. 228. 'I do not know how one can . . .': Duka, 180 (Tr.).

p. 230. 'it is in any case certain . . .': de Lubac, 116 (Tr.).

p. 230. 'the *bauddhistes*, among whom the view . . .': de Lubac, 116 (Tr.).

p. 230. 'that Sanskrit belonged to . . .': de Lubac, 111 (Tr.).

p. 232. 'both in the roots of the verbs . . .': Schwab, 41.

p. 233. 'our familiarity, not merely . . .': Said, 214.

p. 234. 'system of knowledge about . . .': Said, 6.

p. 234. 'I content myself with noting, . . .': Said, 39.

p. 236. 'like one of the sages, . . .': Duka, 84.

p. 236. 'scrupulously tenacious of correctness . . .': Duka, 85 and 92.

p. 236. 'Mr Csoma has no selfish . . .': Duka, 85.

p. 236. 'matter [of] national interest . . . .': Duka, 116.

p. 237. 'the Tibetan faith . . .approaches nearer . . .': Duka, 94.

p. 237. 'will excuse them in some degree . . .': Duka, 108.

p. 238. 'I had been for several years . . .': Bishop (1), 98.

p. 238. 'part of a systematic scheme . . .': Welbon, 34.

p. 238. 'no purpose to meddle . . .': Welbon, 36.

p. 239. 'We should not close our eyes . . .': Welbon, 57–8.

p. 240. 'a completely new subject . . .': Burnouf, 61 (Tr.).

p. 241. 'spiritual, amiable and thoroughly French, . . .': quoted by Guy Welbon in the *Encyclopedia of Religion*, vol. II, p. 581.

p. 241. 'in listening to your lectures . . .': de Lubac, 144 (Tr.).

p. 241. 'among all the philologists . . .': from the preface to the 2nd edition of Burnouf's *L'Introduction*, ii (Tr.).

p. 242. 'if philology has its own peculiar . . .': de Lubac, 143 (Tr.).

p. 242. 'their true and most solid base . . .': Burnouf, 9 (Tr.).

p. 242. 'One has to admire with what speed, . . .': de Lubac, 151 (Tr.).

p. 243. 'the only moral adversary . . .': de Lubac, 184 (Tr.).

p. 243. 'for certain people all questions . . .': Burnouf, 61 (Tr.).

p. 243. 'The appearance of this . . .': de Lubac, 152n (Tr.).

p. 244. 'the bounden duty of the government . . .': Almond, 134.

p. 245. 'must end in the total discomfiture . . .': Almond, 134.

p. 245. 'this hideous system . . .': de Lubac, 158 (Tr.).

p. 245. 'Buddhism has nothing in common . . .': de Lubac, 158 (Tr.).

p. 248. *'definite methodical procedure, . . .*': Johnson, 812.

p. 248. 'an abstraction . . .in each individual, . . .': Marx, Engels, 63–4.

p. 248. 'the philosophers have only *interpreted* . . .': Marx, Engels, 64.

Chapter 15. Arthur Schopenhauer:
The Oriental Renaissance

p. 250. 'Hurl into the water . . .': *La Révolution surréaliste*, 22 (Tr.).

p. 252. 'a mine that is rich . . .': Schwab, 227.

p. 252. 'our religion was hidden . . .': Schwab, 258.

p. 253. 'May Indic studies find . . .': Schwab, 12.

p. 253. 'Whoever knows others . . .': Schwab, 60.

p. 254. 'vogue of oriental prophets, . . .': Jean Filliozat, in Schwab, 248.

p. 255. 'Life is a wretched business, . . .': Magee, 9.

p. 255. 'Sanskrit literature will be . . .': Schwab, 13.

p. 256. 'till 1818, when my work appeared . . .': Schopenhauer (2), 169.

p. 256. 'You will arrive at Nirvana, . . .': Schwab, 427.

p. 256. 'In any case, it must be a pleasure . . .': Schopenhauer (2), 169.

p. 257. 'honest but shallow people . . .': Schopenhauer (1), 195.

p. 257. 'the primitive wisdom . . .': Schwab, 427.

p. 257. 'growing out of religion . . .': Schopenhauer (1), 197.

p. 257. 'necessary for the people . . .': Schopenhauer (2), 168.

p. 257. 'a giant to put on the shoes . . . .': Schopenhauer (2), 168.

p. 257. 'Our existence resembles . . .': Schopenhauer (1), 52.

p. 258. 'the barrier between the ego . . .': Magee, 196.

p. 258. 'It goes without saying . . .': Schopenhauer (1), 61.

p. 259. 'the great event in Wagner's life . . .': Magee, 335–6.

p. 259. 'Burnouf's *Introduction* . . .': Schwab, 439.

p. 259. 'the most difficult thing . . .': Schwab, 440.

p. 260. 'Everything is strange to me . . .': Schwab, 441.

p. 260. 'can and ought to reconcile himself . . .': Chadwick, 111.

p. 260. 'I am impressed, almost frightened . . .': Schwab, 386.

p. 261. '*J'ai l'esprit occupé de Bouddha* . . .': Schwab, 383.

p. 261. 'a religion too pure for the human race . . .': Schwab, 384.

p. 261. 'Of all the events in history . . .': Schwab, 250.

p. 262. 'Hindu Luther . . .': Almond, 74.

p. 262. 'a simple worshipper of the eternal Buddha . . .': Batchelor and Brown, 67–8.

p. 262. 'we see a man who is undoubtedly wise . . .': Batchelor and Brown, 68.

p. 262. 'Isn't it almost a true religion . . .': Batchelor and Brown, 68.

p. 263. 'the would-be similarity . . .': Schwab, 254.

p. 264. 'encounter an invalid or an old man . . .': Nietzsche (1), 72.

p. 264. 'active sympathy for the ill-constituted . . .': Nietzsche (2), 126.

p. 265. 'belong together as nihilistic . . .': Nietzsche (2), 139.

p. 265. 'an overwhelming desire to do harm . . .': Nietzsche (2), 142.

p. 265. 'a religion for *late* human beings . . .': Nietzsche (2), 142.

p. 268. 'to form the nucleus . . .': Fields, 90.

p. 269. 'a science of the methodical . . .': de Lubac, 210 (Tr.).

p. 269. 'incomparably higher, more noble . . .': de Lubac, 212 (Tr.).

p. 271. 'O Great Lama! . . .': *La Révolution surréaliste*, 17 (Tr.).

Chapter 16. Everyman:
The Awakening of the West

p. 272. 'The scandal redoubled . . .': de Lubac, 170 (Tr.).

p. 273. 'It is a post-structuralist commonplace, . . .': David Lodge. *New York Review of Books*, 13 Feb. 1992.

p. 274. 'The forms of Buddhism . . .': Nhat Hanh (3), 94.

p. 279. 'One day an old man was circumambulating . . .': Geshé Wangyal, 141. [I have adapted the body of the text and changed the final reply of Drom according to a version heard orally from Tibetan lamas.]

Chapter 17. Bidiya Dandaron:
Russian Connections

p. 290. 'I was struck . . .': Benjamin, 228.

p. 296. 'on the interpretation of . . .': Piatigorsky, 179.

p. 296. 'it was not they who . . .': Piatigorsky, 178.

p. 297. 'They hated him . . .': Piatagorsky, 178.

p. 297. 'If we look carefully at . . .': Buryaad Unen, 18/1/73, quoted in *Soviet Analyst*, vol. 3, no. 23, 1974, 5.

p. 298. 'We, the Buddhists of the Soviet . . .': Snelling (2), 263.

Chapter 18. Alexandra David-Neel:
The Razor's Edge

p. 303. 'I can't tear myself away . . .': Foster, 176.

p. 303. 'Things seem to be strangely . . .': Brosse, 221 (Tr.).

p. 303. 'Just know that today . . .': Brosse, 238 (Tr.).

p. 304. 'I went there because . . .': Brosse, 239 (Tr.).

p. 304. 'was so shattering in its impact . . .': Alan Bullock, in Bradbury and Macfarlane, 58.

p. 304. 'A conversion to Theosophy . . .': Spengler, 346.

p. 305. 'It is the soul of the West . . .': Massis, 231.

p. 306. 'Western man has no more . . .': Massis, 491.

p. 306. '"I had a sense, . . .': Maugham, 298.

p. 306. 'My taxi, . . .': Maugham, 307.

p. 309. 'I warned you in advance . . .': Brosse, 50 (Tr.).

p. 310. 'Oh! How can I even describe . . .': Brosse, 69 (Tr.).

p. 310. 'had set out on a path . . .': Brosse, 86 (Tr.).

p. 311. 'I don't like popes, . . .': Brosse, 118—9 (Tr.).

p. 311. 'truly ugly and dressed . . .': Foster, 141.

p. 313. 'opportunity to uphold . . .': Govinda (1), 13.

p. 314. 'that if any religious reform . . .': Govinda (1), 104.

p. 314. 'producing Buddhists, unafraid . . .': Humphreys, 21.

p. 319. 'the authentic and rational . . .': de Lubac, 241 (Tr.).

p. 321. 'I am the prisoner of a dream, . . .': Brosse, 306 (Tr.).

p. 321. 'Some inexplicable force . . .': Govinda (1), 13.

p. 322. 'Don't you think, *messieurs*, . . .': Brosse, 294 (Tr.).

Chapter 19. Sangharakshita: Adaptation

p. 323. 'having read it straight through . . .': Sangharakshita (4), 1.

p. 324. 'they demonstrated that . . .': Sangharakshita (4), 3.

p. 324. 'far from being a help . . .': Sangharakshita (4), 97.

p. 327. 'It is far better to approach . . .': Sangharakshita (1), 265.

p. 328. 'my feeling that we were kindred . . .': Sangharakshita (1), 270—1.

p. 328. 'Sangharakshita I wanted to enjoy . . .': Sangharakshita (4), 292.

p. 329. 'Art and meditation are creative states . . .': Sangharakshita (1), 272.

p. 330. 'Far from being an activist . . .': Sangharakshita (1), 414—5.

p. 330. 'I was concerned to see Buddhism . . .': Sangharakshita (3), xii.

p. 332. 'more convinced than ever . . .': Sangharakshita (2), 119.

p. 334. 'that of Yeats' butterfly . . .': Sangharakshita (2), 18 and 120.

p. 334. 'central and decisive, indeed . . .': Sangharakshita (2), 26.

p. 335. 'Each form of life aspired . . .': Sangharakshita (2), 103.

p. 335. 'the process of development . . .': Sangharakshita (2), 95.

p. 336. 'a free association of . . .': Mitrata, 15.

p. 338. 'as a bridge that over . . .': Govinda (2), 29.

p. 338. 'a brotherhood of mind and heart . . .': Govinda (2), 7.

p. 338. 'of no consequence . . .': Govinda (2), 6.

p. 339. 'There are thousands of people . . .': Mitrata, 37.
p. 339. 'The enemies to be attacked . . .': Subhuti, 175–6.
p. 339. 'Then we [will] have to start . . .': Mitrata, 27.
p. 340. 'I am a great admirer . . .': Winkler, 168.

Chapter 20. Satipatthana: Mindful Awareness

p. 341. 'the most important discourse . . .': Rahula (1), 69.
p. 342. 'There is, monks, . . .': Walshe, 335 (adapted after Nanamoli, Anon., 371).
p. 342. 'mindfully he breathes in . . .': Walshe, 335.
p. 348. 'It is not necessary to call . . .': Hart, 17.
p. 348. 'I teach Dharma, . . .': Hart, 18.
p. 351. 'In Europe intellectualism . . .': Anon., 305.
p. 352. 'The first three . . .': Khema (2), 141.

Chapter 21. Nhat Hanh: Engagement

p. 353. 'I have far more in common . . .': Merton, 108.
p. 354. 'moving the hearts . . .': Nhat Hanh (3), 106.
p. 358. 'train rural development cadres . . .': Nhat Hanh (3), 48.
p. 358. 'his soul and body have obviously . . .': Nhat Hanh (3), 77.
p. 362. 'the gradual establishment . . .': Jones, 274.
p. 362. 'as long as its intuitive teaching . . .': Suzuki, 63.
p. 363. 'Our society is a difficult place . . .': Nhat Hanh (1), 49.
p. 366. 'The creation of a New Society . . .': Subhuti, 129 and 174.
p. 366. 'directed to reforming . . .': Jones, 266.
p. 367. 'The Shambhala teachings are founded . . .': Trungpa (3), 28.
p. 368. 'At that time we were caring . . .': Batchelor and Brown, 104.
p. 368. 'Peace work means, first of all . . .': Nhat Hanh (1), 80, 9.
p. 369. 'Inner peace is the key . . .': Batchelor and Brown, 111–2.
p. 369. 'Life is filled with suffering . . .': Nhat Hanh (1), 3, 4.
p. 369. 'How can we practise at the airport . . .': Nhat Hanh (1), 53.

BIBLIOGRAPHY

Abbott, Walter M. (ed.) *The Documents of Vatican II*. London, 1967.

Almond, Philip C. *The British Discovery of Buddhism*. Cambridge, 1988.

Anesaki, Masaharu. *Nichiren: The Buddhist Prophet*. Cambridge, Mass./London, 1916.

Anon. (ed.) *Clearing the Path: Writings of Nanavira Thera (1960–1965)*. Colombo, Sri Lanka 1987.

Batchelor, Martine and Brown, Kerry (eds) *Buddhism and Ecology*. London, 1992.

Batchelor, Stephen. *The Tibet Guide*. London/Boston, 1988.

—. (ed.) *The Jewel in the Lotus: A Guide to the Buddhist Traditions of Tibet*. London/Boston, 1987.

Baumann, Martin. *Deutsche Buddhisten: Geschichte und Gemeinschaften*. Marburg, Germany 1993.

Benjamin, Walter. *One-Way Street and Other Writings*. London, 1979.

de Béthune, Pierre-Francois (1). 'Commission for Interfaith Monastic Dialogue: History, Aims and Methods of the Monastic Encounter in Europe.' Unpublished paper, 1987.

— (2). 'Some Perspectives Opened by "Spiritual Exchange".' Unpublished paper, 1987.

Bishop, Peter (1). *The Myth of Shangri-la: Tibet, Travel Writing and the Western Creation of Sacred Landscape*. London, 1989.

— (2). *Dreams of Power: Tibetan Buddhism and the Western Imagination*. London, 1993.

Boxer, C.R. *The Christian Century in Japan*. Berkeley, Cal. 1951.

Bradbury, Malcolm and McFarlane, James (eds). *Modernism 1890–1930*. London, 1976.

Brosse, Jacques. *Alexandra David-Neel*. Paris, 1991.

Burnouf, Eugène. *L'Introduction à l'histoire du Buddhisme indien*. Paris, 1844.

Causton, Richard. *Nichiren Shoshu Buddhism: An Introduction*. London, 1988.

Chadwick, Owen. *The Secularization of the European Mind in the 19th Century*. Cambridge, 1975.

Chah, Ajahn (1). *Bodhinyana: Teachings of Ven. Ajahn Chah*. Bung Wai Forest Monastery, Thailand, 1982.

— (2). *A Taste of Freedom: Selected Dhamma Talks*. Bung Wai Forest Monastery, Thailand, 1982.

Chang, Garma C.C. (1) *The Hundred Thousand Songs of Milarepa*. (2 vols) New York, 1962.

—. (2) *Six Yogas of Naropa and Teachings on Mahamudra*. Ithaca, 1977.

Ch'en, Kenneth. *Buddhism in China: A Historical Survey*. Princeton, N.J. 1964.

Cleary, Thomas. (tr.) *Shobogenzo: Zen Essays by Dogen*. Honolulu, 1986.

Crépon, Pierre. 'Biographie de Taisen Deshimaru'. Pamphlet distributed by the Dojo Zen de Paris.

Cronin, Vincent. *The Wise Man from the West: Matteo Ricci and his Mission to China*. London, 1955 and 1984.

Crook, John. *Catching a Feather on a Fan: A Zen Retreat with Master Sheng Yen*. Shaftesbury, Dorset 1991.

Croucher, Paul. *Buddhism in Australia (1848–1988)*. Kensington, New South Wales 1989.

Dawson, Christopher. (ed.) Tr. a nun of Stanbrook Abbey *The Mongol Mission*. London, 1955.

Deshimaru, Taisen. (1) *Autobiographie eines Zen-Mönches*. Munich, 1990.

—. (2) ed. Phillipe Coupey. *The Lion's Roar*. Unpublished manuscript.

—. (3) tr. and ed. Nancy Amphoux. *Questions to a Zen Master*. London, 1985.

—. (4) ed. Phillipe Coupey. *The Voice of the Valley*. New York, 1979.

Deutsche Buddhistische Union. (ed.) *Chronik des Buddhismus in Deutschland*. DBU, 1985.

Disciples of Ajahn Chah. *Seeing the Way*. Amaravati, Herts. 1989.

Dodds, E.R. *Pagan and Christian in an Age of Anxiety*. Oxford, 1965.

Douglas, Nik and White, Meryl. *Karmapa: The Black Hat Lama of Tibet*. London, 1976.

Dowman, Keith. *The Masters of Mahamudra: Songs and Histories of the Eighty-four Buddhist Siddhas*. New York, 1985.

Duka, Theodore. *Life and Writings of Alexander Csoma de Körös*. London, 1885.

Dumoulin, Heinrich. *A History of Zen Buddhism*. Boston, 1963. (Extensively revised as *Zen Buddhism: A History. Vol. 1: India and China; Vol. 2: Japan*. New York/London, 1988 and 1990.)

Dutt, Sukumar. *Buddhism in East Asia*. Bombay, 1966.

Eliot, T. S. *Collected Poems 1909–1962*. London, 1974.

Elison, George. *Deus Destroyed: The Image of Christianity in Early Modern Japan*. Cambridge, Mass., 1988.

Ellman, Richard. *James Joyce*. New York, 1982.

The Encyclopedia of Religion. General Editor: Mircea Eliade. 16 vols. London/New York, 1987.

Endo, Shusaku. *Silence*. London, 1978.

Evola, Julius. *The Doctrine of Awakening*. London, 1951.

Feuerbach, Ludwig. *The Essence of Christianity*. New York, 1957.

Fields, Rick. *How the Swans Came to the Lake: A Narrative History of Buddhism in America*. Boston and London, 1986.

de Filippi, Filippo. (ed.) *Desideri: An Account of Tibet: The Travels of Ippolito Desideri of Pistoia, S.J., 1712–1727*. London, 1932.

Foster, Barbara M. and Michael. *Forbidden Journey: The Life of Alexandra David-Neel*. San Francisco, 1987.

Fujii, Nichidatsu. *Buddhism for World Peace*. Tokyo, 1980.

Gernet, Jacques. *China and the Christian Impact: A Conflict of Cultures*. Cambridge, 1985.

Godet, Gérard. 'Memoir'. Unpublished manuscript.

Gombrich, Richard. *Theravada Buddhism: A Social History from Ancient Benares to Modern Colombo*. London, 1988.

Govinda, Lama Anagarika. (1) *The Way of the White Clouds*. London, 1965.

—. (2) *A Living Buddhism for the West*. Boston/Shaftesbury, Dorset 1989.

Grousset, René. *The Empire of the Steppes*. London, 1980.

Guenther, Herbert V. (1) *Jewel Ornament of Liberation*. London, 1959.

—. (2) *The Life and Teachings of Naropa*. Oxford, 1963.

Gyatso, Tenzin, the XIV Dalai Lama. *Freedom in Exile: The Autobiography of the Dalai Lama of Tibet*. London, 1990.

Hart, William. *The Art of Living: Vipassana Meditation as Taught by S.N. Goenka*. San Francisco, 1987.

Hayward, Jeremy W., and Varela, Francisco J. (eds) *Gentle Bridges: Conversations with the Dalai Lama on the Sciences of Mind*. Boston/London, 1992.

Hearnshaw, F.J.C. (ed.). *The Social and Political Ideas of Some Great French Thinkers of the Age of Reason*. London, 1930.

Hecker, Hellmuth. *Lebensbilder Deutscher Buddhisten: Ein Bio-Bibliographisches Handbuch. Band 1: Die Gründer*. Konstanz, Germany 1990.

—. *Lebensbilder Deutscher Buddhisten: Ein Bio-Bibliographisches Handbuch. Band 2: Die Nachfolger*. Konstanz, Germany 1992.

Hick, John and Knitter, Paul F. (ed.). *The Myth of Christian Uniqueness*. London, 1987.

Hopkirk, Peter. *The Great Game: On Secret Service in High Asia*. London, 1990.

Horner, I.B. (tr.) (1). *The Middle Length Sayings (Majjhima Nikaya)* vol. II. London, 1957.

——. (2). *Milinda's Questions (Milindapanha)*. London, 1963.

Humphreys, Christmas. *Sixty Years of Buddhism in England (1907–1967)*. London, 1968.

Hurvitz, Leon. (tr.). *Scripture of the Lotus Blossom of the Fine Dharma (The Lotus Sutra)*. New York, 1976.

Jackson, Peter with Morgan, David. *The Mission of Friar William of Rubruck*. London, 1990.

Jaffe, Paul D. 'Rising from the Lotus: Two Bodhisattvas from the Lotus Sutra as a Psychodynamic Paradigm for Nichiren.' Unpublished manuscript.

Jiyu-Kennett, Roshi P.T.N.H. (1). *Zen is Eternal Life*. Mt. Shasta, Cal. 1987.

—— (2). *The Wild, White Goose: The Diary of a Zen Trainee*. (2 vols) Mt. Shasta, Cal. 1977.

—— (3). *How to Grow a Lotus Blossom or How a Zen Buddhist Prepares for Death*. Mt. Shasta, Cal. 1977.

Johnson, Paul. *The Birth of the Modern: World Society 1815–1830*. London, 1991.

Johnston, William. *Christian Zen*. Dublin, 1979.

Jones, Ken. *The Social Face of Buddhism*. London/Boston, 1989.

de Jong, J.W. *A Brief History of Buddhist Studies in Europe and America*. New Delhi, 1983.

Kapleau, Roshi Philip. *The Three Pillars of Zen*. New York, 1980.

Kappler, Claude-Claire and René (tr.). *Guillaume de Rubrouk: Voyage dans l'Empire Mongol – 1253–1255*. Paris, 1993.

Kato, Bunno et alia (tr.). *The Threefold Lotus Sutra*. Tokyo, 1975.

Kennedy, J. 'Buddhist Gnosticism, the System of Basilides.' *Journal of the Royal Asiatic Society*, 1902.

Khema, Ayya. (1) *Being Nobody, Going Nowhere*. London/Boston, 1987.

——. (2) *When the Iron Eagle Flies: Buddhism for the West*. London, 1991.

Kim, Hee-jin. *Dogen Kigen – Mystical Realist*. Tucson, Ariz. 1975.

Kirimura, Yasuji. *The Life of Nichiren Daishonin*. Tokyo, 1980.

Kodera, Takashi James. *Dogen's Formative Years in China*. London, 1980.

Koestler, Arthur. *The Lotus and the Robot*. London, 1960.

Kornfield, Jack. *Living Buddhist Masters*. Santa Cruz, Cal. 1977.

Lamotte, Etienne. *History of Indian Buddhism*, Louvain, Belgium 1988.

Lang, D.M. *The Wisdom of Balahvar*. London, 1957.

Lassalle, Hugo-Enomiya (1). *Zen – Way to Enlightenment*. London, 1966.

— (2). *Am Morgen einer Bessern Welt: Der Mensch im Durchbruch zu einem neuen Bewusstsein*. Zürich/Köln, 1981.

Lhalungpa, Lobsang P. (1) *The Life of Milarepa*. St Albans, Herts. 1979.

—. (2) *Mahamudra: The Quintessence of Mind and Meditation*. Boston, 1986.

Lieu, S.N.C. *Manichaeism in the Later Roman Empire and Medieval China*. Manchester, 1985.

Ling, Trevor. *The Buddha: Buddhist Civilisation in India and Ceylon*. Hounslow, London 1973.

de Lubac, Henri. *La Rencontre du Bouddhisme et de l'Occident*. Paris, 1952.

Lustig, Friedrich V. *Biography of Karlis Alexis Tennisons*. Unpublished manuscript.

Mackenzie, D.A. *Buddhism in Pre-Christian Britain*. Oxford, 1928.

Mackenzie, Vicki. *Reincarnation: The Boy Lama*. London, 1988.

Magee, Bryan. *The Philosophy of Schopenhauer*. Oxford, 1983.

Marx, Karl and Engels, Frederick. *On Religion*. Moscow, 1975.

Massis, Henri. 'Defence of the West'. *New Criterion*, vol. 4, nos 2–3. London, 1926.

Matsunaga, Alicia and Daigan. *Foundation of Japanese Buddhism. Volume II: The Mass Movement*. Los Angeles/Tokyo, 1976.

Maugham, W. Somerset. *The Razor's Edge*. London, 1944.

McCrindle, E.M. *Ancient India as described by Megasthenes and Arrian*. London, 1877.

Mehta, U. *Kautilya and his Arthashastra*. 1980.

Merton, Thomas. *Faith and Violence*. Notre Dame, Ind. 1968.

The Middle Way, vol. 62, no. 1. 'H.H. Dudjom Rinpoché, 1904–87.' London, 1987.

Mitrata, no. 64. 'What is the FWBO?' Glasgow, 1991.

Montgomery, Daniel B. *Fire in the Lotus: The Dynamic Buddhism of Nichiren*. London, 1991.

Morreale, Don. (ed.) *Buddhist America: Centers, Retreats, Practices*. Santa Fe, N.M. 1988.

Mu Soeng Sunim. *Thousand Peaks: Korean Zen – Tradition and Teachers*. Berkeley, Cal. 1987.

Myodo, January 1992. Pinole, Cal. 1991.

Nalanda Translation Committee. *The Rain of Wisdom*. Boulder, Colo. 1980.

Nanananda, Bhikkhu. *Concept and Reality*. Kandy, Sri Lanka 1971.

Nanamoli, Bhikkhu. *The Life of the Buddha*. Kandy, Sri Lanka 1978.

Narain, A.K. *The Indo-Greeks*. Oxford, 1957.

Nesterenko, Michel (ed.). *The Karmapa Papers*. Paris, 1992.

Nietzsche, Friedrich. (1) *Thus Spoke Zarathustra*. London, 1961.

——. (2) *Twilight of the Idols/The Anti-Christ*. London, 1968.

Nhat Hanh, Thich. (1) *Being Peace*. Berkeley, Cal. 1987.

——. (2) *The Miracle of Mindfulness*. Boston, 1975/76.

——. (3) *Vietnam: Lotus in a Sea of Fire*. New York, 1967.

Norbu, Namkhai. *The Crystal and the Way of Light*. London, 1986.

NSUK Bulletin, no. 84. Taplow, Bucks. 1991.

Nyanaponika Thera. *The Heart of Buddhist Meditation*. London, 1962.

——. 'Nyanatiloka Mahathera: His Life and Work.' *Nyanatiloka Centenary Volume*. Kandy, Sri Lanka 1978.

Obermiller, E. (tr.) *The History of Buddhism in India and Tibet by Bu-ston*. New Delhi, 1986.

Oliver, Ian P. *Buddhism in Britain*. London, 1979.

Piatigorsky, Alexander. 'The Departure of Dandaron.' *Kontinent II*. London, 1978.

Olschki, Leonardo. *Marco Polo's Asia*. Berkeley, Cal./Los Angeles, 1960.

Rabten, Geshé. *Song of the Profound View*. London, 1989.

Race, Alan. *Christians and Religious Pluralism*. London, 1983.

de Rachewiltz, Igor. *Papal Envoys to the Great Khans*. London, 1971.

Rahula, Walpola. (1) *What the Buddha Taught*. Bedford, Beds. 1967.

——. (2) *The Heritage of the Bhikkhu: A Short History of the Bhikkhu in Educational, Cultural, Social and Political Life*. New York, 1974.

Randall, Richard. *Life as a Siamese Monk*. Bradford on Avon, Wilts. 1990.

Ratzinger, Cardinal Joseph. *Letter to the Bishops of the Catholic Church on Some Aspects of Christian Meditation*. Vatican City, 1989.

La Révolution surréaliste. no. 3. Paris, 1925.

Richardson, Hugh M. *Tibet and Its History*. Boulder, Colo./London, 1984.

de Rosa, Peter. *Vicars of Christ: The Dark Side of the Papacy*. London, 1988.

Rossabi, Morris. *Khubilai Khan: His Life and Times*. Berkeley, Cal./Los Angeles, 1988.

Russell, Bertrand. *A History of Western Philosophy*. New York, 1945.

Said, Edward W. *Orientalism: Western Conceptions of the Orient*. London, 1978.

Sangharakshita. (1) *Facing Mount Kanchenjunga*. Glasgow, 1991.

——. (2) *The History of my Going for Refuge*. Glasgow, 1988.

——. (3) *A Survey of Buddhism.* Boulder, Colo./London, 1980.

——. (4) *The Thousand Petalled Lotus.* Gloucester, 1988.

Schenk, H.G. *The Mind of the European Romantics: An Essay in Cultural History.* Oxford, 1979.

Schloegl, Irmgard. *The Zen Way.* London, 1977.

Schopenhauer, Arthur (1). *Essays and Aphorisms.* London, 1970.

—— (2). *The World as Will and Representation* (vol. II). New York, 1958/1966.

Schumann, Hans Wolfgang. *Buddhism and Buddhist Studies in Germany.* Bonn-Bad Godesberg, Germany 1972.

Schwab, Raymond. *The Oriental Renaissance: Europe's Rediscovery of India and the East, 1680–1880.* New York, 1984.

Sedlar, Jean W. *India and the Greek World: A Study in the Transmission of Culture.* Totowa, N.J., 1980.

Seikyo Times/Gosho Translation Committee. (ed. and tr.) *The Major Writings of Nichiren Daishonin (Vols. 1–6).* Tokyo, 1979—90.

Sèngué, Tcheukyi and Tsomo, Rintchèn. *Vie de Kalou Rinpotché (Texte).* Arvillard, France 1984.

Shakabpa, Tsepon W.D. *Tibet: A Political History.* New York, 1974.

Shantideva. *Bodhicaryavatara.* (1) English: Tr. Stephen Batchelor. *A Guide to the Bodhisattva's Way of Life.* Dharamsala, 1979. (2) French: Tr. Comité de Traduction Padmakara based on the version of Louis Finot (1920). *La Marche vers l'Eveil.* St Léon sur Vézère, France 1991. (3) German: Tr. Ernst Steinkellner. *Eintritt in das Leben zur Erleuchtung.* Düsseldorf/Köln, 1981.

Shore, Jeff. 'Japanese Zen and the West: Beginnings.' Unpublished paper.

Snelling, John. (1) *The Buddhist Handbook: A Complete Guide to Buddhist Teaching and Practice.* London, 1987.

——. (2) *Buddhism in Russia: The Story of Agvan Dorzhiev – Lhasa's Emissary to the Tsar.* Shaftesbury, Dorset 1993.

Solé-Leris, Amadeo. *Tranquillity and Insight.* London, 1986.

Spence, Jonathan D. *The Memory Palace of Matteo Ricci.* London, 1985.

Spengler, Oswald. *The Decline of the West.* London, 1926.

Subhuti, Dharmachari (Alex Kennedy). *Buddhism for Today: A Portrait of a New Buddhist Movement.* Tisbury, Wilts. 1983.

Sugawara, Makoto. *Lives of Master Swordsmen.* Tokyo, 1988.

Sumedho, Ajahn. *Cittaviveka: Teachings from the Silent Mind.* Petersfield, Hants.1983.

Suzuki, Daisetz T. *Zen and Japanese Culture.* Princeton, N.J. 1970.

Tanahashi, Kazuaki. (ed.) *Moon in a Dewdrop: Writings of Zen Master Dogen.* Shaftesbury, Dorset 1988.

Tarn, W.W. *Greeks in Bactria and India.* Oxford, 1951.

Tarthang Tulku. 'The Life and Liberation of Padmasambhava'. *Crystal Mirror*, vol. IV. Berkeley, Cal. 1975.

Thinley, Karma. *The History of the Sixteen Karmapas of Tibet*. Boulder, Colo. 1980.

Tillich, Paul. *Christianity and the Encounter of the World Religions*. New York, 1963.

Toscano, Giuseppe (tr.) *Il T'o-Rangs (L'Aurora)* (by Ippolito Desideri S.J.). Rome, ISMEO, 1981.

Triet, Raphael. 'Maître Taisen Deshimaru.' Pamphlet distributed by the Dojo Zen de Paris.

Trungpa, Chögyam. (1) *Born in Tibet*. London, 1966.

——. (2) *Cutting Through Spiritual Materialism*. Boulder, Colo. 1973.

——. (3) *Shambhala: The Sacred Path of the Warrior*. Boulder, Colo./London, 1984.

Tuck, Andrew. *Comparative Philosophy and the Philosophy of Scholarship: Western Interpretations of Nagarjuna*. New York, 1990.

Tulku Thondup Rinpoché. *Buddha Mind: An Anthology of Longchen Rabjampa's Writings on Dzogpa Chenpo*. Ithaca, 1989.

——. *Hidden Teachings of Tibet: An Explanation of the Terma Tradition of the Nyingma School of Buddhism*. London, 1986.

Tworkov, Helen. *Zen in America: Profiles of Five Teachers*. San Francisco, 1989.

The Vajradhatu Sun. vol. 8, no. 5. Boulder, Colo. 1987.

Varela, Francisco, Thompson, Evan and Rosch, Eleanor. *The Embodied Mind*. Cambridge, Mass., 1991.

Vorobyova-Desyatovskaya, M.I. 'List tibetskoy rukopisi iz Ablay-Kita' ('Page of a Tibetan ms. from Ablay-Kita'). *Strany i narody Vostoka*, no. 26. Moscow, 1989.

Wallace, B. Alan. (tr. and ed.) *The Life and Teaching of Geshé Rabten*. London, 1980.

Maurice Walshe. (tr.) *Thus I Have Heard: The Long Discourses of the Buddha (Digha Nikaya)*. London, 1987.

Wangyal, Geshé. *The Door of Liberation*. New York, 1973.

Wasserstein, Bernard. *The Secret Lives of Trebitsch Lincoln*. New Haven, Conn./London, 1988.

Watson, Burton. (tr.) *Chuang Tzu: Basic Writings*. New York, Columbia, 1964.

Welbon, G.R. *The Buddhist Nirvana and Its Western Interpreters*. Chicago/London, 1968.

Wessels, C. *Early Jesuit Travellers in Central Asia 1603–1721*. New Delhi, 1992.

Wilson, Colin. *Aleister Crowley: The Nature of the Beast*. London, 1987.

Winkler, Ken. *A Thousand Journeys: The Biography of Lama Anagarika Govinda.* Shaftesbury, Dorset 1990.

Woodcock, George. *The Greeks in India.* London, 1966.

Yamada, Koun. *Gateless Gate.* Los Angeles, 1979.

Yampolsky, Philip B. (ed. with intro.) (1) *Selected Writings of Nichiren.* New York, 1990.

——. (2) *The Zen Master Hakuin: Selected Writings.* New York, 1971.

Yeshé, Lama Thubten, and Zopa, Lama Thubten. *Wisdom Energy.* London/Boston, 1982.

Yokoi, Yuho. *Zen Master Dogen: An Introduction with Selected Writings.* New York/Tokyo, 1976.

INDEX